Fateful Decisions

APARC
STANFORD
IIS

THE WALTER H. SHORENSTEIN
ASIA-PACIFIC RESEARCH CENTER

STUDIES OF THE WALTER H. SHORENSTEIN ASIA-PACIFIC RESEARCH CENTER
Andrew G. Walder, General Editor

The Walter H. Shorenstein Asia-Pacific Research Center in the Freeman Spogli Institute for International Studies at Stanford University sponsors interdisciplinary research on the politics, economies, and societies of contemporary Asia. This monograph series features academic and policy-oriented research by Stanford faculty and other scholars associated with the Center.

Fateful Decisions

CHOICES THAT WILL SHAPE CHINA'S FUTURE

EDITED BY

Thomas Fingar and Jean C. Oi

Stanford University Press

Stanford, California

Stanford University Press
Stanford, California

This book has been published with the assistance of the Walter H. Shorenstein Asia-Pacific Research Center at Stanford University.

Library of Congress Cataloging-in-Publication Data
Names: Fingar, Thomas, editor. | Oi, Jean C. (Jean Chun), editor.
Title: Fateful decisions : choices that will shape China's future / edited by Thomas Fingar and Jean C. Oi.
Other titles: Studies of the Walter H. Shorenstein Asia-Pacific Research Center.
Description: Stanford, California : Stanford University Press, [2020] | Series: Studies of the Walter H. Shorenstein Asia-Pacific Research Center | Includes bibliographical references and index.
Identifiers: LCCN 2019037230 (print) | LCCN 2019037231 (ebook) | ISBN 9781503611450 (cloth) | ISBN 9781503612228 (paperback) | ISBN 9781503612235 (epub)
Subjects: LCSH: China—Politics and government—2002– | China—Economic policy—2000– | China—Foreign relations—21st century.
Classification: LCC DS779.46 .F38 2020 (print) | LCC DS779.46 (ebook) | DDC 951.06—dc23
LC record available at https://lccn.loc.gov/2019037230
LC ebook record available at https://lccn.loc.gov/2019037231

Cover design: Rob Ehle
Cover photo: Aerial view of highway junction, Shanghai. iStock | zhongguo
Typeset by BookMatters in 10/13 Adobe Garamond Pro

We gratefully dedicate this volume to the memory and legacy of John Wilson Lewis and Michel Oksenberg, teachers, mentors, and pioneers in the field of China studies.

Contents

        Mary E. Gallagher

8   Human Capital and China's Future   200
        Hongbin Li, James Liang, Scott Rozelle, and Binzhen Wu

PART III: EXTERNAL AMBITIONS AND CONSTRAINTS

9   Sources and Shapers of China's Foreign Policy   225
        Thomas Fingar

10 China and the Global South   247
        Ho-fung Hung

11 Bold Strategy or Irrational Exuberance?   272
        Christine Wong

12 All (High-Speed Rail) Roads Lead to China   287
        David M. Lampton

13 China's Military Aspirations   312
        Karl Eikenberry

PART IV: A COMPARATIVE PERSPECTIVE

14 China's National Trajectory   335
        Andrew G. Walder

        Notes   359

        Index   429

Preface

Chinese officials regularly, if not always effectively, assure people at home and abroad that China's rise and return to its proper place in the international system—unspecified but presumably in a, if not the, leading position—will bring mutual benefits to all in a more harmonious world. Their depictions of what that world will be like are largely devoid of specificity but often refer to the development of a harmonious society in China as a model for a postimperial world order. This link increases interest in—and concern about—China's internal evolution and the way in which it addresses common challenges of demographic change, rising expectations, transformative technologies, urbanization, and governance of increasingly diverse and demanding publics. Observers hope that China will provide an attractive and effective model that will help them to address their own challenges. Others fear that China's choices will fail to solve critical problems or produce outcomes that infringe liberties, constrain opportunities, and subordinate the interests of many to the wishes of the few.

For these and similar reasons, government officials, corporate leaders, scholars, and ordinary people want to know how China will evolve and how it will act. Much as they would like to have confident predictions, and despite the willingness of prognosticators to declare with certainty that China will or will not evolve in specific ways, no one has a crystal ball or the ability to know in advance how Chinese decision-makers will perceive, prioritize, and address the many challenges they confront. The challenges are complex, consequential, and interconnected. Choices made in relation to one or a few challenges inevitably impact options and outcomes in other policy arenas. What happens in China and how it acts in the region and around the world will be shaped, driven, and constrained by choices made inside and outside the People's Republic. In a word, China's future—like that of all countries—is highly contingent.

The genesis of this book was a proposal by Jean C. Oi, director of the Shorenstein Asia-Pacific Research Center's China Program, to celebrate the program's tenth anniversary by inviting specialists on different dimensions of contemporary China to speculate about where developments were headed and what China would be like ten years in the future. The presentations identified many challenges and choices that China will face in the years ahead and many ways in which choices in one policy area will affect developments in others. As volume editors, we developed the framework for an integrated study that did not presume or push contributors to predict the choices that Chinese would make or whether individual or aggregate decisions would lead to success, failure, or any other predetermined outcome. The goal was to produce the kind of book that might be written by a single scholar if one could find a scholar with equal understanding of all of the key issues. The efforts of the individual contributors have yielded a well-informed and well-integrated analysis of the challenges, choices, and constraints that Beijing faces.

Thomas Fingar and Jean C. Oi
Stanford, CA

Acknowledgments

This project began as both a question ("What will China be like in the future?") and a conviction that much of what was being written about China's trajectory, intentions, and capabilities was more imaginary than empirical. We knew that we did not have a crystal ball or better imaginations than other scholars who have prognosticated about what China will be like and how it will act in the short or long term, but we knew—or thought we did—that China's future is highly contingent. How it evolves and how it acts internally and on the world stage will be shaped by developments in multiple policy arenas. How developments unfold and interact will be shaped by the constrained choices of decision-makers attempting to manage a host of complex and often interconnected challenges.

We also knew that we were incapable of identifying and analyzing the issues, constraints, and dynamics at play in more than a small subset of the most crucial arenas without considerable help from colleagues. Step one was to prepare a first approximation list of the issue areas we thought would be most important shapers of China's future condition and capabilities; the next step was to identify colleagues with the requisite expertise and experience to analyze and anticipate developments in those key arenas. We needed help from our colleagues and friends, and we got it. The contributors to this volume have deep expertise and years of experience working on the issues explored throughout these pages. Brief biographies can be found following these acknowledgments, but we want to highlight the importance of their contributions to the overall project as well as in their various chapters. Their individual and collective insights made this book possible, and we would be remiss not to acknowledge them here. Thank you to Karen Eggleston, Karl Eikenberry, Mary E. Gallagher, Ho-fung Hung, David M. Lampton, Hongbin Li, James Liang, Alice Lyman Miller, Barry Naughton, Scott Rozelle, Andrew G. Walder, Andrew Wedeman, Christine Wong, Binzhen Wu, and Xueguang Zhou.

We—and other contributors—could not have produced the insights in this volume without critical commentary and suggestions from colleagues throughout the United States and China. In particular, the following participants in an authors workshop at the Stanford Center at Peking University (SCPKU) in November 2017 raised important questions and provided significant suggestions: Fan Jishe, Huang Ping, Huang Yiping, Guo Yong, Adam Liff, Liu Aiyu, Lu Aiguo, Ouyang Wei, Qian Yingyi, Ren Jianming, Wang Jisi, Wang Wen, Xiang Jiquan, Zhao Shukai, Zhou Li-An, Zhang Changdong, Zhang Qingmin, Zhang Xiaobo, and Zuo Xuejin. We give special thanks to Christine Wong for agreeing at the last minute to comment at the Beijing workshop. She did such a great job, we insisted that she contribute a chapter in the book.

We also want to acknowledge the contributions of our colleagues at the Shorenstein Asia-Pacific Research Center (APARC) and the Stanford Center at Peking University. Projects such as this do not just happen; they require a great deal of behind-the-scenes support and assistance. Those who were especially crucial during the production of this book include, first and foremost, Jennifer Choo, associate director of the China Program, who played a crucial role in helping Jean Oi think through the ideas for the original conference to celebrate the tenth anniversary of the China Program, which took place in May of 2017. Jennifer was instrumental in organizing the book workshop at SCPKU and provided insightful editorial comments on the subsequent papers that resulted in this volume. We thank Jennifer for her invaluable academic and administrative contributions. Gi-Wook Shin, director of APARC, also deserves particular thanks for his generous support of the conference that marked the tenth anniversary of the China Program, out of which these chapters evolved. In addition, we simply cannot say thank you enough to SCPKU and its wonderfully capable and welcoming staff. SCPKU provided an ideal venue for the authors and commentators to think about China's possible futures.

Finally, we want to acknowledge the contributions of John Wilson Lewis and Michel Oksenberg to our own intellectual development and to the China field as a whole. They stimulated our intellectual curiosity and gave us many of the analytic tools needed to conduct rigorous research on difficult issues. We think they would be pleased with the objectives and achievements of this volume. To them we dedicate this volume.

Contributors

Karen Eggleston is a senior fellow at the Freeman Spogli Institute for International Studies (FSI) at Stanford University, director of the Stanford Asia Health Policy Program, and deputy director of the Walter H. Shorenstein Asia-Pacific Research Center at FSI. She is also a fellow with the Stanford Center for Innovation in Global Health and a faculty research fellow of the National Bureau of Economic Research (NBER). Eggleston earned her PhD in public policy from Harvard University, studied in China for two years, and was a Fulbright scholar in South Korea. Her research focuses on comparative health systems and health reform in Asia, especially China; government and market roles in the health sector; supply-side incentives; health-care productivity; and economic aspects of demographic change.

Karl Eikenberry is the former United States ambassador to Afghanistan and a lieutenant general, US Army, retired. He was previously the director of the US-Asia Security Initiative at Stanford's Asia-Pacific Research Center and a Stanford University Professor of Practice. His military assignments included postings as commander of the American-led Coalition forces in Afghanistan and Defense Attaché in Beijing. He is a graduate of the US Military Academy, earned master's degrees from Harvard University in East Asian studies and Stanford University in political science, was awarded an Interpreter's Certificate in Mandarin Chinese from the British Foreign and Commonwealth Office, and has an advanced degree in Chinese history from Nanjing University. His articles on US and international security issues have appeared in the *New York Times, Foreign Affairs, Wash-*

ington Quarterly, American Interest, the *Washington Post*, and the *Financial Times*.

Thomas Fingar is a Shorenstein Distinguished Fellow in the Shorenstein Asia-Pacific Research Center at Stanford University. From May 2005 through December 2008, he served as the first deputy director of national intelligence for analysis and, concurrently, as chairman of the National Intelligence Council. Previous positions include assistant secretary of state for Intelligence and Research (2000–2001, 2004–2005), principal deputy assistant secretary (2001–2003), deputy assistant secretary for analysis (1994–2000), director of the Office of Analysis for East Asia and the Pacific, and chief of the China Division. Fingar is a graduate of Cornell University (AB in government and history) and Stanford University (MA and PhD, both in political science). His most recent books are *Uneasy Partnerships: China's Engagement with Japan, the Koreas, and Russia in the Era of Reform* (editor) (Stanford University Press, 2017); *The New Great Game: China's Relations with South and Central Asia in the Era of Reform* (editor) (Stanford University Press, 2016); and *Reducing Uncertainty: Intelligence Analysis and National Security* (Stanford University Press, 2011).

Mary E. Gallagher is the Lowenstein Chair of Democracy, Democratization, and Human Rights in the Department of Political Science at the University of Michigan as well as the director of the Kenneth G. Lieberthal and Richard H. Rogel Center for Chinese Studies. She received her PhD in politics from Princeton University and her BA from Smith College. She was a foreign student at Nanjing University in 1989, taught at the Foreign Affairs College in Beijing from 1996 to 1997, and was a Fulbright Research Scholar at East China University of Politics and Law from 2003 to 2004. In 2012–13 she was a visiting professor at the Koguan School of Law at Shanghai Jiaotong University. Her most recent book, *Authoritarian Legality in China: Law, Workers, and the State*, was published in 2017. She is the author or editor of several other books, including *Contagious Capitalism: Globalization and the Politics of Labor in China* (2005), *Chinese Justice: Civil Dispute Resolution in Contemporary China* (2011), *From Iron Rice Bowl to Informalization: Markets, Workers, and the State in a Changing China* (2011), and *Contemporary Chinese Politics: New Sources, Methods, and Field Strategies* (2010).

Ho-fung Hung is the Henry M. and Elizabeth P. Wiesenfeld Professor in Political Economy at the Sociology Department and Nitze School of Advanced International Studies, Johns Hopkins University. He is the author of award-winning books *The China Boom: Why China Will Not Rule the World* (2015) and *Protest with Chinese Characteristics: Demonstrations, Riots, and Petitions in the Mid-Qing Dynasty* (2011). His research publications have appeared in *Asian Survey, American Sociological Review, American Journal of Sociology, Development and Change, Review of International Political Economy, New Left Review*, among others, and have been translated into nine languages. His analyses of the Chinese political economy and Hong Kong politics have been featured or cited in the *New York Times*, the *Financial Times*, the *Wall Street Journal*, and several other publications.

David M. Lampton is Oksenberg-Rohlen Fellow at Stanford University's Asia-Pacific Research Center (APARC) and Hyman Professor and director of China studies emeritus at the Johns Hopkins University School of Advanced International Studies (SAIS). Having started his academic career at The Ohio State University, Lampton is former chairman of The Asia Foundation, former president of the National Committee on United States–China Relations, and former dean of faculty at SAIS. Among his other works, he is the author of *Same Bed, Different Dreams: Managing U.S.-China Relations, 1989–2000* (2001); *The Three Faces of Chinese Power: Might, Money, and Minds* (2008); and *The Making of Chinese Foreign and Security Policy* (editor, Stanford University Press, 2001). He received his BA, MA, and PhD degrees from Stanford University and an honorary doctorate from the Russian Academy of Sciences' Institute of Far Eastern Studies. His newest book, *Following the Leader: Ruling China, from Deng Xiaoping to Xi Jinping*, initially was published in 2014 and was issued in a second edition with a new preface in 2019.

Hongbin Li is the James Liang Director of the China Program at Stanford's King Center on Global Development, and a Senior Fellow of Stanford Institute for Economic Policy Research (SIEPR). He obtained his PhD in economics from Stanford University and was C. V. Starr Chair Professor of Economics in Tsinghua University (until 2016) and full professor of the Chinese University of Hong Kong (until 2007). He founded the China Data Center at Tsinghua and codirects the China Enterprise Survey and

Data Center at Wuhan University, which conducts the China Employer–Employee Survey (CEES). He is the coeditor of the *Journal of Comparative Economics*, on the editorial board of China Economic Review, on the editorial advisory board for the *Journal of Economic Perspectives* and *China Agricultural Economic Review*, and was an associate editor of *Economic Development and Cultural Change* (2016). He received the Changjiang Scholarship in China in 2009, the National Award for Distinguished Young Scientists in China in 2010, and the McKinsey Young Economist Research Paper Award in 2012.

James Liang received his PhD in economics from Stanford University and master's and bachelor's degrees from the Georgia Institute of Technology. He attended the "China Gifted Youth Class" at Fudan University. He is a cofounder and executive chairman of the Board of Ctrip.com International, Ltd. In addition to leading one of the world's largest online travel agencies, Liang is an economics professor at Peking University. A leading expert in China's demographic studies, he has played an important role in shaping China's population policies as well as generating public interest in education and urban planning. He has multiple publications, including *Too Many People in China?* (*Zhongguo ren tai duole ma?*) (2012), which analyzes the impact of the one-child policy and the adverse effects of demographic changes on China's economy, as well as *The Rise of the Network Society* (*Wangluo shehuì de jueqi*) (2000) and most recently *The Demographics of Innovation* (2018).

Alice Lyman Miller is the John H. Zhao Fund lecturer in East Asian Studies at Stanford University. She holds a BA from Princeton and MA and PhD degrees in history from George Washington University. Miller was a US government China analyst from 1974 to 1990 and taught at Johns Hopkins School of Advanced International Studies, Georgetown, and the Naval Postgraduate School. From 2001 to 2018, she was editor and contributor to the Hoover Institution's *China Leadership Monitor* and is the author of *Science and Dissent in Post-Mao China: The Politics of Knowledge* (1996) and coauthor of *Becoming Asia: Change and Continuity in Asian International Relations since World War II* (Stanford University Press, 2011).

Barry Naughton is the So Kwanlok Professor at the School of Global Policy and Strategy, University of California–San Diego. Naughton's work on the Chinese economy focuses on market transition; industry and technology; foreign trade; and political economy. His first book, *Growing Out of the Plan*, won the Ohira Prize in 1996, and a new edition of his popular survey and textbook, *The Chinese Economy: Adaptation and Growth*, appeared in 2018. Naughton did his dissertation research in China in 1982 and received his PhD in economics from Yale University.

Jean C. Oi is the William Haas Professor of Chinese Politics in the Department of Political Science and a senior fellow in the Freeman Spogli Institute for International Studies at Stanford University. She directs the China Program at the Walter H. Shorenstein Asia-Pacific Research Center and is the Lee Shau Kee Director of the Stanford Center at Peking University. Oi has published extensively on China's reforms. Recent books include *Zouping Revisited: Adaptive Governance in a Chinese County*, coedited with Steven Goldstein (Stanford University Press, 2018), and *Challenges in the Process of China's Urbanization*, coedited with Karen Eggleston and Yiming Wang (2017). Current research is on fiscal reform and local government debt, continuing SOE reforms, and the Belt and Road Initiative.

Scott Rozelle holds the Helen Farnsworth Endowed Professorship at Stanford University and is a senior fellow and professor in the Freeman Spogli Institute for International Studies. His research focuses on the economics of poverty, with an emphasis on the economics of education and health. He is the codirector of the Rural Education Action Project (REAP) and is an adjunct professor in eight Chinese universities. In 2008 he was awarded the Friendship Award—the highest honor that can be bestowed on a foreign citizen—by Premier Wen Jiabao. His most recent book is *China's Invisible Crisis* (2019).

Andrew G. Walder is the Denise O'Leary and Kent Thiry Professor of Sociology in the School of Humanities and Sciences, and a senior fellow in the Freeman Spogli Institute for International Studies at Stanford University. A political sociologist, Walder has long specialized in the study of contemporary Chinese society and political economy. After receiving his PhD at the University of Michigan, he taught at Columbia, Harvard, and the Hong Kong University of Science and Technology. At Stanford he has served as chair of the Department of Sociology, director of the Asia-Pacific Research Center, and director of the Division of International, Comparative, and Area Studies in the School of Humanities and Sciences. His most recent books are *Fractured Rebellion: The Beijing Red Guard Movement* (2009), *China under Mao: A Revolution Derailed* (2015), and *Agents of Disorder: Inside China's Cultural Revolution* (2019).

Andrew Wedeman received his doctorate in political science from the University of California–Los Angeles and is a professor of political science at Georgia State University, where he heads the China Studies Initiative. He taught previously at the University of Nebraska–Lincoln, where he also served as the director of the Asian Studies Program and the director of the International Studies Program. He has been a visiting research professor at Beijing University, a visiting associate professor at the Johns Hopkins Nanjing University Center for Sino-American Studies, and a Fulbright Research Professor at Taiwan National University. During 2016 and 2017 he was a fellow in the Kissinger Institute on China and the United States of the Woodrow Wilson Center for International Scholars. His publications include *Double Paradox: Rapid Growth and Rising Corruption in China* (2012) and *From Mao to Market: Rent Seeking, Local Protectionism, and Marketization in China* (2004).

Christine Wong is a professor of Chinese studies and the director of the Centre for Contemporary Chinese Studies at the University of Melbourne. She taught previously at the University of Oxford, where she was a professor and the director of Chinese studies and a fellow at Lady Margaret Hall; she was the Henry M. Jackson Professor at the Henry M. Jackson School of International Studies at the University of Washington; and she taught economics at the University of California–Santa Cruz and Berkeley campuses and at Mount Holyoke College. She has also held senior staff positions at the World Bank and the Asian Development Bank, and she has worked with many other international agencies including the IMF, OECD, and UNDP. Her most recent publications cover topics that include fiscal reform under Xi Jinping and how China's decentralized fiscal system affects implementation of policies for education, air pollution, and urbanization.

Binzhen Wu is an associate professor in the Department of Economics, School of Economics and Management, Tsinghua University. She also is a research fellow at the National Institute for Fiscal Studies and the China Data Center at Tsinghua University, and was a visiting scholar at Stanford University's Freeman Spogli Institute for International Studies. Her research interests include public economics, development economics, and applied microeconomics. She received her PhD in economics from the University of Wisconsin–Madison in 2006. She has published in leading journals, including the *Journal of Development Economics, Games and Economic Behavior*, the *Journal of Economic Perspectives*, the *Journal of Comparative Economics, Economic Development and Cultural Change*, and *China Quarterly*.

Xueguang Zhou is a professor of sociology at Stanford University, where he is also the Kwoh-Ting Li Professor in Economic Development and a senior fellow at Freeman Spogli Institute for International Studies. His main areas of research are institutional changes in contemporary Chinese society, Chinese organizations and management, the Chinese bureaucracy, and governance in China. He currently conducts research on the rise of the bureaucratic state in China. He works with a research team to examine patterns of personnel flow among government offices to understand intraorganizational relationships in the Chinese bureaucracy. He also studies the historical origins of the Chinese bureaucracy. His publications include *The State and Life Chances in Urban China* (2004) and *The Institutional Logic of Governance in China* (2017).

Fateful Decisions

Introduction

Thomas Fingar and Jean C. Oi

Speculating about China's future is a game that anyone can play and many do. Predictions about China's future evolution range from breathless (or dire) projections of sustained high rates of growth, ever-increasing power, and inevitable displacement of the United States as leader of the global system, to cautionary (or gleeful) arguments anticipating imminent or inevitable collapse.[1] For some analysts and commentators, China is an unstoppable juggernaut; for others, it is a flash-in-the-pan phenomenon that is already running out of gas and doomed to fail because of inherent and irreconcilable contradictions. Official Chinese projections of the country's future envision slower but sustained progress toward high-income status, global leadership, and a more prosperous and harmonious world.[2] Others view Chinese actions, intentions, and implications for other countries as more malign.[3]

For some, China's evolutionary trajectory is inevitable; it will succeed or fail, act with beneficence or malevolence, and be admired or feared because of what it is (e.g., a Communist Party–led authoritarian state determined to regain China's rightful place as hegemon of "everything under heaven"). Others eschew essentialist projections in favor of alternative choice-determined trajectories leading to quite different versions of what China would be like and how it would act on the world stage.[4] Taken together, the sprawling literature on China's future contains numerous insights, more than a few thought-provoking ideas, and many confidently asserted judgments and recommendations. But the analyses and predictions are so diverse that it is difficult to determine which are most/least accurate and which assurances, alarms, and advice warrant serious consideration.

No one can predict with precision how China will evolve over the next few years or decades, and this book certainly does not claim to do so. Beijing has articulated numerous, specific, and ambitious economic, social, and other goals that it intends to achieve by 2021 (the one hundredth anniversary of the founding of the Chinese Communist Party) and 2049 (the centenary of the People's Republic of China [PRC]). These official projections of what China will be like in 2021 and 2049 differ from others in two important respects. One is that they constitute de facto promises to the Chinese people for which, at least in theory, party and government officials and institutions can be held accountable. The second is that they provide extensive lists of tasks—albeit without priorities or detailed plans to achieve them—that can be used to anticipate and assess the feasibility and efficacy of proclaimed objectives and policies to achieve them.[5]

That China will attempt to achieve the ambitious goals outlined in 2012 and reaffirmed in 2017 and 2018 is certain. How they will be pursued and whether they will be achieved are not. Whether all of these goals are realized may be less important than progress in specific areas. Improvements in health care and elder care will probably be more important to ordinary Chinese than the enhancement of military capabilities or the achievement of advanced technology objectives. Significant improvements in education, especially primary and secondary education in rural areas, may be more important for sustained economic growth than reforms intended to reduce debt or tighten central control over local governments. Some objectives must make progress in tandem if they and other linked goals are to be achieved (e.g., advances in secondary education and innovative capabilities will be required, among other things, for the achievement of military modernization and "Made in China 2025" goals), but whether China has the human, fiscal, and institutional capacity to pursue all at the same pace is far from certain.[6]

That China's goals are numerous and ambitious does not automatically make them unachievable. China has outperformed expectations during most of the "Reform and Opening" period. But, as with stock portfolios, past performance does not ensure comparable returns in the future. China has greater wealth, experience, and capacity than in any previous period, but the challenges ahead are more numerous, complex, and interconnected than those of the past. Perhaps the biggest and most consequential challenge will be to devise mechanisms and policies to ensure effective implementation of political decisions, to achieve desired outcomes, and to maintain adequate control and coordination without stifling initiative and adaptation to local conditions. We could speculate almost endlessly about what might happen and how different combinations of choices and contingencies could affect the trajectory of China's evolution, but doing so would, we believe, be less useful than underscoring the magnitude and complexity of the challenges facing PRC leaders and the contingent nature of every choice they make. A primary objective of this book is to identify where to look and what to watch, not to predict cumulative effects in a few years or decades.

China's future is neither inevitable nor immutable. How it evolves will be determined by how—and how effectively—Chinese actors manage hundreds of complex interconnected challenges. Rather than predicting the net outcome of myriad decisions made at different levels of the system by diverse actors with different interests and objectives, and the impact of changing international conditions, we focus on illustrative challenges and factors likely to shape decisions on how to manage them. Doing so underscores the contingent nature of China's future. The chapters that follow examine constraints that will shape both policy choices and their efficacy. They ask such questions as: Does China have the resources to achieve Beijing's ambitious domestic and international goals? Is money the most important constraint, or are human and structural factors even more important? Such questions cannot be answered definitively, but exploring them helps to clarify what to watch and watch for in the years ahead. It also underscores how complex China has become, and how choices made at different levels of the system by actors with diverse interests and information can affect attainment of leadership priorities. The focus on challenges, constraints, choices, and contingencies helps illuminate similarities, differences, interconnections, and contradictions within and across policy arenas. The intended result is greater insight into what is happening and what will shape future trajectories. We hope that the insights generated by this project will help officials, scholars, firms, nongovernmental organizations, and others to anticipate, interpret, and respond to developments in and by China.

The central premise of this edited volume is that specific policy choices will provide important clues about the extent to which top leaders have decided to stick with, reinvigorate, or depart from the model that has yielded success during the past four decades. The choices they make will be shaped by their perceptions of the international situation and judgments about what is required to sustain growth, maintain domestic stability, and preserve party primacy. China's own actions since the global financial crisis have changed the way other nations perceive PRC intentions and capabilities, and changes in both the international situation and the policies of key actors, notably the United States, have created new obstacles and opportunities affecting what Beijing must and can seek to achieve. Similarly, the cumulative domestic effects of sustained growth and societal change require review and possible revision of priorities and policies adopted earlier in the reform period.

The contributors to this book see many signs that past practices are losing efficacy and that China's leaders are searching for alternatives that will sustain growth and continue China's acquisition of wealth and power. There is little question that all party leaders want to do so in a way that preserves party rule and other key features of the existing system. Some seek more rapid and fundamental changes; others worry that deeper reform will undermine Chinese Communist Party (CCP) control. All agree that further reforms are needed, but there appears to be little consensus on what to change, what to preserve, how fast or how far to go in making changes to the system, or even on what the ultimate destination should be. The findings in this book point to both the need for fundamental reforms in many policy areas and a current inclination to defer tackling them for as long as possible. Indeed, much of what Beijing is doing, both internally and externally, seems intended to buy time by reverting to recentralization, tighter control, and the export of excess capacity while hoping that conditions will become more propitious for deeper reform in the future.

The First Forty Years of Reform

The reform era began with conscious choices to abandon the experimentation and campaign style of development that characterized the Maoist era (1949–76) in favor of adopting and sticking with the export-led growth model used by Japan and Taiwan. Deng Xiaoping and other veteran cadres initiated reform by adapting core institutions created in the 1950s. However, to win the policy debate that ensued after Mao's death, Deng assured other veteran cadres that proposed reforms would enhance the power and legitimacy of the party and preserve the "socialist" character of the state. This constrained reform options and precluded fundamental changes such as privatizing the means of production.

Early in the reform era, policy choices were shaped by a strong sense of urgency to make up for lost time, take advantage of opportunities created by developments in the international system, and restore social stability and party legitimacy. Repurposing existing institutions, even those degraded by the Cultural Revolution, seemed a better way to get the system up and running than delaying the process to design, debate, and deploy new ones. Difficult and fundamental changes were deferred until party and governmental institutions had been resuscitated, the economy was stronger, and leaders were more confident of their ability to manage the risks of transformation.

Deng's strategy of "feeling for stones to cross the river" facilitated economic growth while sidestepping fundamental institutional reforms. Agricultural reforms led the way because they could be implemented without abolishing collective ownership of the means of production. Markets were reopened and state procurement prices were increased to encourage rural households to grow and sell more of their harvest. The approach produced tangible results, and built confidence and legitimacy. As the need—and opportunities—for further change became apparent, the reform wheel moved forward and more demanding changes were undertaken. Reforms that required more fundamental change of the socialist system, like those in state-owned enterprises (SOE), progressed more slowly.[7] Corporate restructuring was undertaken, but SOE reforms were incomplete and remain so today.

Compromises made in the limited SOE reforms (and even in the more successful agricultural reforms) resulted in halfway measures that were politically expedient but created future challenges. Though understandable and defensible when such compromises were adopted, they often made it more difficult to achieve longer-term objectives. After three decades, most of the "easier" reforms had been undertaken. By the first decade of the current century, institutional changes remaining on the to-do list were difficult, demanding, and dangerous to continued party rule. Examples of the latter include movement toward an independent judiciary and rule of law, managing the privatization of land, reforming the *hukou* (household registration) system, and completing SOE reform. With only difficult reform challenges on the agenda, the process of reform bogged down during Hu Jintao's "lost decade" (2002–12).[8]

Architects of the Reform and Opening strategy were determined to limit intraparty disputes and prevent policy disagreements (and personal feuds) from spilling into the streets. Invocation of party discipline was reinforced by systems of promotion designed to limit infighting among factional groups and advocates of different policy prescriptions. These arrangements drove the policymaking process toward consensus and preservation of the status quo.[9] This reinforced other measures to ensure stability and policy continuity but also made it harder to tackle more difficult reform challenges. Intended to minimize the danger that policy disputes and personal rivalries would impede steady growth and advances on the quest for modernization, these measures made it increasingly difficult to implement additional structural and procedural reforms essential for sustained growth.

The decision to pursue rapid growth and technological modernization by following the export-led growth model utilized by Japan and Taiwan shaped a wide range of domestic and foreign policies. Following the Japanese model required access to markets, capital, technology, and training that was most readily—or only—available in the US-led "free world." Gaining access required the acquiescence and assistance of the United States. That, in turn, required moving beyond the "enemy of my enemy is my friend" relationship forged by Mao Zedong and Richard Nixon. To achieve that instrumental goal, Deng acquiesced to Washington's insistence on maintaining extensive albeit nonofficial relations with Taiwan.[10]

Reducing the priority of military modernization, symbolized by making the military the last of the "Four Modernizations," was a foreign policy gesture intended to reassure the United States, Japan, and other essential partners that China's self-strengthening strategy would not threaten them. It was also a key shaper of domestic investment decisions.[11] Indeed, the entire spectrum of domestic and foreign policies was intended to facilitate rapid economic growth, sometimes with unanticipated and undesirable consequences. For example, according higher priority to growth and job creation than to environmental protection has had highly negative and increasingly resented impacts on health and quality of life. The devolution of authority and resources to lower levels of the system allowed for initiative and entrepreneurial behavior but also created opportunities for abuse of power, corruption, and excessive focus on short-term gains at the expense of long-term requirements.[12]

The economy grew impressively for more than three decades and is still growing at a rate to which most countries can only aspire. But China has changed in fundamental ways over the course of reform. The once over-whelmingly rural population is now more than 50 percent urban. Regional, sectorial, class, educational, and myriad other social divisions have become deeper and more consequential. Interests, needs, and expectations have changed dramatically, reflecting the much greater complexity of the economy and society. People are now better educated, more mobile, and more aware and connected than ever before. Everything has changed and continues to evolve, but changes are occurring throughout China at different rates in different regions and sectors. As a result, many aspects of the system are out of synch and out of balance.[13] Interests, expectations, and aspirations have changed more rapidly and extensively than has the political system. Government institutions and instruments have demonstrated a surprising degree of agility and ability to adapt, but they have evolved more slowly than the sectors and activities they facilitate and manage.[14] The combination of greater complexity and more difficult challenges is straining the ability of the system to manage the more modern country.

China's success has elevated it to the status of an upper middle-income country.[15] Achieving high-income status is one of China's centenary goals, but most countries have found it difficult to make the transition.[16] Most of the fewer than three dozen countries that have done so have had much smaller populations than China; only Poland, Russia, and South Korea had populations larger than 35 million when they graduated to high-income status, and only Russia had more than 140 million.[17] China's population is ten times larger than Russia's was. Perhaps more people will make it easier for China to make the transition, but greater difficulty seems more likely. Per capita gross domestic product (GDP) is an indicator not only of living standards but also of readiness for transition from autocracy to democracy. As China approaches the threshold for graduation to high-income status (currently $12, 235), it will enter the zone in which many countries have experienced and yielded to internal pressures for more accountable and responsive governance.[18] However, allegedly to sustain economic growth, Beijing has reinstituted various forms of political study and issued at least one directive to guard against "political perils," including promotion of Western constitutional democracy.[19]

New Constraints and Choices as China Enters Deep-Water Reform

China's rise was facilitated by good leadership, good policies, and good fortune. All three fortuitous circumstances contributed to the success China has achieved, but at least one (and possibly all three) of these circumstances can no longer be taken for granted. When Beijing launched its reform and opening strategy, China had the field to itself. It was the only large developing country admitted to the "free world" economic system, and its entry occurred when the West was willing to overlook China's ideology, human rights practices, and other blemishes to secure a large partner in the seemingly endless competition with the Soviet Union. The onset of reform and opening also coincided with a period during which Western firms had the wherewithal and desire to expand abroad, and advances in computers and information technology were making it easier to subdivide production into multiple phases that could be located in many different locations.[20]

China caught the wave and, for more than a decade, had essentially no competition. Foreign direct investment flowed into the country, which rapidly gained a place, usually at or near the final assembly stage of manufacture, in a growing number of production and supply chains. Its place at the end of production chains often made China the largest export destination of many developing countries, and the largest exporter to the major markets of North America, Europe, and Japan. China's success, in combination with the demise of the Soviet Union, provided an attractive model for dozens of "nonaligned" nations that had adopted socialist economic systems after gaining independence. When the Cold War ended, most of these countries decided to reform their economic systems and to emulate China's pursuit of wealth and power through export-led growth. Today China has many formidable competitors with large reserves of low-cost labor.

A second deleterious development is the exhaustion of China's own once seemingly limitless supply of low-wage workers. During the first four decades of reform, China's population grew by approximately 380 million people, and hundreds of millions moved from farms to factories. But China will soon reach the so-called Lewis Turning Point at which the ability to increase growth and productivity by moving labor from agriculture to industrial production is exhausted.[21] A third development that bodes ill for China's future is the way in which it has alienated foreign firms by stealing intellectual property, demanding transfers of technology as a condition for establishing or expanding operations in China, and generally failing to honor contracts and trade commitments. Rather than build new facilities in China, companies increasingly forego the advantages of familiarity with conditions in China to pursue better opportunities elsewhere.[22]

Effective leadership has been critical to China's rise, but the ability to push through difficult reforms began to wane during the Hu Jintao era. The jury is still out on the question of whether current efforts to overcome structural and contextual challenges by empowering Xi Jinping will prove adequate to manage China's increasing diversity and multiplicity of interests. As the chapters in this book demonstrate, the existing system has inherent problems that impede effective responses to many economic, political, and societal challenges. To buy time to work on those problems, the party appears to have decided to expand the responsibilities, if not the authority, of its "core" leader, Xi Jinping (see chapter 1 by Alice Lyman Miller). Whether empowering Xi Jinping and reasserting party and central control will be effective is still an open question. But concentrating power puts responsibility for good leadership squarely on Xi. Every "crisis," such as the scandal over the dissemination of bad vaccines for children, causes ordinary Chinese and elites alike to have doubts about the efficacy of the system and the abilities of its leader.[23] The selection of Xi Jinping was supposed to reinvigorate the system after the "lost decade" under Hu and Wen. Xi has more titles and more authority but has yet to demonstrate that he is more effective than his predecessors.

Party leaders have essentially three broad options for addressing the challenges they face. One is to reinvigorate the process of synchronized gradualist and comprehensive reform adopted in the late 1970s by implementing more fundamental reforms (essentially the course that was followed from 1979 through 2008). A second option is to slow and disaggregate the reform process to sustain benefits, fix specific problems, and minimize risks (the apparent strategy during the Hu Jintao administration). The third option is to abandon and replace the logic and modalities of the East Asian developmental model adopted in 1978. What must be done is often unclear, how best to do it is subject to debate, and whether the options chosen will alleviate specific problems or make others worse is hard to anticipate. Moving ahead entails risks, but so does attempting to prolong arrangements that do not and probably cannot sustain growth or satisfy escalating public demands. To a perhaps increasing degree, the Xi administration seems to be using old playbooks to address new challenges.

The success of reform and opening policies has transformed the PRC but left unclear whether China must resume, revise, or retreat from policies that made success possible. American and other foreign officials and analysts who championed engagement as a strategy to transform the People's Republic into a more modern, prosperous, rule-abiding, and democratic country envisioned—and many still envision—reform as a continuing process in which economic transformation eventually and inevitably leads to political transformation. Their expectation assumed that if China halted reform, modernization and economic growth would stall. A number of Chinese analysts seem to have adopted a similar view, perhaps influenced or rationalized by Marxist theories of development.[24]

Other Chinese observers—for ideological, political, or self-interested reasons—became troubled by the duration and growing extent of dependence on the US-led, rules-based international order and the extent to which successive waves of reform were taking the country further away from core features of the party-led, centrally administered, authoritarian system envisioned by the founding fathers.[25] In their view China was becoming more prosperous, modern, secure, and influential, but it was also becoming less socialist and "less Chinese" (as they defined those concepts). They wanted to slow or halt reform and were willing to accept slower growth as a necessary cost. Over time, their arguments against continuing the approach adopted in the late 1970s were reinforced by perceptions of greater Western hostility toward China, decreased willingness on the part of other countries to accommodate China's interests, and the consequences of reform-facilitated changes in PRC society. Debate between advocates of these two imputed schools of thought surfaced occasionally but occurred largely behind the façade of party unity that all members of the political elite agreed must be maintained. Determination to prevent inner-party disputes from spilling out into the public arena stalled the reform process and resulted in more attention being paid to balancing interests and preserving cohesion, if not consensus, than to making changes necessary to sustain growth and modernization.

What is happening in China now as well as decisions being made today that will shape China's future character and behavior for years to come appear to be the product of circular logic and a back-to-the-future approach evincing more confidence in the decisions of past leaders than in the ability of contemporary officials to devise fresh solutions to new challenges. What we mean by "circular logic" can be summarized as an approach to decision-making that begins from the premise that "only the Communist Party can save China" and produces policies designed to preserve the party's monopoly of political power. This logic allows no room for consideration of whether or under what circumstances or to what extent continued party rule and perpetuation of the institutions and procedures undergirding the party's monopoly might actually be an impediment to sustained growth and comprehensive modernization. Under this logic anything that imperils or even challenges party rule threatens realization of the China dream.[26]

When Chinese leaders look to the future, they see a host of daunting challenges, and every challenge is viewed through the lens of implications for continued party rule. As a result, decisions on how to respond to or manage each challenge seem to have a bias for minimizing the threat to the status quo rather than maximizing opportunities and advantages for groups outside the party and the entrenched elite it represents. This approach and bias explain, in part, why Beijing looks to the past for solutions to future problems. A bit of history will help to clarify what we mean.

The Chinese Communist Party was born in the context of intellectual ferment and political competition centered on the quest for an ideology and blueprint to overcome China's backwardness and vulnerability. Memories, embellished by mythology about China's past greatness, reinforced preferences for a strong unitary state with a single ideology and greater reliance on the inculcation of shared values and strict social codes than on laws, courts, elections, or other methods of accountability. Marxist ideology, Leninist organizational principles, and Stalinist methods of control and forced modernization fit well with traditional Chinese notions of governance. When the CCP took power in 1949, it established a system of governance designed to achieve rapid modernization under the leadership and control of the party. Mao disrupted the new/old system repeatedly but failed to establish an alternative way to lead and control the diverse and sprawling country.[27]

"Reform and opening" was adopted and presented as a temporary expedient to jumpstart modernization, make China richer and stronger, and create the foundation for greater reliance on the "scientific socialist" model that had been abandoned by Mao. The steps taken to achieve rapid growth and sustained development included extensive devolution of authority and funds to lower levels of the system, abandonment of central planning, and substantial relaxation of social controls with the twin goals of incentivizing experimentation and innovation as well as producing tangible results that would improve livelihoods and help restore party legitimacy. The approach was highly successful and transformed virtually all aspects of China's economy and society. But the transformation of China's economy, society, and relationship with the rest of the world has sharpened the contradiction between those wishing to press on and those wishing to pause, if not halt entirely, key components of the reform process.

We do not know what positions have been championed by individuals or groups at the apex of the system, what arguments they have used to justify or oppose particular policy proposals, or even the scope or intensity of this imputed debate. But we do know that reform has slowed and become more disjointed, that performance has waned as expectations have risen, and that Beijing has reverted to methods of direction and control reminiscent of the pre-reform era. One way to explain these and related phenomena is to view them as the response of leaders worried that slowing growth and rising demands jeopardize social stability and party legitimacy in ways that imperil the quest for wealth and power.

The system and approach adopted after Mao's death have become victims of their own success. China and the world have changed so much that the arrangements put in place forty years ago are losing efficacy. But there seems to be no consensus on what to preserve, what to reform, and what to replace. In the absence of confidence in—or even the existence of—an alternative model capable of maintaining growth without further entrapping China in relationships and arrangements judged hazardous to continued party rule, Beijing seems to have decided that the most prudent course is to play for time by trying to prolong the efficacy of increasingly outmoded methods and mechanisms.

Illustrative manifestations of this include efforts to reassert party control (including reversal of the separation of party and state initiated by Deng) and mitigate threats to the party from civil society, social media, and calls to subordinate the constitution, the courts, and even foreign NGOs to the party. Another set of back-to-the-future moves includes the tightening of central control over localities and increased "steerage" of the economy (see chapter 2 by Barry Naughton, this volume). Chinese leaders recognize the magnitude and risk inherent in rapidly accumulating challenges but are reluctant to allow events to progress on the trajectories they have followed for more than three decades and fearful of making matters worse by attempting bold reforms. The alternative they appear to have chosen is to revitalize institutions and methods from the past.

During the first decades of the reform era, Beijing devolved considerable authority and resources to lower levels of the system. Doing so unleashed initiatives that contributed to sustained high rates of growth but at the cost of severe environmental degradation and dramatic increases in debt and questionable activities by cadres. As the economy (and society) became more diverse and interconnected, weak coordination across bureaucratic and sectorial boundaries facilitated behaviors now declared to have been "corrupt" and detrimental to growth, social harmony, and system legitimacy.

Rather than adopt reforms that would necessitate fundamental structural changes to address problems, current leaders seek to strengthen party control. Political power and financial resources are being recentralized, central directives restrict the use of funds and mandate activities at local levels, controls have been tightened on social media and civil society more broadly, and the role of state-owned enterprises is increasing. Beijing seemingly feels an urgency to reassert central control to overcome resistance from vested interests, reign in overextended local finance, eradicate corruption, manage urbanization and structure social welfare to prevent localism, preempt destabilizing forces unleashed by new social media, and so on. However, decentralization remains necessary to energize and incentivize local agents, allow market forces to allocate risks and resources efficiently, and promote an innovative economy. Finding the right balance between central control and local discretion is a continuing challenge. China and the Chinese people have changed greatly since 1978, and so have the requirements for effective governance and management of the economy. But Beijing seems to have decided to pursue modernity and high-income status by resurrecting institutions, personnel systems, and approaches developed for a very different time and stage of development.

A theme that runs through this book is that when the levers of control are overcentralized in the party-state, allocation of investment and risk lacks the finesse, speed, agility, objectivity, and efficiency that China's economy, politics, and society require. Political spillover from overcentralization could lead to increased factionalism, succession crises, or the demise of institutional constraints. A number of authors see big risks in China's current trajectory of hard recentralization, the Belt and Road Initiative (BRI), and "grand steerage." The implication is that the party-state needs to relax its grip and take a more open, liberal, market-based approach to development because its economy, society, and politics are becoming ever more complicated.

China's attempt to achieve modernity and high-income status without fundamental transformation of its 1950s political system is arguably the most unique feature of its version of the export-led growth model developed by Japan, Taiwan, and South Korea. Observers, both inside and outside China, now describe the Chinese experiment as a proven—if not superior—alternative to the "Washington consensus" model of development, but that judgment is premature at best.[28] If the People's Republic of China meets its centenary targets while relying more on party discipline than rule of law, substantially restricting the scope of private sector activities, and maintaining tight control of an increasingly diverse and demanding citizenry, it will be able to make a strong case for the efficacy of its alternative model. But even if it achieves modernity, democracy, and social harmony with Chinese characteristics, China might well continue to have limited soft power because there is much about the Chinese system and behavior that has little appeal for countries with liberal democracy, and discomfort with China's brand of big power behavior seems to be growing.

Back to the Future with Chinese Characteristics

What worked in the past for China appears increasingly inadequate to meet current and looming challenges. Although China's performance has surpassed expectations and forty years of reform have transformed the PRC from a poor, underdeveloped country into the world's second largest economy, key facilitating factors are disappearing. The challenges examined in this book illustrate how much China has changed; the range, complexity, and consequences of past and future choices; and tensions resulting from the use of old mechanisms to solve new problems. The developmental strategy adopted in the late 1970s has produced extraordinary growth and social change, but growth is slowing and citizens expect and demand more and different things from the party-state system. Legacy institutions and proven methods are becoming less appropriate and less effective.

The chapters in this book—written by economists, political scientists, historians, and sociologists—examine key challenges facing China as it negotiates what promises to be a difficult transition. The analysis is divided into four parts: (I) Institutions and Instruments of Governance; (II) Domestic Policy Choices and Constraints; (III) External Ambitions and Constraints; and (IV) A Comparative Perspective. Each chapter outlines possible choices and assesses the implications. The goal is not to predict what choices China will make but to illuminate how challenges and choices will affect what China becomes and how it will act.

The Institutions and Instruments of Governance part examines elite politics, center-local relations, and state attempts to control social media and reassert control of the economy. In chapter 1, Alice Lyman Miller examines the selection, mandate, and actions of Xi Jinping, including developments that many observers see as undermining institutionalization of the Chinese political process. Miller, however, argues that the reassertion of party primacy, the recentralization of power, and the enhancement of Xi's authority as China's "core" leader reflect consensus among top leaders who see these steps as essential to revitalize the system and preserve the party's leading role. She argues that Xi's increasing prominence is intended to overcome the decision paralysis that plagued Hu Jintao's second term and prevented an adequate response to slowing growth and other new challenges.

The ultimate purpose of Xi's mandate to get the country moving again is to prevent erosion of and challenges to the party's leading role and, not coincidentally, the perquisites of the party elite. The logic of this strategy is clear, but its efficacy is not. Miller acknowledges that recentralization is a high-risk strategy because it resurrects classic dangers of the Stalinist political system China adopted in the 1950s. Those dangers include the potential for arbitrary leadership, power struggles, uncertainties in succession politics, decision paralysis at lower levels of the system, and a progressively sclerotic policymaking process.

In chapter 2, Barry Naughton examines the approach Beijing has developed since 2005 to mitigate slowing growth and achieve ambitious economic goals. This approach, which Naughton calls "grand steerage," utilizes techno-industrial policies that will funnel 3–5 percent of China's GDP into such visionary projects as "Made in China 2025," the "Strategic Emerging Industries" initiative, and the Belt and Road Initiative. Naughton assesses that China currently has the financial resources to implement these plans, but suggests that "grand steerage" of China's high-tech future has perhaps a ten-year runway to take flight before demographic pressures force the government to make difficult trade-offs between investments in high-tech industrial policies and spending on social welfare and health care.

Naughton judges that China has the potential to succeed in many sectors, but converting these individual successes into overall developmental success will require policymakers to allow greater scope for open, market-based approaches. He predicts that some "grand steerage" projects will succeed and some will fail completely. He does not speculate about which those will be, but he predicts that many projects will experience prolonged and extensive gridlock caused primarily by the lack of diverse policy views, formation of vested interests, and reluctance to terminate failing projects endorsed by Xi Jinping. This could create myriad underperforming "zombie" enterprises that squeeze out private entrepreneurs. The fact that this is an unprecedented gamble precludes confident predictions about the outcome, but Naughton notes the critical importance of the next decade during which China's labor force will shrink and the population ages. If "grand steerage" succeeds, the PRC will be the world's dominant economy. If China loses this gamble, however, the country will be plagued by excess capacity, sizable debt, and an underperforming economy. China is at a critical juncture in its economic development. Naughton, like other authors in this volume, argues that political factors will be more important than financial and technical determinants of success, failure, or stagnation.

The contribution by Andrew Wedeman, chapter 3, compares Xi Jinping's anticorruption campaign to earlier ones undertaken in the 1980s and 1990s, and analyzes Xi's motivation for the current crackdown. Wedeman argues that despite much fanfare, Xi's crackdown represents only a minor escalation of Deng's 1980s war on corruption, although the focus on "tigers" (i.e., high-level officials) is distinctive. Some think Xi's anticorruption campaign is a ruse to purge his opponents but Wedeman raises significant doubts about factional analysis. He argues that major tigers, such as Zhou Yongkang, are better seen as leaders of bands of bandits rather than heads of factions. Wedeman maps the connections between big tigers (i.e., senior officials) at the center of networks that included both other tigers and nontigers. He shows that each of these big tigers were linked to a core group of other senior officials and connections into a wide web of relationships, but

Wedeman is careful to stress that not all within these networks were necessarily of the same faction or coconspirators in crime.

Rather than a ruse to purge his opponents, Wedeman argues that Xi felt compelled to launch the anticorruption campaign when he faced sobering evidence that corruption had spread to the very core of China's leadership structure. Wedeman judges that Xi initiated the campaign and sustained his attacks against high-level "tigers" because failure to take action on cases publicized via social media would undermine the party's reputation and his own authority. However, Wedeman finds that the numbers of officials indicted and convicted in the latest campaign were only modestly greater than those of earlier ones. Moreover, he is skeptical that this campaign or the new National Supervisory Commission established at the 13th National People's Congress will produce results much different than China's previous efforts to eradicate corruption. Wedeman concludes that Xi and his allies are unlikely to solve the problems of corruption as long as the incentives and opportunities induce officials to accept bribes or ignore regulations to "pursue acceptable goals through unsanctioned means."

In chapter 4, Jean C. Oi examines the enduring and emerging challenges in China's central–local relations in balancing central control and local autonomy. Decentralization and incentives for local state–led development have been critical to the past forty years of growth, but under Xi the pendulum is swinging decisively toward more centralization and tightened control over the localities. The question is whether Xi's sweeping recentralization and reliance on punishment of local-level officials will allow China to achieve its ambitious goal of becoming a moderately prosperous society. The division of fiscal revenues between the center and the localities has been at the heart of incentives that spurred China's economic miracle, but the failure to reform that same fiscal system reveals the deep institutional flaws that now plague this system and require deep reforms. Oi examines the causes of local government debt as a case study to assess which of Xi's policies to reign in local government debt are likely to be effective and which may cause unintended consequences that might dampen the incentive of local state agents and put the entire system at risk by further slowing economic growth.

Oi describes growth and debt as conjoined twins in China's developmental model and argues that local government debt is more the result of institutional factors than lavish spending by local officials. The chapter highlights the importance and consequences of the informal, hidden bargain that Zhu Rongji struck with local officials in 1994 to secure their support for his fiscal reforms. That deal gave local officials increased ability to raise funds locally to promote growth and pay for operating expenses and unfunded mandates, but it also opened the door to massive local government debt. This is an important finding because Xi Jinping's cure for the explosive local debt has been to ratchet up the anticorruption campaign and impose greater top-down regulation. Oi argues that flawed fiscal institutions are the root of the problem. A cure that blames "bad people engaging in bad behavior" will sap local initiative, which has been the key to China's economic success. The chapter ends by asking whether China can continue to operate with Leninist institutions or has reached the limits of what is possible without deep systemic reforms.

Chapter 5, Xueguang Zhou's contribution, examines tensions between the modus operandi of an authoritarian state that seeks to monopolize information and the organizing principles of the Internet and social media, which feature dense networks of multilayered, interlinked, and decentralized channels of communication that defy control. He notes the double-edged sword of social media that provides a valuable channel of communication and source of information about citizen concerns and complaints but also constitutes a worrisome mechanism for disseminating information officials would prefer to conceal and a vehicle for organizing collective action. Zhou argues that the Internet challenges the hierarchical, locality-based logic of the authoritarian state because it allows people who are similarly aggrieved to discover one another, link up, and make highly visible political demands. This makes it more imperative, more difficult, and potentially more risky for authorities to repress or meet the demands of the aggrieved. The reach and pervasive use of social media make it difficult for the government to contain local discontent because information (accurate and distorted) about events anywhere can instantly be communicated to netizens everywhere.

Zhou cites ways in which the Chinese state has manipulated social media to achieve its objectives and illustrates how officials have used intimidation and harassment to silence public intellectuals. He argues that despite the regime's success to date in controlling its netizens, social media is changing the way the government relates to its citizens and the increasing ability of citizens to hold officials accountable for their actions. His chapter illustrates the continuing contest between government controls and citizen ingenuity facilitated by advances in technology. How effectively the CCP manages China's social media, Zhou argues, will have a profound effect on the country's future.

The second part of the book, Domestic Policy Choices and Constraints, examines some of the many challenges derived from and shaped by the needs and demands of China's huge and changing population. The size of China's population was a valuable asset during the first four decades of reform, when the country capitalized on the so-called "demographic dividend." Hundreds of millions of workers moved from farms to cities, and population growth added almost four hundred million consumers and potential workers. But that fortuitous situation is now over. China's population has plateaued and will soon begin to decline. It is also aging, becoming more urban, better informed, better connected, and more demanding.

Karen Eggleston, in chapter 6, examines the interplay of China's rapidly aging population, changing health-care needs, gender imbalance, and urbanization—a combination of forces that generates a complex array of challenges such that choices in one area entail inescapable consequences in others. The challenge Eggleston addresses is how China must soon achieve economic growth with a shrinking workforce burdened with a growing population of elderly dependents. The aging population will require more and different health care. China's health system must provide more preventive care; treat multiple, chronic illnesses; offer elderly long-term care; and offer equitable access to both rich and poor as well as rural and urban populations. The cost of medical care in China, as elsewhere, will rise because treating chronic conditions is more expensive than providing basic care (which must continue to be provided), and medical technologies are becoming more expensive. Add to this the challenges of devising ways to allocate costs among individuals/families, workplaces, and the government.

Eggleston highlights the need to contain health expenditures, which have been rising at double-digit rates, to ensure adequate funding for education, elder care, and other social programs. The connections are multiple and critical. For example, with a smaller and more elderly workforce overall, having healthy workers will be critical for sustained growth and rising productivity. Good health is a requisite for effective learning and enhancement of China's social capital for the more technologically demanding jobs of the future. The structure of China's system and the challenges of coordinating programs spanning different levels of government, overlapping jurisdictions and functions, and the interests of multiple stakeholders, both private and public further complicates cost management. Eggleston underscores the difficulty of meeting these challenges when China is transitioning away from a system in which responsibility for health care and elder care rests almost entirely with families toward one with more government-designed and publicly financed health-care programs. Moreover, China's health-care reform is occurring concurrently with rapid urbanization and the expansion of other programs to alleviate access disparities. The future character of China's health care and elder care, Eggleston concludes, will require and reflect trade-offs to balance conflicting interests and priorities in the allocation of risks and responsibilities among households, local governments, and the central government.

Mary Gallagher's contribution, chapter 7, looks explicitly at issues related to urbanization and access to social benefits and public goods. She focuses on the challenges of achieving inclusive and sustainable urbanization in ways that provide equal citizenship benefits to rural, migrant, and urban residents. A major factor—and impediment—is the *hukou* (household registration) system that bifurcates workers into urban residents entitled to social benefits (including health care, education, and pensions) and migrant workers whose rights are tied to their native villages even though they live and work in cities. Gallagher analyzes the two most common modes of urbanization in China today: those based on workplace and those based on citizenship. She examines their different logics, costs, and benefits as well as their effects on welfare and citizenship inclusion. She demonstrates that workplace-based citizenship, the dominant model in China today, marginalizes those with lower education and skills and those who work in informal sectors. Citizenship-based urbanization extends urban *hukou* to rural citizens who share the same location but live on the outskirts of cities. However, to obtain the benefits of "legal" urban residence, these migrants must surrender their rural land-use rights. This policy has engendered widespread disputes because rural land has increased significantly in value and local governments often use top-down measures to compel villagers to relinquish their land-use rights. Rural residents who relinquish their land rights to gain urban *hukou* are often left with inadequate guarantees of employment or social welfare. Gallagher argues that China's decentralized governance is a further barrier to sustainable and inclusive urbanization. Local officials act in ways shaped by incentives to promote local growth and recover land-use rights that can be used to supplement funds for operating expenses and unfunded mandates.

Hongbin Li, James Liang, Scott Rozelle, and Binzhen Wu, in chapter 8, examine human capital as a critical factor in China's ability to sustain rates of growth necessary to achieve national objectives. With the end of China's demographic dividend the country must rely more on increases in human capital, achieved primarily by expanding and enhancing education. Their analysis argues that the favorable global and domestic conditions that enabled the PRC to sustain high growth for more than three decades no longer exist. China, according to the authors, has reached a stage of development that makes future growth at the 6 percent rate projected by Beijing unattainable for more than another few years. Achieving growth at even 3–4 percent will be difficult and require substantial and steady improvements in human capital. That, in turn, will require significant improvements in rural schools, which will prepare more than half of future entrants into the workforce. Based on cost estimates, the authors think it is financially feasible to expand education. However, a key takeaway of the chapter is that simply expanding the budget to increase the number of schools or teachers will not solve China's human capital challenge, especially in the rural areas, which the authors see as a key determinant to future development. There is the more difficult challenge of recruiting and keeping better, more highly trained teachers to improve the quality of education so that students will want to go to (and stay in) school. The chapter enumerates the need for improvements in nutrition, health care, and changes in childrearing practices, and the authors underscore the daunting challenges of creating incentives for parents to keep their children in school and delay entry into the workforce.

• Together, the chapters in the first two parts of the book highlight the need for China to better coordinate the diverse and often contradictory interests of political actors at different levels of government who must deal with numerous and varied sectors of the economy while coping with the rising expectations of an increasingly sophisticated and demanding population and a society that has become much more complex. The chapters by Oi, Zhou, Eggleston, and Gallagher highlight key constraints and policy choices faced by policy makers who have to operate with and within flawed and sometimes ineffective institutions created for very different economic and social conditions. Advances in particular areas have been facilitated by developments in others, and truncated reforms or retreats in some areas constrain possibilities in the system as a whole. Managing the interconnected whole will be increasingly difficult if Beijing continues to rely on old institutions and approaches to address new challenges. The authors of these chapters are neither optimistic nor pessimistic about Beijing's ability to manage the challenges in the sectors they examine, but all note that the task will be difficult.

The third part of the book, External Ambitions and Constraints, examines some of the ways Beijing is attempting to sustain growth, preserve domestic stability, and buttress China's security and party legitimacy through international engagement. It illustrates some of the ways that external conditions and actors drive, shape, and constrain China's ambitions and actions. As China has become stronger and more prosperous, it has become more ambitious and assertive, able to do more for other countries but also able—and sometimes demonstrably willing—to use its greater economic and military power. If nationalism remains the principal secondary pillar of legitimacy—secondary to economic growth and delivery of material benefits—Beijing could act more assertively to compensate for the diminished efficacy of renminbi (RMB) diplomacy. If foreign companies redirect investment to other countries or adjust production chains in ways that shift final assembly operations to countries other than China, Beijing's image and influence could suffer. But the opposite is also possible. If Beijing chooses to open the economy further, to create and rely on an independent judiciary and rule of law, and to adopt other reforms that make China a more attractive venue for foreign businesses, both the economy and China's influence could grow.

These chapters examine how Beijing's foreign and security policies fit into the larger matrix of national objectives and their role in achieving those objectives. Four decades of reform and opening enmeshed China in the global system in ways that have facilitated the country's rise but also constrain what it can, wants to, and must do internationally. Beijing has endeavored to increase China's influence and leverage while minimizing its dependence on and vulnerability to developments beyond its borders. In chapter 9, Thomas Fingar argues that China's foreign policy and international behavior are key components of Beijing's overall strategy to achieve greater wealth, power, and influence. Pursuit of the export-led growth strategy adopted in 1978 requires a reasonably stable and peaceful international environment; access to the markets, technology, and production chains of the most developed countries; and, increasingly, access to and influence in what used to be called the "Third World." Fingar argues that what China needs to sustain growth and domestic stability shapes Beijing's foreign policy priorities and behavior. Contrary to the aspirations of Chinese leaders in the 1970s and since, export-led growth facilitated by participation in the liberal order has made China more, not less, dependent on and vulnerable to decisions made beyond its borders.

As growth slows and Beijing finds it increasingly difficult to meet its domestic challenges, incentives to work with and within the US-led international order remain compelling. Fingar's bottom-line assessment is that domestic pressures on the regime push the country to adopt more assertive rhetorical positions on international issues, but the realities of interdependence and the perceived need to maintain high rates of growth and ambitious developmental targets constrain Beijing to maintain more-or-less the same foreign policy priorities and practices it has followed since 1978. China wants to be seen to have a larger say in international affairs, but it does not (yet) want to lead or change fundamentally the way the rules-based order operates. His analysis underscores the critical importance of China's relationship with the United States to the success of Beijing's security and developmental strategies. During the first thirty-five years of reform, Beijing repeatedly and effectively adjusted its policies and behavior to ensure continued US support for China's quest for wealth and power despite Tiananmen, the end of the Cold War, and numerous incidents involving the militaries of both countries. Fingar argues that meeting China's domestic challenges will compel Beijing to maintain essentially the same security and foreign policies into the future, but Xi Jinping has adopted a more confrontational posture and Donald Trump has responded very differently than his predecessors. Whether Beijing and Washington will revert to the policies of hedged engagement that have been important to both countries remains an open question. The analyses in this book suggest strongly that China will need a stable and predictable international environment for many years to come if it is to meet its domestic challenges. How easy or difficult it is to meet those challenges will be strongly influenced by the character of China's relations with the United States and a host of other countries.

Complementing Fingar's chapter on engagement with the major powers, chapter 10, by Ho-fung Hung, looks primarily at China's relations with the "Global South." Hung finds that despite continued incantation of Chinese rhetoric about solidarity with other developing countries, Beijing takes a very instrumental view of its relationships with the Third World, viewing individual countries primarily through a lens that identifies what the country can do to advance China's quest for wealth and power. What a country can do for China is more important in shaping the bilateral relationship than ideological similarities, comparable histories, or common positions on international issues. Hung further argues that China's engagement is driven by essentially the same factors as have driven other rising powers toward greater international engagement, including excess productive capacity at home and desire to lock in access to markets and resources abroad. However, powerful forces outside its control—for example, backlash from other countries leery of China's intentions, the continuing geopolitical predominance of the United States, pushback by other nations and multinational firms, and even some multilateral institutions—constrain China's policy options.

The fact that China's economic dynamism depends on exports to highly developed countries and adherence to the rule-based, neoliberal order will continue to constrain Beijing's actions and ambitions. Hung's chapter demonstrates that China's engagement with what was once called the nonaligned world is and will remain less unique than many observers, including many Chinese, have claimed it to be. His comparison of China's reported pledges of support for overseas projects and what has actually happened shows that the latter is only a small fraction of the former and provides a useful corrective to journalistic reports about China's engagement with developing countries. Equally revealing is his analysis of where China's overseas investments are concentrated. Contrary to many depictions of Chinese investment, the vast majority goes to Hong Kong and Caribbean tax havens as well as to the most highly developed countries.

Hung argues that China's outgoing investment has been driven by the desire to lock in access to energy and raw material supplies, and to export China's excess capacity in construction and related industries like cement and steel. Chinese investment in wholesale and retail trade is likely intended to facilitate importing raw materials from and exporting manufactured products to other developing countries. His fine-grained analysis of different types of foreign aid provides insight into how China has acquired control of projects when recipient countries have been unable to repay loans from the PRC.

Christine Wong's contribution, chapter 11, narrows the focus from the developing world as a whole to those targeted or encouraged to take advantage of China's Belt and Road Initiative (BRI) and explores the critically important question of whether Beijing can afford the projected scale of engagement in the new era of slower growth. Wong points to China's $13 trillion economy and assets of more than RMB 300 trillion in its financial sector to support her fairly optimistic judgment that China can easily absorb the projected $10 billion to $15 billion ("or even $100 billion") per year investment in BRI. However, she qualifies her optimism by identifying long-standing flaws in China's fiscal institutions. Wong, whose analysis of the point is similar to Oi's, iterates how China's fiscal decentralization poses risks to China's macroeconomic management—as evinced during China's 2008 stimulus program when local governments and SOEs overinvested and went offbudget. Unlike some of the authors in this volume, however, Wong expresses confidence that recent reforms and the anticorruption campaign have strengthened public financial management sufficiently to enable Beijing to discipline local spending associated with BRI. However, she points to hubris on the part of central ministries, large SOEs, and even the topmost leadership as a factor that has emboldened Beijing to pursue an overly ambitious foreign policy. Wong's analysis of China's financial capacity to support and sustain the BRI is also germane to the assessment of possibilities, constraints, and trade-offs in each of the other policy areas discussed in this book. Her judgment that Beijing can afford BRI if it chooses to do so probably pertains, mutatis mutandis, to education, military modernization, and other challenges, but only if the share of expenditure on other priorities is constrained.

In chapter 12, David M. Lampton narrows the focus even further to examine the high-speed rail component of BRI in Southeast Asia that will connect southern China to Singapore through eight countries via three potential rail lines. He provides a granular analysis of the people, organizations, and institutions within China who support, oppose, or remain purely instrumentalist in their orientation toward BRI. Xi Jinping's personal endorsement and the high profile of the undertaking influences decisions at all levels and in many sectors of the Chinese system. It also illustrates ways in which actual and prospective partners seek to take advantage of Chinese ambitions and to constrain Chinese influence. Lampton describes two major groups arrayed for or against BRI: state-centric actors, like the National Development and Reform Commission (NDRC) and the policy banks, who take the "long view" on infrastructure investments and its potential to bring about growth, and those like market-oriented banks, profit-minded actors, and China's civil society organizations who look at "short-term" results and question the ability of BRI projects to turn a profit and/or its negative externalities.

The potential gains from the BRI and the high-speed rail (HSR) system are massive, but Lampton's detailed case study illustrates that the challenges and uncertainties are enormous as well. Potential—even probable—problems include loan delinquencies and increasing security risks to Chinese personnel and property overseas. China must address these problems as it attempts to secure resources and influence abroad. Success will depend not only on China's economic capacity and wisdom but also on its political skill. Like the chapters on domestic issues, this one illustrates and underscores the complexity of contemporary China's multiple actors, competing interests, imperfectly coordinated systems, and sometimes soaring ambitions. Risks and difficulties that Hung and Wong discuss are underscored by specific examples in Lampton's chapter. Whether the HSR (and by extension the BRI) will deepen integration among neighboring countries and enhance stability and growth, or whether it will promote China's strategic domination, remains to be seen.

Karl Eikenberry, in chapter 13, examines the drivers and consequences of China's military modernization and buildup and emerging strategy that have changed the region's security situation and altered global perceptions of the PRC, the United States, American alliance commitments, and US–China relations. He looks at the relationship between growing global engagement and Beijing's perceived need to be able to protect its overseas interests. Eikenberry argues that China's economic success has expanded its perception of what the People's Liberation Army (PLA) must be able to defend. Beijing's judgment that the international environment is hostile and dangerous reinforces the perceived need to strengthen China's military capabilities. But the author also points to the near certainty of budgetary constraints resulting from slowing growth, political pressures to reduce debt, and competing demands to increase funds for education, health care, and other civilian programs.

Eikenberry describes causal chains in which expanding interests give rise to new military missions requiring new equipment, doctrine, and deployments, and increased capabilities that trigger international and regional backlash and security dilemmas. Persuading other countries that China's rise did not threaten them was a key pillar of China's modernization strategy for more than three decades, but worry on the part of Chinese officials that success has made China a more lucrative and likely target for jealous rivals caused them to undertake military developments that have deepened suspicion and fear of PRC intentions. He notes that expanding military missions and acquisitions carry an ever-larger price tag demanding ever-larger shares of the national budget. Sustaining the buildup already achieved will cost more in the future and make it more difficult to pay for other necessary expenditures.

In the final part of the book, A Comparative Perspective, Andrew G. Walder examines ways in which China is and is not unique. In chapter 14 the author suggests lessons from the experience of other Asian developmental states (such as Japan, South Korea, and Taiwan) and other states transitioning out of Soviet-type socialism (Russia and the Central European states) to better understand the consequences of China's choices at this critical juncture in its reforms. He examines the impact of China's economic evolution on its politics, as do Naughton, Oi, Eggleston, and Gallagher. Walder notes that Deng Xiaoping was able to implement his radical reforms in 1978 more easily than Russia in the 1990s because Mao's policies during the Cultural Revolution had destroyed what in Russia was an entrenched elite with vested interests in preserving the existing system. But that situation has changed dramatically after forty years of reform. He argues that China now has overlapping political and economic elites that dominate all aspects of the system and would be disadvantaged by the kinds of changes many think necessary to ensure healthy economic growth. Walder's analysis suggests that deep structural reforms that can move China away from reliance on high levels of investment and impose market discipline on state-owned enterprises have been and will be impeded by this elite, who have derived tremendous wealth from the existing system. The author predicts that unless China can wean itself away from legacy institutions and implement reforms to curtail its mounting debt and reorient the economy toward efficiency and innovation, the country will struggle to reach even the lower projected growth rate of 2 percent to 3 percent within the next decade.

The crux of Walder's analysis is that slowing growth will have a profound impact on Chinese politics. The party and party leaders have reaped a tremendous political dividend from thirty years of growth and rising incomes. That dividend will surely dissipate as China enters an era of slower growth. The rate at which political support fades and the level it reaches will depend on how much growth the country is able to sustain. Whether this leadership is able to achieve its ambitious goals will in turn depend on whether party leaders are able to implement policies that allow China to avoid stagnation and/or financial instability. Walder sees Beijing's recent reversion to greater party control, strengthening of the SOE sector, and launching of the Belt and Road Initiative (which he describes as another way to delay state-sector reforms) as portents of stasis and stagnation. As other authors in this volume (Eggleston and Gallagher) argue, the "new normal" of China's political economy—that is, growing popular expectations as manifested in the principal contradiction "between unbalanced and inadequate development and the people's ever-growing needs for a better life[—]will be a critical determinant of what Beijing must and can do."[29]

The challenges facing China are enormous, and managing them is complicated by structural features, entrenched interests, and increasingly zero-sum relationships that require reducing expenditures in some policy areas to free resources for other priorities. China's road ahead will be more difficult than the one it has traveled since 1978. Past successes have transformed the country in ways that make it both more difficult and more critical to make correct choices, and more costly to make incorrect ones. China's future is not foreordained; it is a work in progress that will be shaped by these choices.

Though rich in insight and research findings, this book similarly is a work in progress because it examines only a subset of the challenges and contingencies certain to confront Chinese officials and other actors in the years ahead. We think we have included the most important and consequential policy arenas but are very aware how many others have been omitted (e.g., consequences of enterprise debt, severe water shortages in agricultural regions and major urban centers, and managing the expectations and demands of increasingly connected citizens, to name a few). We hope that other scholars will adapt the approaches used in this book to examine challenges that we have omitted, and that the result will be a cumulatively more complete and insightful understanding of the drivers, shapers, and consequences of decisions that will determine China's possible futures.

PART I

Institutions and Instruments of Governance

CHAPTER I

Xi Jinping and the Evolution of Chinese Leadership Politics

Alice Lyman Miller

In recent decades, leaders of the People's Republic of China (PRC) have typically described the agenda of the Chinese Communist Party (CCP) in terms of "opportunities" and "challenges." In his report to the 19th Party Congress in October 2017, CCP General Secretary Xi Jinping also deployed this framework. "China and the world are in the midst of profound and complex changes," he observed. "China is still in an important period of strategic opportunity for development," he said, noting that "the prospects are bright but the challenges are severe."[1] Public statements by Xi Jinping frequently convey a confident tone of triumph in seizing the opportunities before the regime. The pursuit of reform by successive CCP leaderships, Xi claimed at the 19th Congress, has enabled Chinese socialism to cross the threshold of a "new era." China is now at a "critical stage," poised to win a "decisive victory" in the struggle to establish a "moderately prosperous society" by the party's hundredth anniversary in 2021. It will soon begin an "all-out effort" to build a "modern socialist country" by midcentury. "We are closer, more confident, and more capable than ever before of making the goal of national rejuvenation a reality," he declared.

Nevertheless, a perceptible undercurrent of insecurity underlies the confidence of Xi's pronouncements. As China embarks on the "last leg of the journey" to national rejuvenation, Xi warned at the party congress, "it will take more than beating drums and clanging gongs to get there." It will require struggle. Specifically, the Xi leadership complains incessantly about the difficulty of overcoming blocs of "vested interests" that have stymied economic reform and about its frustrations in gaining compliance with central policies from unresponsive officials further down the political system who go their own way. More fundamentally still, leadership statements and actions betray a foreboding sense of precariousness about the party's hold over a diverse, restive, and wired society. Xi has repeatedly warned that the party's survival is in doubt if it cannot push through long debated and long stalled reforms in several policy sectors that he has been mandated to achieve. In that regard, in December 2012, on his first trip outside Beijing after becoming the CCP's top leader, Xi laid a wreath at a monument to Deng Xiaoping in Shenzhen and admonished his colleagues that the collapse of the Soviet Union was the consequence of the failure of strong leaders to stand up in the face of the challenges of their time.

Since taking power in 2012, Xi Jinping has pursued a policy agenda based on the same overarching goals that guided the policies of his two predecessors, Jiang Zemin and Hu Jintao, during the preceding two decades. More broadly, Xi's agenda has been squarely consonant with the "wealth and power" ideology of "socialism with Chinese characteristics" that Deng Xiaoping set down to undergird policies of reform forty years ago. Judging by pronouncements at the 19th Party Congress and at the March 2018 13th National People's Congress (NPC), the Xi leadership's policies may be expected to proceed on that basis, not only for the coming five years until the next party and people's congresses but beyond to the PRC's centenary in 2049.

These themes of opportunity and challenge have provided Xi Jinping both the impetus and the rationale to skew the party's leadership system increasingly in directions that at first glance seem at odds with that established by Deng Xiaoping and adapted by his successors. Xi justifies his relentless centralization of power in the party leadership across political hierarchies and policy sectors, his rapid accumulation of authority in his own hands, and his tactical constriction of the limits of political discourse as necessary in the concerted pursuit of his reform agenda, however much they may also serve his own personal ambitions for power. This agenda requires, in the view of Xi and his backers, aggressive leadership to galvanize a party grown lethargic and corrupt, to catalyze long-term economic growth and avoid stagnation, and to sustain stability in a society undergoing rapid change.

But Xi's concentration of power also debilitates the decentralization of decision-making authority and the incentives for risk and innovation that the economic reforms are intended to facilitate. They invite personalistic distortions of political behavior that undermine the relative stability of institutionalized politics that has served China well and for which Xi stridently espouses support. A central part of the story of Xi's pursuit of the "China dream" will be whether and how far the political steps Xi has taken to achieve his reform agenda will hinder its realization.

Genesis of the Xi Jinping Agenda

The politics of the Xi Jinping leadership grew out of the stagnation in decision-making and the frustrations of policymaking in the late Hu Jintao period. In hindsight, the readiness of some Chinese observers to dismiss the entire 2002–12 Hu era as a "lost decade" appears more a measure of those frustrations than an accurate assessment of the period.[2] Hu's first term as party leader saw several policy initiatives to address some of the social side-effects of lopsided emphasis on economic growth under various ideological rubrics—the "scientific development concept" (2003), "building a socialist harmonious society" (2004 and 2006), and the "new socialist countryside" (2005).[3] The agricultural tax was abolished altogether in 2006, the regime delivered in short order a major stimulus package in November 2008 to counter the impact of the world financial crisis, and China's GDP more than quadrupled over the decade.

But in comparison with the first, Hu's second term saw neither major ideological initiatives nor new major policy departures. Instead, the leadership seemed paralyzed in the face of looming policy issues. The injection of a major stimulus to the economy in November 2008 stanched the impact of the emerging world financial crisis but it also benefitted the state sector of the economy over the more productive private sector, setting back progress toward economic reform. Obdurate blocs of "vested interests" consolidated, blunting any effort by an already lethargic party apparatus to press new reforms (see chapter 14 by Andrew G. Walder, this volume). In that context, already rampant corruption networks expanded dramatically, not only in the economy but also in the party, the media, the judiciary, and other realms.[4]

The Hu leadership also saw considerable slowing in economic growth beginning in 2010, as GDP growth slid from 9–10 percent to 6–7 percent annually. This slowdown came in the aftermath of the global economic crisis and a drop in export demand, but it also reflected long-term trends, including the depletion of China's surplus labor pool and rising labor costs at a time when foreign labor markets offered cheaper alternatives. Together with the graying of China's population, Beijing needed to push the economy up the value-added ladder of industrial production through investment and innovation (see chapter 6 by Karen Eggleston and chapter 8 by Hongbin Li et al., this volume).

Other problems compounded the challenge. Eruptions of ethnic and religious violence in Tibet and Gansu in 2008 and in Xinjiang in 2009 intensified leadership worries about the potential for a "color revolution" like those in Georgia, Ukraine, and Kyrgyzstan earlier in the decade, and like the Arab Spring in Egypt in 2011. Party leaders appeared unable to devise a consistent and effective approach to dealing with the political implications of the explosion of social media since the mid-2000s (see chapter 5 by Xueguang Zhou, this volume). Debates over how to reform the People's Liberation Army (PLA) to meet the challenges of China's expanding interests and contemporary developments in warfare seemed to go nowhere.[5] In foreign policy, clear indications of miscoordination appeared in managing maritime territorial disputes in the East and South China Seas.[6]

All of these developments indicated problems in the party's Politburo and its decision-making core, the Standing Committee. There were no open splits among the elite, as occurred often in Mao's day and to some degree in the Deng era, but policy stagnation in response to the growing challenges suggested deadlock in the leadership. In this context, Premier Wen Jiabao made repeated calls for renewed political reform. Finally, only months before the party's 18th Congress opened, Chongqing party chief Bo Xilai was suspended from the Politburo, expelled from the party, and handed over to civil authorities for prosecution on several counts of crime.[7] The 18th Party Congress, held November 8–15, 2012, offered the opportunity to address these challenges and renew momentum behind long-stalled reforms. Much of the overarching agenda that the new Xi Jinping leadership subsequently pursued was set down or foreshadowed in Hu Jintao's political report delivered at the congress.[8] This agenda called on the party to pursue the construction of a "moderately prosperous society" (*xiaokang shehui,* 小康社会) through "comprehensively deepening reform."

This was announced as the congress's main theme in the title of Hu's report and in the heading of its chapter on the main tasks the party should undertake. These tasks were spelled out in more detail at the November 2013 Third Plenum, which cited impetus from the party congress (the plenum was convened "in order to implement the 18th CPC National Congress strategic plan for the comprehensive deepening of reforms"). The plenum adopted a sixty-point decision that listed some three hundred reforms in seven policy sectors—economy, ecology, law, culture and media, social management, military, and party—all to be completed by the party centenary in 2021.[9]

The 2021 "comprehensive reform" goal of achieving a "moderately prosperous society" was first set down in Jiang Zemin's report to the 15th Party Congress in 1997. Jiang spelled it out in detail at the 16th Congress in 2002. Hu Jintao strongly reaffirmed it in his report at the 17th Congress in 2007 and again at the 18th in 2012.[10] As in 2012, each of the previous party congresses laid out broad strategies and guidelines and set the agenda based on the 2021 goal for the leaderships they appointed. In addition to prescribing the overarching policy agenda, the 18th Party Congress also set the schedule of subsequent Central Committee plenums to address it.[11] The congress agenda was encapsulated by Xi Jinping during inspection tours of Fujian and Zhejiang in 2014 under the umbrella formulation of the "four comprehensives" (*si ge quanmian,* 四个全面—comprehensively building a moderately prosperous society, comprehensively deepening reform, comprehensively administering the country by law, and comprehensively managing the party strictly). As Xi explained later in remarks to the Sixth Plenum in November 2016, the party congress and the new Central Committee set the agenda of Central Committee plenums that rolled out according to this sequence, addressing "comprehensive reform" (the Third and Fourth), legal reform (the Fifth), and party discipline (the Sixth).[12]

Hu's report to the 18th Party Congress also called for several specific initiatives—often quite explicitly—that emerged under Xi's leadership. These included:

- Foreshadowing the upgrading of the National Security Leading Small Group into the National Security Committee, the report called on the new leadership to "improve the national security strategy and its work mechanism, and keep high vigilance against and resolutely forestall separatist activities and activities of infiltration and subversion carried out by hostile forces."

- A call for "intensive activities throughout the Party to study and practice the mass line," a task that the Xi leadership implemented in 2013–14. A Politburo meeting on April 19, 2013, laid out the agenda of the campaign, and a work conference addressed by Xi formally launched it at central and provincial levels. The second stage, focused on subprovincial units, began in January 2014 and ended the following September.[13]

- Mandating "determined efforts to improve the style of writing and the conduct of meetings, and rejecting undesirable practices such as mediocrity, laziness, laxity and extravagance, the practice of just going through formalities, and bureaucratism." The Xi leadership undertook this task almost immediately at a Politburo meeting on December 4, 2012, that adopted an eight-point set of regulations to improve party work style for the Politburo to model for the entire party.

- Hu's report called for accelerated efforts to "establish and strengthen Party organizations in nonpublic economic entities and social organizations," a task that the Xi leadership undertook soon after the congress.

- A call for intensified efforts to enforce discipline behind the party's central leadership, which anticipated the "four consciousnesses" theme that emerged from a December 2015 Politburo meeting. All party organizations, the report said, "must resolutely uphold the authority of the Central Committee and maintain a high degree of unity with it theoretically, politically, and in action," and "faithfully implement the Party's theories, line, principles, and policies and ensure that the decisions of the Central Committee are carried out effectively." "We will never allow anyone to take countermeasures against them or disregard them," calling on the party to "strengthen oversight and inspection, strictly enforce Party discipline, political discipline in particular, and take stern actions against violations of Party discipline."

The coherence of this broader policy context invites the inference that the 18th Party Congress also gave the new Xi leadership the necessary tools to pursue this "comprehensive reform" mandate, including:

- Authorization of efforts to revitalize and recentralize the party apparatus as a more responsive and more effective driver of reform;

- Authorization of a far-reaching campaign against corruption aimed principally at attacking blocs of "vested interests" (*you liyi zhe,* 有利益者) that established themselves in recent years and that impeded reform; and

- Tightened constraints on political discourse and a tough crackdown on dissent on both the left and right ends of the spectrum—a tactic that party leaderships frequently deployed while initiating new rounds of reform in the past.[14]

Efforts to recentralize power in the hands of the party leadership emerged in lockstep thereafter. Most prominently, following the adoption of the sixty-point "comprehensive reform" plan at the November 2013 Third Plenum, a Central Committee Leading Small Group for Comprehensively Deepening Reform was established in January 2014 to coordinate implementation of the reforms across six of the seven major policy sectors called for at the plenum. A seventh leading small group was established under the party's Central Military Commission to coordinate the reforms in the PLA called for at the plenum. Some of the existing Central Committee leading small groups—such as the Finance and Economy group—were subsumed (though not dissolved) under the new "comprehensive reform" super group. The resulting group was led by Xi Jinping and included three Politburo Standing Committee members as his deputies, constituting a majority of the Standing Committee's seven members. During the new group's first four years, the group held more than thirty publicized meetings to adopt guidelines and directives for reform.

The campaign against party corruption was conducted with aggressiveness unprecedented in recent decades (see chapter 3 by Andrew Wedeman, this volume). Discipline inspection teams under the direction of Central Discipline Inspection Commission Chairman Wang Qishan, a close crony of Xi's, fanned out through central and provincial party and state bodies, while central media regularly reported on the cashiering of "tigers," "flies," and "foxes" snared in the campaign. Though often portrayed in foreign media accounts as a throwback to Mao-era purges, the campaign was deployed in a thoroughly Dengist organizational fashion, working entirely within party disciplinary and state legal frameworks. There was no resort to Mao's classic tactics of inciting the ranks of society to rise up and attack the party—surely, the last thing the current leadership wants when facing a restive populace. Moreover, the campaign charged over 750,000 party cadres in its first three years—a number far too large to be simply Xi's attempt to root out factional opposition to his leadership.

The 19th Party Congress and the 13th National People's Congress

The concerted program of reform and the party discipline and anticorruption drives authorized at the 18th Party Congress received an energetic launch in Xi Jinping's first term as party leader, but real progress in several areas was halting at best. The advance of the economic reforms spelled out at the Third Plenum was stalled by the economy's troubles during the summer of 2015, and the subsequent policy adjustment calling for "supply-side structural reform" produced contradictory results as provincial leaders skewed the policy to their own regional agendas.[15] The aggressive campaign against corruption and the drive to revitalize party work style cracked down hard on the party apparatus, but it also intimidated leaders and cadres at various levels, freezing incentives for any creative initiative and inviting passive compliance with central directives (see chapter 4 by Jean C. Oi, this volume). Reforms launched in December 2015 reorganized the PLA's central command structure and transformed its seven military regions into five theaters, all to enhance its ability to wage joint warfare. But the purge of higher-level officers on charges of corruption and the scrambling of career paths by the sweeping reorganization reforms led to perceptible grumbling and foot-dragging.[16]

The 19th Party Congress in October 2017 and the 13th National People's Congress held March 5–20, 2018, adopted a set of supplementary steps to redouble the Xi leadership's efforts behind the reforms mandated at the 18th Congress in 2012 and to reinforce the tools and tactics to pursue them. All of these steps were presented as necessary to achieve the first centenary goal of building a "moderately prosperous society" by 2021 and to lay the foundations for achieving the second centenary goal by 2049, and as suited to the "new era in socialism with Chinese characteristics."

What is different about the "new era," as Xi explicated it using Deng's orthodox logic of dialectical materialism at the party congress, is that the party now faces a new "main contradiction" as the organizing principle guiding its overarching agenda.[17] Since the beginning of the reform era, the party defined the "main contradiction" that the party must address as that "between the people's growing material and cultural needs and the backward level of our social production"—a judgment that the "basic needs" of China's people have yet to be satisfied and that China's level of development was still low. The new "main contradiction" that the party must focus on, Xi asserted, is that "between unbalanced and inadequate development

and the people's ever-growing needs for a better life." Forty years of reform
has met the "basic needs" of China's people, although the level of prosperity is uneven across society, and the standards of living that Chinese people
now seek have elevated. "We must recognize," Xi stated, "that the evolution
of the principal contradiction facing Chinese society represents a historic
shift that affects the whole landscape and that creates many new demands
for the work of the party and the country."

On the basis of this new ideological platform, the 19th Central Committee held two plenums—one in January 2018 and another in February—to
prepare revisions to the PRC constitution and to lay out a plan for sweeping
changes to China's political order for adoption at the 13th NPC in March.[18]
Two changes to the PRC constitution—the first since 2004—were essential to advancing the Xi leadership's agenda. First, "Xi Jinping Thought for
the new era of socialism with Chinese characteristics" was written into the
constitution's preamble, strengthening the fundamental legal foundations
of the Xi leadership's reform agenda. Second, Article 1 of the constitution,
which stipulated that socialism is the "fundamental system" of China,
was revised to incorporate the additional statement that "the leadership
of the CCP is the most essential characteristic of socialism with Chinese
characteristics"—a proviso that enhances the authority of the Xi leadership's extension of the party's reach into the political order and its effort to
concentrate power in the central leadership.

Similarly, some of the organizational changes adopted at the NPC
advanced the efforts of the Xi leadership to centralize power. The most
striking of these was the formalization of the Central Committee's leading
small groups—the previously informal groups that coordinated policy implementation—into party commissions. Four Central Committee leading
small groups—the Leading Small Groups for Comprehensively Deepening Reform, for Finance and Economy, for Cybersecurity, and for Foreign
Affairs—were elevated in status to Central Committee commissions. In
addition, three new Central Committee commissions—a Comprehensively
Governing according to Law Commission, an Audit Commission, and a
State Supervisory Commission—were established. The latter appears to
combine processes managed by the party's Central Discipline Inspection
Commission and the Ministry of Supervision under the State Council to
enhance the efficiency of the anticorruption campaign (see Wedeman chapter, this volume).

Party Central Committee departments were given more direct roles in "uniformly managing" the relevant sectors they guide. Thus the Organization Department was given enhanced authority to manage civil servants, the Propaganda Department was given a more direct reach in managing news, publishing, and filmmaking institutions; and the United Front Work Department was given a greater hand in minority affairs, religion, and overseas Chinese policy. Finally, the Central Party School will become the State Academy of Governance.

Xi Jinping and the Party Leadership

The prominence of Xi Jinping from the very beginning of his tenure as top party leader has led many observers to describe him as the most powerful Chinese leader since Mao. His immediate succession to the top party, military, and state posts, the proliferation of other titles he has gained, his designation as "core leader," the emergence of a cult of personality around Xi, the publication of two volumes of his speeches, the writing of "Xi Jinping Thought" into both the party and state constitutions, and the lifting at the 13th NPC of the constitutional term limit on his post as PRC president have all been interpreted as indications of his relentless drive for supreme power as a new Mao.

This interpretation exaggerates Xi's power, however. First, this account provides no explanation for how Xi Jinping achieved such supreme power so early. His power grab supposedly surprised everyone, including his leadership colleagues who, despite working alongside him for five years before his ascension, had no inkling of his grandiose ambitions. Second, Xi is not, as often asserted, chairman of everything. The two groups that Xi leads and that Hu did not are both new—the Leading Small Groups for Comprehensively Deepening Reform and for Internet Security and Informatization. The former, established early in 2014, guides implementation of the Third Plenum's sixty-point decision for reform across seven policy sectors—including economy, political and legal affairs, social management issues, culture, military affairs, environment, and party affairs. Under principles of collective leadership, only the general secretary could preside over reforms that span so many major policy sectors. As noted earlier, three other senior leaders who preside over relevant policy sectors also serve as deputies, and, taken together, they comprise a majority of the seven-member Politburo

Standing Committee, so the group's deliberations cannot be guided solely by Xi's whims.

Third, the collective leadership work system, restored by Deng Xiaoping in the 1980s and elaborated under Jiang Zemin and then Hu Jintao, remains in operation under Xi Jinping. This is clear in the policy sector assignments that each Politburo Standing Committee member oversees within the leadership's division of policy labor and in the corresponding leading small groups each directs. In addition, PRC media reporting on Politburo processes under Xi has given no hint of change from the patterns in the Hu era, when such reporting began.

Xi's designation as leadership "core" at the Sixth Plenum in November 2016 did not signal the demise of collective leadership. The concepts of "core" leader and collective leadership are not contradictory, in principle at least, as apparent in Deng Xiaoping's June 1989 talk establishing the idea of a "core": "A collective leadership must have a core."[19] The Sixth Plenum underscored this principle by revising the 1980 party regulations to strengthen provisions for collective leadership while naming Xi "core." For example, the 1980 guidelines had warned against overriding the role of the first secretary of a party committee or party group:

> The first secretary bears the main responsibility of organizing the party committee's activities and handling its day-to-day work. The important role of the first secretary must not be downgraded or even written off under the pretext of collective leadership.[20]

By contrast, the revised "Guidelines" adopted at the Sixth Plenum stressed the opposite:

> The principal responsible comrades of the party committees and party groups should foster democracy, be adept in uniting and dare to assume responsibility. When studying and discussing problems, they should consider themselves to be equal members of the body, fully promote democracy, make decisions strictly according to the procedures and act according to the rules, pay attention to divergent views, correctly deal with the views of the minority, and refrain from enforcing in an authoritarian and even a patriarchal system. Members of the body should be supported in assuming sole responsibility in initiating work within the scope of their responsibilities. It is necessary to firmly prevent and overcome the practice of an individual or a handful of people deciding matters in fact but under the guise of collective leadership and of collective responsibility in name but no one assuming responsibility in fact.[21]

In addition, the long-standing stipulation that the party practices collective leadership remains unrevised in the party constitution.

Fourth, the Sixth Plenum renewed the 1980 regulations' injunction against leadership personality cults. Attention to Xi Jinping in PRC media, in that regard, seems to reflect less a growing cult of personality around Xi than focus on his role as the front man for pressing the package of reforms sketched at the 18th Party Congress and laid out at the November 2013 Third Plenum. Leadership speeches and authoritative press commentary endlessly call on party members to "implement the spirit of the series of important speeches of General Secretary Xi Jinping and the new concepts, new thinking and new strategies" in pursuit of the "four comprehensives" (the reforms mandated by the 18th Party Congress). But they attribute that "spirit" and those concepts, thinking, and strategies to the 18th Central Committee leadership as a whole, not just Xi. In the same vein, the prefaces to Xi's two collections of speeches and talks, *The Governance of China*, underscore the collective authority of its contents, stating that Xi's speeches "embody the philosophy of the new central leadership." Similarly, "Xi Jinping Thought for the new era of socialism with Chinese characteristics" is not credited personally to Xi's innovative genius in the revised party and state constitutions but rather is described as the "crystallization" of the wisdom of the entire leadership collective and the party as a whole.

Meanwhile, media attention to Xi's public persona—eating pork dumplings at a western Beijing restaurant or kicking a soccer ball around, for example—is not altogether unique to him. There was comparable reporting on Hu Jintao eating with peasants in Inner Mongolia and other "close to the people" activities during his time.[22] What we don't hear about is Xi Jinping as "the reddest red sun in our hearts" or his thought as "a spiritual atom bomb of infinite power," as we did about Mao in his heyday.[23] Nor do we hear about Xi shooting thirty-eight strokes over eighteen holes of golf, including eleven holes-in-one, as Kim Chong-il reportedly did in Pyongyang, where a real cult of personality prevails.[24]

Fifth, the abolition of a term limit on the post of PRC president at the 13th NPC in March 2018 did not signal the wholesale dissolution of term limits or abandonment of long-standing norms of leadership retirement. In revising the PRC constitution, the NPC did not end term limits on the posts of NPC chairman and vice chairmen and of premier and vice premiers. In addition, the NPC also established term limits on leadership of the new State Supervision Commission. Nor were long-standing age-based norms of retirement abandoned in the appointment of members of the Politburo at the 19th Party Congress the preceding October, as noted earlier. The change in term limits on the post of president really was all about Xi Jinping specifically. The purpose was obviously to extend Xi's tenure beyond 2022, complementing the decision at the 19th Party Congress not to appoint a successor to Xi as party leader in 2021.

Authoritative commentary has hastened to point out that the constitutional revision does not signal Xi is "president for life." A long article in *People's Daily* on March 1, 2018, under the byline "Xuan Li"—a pseudonym for the party Propaganda Department's Theory Bureau—adhered to the standard line that the abolition of the term limit is "conducive to maintaining the stability" of China's unitary leadership system, by which the incumbent post of party general secretary serves concurrently as top military leader and head of state. But "Xuan Li" went on to note that the change does "not signify changing the retirement system for leading cadres of the party and the state, nor does it signify life tenure for offices of leading cadres."[25] In addition, the party constitution continues to stipulate that leaders may not expect lifetime tenure in their posts.

Finally, so much of what is adduced as evidence of Xi's supreme power may be turned around. For example: If Xi is so powerful, why does he need so many titles? Neither Mao nor Deng Xiaoping had many—just one or two key titles. In Deng's case, these were a seat on the Politburo Standing Committee and chairman of the party Central Military Commission. Furthermore, Deng resisted taking supreme positions himself. After pushing Hua Guofeng out of power, Deng allocated the post of party general secretary—a post he had occupied for ten years prior to the Cultural Revolution—to his lieutenant, Hu Yaobang, and the post of premier to Zhao Ziyang. Heading into the 11th Central Committee's Fifth Plenum in February 1980, Deng squashed calls on him to take the post of party chairman. Instead, he pressed for abolition of the post, which the party finally did in 1982.

There is no denying that Xi has gathered great authority—and responsibility—in the array of posts he has assumed. But does he have correspondingly great power? If Xi's so powerful, why hasn't he been able to get anything done? On his own authority, Mao laid the groundwork for the Great Leap Forward at the 8th Central Committee's Third Plenum in

September 1957 and launched the disastrous movement in 1958. With the aid of his closest comrade-in-arms, Lin Biao, he engineered the hideous Great Proletarian Cultural Revolution in the spring and summer of 1966. Deng Xiaoping launched the battle for control over the CCP's ideological platform with the 1978 campaign to "take practice as the sole criterion for testing truth," triumphing at the December 1978 Third Plenum and launching the era of "reform and opening up." Surely, if Xi has acquired supreme control over the party, he could initiate something of comparable scale. Instead, what we hear about loudly in the press is the opposite—how hard it is to push the reforms in the face of deep resistance from "vested interests," from party and state leaderships up and down the institutional hierarchy who ignore central direction and go their own way, and from corrupt cadres who skew central policies for profit.

If Xi enjoys absolute authority over and support from the People's Liberation Army, why does the Xi leadership demand at every turn the army's "absolute loyalty" to the party persist as vigorously as ever? Why convene a conference commemorating the eighty-seventh anniversary (did they ever observe a previous one?) of the December 1929 Gutian conference to stress again that the party controls the gun in November 2015, a month before announcing sweeping military reforms that have scrambled PLA missions, officer promotion prospects and career pathways, command-and-control procedures, and interservice relationships if Xi is confident of PLA loyalty? If the army is completely loyal to Xi and the party leadership, why does he need a Central Military Commission chairman responsibility system to reinforce responsiveness to central command? All of this impresses as intimations of insecurity on the part of Xi and the party leadership, not confidence in Xi's absolute authority over the military.

A better approach is to situate Xi Jinping's prominence squarely in the context of the reform agenda he was mandated to pursue when he was appointed the party's top leader. Xi's enhanced role thus reflects a consensus among the broader party elite—active and elders—in the run-up to the 18th Congress to strengthen the role of the party general secretary, enabling him to break the policy deadlocks that paralyzed the later years of Hu Jintao's tenure. By this logic, the drive to push through a broad array of long debated and long stalled reforms deemed critical to the party's survival requires a stronger leader, though not a strongman leader unconstrained by the tenets of collective leadership.

In that light, Xi Jinping does not seem a Mao-like power monger and anti-institutionalist rule-breaker. Instead, he has worked in a thoroughly straightforward Dengist fashion, relying on party disciplinary institutions to break opposition to the reform effort. More broadly, a hallmark theme of Xi's leadership recurring in his speeches and in his *Governance of China* volumes has been "putting power within a cage of institutions" ("*ba quanli guan jin zhidu de longzi li*," 把权利关进制度的笼子里), an emphasis consistent with a Dengist institution-builder rather than a Maoist norm buster. Xi's stress on study of the party constitution—mandated in 2016 as a permanent feature of party life—and his modeling for all officialdom taking an oath of allegiance to the PRC constitution on reappointment as head of state at the 13th NPC underscore this same commitment to institutions.

From that perspective, Xi's predominating role in the leadership appears less a break from the leadership system Deng Xiaoping established in the early 1980s than the latest adaptation of it to prevailing party circumstances. That system has not been static. The system Deng initially established was a simple restoration of the leadership structure and processes set down at the CCP's 8th Congress in 1956, a framework that was overthrown by Mao on the road to the Cultural Revolution. The early 1980s system had to be altered at the party's 13th Congress in 1987 following the demotion of Hu Yaobang because of alleged abuse of his role as party general secretary and as head of the Secretariat. It was modified again in 1992–93 at the 14th Congress and 8th NPC, when the post of PRC president was given to the general secretary, to strengthen Jiang Zemin's authority as an emergency choice as top leader in the wake of the 1989 Tiananmen crisis. The system was modified further at the 15th Congress in 1997, when age-based retirement provisions were introduced, and these provisions were refined at the 16th Congress in 2002. Notably, the Xi leadership continues to uphold these retirement norms, as evidenced by the leadership changes at the 19th Party Congress.

Risks and Challenges

The adjustments to the collective leadership system introduced at the party's 18th and 19th Congresses that have accentuated Xi Jinping's stature in the party leadership appear to be accommodations to the "critical stage"

that CCP faces in pushing through "comprehensive" reforms deemed necessary for the party's survival. The suspension of retirement norms that may
allow Xi to extend his tenure as China's top leader recalls the exception
made for Jiang Zemin at the 15th Party Congress in 1997, when he was
exempted from a new norm requiring retirement from the Politburo at age
seventy or older, as the party worked through wrenching reforms of China's
state-owned enterprise sector while simultaneously applying for accession
to the World Trade Organization. In the early 1980s the Deng leadership
coalition restored the collective leadership approach to oligarchy that the
CCP originally implanted at the 8th Party Congress in 1956 for two purposes. One was to inhibit a return to arbitrary personalistic politics of the
sort that plagued China under Mao in his later years. The other was to
foster effective leadership decision-making to guide a country undergoing
rapid modernization, with all its diverse and complex consequences. The
growth of Chinese wealth and power over the past four decades means that
the leadership's stake in stability, predictability, and consistency has grown
with it.

The provisions to strengthen Xi Jinping's authority, to enhance his
charisma, and to extend his tenure appear to have been justified as necessary to sustain the party's hold over a rapidly changing Chinese economy and society. If, with these adjustments, leadership politics continues
along lines of institutionalized oligarchic authoritarianism implanted in
the 1980s under Deng Xiaoping, then the relative stability and predictability of politics and policy that have prevailed since Deng's time period
will continue. Nevertheless, oligarchic politics brings its own dilemmas,
as Aristotle delineated long ago. One is the prevention of the rise of single
leader dominating all the others. In that regard, the enhanced stature of
Xi Jinping and the relentless concentration of power in the party that he
has promoted in the cause of reform vital to longer-term regime survival
bring considerable risks. These steps invite a return to autocratic strongman
politics of the kind that pervaded Chinese leadership politics in the later
Mao era, and the political and policy costs of arbitrary leadership would
be exorbitant. Some in the party may question why the suspension of retirement norms extends only to Xi Jinping, and so the Xi exception may
unravel in a trickle and then a cascade of exemptions for other leaders from
retirement norms. The demise of institutionalized constraints on leadership
retirement norms may bleed into other constraints on leadership conduct

that will in turn foster a personalistic politics of cronyism, factionalism, and free-form struggles for power and position.

The Xi leadership's abandonment of the succession mechanism that provided for the orderly transfer of power from Jiang Zemin to Hu Jintao in 2002–2004 and then from Hu Jintao to Xi Jinping in 2012–2013 may open the way to the uncertainties in power transition that plagued China under Mao and Deng Xiaoping, not to mention in the experience of most other Communist systems. As China approaches the "critical stage" of essential reforms, Xi may well have wanted to avoid the frustrations and decision-making stagnation that Hu Jintao endured as lame duck in his second term as general secretary. But uncertainties about succession to Xi may also catalyze competition among leaders and their factions as they jockey for favor and position, disrupting the stable career paths and prospects that institutionalization fostered. Policy alternatives will become more sharply contested as instruments of factional competition of the sort that made China-watching in the later Mao years and the early Deng period easier than now.

The Xi leadership's centralization of power in the party invites self-defeating consequences for reform. Concentration of decision-making at the top invites bumping decisions that ought to be made at lower levels upward, clogging the agenda of the central leadership with issues about which it has little direct knowledge. It accordingly paralyzes incentives for the policy innovation and experimentation at local levels needed for effective reform (see Oi, this volume). In extreme cases it magnifies the possibilities for policy error of potentially disastrous proportion. These are all classic faults of Stalinist political systems, and they are all the more out of step with an economy and society as diverse and complex as China's has become.

Predictably, Xi's drive for "comprehensive reform" provoked resistance from the "vested interests" that it was intended to overcome. This was already clear by the end of his first term as top leader. The apparent doubling down on the agenda at the 19th Party Congress in 2017 and the 13th NPC in 2018 and their further accentuation of party centralization and Xi's leading role confirmed it. Since those meetings, sharp attacks on "vested interests" in PRC media persist, while foreign media register complaints by liberal intellectuals, the business community, and retired party leaders that Xi has pressed his mandate too far and has run away with it to benefit his personal power. This resistance, added to the fundamental contradiction in the Xi leadership's tactics of centralizing power in the party in order to advance "comprehensive reform," lends weight to the likelihood that the reform agenda will fall short of achieving its goals. Such failings open the door to attacks on Xi's leadership. Nevertheless, given the original consensus on behalf of the mandate he received at the start of his tenure, it seems unlikely that he can be easily unseated except through ordinary succession processes such as at a party congress. If so, the prospect looms of a stagnant central leadership sustaining a system of excessively centralized party domination and presiding precariously over a society chafing at the consequences of stalled or incomplete reforms.

CHAPTER 2

Grand Steerage

Barry Naughton

The starting point for any discussion of China's economic future is the end of the "miracle growth" era. Around 2010, China exited the era of 10 percent annual growth and entered a "new normal" phase of moderately rapid growth. In the four years since mid-2015, GDP growth has been in a narrow range of 6.4 percent to 6.9 percent every quarter, which is close to the maximum possible growth rate under current conditions. Based on simple projections of the future growth of capital, labor, and productivity, growth will gradually trend down to about 4 percent annually—if things go well—over the next decade or two (see chapter 8 by Hongbin Li et al., this volume). The transition to slower growth, as pointed out by Andrew G. Walder (chapter 14, this volume), presents a series of social and political challenges to the Chinese growth model and social compact.

China's leaders clearly do not accept the idea that their economy is condemned to ponderous middle age, much less early senescence. Xi Jinping firmly embraced a target of doubling GDP by 2020—from a 2010 base—which implied an average annual growth rate of 7.2 percent for the decade. Given that growth exceeded this rate in 2010–12, current growth rates should be enough to achieve this doubling target. Although Chinese growth rates are lower than before, they are still higher than those of all but a handful of economies. Accompanying this push for continued rapid growth is an extraordinarily ambitious program to shape economic development and guide China to a high-tech economic future. Starting in 2005, China has launched new industrial policy initiatives, at first rather tentatively but steadily increasing both in the number of initiatives and in the volume of resources devoted to each one. At the same time, new ideas about future possibilities seem to be gathering force as actors in government and business contemplate potential implications of new technologies, especially artificial intelligence. This combination of practical initiatives and utopian-fringed visions is propelling China toward a program I label "grand steerage."

Because China's industrial initiatives were initiated comparatively recently and are expanding rapidly, we cannot simply extrapolate from past experience to divine China's future. In essence, China is engaging in an unprecedented gamble. If it succeeds in steering its economy to a high-tech future, China's already large economy will achieve a sort of global dominance (perhaps shared with the United States, or perhaps not). If it fails, China will be condemned to awkward second-tier status as it grapples with difficult economic problems while unpleasant demographic realities start to kick in. In this chapter, I first set the scene by pointing out the strong strand of utopian dreaming that tends to normalize the gamble that China is making. I then describe the main components of the policies currently being adopted and stress their departure from the "old normal" of a reforming China. Next I describe these policies further by asking and answering three questions: Are there adequate resources to carry out grand steerage? Is grand steerage compatible with China's market-based economy? What are the rationales for the policies of grand steerage?

On the basis of these three questions, I pose a final query that does not have a definite answer: Will it work? Of course, the fact that this is a gamble implies that we do not know whether it will work or not, any more than Chinese policymakers themselves know. Instead, to clarify the probabilities of success, I provide three simple definitions of success, failure, and gridlock. Because China's economy is so large and complex, the simple idea of success and failure can be applied only to sectors—to industries and sometimes regions—rather than to China as a whole. However, an understanding of how effectively China navigates the trade-offs between success and failure in *individual sectors* will help us evaluate the prospects for grand steerage as a whole. China's technological potential is enormous. It has the potential to succeed in many sectors, but converting these individual successes into overall developmental success will require that policymakers step back and take a more open and market-based approach to development than is currently in evidence.

The Temptation of the Plan

One of the many differences between the mind-set of the average Chinese and that of the average American involves judgments about the ability of government to shape the future. Many Americans express feelings of passivity and helplessness in the face of impending technological change and are deeply skeptical of the ability of government to change or shape the future. By contrast, many Chinese seem to assume that government will shape the future and accept that government "knows more" about the future than they do. As a result, they tend to passively or actively support the idea that their government will steer the economy into the future. Of course, the difference in mind-set is easily traced to the contrasting experiences of economic growth over the past forty years: while the median American wage has stagnated, household incomes in China have doubled each decade. Both Chinese and Americans have experienced disorienting technological change over the past two decades, but the experience for Chinese has been overwhelmingly positive. Projecting their recent pasts into the future, it is no surprise that Chinese residents are more upbeat about the future and receptive to grand government schemes than are ambivalent Americans.

An impending wave of technological change—marked by artificial intelligence (AI), ubiquitous sensors, and robots and autonomous vehicles—has given this generalized optimism a new utopian flavor. Billionaire businessman Liu Qiangdong, the founder and CEO of Jingdong.com, a Fortune Global 500 company, has said:

> In the past a lot of people thought communism was completely unattainable, but seeing our technological achievements in the past 2-3 years, I think we can achieve communism in this generation. Since [in the future] robots will be doing all the work, enormous wealth will have been created, and the government can distribute it to everyone, with no more rich or poor. All companies can be nationalized. China will only need one e-commerce company, one sales company, and [communism] can be realized.[1]

In Liu's vision, humanity will be freed from physical labor and thus able to engage in spiritual, artistic, and emotional pursuits. In essence, this is the idealist and utopian vision suggested by Karl Marx 175 years ago, for which we have been waiting ever since.[2]

Even though Xi Jinping's commitment to government planning operates in an utterly different dimension from that of Liu Qiangdong, it partakes of a similarly vast scope. At the 19th Party Congress in October 2017, Xi reported that the party has now "drawn up a two-stage development plan," to develop by 2050 "a great modern socialist country that is prosperous, strong, democratic, culturally advanced, harmonious, and beautiful."[3] Neither of these vision statements is a "plan," but both show that the vision of grand steerage has a significant hold on many important Chinese decision-makers. They fit into a broader narrative of China's rise that many people find congenial. This intellectual environment is the backdrop for the discussion of "plan" and "steerage" used in this chapter.

The "plans" referred to in this chapter are initiatives that involve real expenditure of resources to achieve concrete outcomes. These plans are operational: they push resources into specific sectors, either directly or indirectly, and thus create an allocation of resources that is different from that which would have occurred under pure market forces. When we define planning in this way, we discover something surprising: fifteen years ago, China had no plans; today China has scores, certainly more than a hundred. This enormous change has scarcely been noticed, much less understood, but it is essential to understanding China's potential futures. Vague vision statements are not new. What is new is the steady accumulation of real programs that in aggregate magnitude have exceeded some notional threshold and transformed into something qualitatively different. This unprecedented new phenomenon calls for a new term, and I provisionally call it "grand steerage."

From Planning Degree Zero to Today's China

Back in 2002, China had no plans. While there were programs linked to broad objectives—sometimes called "long-range plans" (*guihua*)—these involved modest budgetary outlays and were rarely tied to concrete outcomes.[4] The attention of policymakers was concentrated on breaking through barriers to the creation of a market economy. From 2005, China began to accumulate planning initiatives. From relatively tentative beginnings, the growth has been steady, both in the number of initiatives and in the volume of resources devoted to each one. The initiatives can be grouped into three baskets: techno-industrial policies, infrastructure plans, and urban reconstruction.

TECHNO-INDUSTRIAL POLICIES

China resumed planning in a big way in 2005 and 2006, with the promulgation of "techno-industrial policies" as part of the Medium and Long-term Plan (MLP) for Science and Technology Development.[5] Altogether, three waves of techno-industrial policies can be identified, adding cumulatively to a steady increase in the priority given to development of industrial technology. The promotion of high-technology industry has become a master key and guiding passion for Chinese leaders.

The Medium and Long-term Plan (2006). The MLP included sixteen primarily government-funded megaprojects. These were long-term research and development programs but with clear industrial policy applications. One megaproject was the civilian jetliner, the C919, which completed its first test flights during 2017. Other megaprojects covered nuclear reactors, mobile broadband telecom, and manned space flight, while more diffuse programs were launched in drug discovery, pollution control, and transgenic plant breeding. The megaprojects started slowly but in February 2009, in the wake of the global financial crisis, spending on the megaprojects was accelerated. The megaprojects were merged into a broad range of sector-specific industrial policies that combined economic stimulus and industrial restructuring.

Strategic emerging industries (SEIs). During 2009 the industrial policy implications of the MLP were gradually developed into a set of structured initiatives. In 2010 these coalesced into a formalized set of twenty targeted industries (in seven categories) for which substantial subsidies and preferential policies were provided. Unlike the megaprojects, in which government entities directly carried out most activities, in the SEIs, government was to "make the market" and provide support for leading companies, which were frequently private. A formal SEI plan was published in mid-2012, catching up with the other plans for the 12th Five Year Plan (2011–15). Expenditure on the SEIs expanded massively in subsequent years. The most striking example is the semiconductor industry, which had $65 billion (in US dollars) in dedicated investment funds by the end of 2016, and well over $100 billion by early 2018.[6] Commitments on a similar scale are evident in electric ("new energy") vehicles. An early developer among the SEIs was solar panels, which surged in 2010–11 before running into problems with excess capacity and import barriers among developed country markets, including the United States.

Innovation-Driven Development Strategy (IDDS). During 2015 through 2017 a whole series of new industrial policies were rolled out under the umbrella of the Innovation-Driven Development Strategy (IDDS).[7] The most well-known of these (in the West) is "Made in China 2025," which described a program of industrial robotics and intelligent manufacturing, modeled on Germany's "Industry 4.0" program. However, "Made in China 2025" was just one of many programs, including "Internet+" (2015), Artificial Intelligence (2017), and Military-Civilian Fusion (2017). While these industrial policies are designed to foster specific sectors, such as robotics and artificial intelligence, these programs differ from the SEIs in that they envision using new technologies to transform traditional industrial sectors.[8] In a sense, each generation of techno-industrial policy has been more sophisticated than the preceding one (and to a certain extent may be seen as a response to the failings of the previous generation).

These techno-industrial policies are proliferating initiatives. When new initiatives are introduced, the old ones don't disappear. These initiatives generally do not have sunset provisions. Instead, when problems emerge with excess capacity, ad hoc adjustments are made to scale back subsidies (for example, in solar power and electric vehicles). As the initiatives are rolled out, they are incorporated into successive Five Year Plans. This gives an impression of continuity, since Five Year Plans had never disappeared. But the Five Year Plans for 1996–2000 and 2000–2005 were indicative, vague guidance plans articulating developmental goals. Since 2005, these plans have bulked up and gotten much more concrete content, most obviously in the number of subsidiary plans (sectoral and regional), which have increased dramatically and are being taken much more seriously. Indeed, the Five Year Plan itself is a kind of "stamp of approval" that attempts to wrap the techno-industrial initiatives into some kind of coherent framework. Only after an initiative has been approved and launched is it woven into a Five Year Plan.

INFRASTRUCTURE PLANS: BELT AND ROAD INITIATIVE

Ambitious infrastructure construction has been a feature of the Chinese economy since 1998. Construction of highways and expressways accelerated around the turn of the century, such that China was building about 10,000 kilometers of expressway annually by 2010. High-speed rail (HSR) construction was ramped up rapidly in 2009, and about 3,000 kilometers of HSR have been completed annually since 2010. Both these remarkable programs reached peaks around 2014 and 2015, after which the pace of construction has leveled off as the national network neared completion.

It is not much of a stretch to see the Belt and Road Initiative (BRI) as a continuation of this domestic effort, but with a new level of international commitment. Crucially, the BRI envisions China as the hub of a radiating system of transport and communication spokes. David M. Lampton (chapter 12 in this volume) shows the substantial investment envisioned in one of the most important "spokes": that reaching down to Singapore. However, this is just one of six land spokes that will link China to its neighbors in three directions. BRI is an enormous program with potential implications across many spheres. Suffice it to say that BRI is a program that inevitably starts slow, because each individual project must first be selected in a binational agreement, and there must be bilateral planning processes. The program will, however, gradually gain momentum (see Lampton and chapter 11 by Christine Wong, this volume).

URBAN RECONSTRUCTION: XIONGAN, YANGTZE BELT, AND THE "GREATER BAY AREA"

While most attention has been focused on China's techno-industrial and infrastructure ambitions, China has also been gradually laying out increasingly ambitious plans to reconstruct its most important urban areas. These are also infrastructure plans, of course, but programs in which infrastructure construction is tied to the creation of a planned urban environment. There are three national plans to reconstruct urban regions, or agglomerations, each an expansion of the most important existing "traditional" cities: Beijing, Shanghai, and Hong Kong.

The program that has attracted the most attention is certainly the Xiongan New District, an entirely new city to be built about 100 kilometers south of Beijing. Planning for Xiongan seems torn between three competing inspirations: Xiongan is to be the receptacle for the "noncore" functions of Beijing, relieving pressure on the national capital;, it is to be a kind of prototype "smart city"; and it is to be an exemplary "green" city.[9] These conceptions ensure that a lot of expensive infrastructure will be built, including rapid and high-quality transport and communications. However, they cannot ensure that a vibrant and economically productive city will be created (for more on challenges of urbanization see chapter 7 by Mary

E. Gallagher and chapter 6 by Karen Eggleston, this volume). The other two regional urbanization plans are more straightforward, because both regions are already characterized by diverse clusters of medium-sized and larger cities. The "Yangtze Economic Belt" includes the highly productive midsize cities of the Lower Yangtze along with provinces up the Yangtze to Sichuan. The "Greater Bay Area" program is particularly ambitious, since it includes Hong Kong and Macau, as well as Shenzhen, Zhuhai, and Guangzhou, pushing the economic integration of cities that are under different political administrations. In both regions the urbanization plans are based on building infrastructure to link existing cities more closely. This forthright rationale underpins the planning effort and may contribute to improved productivity.

This is a large menu of government plans, and the list is getting longer on an almost daily basis. Put together, these initiatives add up to an extraordinary commitment of economic resources. In fact, we do not have a very accurate assessment of the total volume of these investments. In part, this is because the plans, their definitions, and the priorities put on them are in a constant state of flux. Judging from official Chinese media, one would think that the Belt and Road Initiative is the largest or most important of these initiatives, but it is at most only as big as one or two of the industrial policy initiatives put together. A lack of precision is due in part to the fact that many different instruments are being used to foster industrial policies, and many different channels are being used to provide funding, so we are far from having a comprehensive accounting. Most of all, though, quantitative accuracy is impossible simply because the programs are growing so rapidly that two- or three-year-old data substantially understates the level of commitment.

However, we can postulate a rough order of magnitude for these programs in the aggregate. China's 2018 GDP was about $13 trillion. As discussed below, China has already set aside $1.34 trillion in state-run "industrial guidance funds," which is 10 percent of GDP. This figure denotes the total fund-raising scope, not how much will actually be spent in a given year, which we need to estimate. The "industrial guidance funds" will invest in twenty to twenty-five industrial sectors, and some will require very substantial commitments. Recent estimates of the scope of electric vehicle industrial support, for example, range upwards of $100 billion over several years. Thus a very rough estimate of an average commitment of $10 billion annually to each of twenty to twenty-five sectors is realistic and produces an estimate of $200 billion to $250 billion annual investment for all techno-industrial policies. The Belt and Road Initiative is spending only $25 billion to $50 billion per year right now but is expected to double that figure relatively quickly.

China also reports spending about $2 trillion annually on total transport, urban, and environmental infrastructure investment. Half of this amount (about $1 trillion) is spent on land purchase and many necessary and routine investments, leaving about $1 trillion in real new infrastructure investment. If we guess that 30–40 percent of this goes to large-scale government initiatives such as high-speed rail and urban reconstruction, that gives an additional $300 billion to $400 billion. Summing these three categories provides a rough estimate of expenditures for "grand steerage" of somewhere between $525 billion and $750 billion a year. This implies China is, or will soon be, spending 4–6 percent of GDP for grand steerage initiatives. More than half a trillion dollars a year—plus clear signals of intent to grow these programs—indicates the magnitude of China's ambition.

Are China's Resources Adequate for Grand Steerage?

Although the sums envisaged for China's grand steerage are large, China generally has the resources to spend. However, it will be impossible to avoid difficult future trade-offs. The recovery of China's fiscal revenue base between the 1990s and the 2010s provides the basic context for the revival of planning. Back in the late 1990s, China simply did not have sufficient budgetary resources to carry out ambitious plans. Budgetary inadequacy combined with the need to tame out-of-control inflation made then premier Zhu Rongji allergic to all types of grandiose projects. By the turn of the century, though, budgetary revenues were reviving strongly (see Wong, this volume). With successful fiscal reforms the government's "take" from the economy—fiscal revenues as a share of GDP—doubled between 1995 and 2012, from 11 percent to 22 percent—before stabilizing (this consolidated budget includes central and local governments). This remarkable doubling of the fiscal share doesn't capture the whole story, though, because China also raised revenues from two substantial sources that were insignificant in the 1990s. First, social insurance premiums—included in the budget by every other country but segregated into a special government fund in

China—increased rapidly to 8 percent of GDP in 2017–18. Second, local government land revenues are volatile but have increased rapidly to a range today from 5 percent to more than 7 percent of GDP. These two special revenue sources have grown from almost nothing, so if we combine them with standard budgetary receipts to create "augmented government revenues," that sum has much more than doubled as a share of GDP. Moreover, whereas regular budgetary revenues stabilized as a share of GDP and began to decline after 2015, augmented revenues have continued to increase and reached 36 percent of GDP in 2018.[10]

This gives a sense of the amount of room for maneuver that Chinese policymakers have today: 36 percent of GDP in government hands is very substantial, comparable to high-income welfare states, and significantly higher than the comparable ratio in the United States.[11] These comparative figures come without considering the impact of state ownership on the economy. Virtually all of China's financial system is state-owned, which means that the scope for channeling abundant household saving into government priorities is very substantial. Control by state-owned enterprises of strategic sectors such as energy, electricity, and telecom can potentially be used to further government priorities. In short, these steerage ambitions are broadly within the capabilities of the Chinese government. If we make a comparison with the United States, the war in Iraq was within the capabilities of the US government, even though it absorbed similarly huge sums and was far less productive. Another comparison would be the US Apollo (moon-landing) program, which cost a total of 2 percent of the United States's 1970 GDP, spread out over several years. The Chinese economy is big and the government's tax take is large, so the government can afford these programs if it wants them.

Yet costs should not be measured purely in terms of ability to pay. Chinese policymakers for years have talked of "rebalancing" the economy, but in truth China maintains by far the world's highest investment rate. Fixed capital investment's share of GDP soared to 45.2 percent in 2010 and then plateaued; it started only to decline in 2014 and in 2017 was 42.7 percent of GDP.[12] If this is "rebalancing," it is occurring extremely slowly and gradually. In fact, every one of the ambitious initiatives described here sustains the high investment rate and thus reduces the share of national income that can be made available for consumption. More concretely, the flow of resources into industry and infrastructure reduces the funds available for medical care and retirement support, crucial given China's aging population (see Eggleston, this volume). Of course, resources cannot just be transferred from investment to consumption without considering the impact on the trajectory of growth. Still, at the end of the day, resources have an opportunity cost, and the cost of China's ambitious initiatives is the lost ability to improve consumption and social security more rapidly.[13]

Underspending on social services can be sustained for a while but not indefinitely. Chinese people are accustomed to poor public services, but their patience is not unlimited. More fundamentally, China is still in a stage of its demographic trajectory where dependency rates are quite low and the share of the population working is very high. During this phase, governments can get away with poor public services and unrealistic retirement programs, because the population is young, healthy, and predominantly working. Today in China the turning point toward a slower growing labor force and an aging population has already been reached, but these changes don't become quantitatively large for another decade. In 2027, according to the best projection, two things happen: China's total population will peak and begin to inch downward. At the same time, the total population at working age (sixteen through sixty-four), having plateaued since 2014, will begin to decline briskly. Not surprisingly, old-age dependency ratios will begin to increase sharply about that time, and China will enter the category of an aging society (see Eggleston, this volume).[14]

This emerging demographic reality will force some tough choices on China. By 2030 there will be only four working-age adults for every old person. The generous retirement program currently in place for fully vested urban workers cannot possibly be extended to all workers (rural–urban migrants, informal sector workers, and farmers). Medical expenses are likely to grow rapidly as the population ages. These challenges loom in the medium term, but China can defer them for another decade. In a way, one could look at China's "grand steerage" today as an effort to exploit a window of opportunity, the coming ten years (2018–28) when overall demographic conditions will still be favorable and the supply of young and experienced workers is still growing rapidly. For now, there is no absolute obstacle to China spending 4–6 percent of GDP on visionary projects. Over the long run, however, China's grand steerage inevitably heightens the "principle contradiction" that Xi Jinping articulated in 2017: that "between unbalanced and inadequate development and the people's ever-growing needs for a better life." It is a gamble, the terms of which start to become markedly less favorable in a decade.

However, none of the political constituencies that would be expected to restrain aggressive spending has much voice in China. Ordinary Chinese citizens have no role in determining their level of taxation. Perhaps feeling powerless about their overall direct and indirect tax burden, Chinese urban citizens sometimes voice qualified support for techno-industrial policies. "The government will spend the money anyway," one often hears, "they might as well spend it here at home on something that might have beneficial effects." Besides, few people have a sense of the sums of money involved because they are so enormous. Meanwhile, the Ministry of Finance, which is a force for fiscal conservatism in most countries, has been actively involved in crafting the financial mechanisms for these initiatives, and the technocrat most involved in the design process, Liu Kun, was promoted to minister of finance in March 2018. Under today's circumstances China has the resources and the political will to engage in grand steerage.

Is Steerage Compatible with China's Market Economy?

Chinese policymakers have invested substantial time and effort into creating institutions and organizations to keep these ambitious programs compatible with a well-functioning market economy. They may not succeed, but they have approached the issue thoughtfully. Indeed, the belief of policymakers that grand steerage and a market economy are compatible is part of the answer to the obvious question: How can it be that China, after more than thirty years of transition to a market economy, now seems to be tilting toward increased government steerage?

A MARKET ECONOMY AT THE BASE

China's economy is still predominantly a market-based economy. While the intention of Chinese policymakers to steer the economy distorts market signals, it does not squeeze out the market (at least, not yet). Moreover, while the government and Communist Party envision special roles for state-owned firms and provide them with special support, planners do not at all exclude private firms from their ambitions. Quite the contrary: privately owned firms like Alibaba and Tencent, as well as the employee-owned firm

Huawei, are already "national champions," vigorously supported by the Chinese government. Indeed, the goods-producing sectors of the economy, manufacturing and agriculture, are overwhelmingly dominated by private business. Today's ambitious government initiatives are layered onto the foundation of a market economy.

WHAT KIND OF PLANNING IS THIS "STEERAGE"?

China's policymakers today designate industries for favorable treatment; they practice a kind of indicative planning that signals to private and state actors which sectors they view as the industries of the future. Once those decisions are made, they open the taps. Resources flow through a variety of channels, some of which are described in the next section. Central government resources flow through direct investment, tax breaks, special funds, and abundant bank lending. Once the central government signals its intent—and sometimes before—local governments follow with their own programs, often designed to position local firms to join in the government-provided bounty. Little or no attempt is made to control or limit who can partake in these new initiatives. There is no "top-level design," despite frequent use of that term by policymakers. This is certainly not a centrally planned system. Competition is an integral part of the system, at least most of the time.

To be sure, important strategic decisions are made centrally. Initially, this means articulating a vision of the industries of the future, which indicates what industries to support and sometimes which technological solutions to gamble on. But once these crucial designations have been made, actual implementation is competitive and, to a certain extent, chaotic. Multiple local government initiatives complement—or conflict with—central government favorites. There is no attempt to resolve trade-offs between supporting one industry or another. While the government charts the desired direction, it remains agnostic about the specific solutions or even the chances of success. If a national champion seems to be emerging, the government will swing behind it. Sometimes the government will swoop in early, backing early market consolidation (as with Didi Chuxing in ride-hailing, for example). At other times the government waits until dominant firms have emerged through market processes, as happened with Alibaba, Baidu, and Tencent, and then pulls them into a compulsory embrace that both supports and reins them in.

This somewhat chaotic scenario shows how different the current shift toward grand steerage is from the old planning system. First, recall that planning emerged in the Soviet Union precisely because the Soviet government did not have the financial resources to ensure that critical resources went to planners' priorities. Soviet planning began as a series of ad hoc reactions to specific shortages and then, as the Hungarian economist Janos Kornai taught in his 1980 book *The Economics of Shortage*, it became a permanent shortage system. As a result, planners spent all their time making sure today's steel output went to their preferred customers. This was a complete waste of time because markets are perfectly able to distribute steel to all users, provided the budgetary and credit systems ensure that they have adequate funds. China's grand steerage effort is far more efficient than the (failed) Soviet system, because it dispenses with all that waste of planners' time spent reproducing simple production and trade relations, leaving that to the market. This enables planners to focus on the change margin, trying to be effective in setting developmental directions for the economy.

Of course, waste is still enormous. All the Chinese planners and policymakers implicitly acknowledge this. But their attitude to this waste is that of the venture capitalist: most of the new firms will fail, and the money spent on them will be lost, but the few that succeed will become the future national champions. If that occurs, China will have gotten its money's worth, figuratively if not literally. In their view, although the steerage is wasteful, at least the waste is concentrated in the right place.

FINANCIALIZATION OF GOVERNMENT INSTITUTIONS

As the government and party commitment to grand steerage has grown, China's leaders have adapted government institutions to provide the necessary financial support. In short, the Chinese government expects to achieve ambitious objectives because it is prepared to pay for them. Of course, that does not mean that budgetary revenues fund all these initiatives. Rather, the model is that government funding and lending from state-owned banks will "sweeten the pot," attracting additional investment from private and publicly owned businesses. In this way, ample funding for each initiative can be assured.

The realization of this funding objective is closely related to one of the least well-understood objectives of Chinese economic system reform proposed during the 2013 Third Plenum. The reform program that emerged from that meeting called for diffuse and hard-to-define objectives such as "mixed ownership" for state-owned enterprises. In subsequent years the institutional shape of those objectives only gradually came into focus. After 2016 new government-run corporations were created, sometimes from existing state-owned enterprises. This new category of "state capital investment and operations companies" (*guoyou ziben touzi, yunying gongsi* 国有资本投资、运营公司) has been delegated ownership rights from the existing state asset managers.[15] These firms are empowered to make investments in a wide variety of sectors, but, of course, are supposed to follow national policy and support the grand steerage envisioned by planners.

Closely related is the new category of government-run "industrial guidance funds" (*chanye yindao jijin* 产业引导基金). These are government funds that are set up like venture capital firms. That is, there is a managing partner and limited partners. The managing partner, always a state-owned enterprise or government agency, has full responsibility for investment decisions and fulfilling the strategic guidelines specified in a management contract. The limited partners are passive providers of funds, and they may be state enterprises, subsidiaries of state banks, private firms, or even some types of government agencies. These funds are fully empowered to invest in private firms or state-owned enterprises, existing firms or start-ups, and while most are domestically oriented, a few have made significant investment in foreign firms. They can also establish and manage subsidiary funds that operate like venture capital funds, early stage ("angel investor") funds, or private equity funds. Their objective is to fund growing firms, devise appropriate exit strategies, and (eventually) recover their investments.

An example of an "industrial guidance fund" is Guoxin Guotong Zhejiang (国新国同浙江), capitalized with RMB 150 billion. It is managed by Guoxin International (国新国际), a subsidiary of a central government state enterprise (Guoxin 国新, translated as China Reform Holdings) recently converted to a "state capital operations company." Guoxin Guotong Zhejiang has attracted investments from four other central SOEs, including China Aerospace, and nine local Zhejiang firms, a few of which are private. The mission of this fund is to invest in Zhejiang's high-technology enterprises and foster information technology in particular.

In this "financialized" set-up, government agencies foster government investment priorities through a number of different channels. First, as managing partner, a government entity is responsible for choosing investments in line with government priorities. Second, serving as limited partners, government enterprises and agencies act as "patient investors" who will be satisfied with a low rate of return, even a zero rate of profit, so long as they (hopefully) recover their initial investment. In this way the government is hoping there will be more profit left over for the other partners, thus attracting (less patient) private investors to participate. Finally, the government sets up explicit types of fiscal outlays that help to smooth the system. Budgetary expenditures are used both to subsidize interest rates, and to compensate certain investors when their investments fail and must be written off. Through these channels, government policymakers hope to make investments as profitable for private parties as for government firms. They are thus combining government guidance with market orientation. In this sense "mixed ownership" has become a way in which government objectives permeate both public and private sectors of the economy, supported by generous funding. Subsidizing investments, guaranteeing against losses, and reducing the government's take from successful investments, these funds seek to encourage and support both private and government firms to pioneer new areas and business models.

Industrial guidance firms are large and growing quickly. Government-run industrial guidance funds had grown to an astonishing total size of $1.34 trillion (fund-raising scope) as of the end of 2017.[16] This number was almost double that of end-2016, which in turn was more than double the end-2015 figure of "only" about $250 billion. This money was being paid-in and just beginning to be invested. Thus the financial institutions set up implied a substantial acceleration in the steerage effort from the year 2017. This rapid increase in funding certainly risks creating a "bubble," of inflated valuations for new firms, and money squandered on start-ups that in retrospect appear silly. However, these bubbles are not different in kind from those that are blown up in market economies. Indeed, overall, these institutions are intelligently designed and compatible with a market economy. In principle, there is no reason they cannot support accelerated growth by start-up and entrepreneurial firms.

What Is the Rationale for China's Grand Steerage?

China's grand steerage effort ultimately derives from policymakers' response to the end of "miracle growth" in China. By 2005, Chinese policymakers could see that fiscal revenues were recovering strongly, and they were emboldened to take the first tentative steps toward industrial policy initiatives. The unwelcome arrival of the global financial crisis in 2008–2009 gave an additional abrupt and fundamental impetus to the policy calculus. China responded to the financial crisis with a massive domestic demand-side stimulus. Within a few months China pumped bank credit and fiscal outlays into myriad investment projects (including some of the techno-industrial policies described earlier). China displayed a remarkable ability to get shovel-ready projects going in a short time. Roads and new public squares were soon under construction in virtually every Chinese town. Within several months the policies were seen to have been broadly successful. The rapid rollout of this investment-based stimulus program pumped up domestic demand and effectively compensated for the rapid drop-off in export demand caused by the global financial crisis. The beneficial effects spilled over into the global economy as well, because the surge in investment sustained China's demand for imported raw materials, which sent one of the first positive signals that helped the world turn the corner, in the spring of 2009, from the worst phase of the crisis.

At the same time, the global financial crisis deeply undermined the attractiveness of the American model, weakening Chinese advocates of a market-driven, generally hands-off approach to development. The American system had stumbled dramatically, with huge economic and political costs. Moreover, in response to the crisis, the US and European governments embraced government policies to support the development of their solar, wind, and other alternative energy industries. Developed countries did this as part of their stimulus response to the crisis and considered it a temporary, crisis-driven recourse. But to the Chinese, if the free-market paragon of the United States behaved this way "when the chips were down," didn't this show that across-the-board opposition to such government intervention was at best inconsistent and at worst hypocritical? Thus the global crisis contributed strongly to a fundamental shift in the attitude of Chinese policymakers.

After the short-run recovery from the crisis, though, policymakers had to confront the reality of a growth rate that was declining for deeper structural reasons, relating to the declining growth of the labor force, the slowing of rural-to-urban migration, and the completion of industrialization of many traditional sectors. At a comparable stage in their development, forerunner economies like Japan and Korea marked the end of high-speed growth by remaking the relationship between the state and the economy. Dirigiste regimes—that took their authority over private firms for granted—gave way to "light touch" industrial policies. Governments did not become hands-off, but they ceded to corporations and research institutes much of the exploration and guidance activity the government had provided during the growth miracle phases. As their economies approached the technological frontier, government planners lost confidence in their ability to shape future trajectories and allowed corporations to go their own way. Of course, at approximately this stage of development, Korea and Taiwan became democracies, and new constituencies pulled their governments in fundamentally different directions.

Chinese policymakers have resolutely declined to follow a path similar to Japan and Korea when their economies slowed. In the first place, per capita GDP is substantially lower in China than it was at the time of growth slowdown in Japan and Korea. Policymakers were flush with confidence after their success in managing the global financial crisis and, in China's political system, faced few constraints on their desire to push for the highest possible growth rate—that is, to minimize the inevitable slowdown of the economy. In this context policymakers naturally began looking for large-scale aggressive investment programs to prop up the growth rate. The high-speed rail and highway projects could answer this need until about 2015, but there are limits to how many railroads you might want to build. This space could only be filled with the ambition to foster a technological revolution.

Opportunities may be greatest in "emerging industries," because there are no entrenched incumbent competitors. The way may be open for an electric vehicle manufacturer, for example, in a way that it will never be for a producer of old-style gasoline combustion vehicles. Along with the revival in techno-industrial policy in 2006, Chinese planners began to look for emerging industries in which to make their mark. The experience of solar panels seemed to provide proof of concept, since Chinese producers rapidly achieved global dominance. Even more critically, from about 2015 it became plausible that an unprecedented wave of technological change would begin to reshape the global economy, as artificial intelligence and ubiquitous sensors have begun to change how we manage the physical world. Liu He, China's most influential economic adviser, is on record as arguing that technological revolutions develop in tandem with global crises, and that world economic relations realign in the wake of crisis as new technologies are incorporated into the production system. In other words, with the world recovering from the global financial crisis, Liu He predicts that the adoption of a new wave of technologies will drive global realignment.[17] For better and for worse, the perception of a technological revolution fulfilled a perceived need for Chinese planners. They already felt a need for aggressive spending to prop up growth, so it was appealing for them to spend it on a technological revolution in which China was relatively well positioned. The scope of "emerging industries" was expanded to encompass the Internet+, Artificial Intelligence, and "Made in China 2025." The way was open for a steady increase in the volume of resources going to new industries and technologies.

The inevitable growth slowdown can also be seen, from a different perspective, as an intrinsically hard-to-manage problem. Following structural changes in the economy, the sudden downward revision in expectations about growth leads businesses to cut back on their investments. The problem in a way is how to move smoothly from a very high investment rate appropriate in a high-growth environment to a moderate investment rate without triggering a downward spiral and sharp recession. The risk is that as previously profitable investments become unprofitable, the investment rate drops, leading to a self-reinforcing cycle in which reduced demand leads to further cutbacks in investment and a shrinking economy. To different degrees, both Japan and Korea encountered this problem at the end of their miracle growth phases. Chinese policymakers were determined to avoid such a downward spiral, which meant propping up investment for its "demand side" importance. In Keynesian terms, ambitious programs can be a way to manage the investment rate to keep aggregate demand from dropping too rapidly.

However, government-sponsored investment cannot be a long-term growth strategy unless that investment contributes on the supply side as well. Even the boldest investments must ultimately be justified by their creation of new capital that contributes to the productivity of the economy (and thereby generates a return to repay the investor). The risk is that decision-makers will overestimate an investment's contribution to the economy's long-run supply potential because they are focused on propping up demand. In that case, sustaining a high investment rate will only defer problems to a later date, by keeping demand artificially high for a prolonged period. How likely is that outcome? To begin to address this question, it is necessary to first specify more clearly the nature of success and failure on a sectoral level.

What Constitutes Success and Failure?

China possesses numerous technological and economic strengths. To evaluate China's future, I describe three scenarios at a sectoral level: success, failure, and gridlock.

SUCCESS

Success in an industry or service sector can be defined in a straightforward way. After a period of shakeout, in which unsuccessful firms go bankrupt or are acquired by successful firms, a given industrial sector in China emerges with a number of world-leading, Chinese-controlled firms. These firms must be able to survive in fair and open international competition. They do not need to "dominate" their industries (despite the fondness of Chinese planners for this word), but they must be able to control key segments of the production process and innovate continuously to remain competitive. In this scenario the assets of successful firms have real value. Investors can hold on to these assets or get their money back; lenders can be repaid.

FAILURE

Failure is not just the absence of success. Failure means that start-up firms are unable to survive after subsidy and protection are ended. It may be manifest in widespread bankruptcies, or it may be disguised in various ways. Mediocre firms may shelter in low value-added segments of the industrial production chain, cooperating with multinationals to produce commoditized goods. Governments may invoke noneconomic justifications, such as national security, to continue protecting these firms, but they are unable to disguise the lower productivity and innovativeness of the firms. In this scenario the assets of the surviving firms are worth far less than the investment made. Loans cannot be repaid and investors face substantial losses. There is an overhang of bad loans until painful debt restructuring must be carried out.

GRIDLOCK

Gridlock appears when low-performing firms are kept alive, but protection is not explicit. Zombie firms are kept alive by various kinds of regulatory forbearance and discrimination, combined with ad hoc bailouts. However, it is never clear whether these firms could survive in fair-market competition. The degree of protection remains murky, and numerous firms with heterogeneous capabilities remain in the market. Investors face great difficulty in getting their money back, yet the will to carry out decisive debt restructuring is absent because firms seem capable of limping along in the present environment.

Based on these simplifying scenarios, we can make three observations about China's future. First, China is likely to enjoy success in many sectors. Second, the Chinese economy can absorb many cases of both success and failure. Third, the most serious economic risk is the danger of multisector gridlock. Overall, there are four reasons to expect that China will experience a degree of success in many emerging industrial sectors. First, China's human capital base is already substantial and is improving rapidly. The number of students graduating from college has increased steadily, reaching 7.36 million in 2017, of whom 40 percent are in science and engineering. Thus China has a deep pool of relatively inexpensive technical labor and is currently producing twice as many scientists and technicians annually as the United States (there is still a quality differential, of course). China may indeed by *over*investing in highly skilled labor and neglecting basic rural education (see Li et al., this volume), but in terms of the programs under discussion in this chapter, this is not likely to be a problem for at least a decade. Moreover, China's increasing investment in research and development has already reached critical mass. With the steady increase in overall R&D spending, China is on track to catch up with the United States by 2020 (again, quality matters).[18] In addition to the evidence of the aggregate numbers, it is clear that China is already a player in many of the technological fields necessary for emerging industries, an actor of significance second only to the United States.

Second, China possesses a very large market that increasingly serves as the "lead market" for some types of innovative product. Market size is largely dependent on GDP, and China is the second largest GDP in the world. Even more directly, though, China has by far the largest number of mobile phone and Internet subscribers, so it already serves as the lead market for many products and services related to those platforms. It is not accidental that the application WeChat has become the most important social network in the world, or that cell phone–based payments systems are already pervasive in China while they have scarcely taken root in the United States. Demand for security equipment from the Chinese government makes it a large customer for surveillance and big data services, serving as a (chilling) lead market in that important area. Being the lead market is extremely important, because it means that innovative firms are close to the customer and can adapt and fine-tune innovations to meet customer needs most effectively. That gives those innovative firms a first-mover advantage that can often be applied in global competition.

Third, China possesses the world's largest and most diversified manufacturing bases in the Yangtze and Pearl River Delta areas. This factor is a perfect mirror image of the preceding one: proximity to manufacturing means that incremental innovations can be quickly implemented in production, driving down costs and eliciting creative new solutions to production problems. Of course, manufacturing can also be the "lead market" for many innovative products, particularly in the era of robotics and artificial intelligence. The proximity of production and use creates the potential for extremely rapid cycles of innovation, adoption, and adaptation.

Fourth, and finally, it is indeed entirely possible that we are on the cusp of an unprecedented period of technological change. Novel "general purpose" technologies are emerging, in the combination of AI, cloud computing, and the "Internet of Things." China has a strong technological and competitive position in each of these, and if they combine in mutually reinforcing ways, China may be in an especially strong position. In this sense, Liu Qiangdong may not be completely wrong, and new technologies may create the possibility of qualitatively new forms of economic organization.

In short, while money can't buy everything, there are many things that money can buy, and China has many of the prerequisites for supporting success in innovative industries. Thus China's aspirations certainly cannot be dismissed. Quite the contrary, it seems obvious that successful and globally competitive Chinese firms will emerge in many sectors—from electric vehicles to Internet services and AI firms—if they are allowed to do so. Indeed, this would be the case even if China had no industrial policies.

Correspondingly, the Chinese economy is big enough and diverse enough that overt failure in a score of sectors need not be a big threat to overall economic performance. If investors lose money on a case-by-case basis, the government will share in their losses, but they are both consenting adults and there is no reason the investments cannot be quickly liquidated. Failure, allowed to produce its own consequences, is also not a big risk. Rather, the risk is of widespread deadlock. Why might that occur and why might it be damaging and risky to the Chinese economy?

The Risks of Gridlock

The most immediate risk of China's current policies is simply that the productivity of investment will decline and many individual investments will generate little or no return. In this type of outcome, growth will steadily decline as the productivity of investment slides. Financial risks will accumulate as unpaid loans mount and investors are unable to recoup their investments. In assessing the risks of this type of outcome, it is important to keep in mind the fact that the vast majority of investment goes for relatively mundane items: structures, simple machines, and basic infrastructure. Massive as the ambitious grand steerage programs are, they still account for a clear minority of overall investment, and technological revolutions do not happen overnight. In fact, the productivity of China's investment has been declining since 2010, as measured by the simple incremental capital-output ratio. This calculates the number of units of fixed capital that have been required to produce an additional unit of GDP: it shows a steady deterioration as the investment required to increase GDP by one unit has increased from under four to over six. This may reflect the difficulty of shifting gears and coping with a sluggish global economy, or it may be the result of a steady erosion in investment productivity as political direction of investment becomes more prominent and more investment goes into unproductive projects.

There are also many reasons to be skeptical of the likely productivity of the new initiatives themselves. Take urban reconstruction projects for starters. The international record of cities newly built by government planners is far from reassuring. Purpose-built cities like Brasilia, Naypyidaw, or Chandigarh rarely contribute much to a country's economic development.

The enormous investment effort China is likely to put into the new city of Xiongan—and the associated effort to adjust the economic structure of Beijing—is unlikely to increase productivity very much. Xiongan doesn't even exist yet, but it already has a schizophrenic personality of being an ecological, high-technology city (on the one hand), and a repository for the Beijing city functions that are inconsistent with being a gleaming national capital (on the other).

The Belt and Road Initiative aims to create an Asian infrastructure network, with China at the hub, that will lower transport and logistics costs across a broad swath of the world. But transport is already much cheaper by sea than by land, and the economic centers of Asia (including China) are all on the coast. The overland portion of BRI will create expensive land connections to relatively small nearby economies that already have alternative transportation links. While such investments will make a modest contribution, on a case-by-case basis, to the neighboring economy, they are unlikely in the aggregate to have a high payback to the Chinese economy.

In the high-tech areas there is significant new technology risk. By definition, the specific solutions that will emerge at the technology frontier are unknown. Investing too early in unproven technology solutions can be extremely costly. Sometimes it makes sense to be a latecomer and slip quickly into a market with a slightly cheaper version of a technology already proven by somebody else. For example, China is currently investing an enormous amount in NiCad batteries (as is Tesla in the United States). This is a gamble, because it is by no means clear that this is the best battery technology, or even that all-battery vehicles are superior to various hybrid solutions, or to radically different fuel cells. A really good venture capital system allows work to go forward on a diverse portfolio of practical technologies. There is plenty of room for an outsider technological solution to come from behind and surpass the consensus frontrunner. China's system does not preclude such a dynamic in all areas: it is still market-based and subsidies are often available for a range of approaches, so "plans" cannot generally bottle up whole industries. However, in many sectors, industrial policies display significant favoritism to "core technologies" and specific approaches. In electric vehicles, hybrid engines are specifically excluded from most subsidy programs because of fears that Japanese manufacturers are sufficiently advanced in hybrid technology and that domestic companies will never be able to catch up with them.

Similar technological guidance in other industries adds to cost, distortion, and risk.

In short, just as we can have confidence that Chinese entrepreneurs will succeed in many areas, we can be equally confident that much investment will be wasted on shortsighted or misguided initiatives. It is thus of crucial importance how low productivity and failed investments are handled. If a failed investment is matched by extinction of the investors' capital, bankruptcy, and the write-off of bad loans, then the costs can be chalked up to experience and forgotten. Lots of human activities waste resources. Far more consequential is if bad investments and bad lending decisions are allowed to fester in a pattern of widespread gridlock. Investments that have failed to become successful firms in that case may be kept alive as zombie businesses. Zombie businesses would be sustained by a constant drip-feed of credit, tying up resources and skilled labor. Governments, banks, and entrepreneurs have every incentive to collude in this kind of outcome. Banks don't like to have to write off their bad loans; governments face embarrassing questions about failed investments; and entrepreneurs want to hold on to the good times for as long as possible. Zombie infestation is a real risk, and the technical, accounting, and political challenges involved in wrapping up nonperforming firms can be considerable.

This type of outcome would also increase the risk of financial crisis. Outside analysts have warned for years of the problem of excessive debt in China, so far without ever seeing the crises they had predicted come to pass. Indeed, Chinese authorities in 2017–18 made an effort to restrain the growth of credit and begin deleveraging. However, China's ambitious initiatives have the potential to wreck any deleveraging process and establish an even bigger and more dangerous debt burden than before. Even though government guidance funds invest directly in firm equity (rather than bank lending), many of these funds leverage their access to capital through cordial relations with government-run banks. Moreover, the guidance funds are all closely tied to government patrons who will not want to see them lose money or go bankrupt. In the long run, this excess flow of capital to a limited range of sectors may create an even larger financial bubble, contributing to greater risks in the future. The fundamental question is whether investors and regulators have the determination and the tools to liquidate bad investments reasonably promptly. By the evidence of the Chinese system in the past decade, the answer is no.

Are the Risks Increasing?

There are three reasons to believe that there is an increasing risk of the kind of long-term gridlock, eroding efficiency, and financial crisis just described. This is because many of the costs of current policies are hidden; the aggregate effort going into the policies is accelerating; and international conflict is increasing. These adverse trends suggest that a major reorientation of policy may be required.

ACCUMULATION OF HIDDEN COSTS

The expansion of many initiatives and the expenditure of massive amounts of money distort the market environment and lead to the steady accumulation of hidden costs. Government industrial policy, in any economy, tends to draw resources into targeted sectors more rapidly than would otherwise occur, and since China's policies are carried out in uncoordinated fashion by multiple local governments, the experience likely will be replicated in many localities. We have seen a taste of this with the solar panel industry, which experienced rapid entry and then a collapse of profitability. We will surely see similar phenomena in electric vehicles, for example, where many different localities are promoting and protecting their local champions.

In addition, policies that protect one sector inevitably subject some other sector to additional hidden costs. This is one of the key insights of the economics of international trade: tariffs that protect one industry create "negative protection" for downstream sectors that use that industry's product as their inputs. China's industrial policies are so complex and affect so many different sectors, that it is impossible to assess the extent to which other sectors are being disadvantaged. This is especially true when initiatives target so-called "core technologies," such as semiconductors and batteries. Chinese policymakers often describe "core technologies" as key profit centers in production chains, which means these products are key inputs into downstream assembly industries. If planners allow downstream purchasers to buy freely on the world market, then upstream "core" technology producers may never attain profitability; if planners restrict downstream purchasers, they support the upstream core producers but disadvantage the downstream industries. In the short run, this difficult trade-off is submerged by the huge inflows of money into these core sectors, but it will be difficult to avoid the problem forever. In the meantime, no significant cost-benefit analysis is being conducted, so it is hard to know how effectively money is being spent, or what the indirect costs really are. In the end, China is spending trillions of dollars with little serious scrutiny of the value of the investment.

The political commitment to grand steerage is intensifying, the magnitude of the effort is accelerating, and the difficulty of disengaging from any particular initiative is increasing. Xi Jinping has consolidated his political position and the constitution was amended in March 2018 to eliminate term limits on Xi's post as president, thus opening the way to an indefinite hold on power. In addition, Xi launched a government and party rationalization and reorganization that clearly strengthened his ability to exercise top-down power more effectively, often by using direct Communist Party channels (see chapter 1 by Alice Lyman Miller, this volume). Thus, for the coming decade at least, Xi's voice will be by far the dominant one on these grand steerage initiatives. There is no doubt that Xi Jinping strongly favors these ambitious initiatives. Xi has already demonstrated his strong commitment to prestige-enhancing targets and policies, and China's big initiatives are obviously a continuation and expansion of this approach. Xi has personally identified himself with the Belt and Road Initiative and with the construction of a new city at Xiongan, and he seems to feel strongly that the national capital should be a more presentable showcase than it is at present. The links to techno-industrial policy and Five Year Plans are less personal but hardly less strong. Xi has a strong liking for multidecadal goals and anniversaries, and he expects to achieve ambitious goals to mark those anniversaries. He is attracted by the links between techno-industrial policy and military capability, and he supports the goal of steadily making Five Year Plans both more visionary and more authoritative.

Will an unfettered Xi Jinping be willing to restrain or cut back on these ambitious programs? Would his advisers have the nerve to tell him it needs to be done? The most likely answer to these questions is "no," and so we face the likelihood of a steady increase in the commitment of resources to grand projects. From a top-down perspective, Xi is pushing the system to provide greater outputs of power and prestige, and that means more investment in showcase initiatives. At the same time, there is a bottom-up political economy logic that pushes for each individual initiative to be maintained and expanded. There are legitimate objectives linked with each program, and interest groups rapidly form around any existing program. If the goals have not been achieved, the argument can easily be made that the resource input should be increased to overcome this failure.

Indeed, this has already happened at least twice with semiconductor fabrication industrial policy. Each time that policy has failed, it has been relaunched with twice as much money. It might actually be easier to terminate successful programs—which can be spun out into successful businesses—than unsuccessful ones. Programs like these give politicians at many levels resources and a sense of mission and personal self-importance. Big projects generate big patronage and naturally attract support. Without doubt, government agencies like the National Development and Reform Commission (NDRC) and the Ministries of Industry and Information Technology and Science and Technology strongly support the full spectrum of techno-industrial policies. They see themselves as executing the initiatives in partnership with the China Development Bank and other government-run financial institutions. The political economy logic of these programs makes the "zombie infestation" scenario rather more likely.

To be clear, these initiatives also seem to enjoy support among China's rising middle class. The aspiration to make China a modern, civilized, great nation is widely shared. As described earlier, the number of college graduates in the workforce is increasing rapidly. Many of these graduates have technical degrees, and the market for their services is by no means guaranteed. By calculation and aspiration, many of them support a grand steerage role for the state if that will accelerate hi-tech employment growth. The money in, for example, industrial guidance funds is increasing rapidly. The speed, but also the acceleration, of China's effort adds to the overall risks.

INCREASING NATIONALISTIC HOSTILITY

Finally, these initiatives increase international conflict with consequent increased nationalistic hostility on both sides of the conflict. Each of these initiatives—but especially in the fields of techno-industrial policy—involves an element of international competition. Indeed, the articulated Chinese rationale for these policies, as articulated in the program for Innovation-Driven Development Strategy, stress their impact on national competitive strength (or weakness).

During 2018, Sino–US tensions over trade, investment, technology policy, and intellectual property rights burst into open conflict. While

Trump's disruptive approach to international relations is an important factor, the big Chinese push—especially in techno-industrial policy—is clearly destabilizing international economic relations. Worries about Chinese industrial policy have increased in Germany, France, and Japan, and not just in the Trump administration. Parties outside China are worried about those policies that will succeed and also those that won't. Rapid technological progress has the potential to benefit all of humanity, particularly when the most efficient companies and solution providers are allowed to prevail internationally regardless of their national origin. However, China's tip into strongly nationalist industrial policies means that this type of mutually beneficial—but competitive—outcome will be hard to achieve.

Instead, both China and the United States face the clear danger of falling into a vicious cycle of retaliation and protectionism. Even if the current (2018–19) "trade war" is resolved in a negotiated solution, it is hard to see the underlying tensions lessening without a significant shift in Chinese policy. Indeed, it is far easier to envision the opposite outcome: China may double down on techno-industrial policies because it perceives the outside world as increasingly hostile and unreliable. That would further contribute to the acceleration of industrial policies already under way. If China responds by consolidating multiple industrial policies into a system of comprehensive national protection, it will be extremely damaging to long-run productivity growth. In addition, it would also make it much more difficult politically for China to shift its policy stance, and economic damage would spill over to the rest of the world economy. Of course, these effects are not inevitable, but they will require wisdom and statesmanship to avoid—qualities that are in short supply in today's world.

Conclusion

China is taking big risks with its current grand steerage policy. This means that the future is unusually hard to project. It is possible that China will continue to spend large and increasing sums of money and emerge as a world leader in a broad spectrum of newly emerging industries. If Chinese cities are also able to hook into a "smart cities" dividend, create a new model of urban form, and reap a productivity dividend from highly networked and integrated urban clusters, the possibility of broad success cannot be dismissed.

At the same time, the stance of top political leaders today, combined with recent trends in policy and expenditure, suggests that the more likely outcome is that investment will continue to accelerate and resources will be channeled into an excess volume of low-performing projects. There may be no productivity-enhancing breakthroughs for another decade; new cities may turn out to be pleasant backwaters with no significant economic impact. Under these circumstances, aggregate debt would grow, the volume of resources tied up in unproductive projects would grow, and economic performance would deteriorate. Simultaneously, financial risks would grow, and so would risks of international conflict. The possibility of substantial economy-wide failure is not insignificant.

These are not the only options. There is a possible middle path. China could conceivably maintain a substantial but stable aggregate effort at about the level sustained in the past few years, at perhaps 3 percent of GDP. Such an effort, prolonged over several years, is already probably unprecedented outside of wartime, but the Chinese economy could support this for a decade. However, to maintain the overall scope of the program at roughly today's level, some initiatives would be enabled to grow, but other programs would have to be pruned, and cut back as they reach maturity. Decisive action would be required to get rid of the "losers" in overcrowded fields through efficient bankruptcy and prompt debt consolidation. In such a scenario, planners would have to demonstrate convincingly that protection and nurturing of "infant industries" is short-term and that adolescent firms would be required to stand on their own after a maximum of five to ten years. Tough choices would have to be made regularly about the quantity and duration of support for competing projects. This outcome is entirely possible from an economic and technical perspective, and this policy setting would complement China's impressive domestic resources.

The problem is that this "tough love" scenario would require a major policy reorientation and is therefore in the short run politically extremely unlikely. True, China will likely be able to celebrate many successes in the 2020s, including having doubled GDP in the previous decade, substantially reducing poverty, and making a dent in pollution. There will be opportunities to declare a well-earned victory and retreat from the biggest excess of grand steerage. If that doesn't happen, by the late 2020s, China will begin to face a much more difficult set of challenges in the subsequent decade as the labor force shrinks and the population ages. In practical terms, it is entirely possible for China during the next decade to steer a course between Scylla and Charybdis, between overinvestment in grand projects and excess caution and economic slowdown. However, it is much easier to envisage the Chinese steerage trajectory tipping to one extreme or the other, and hard to have confidence in the ability or willingness of the leadership to moderate ambitions and ease into a more sustainable growth path.

China is making an enormous gamble, and we do not know what the outcome will be. If China wins this gamble, it will emerge in twenty years as not just the world's largest economy but as a globally dominant actor. Size will be combined with success in moving to the technological frontier and a position of sufficient centrality in the Eastern Hemisphere to guarantee global predominance. If China loses this gamble, it will be swamped by excess capacity, an extreme debt load, and an underperforming economy that takes decades to work off the burden of low-quality, deteriorating, and ill-designed infrastructure. That would cause an aging China to tumble into a decade of stagnation resembling Japan's 1990s decade, but on a larger scale. Whatever the outcomes, these ambitious policies—this gamble—will have enormous implications for all Chinese, and for everyone on the planet.

CHAPTER 3

Anticorruption Forever?

Andrew Wedeman

Corruption is a multifaceted, long-standing, and integral component of both governance and development with Chinese characteristics. During the transition from the plan to the market, bribes often helped move assets from the plan to the market by giving officials material incentives—albeit illegal incentives—to transfer state assets to entrepreneurs who stood to reap windfall profits from the transfer. Corruption, however, also skewed development and harmed the Chinese economy as well as causing safety and reputational damage. The likelihood of eliminating corruption in China's party-state system is small, but the relative success (and failures) of efforts to bring it under control will have a significant impact on the efficacy of policies to address the other challenges examined throughout this volume and the ways Chinese and foreigners view the system and its leaders.

The current anticorruption campaign has some unique characteristics, including the extent to which it is attributed to Xi Jinping, but efforts to limit the political costs of high-level corruption did not begin with his ascent to power. Members of the Politburo were convicted of corruption during the tenures of Jiang Zemin (Chen Xitong, Beijing party secretary, in 1995) and Hu Jintao (Chen Liangyu, Shanghai party secretary, in 2006), and more than fifty provincial governors, party secretaries, ministers, vice governors, and vice ministers had been removed for corrupt behavior in the decade before Xi Jinping's ascent. Indeed, by 2012 it looked like the party's war on corruption was beginning to achieve at least limited success. The number of party members punished for infractions each year had stabilized at around 140,000 since the mid-2000s, and the number of individuals indicted on corruption charges hovered at about 40,000 a year. According to Transparency International, China had been gradually moving closer to the mean of its Corruption Perceptions Index (CPI), and between 2000 and 2012 China's average score was better than the median.[1] The World Bank's Governance Index also showed improvement as China's score regressed toward the mean.[2] Nevertheless, public opinion in China consistently ranked official corruption as a major problem.[3] Although many ordinary Chinese may have grumbled about official corruption, there were few signs that ire was morphing into demands for high-level intervention.[4]

Despite such indicators that corruption had not become more serious or salient, Xi Jinping appears to have decided during his preparation to succeed Hu Jintao as general secretary of the Chinese Communist Party (CCP) that serious corruption at the heart of the party, state, military, and internal security apparatus had reached a dangerous level. Serious corruption at the core constituted a political threat because it implied that the paramount leadership lacked the ability—or perhaps the will—to enforce discipline at the top. Attacking corruption enabled Xi Jinping to demonstrate to both the party-state and to a cynical public that he could achieve success where others had failed to make much headway in the party's decades-long battle against the "cancer of corruption."

The question addressed in this chapter is whether Xi Jinping's campaign, in practice, differs from those of his predecessor in either effectiveness or focus. While the actual tempo of the war on corruption has not changed much, this campaign is distinctive in its focus. Whereas earlier crackdowns in the 1980s focused on rank-and-file corruption, and those in early 1990s on mid-level corruption, Xi Jinping shifted the focus to high-level corruption in 2013—what is called "hunting tigers." This tiger hunt began in early 2012, when Politburo member Bo Xilai, party secretary of Chongqing, was detained after evidence surfaced that his wife, Gu Kailai, had murdered English businessman Neil Heywood.[5] Available data indicate that the campaign peaked in 2014–15, but the crackdown on high-level corruption continues. The reported takedown of ten tigers in the first three months of 2019 indicates that scrutiny of high-level corruption will likely continue. As of March 2019, 203 tigers had been detained, indicted, sent to prison, received lesser party disciplinary sanctions, or were reported to be undergoing investigation on corruption-related charges. Tigers continue to be bagged, albeit at a lower rate. However, of the recently netted tigers, only Sun Zhengcai, a Politburo member and party secretary of Chongqing who was detained in July 2017, has held a senior party or government position.[6]

This chapter examines who has been targeted, how the tiger hunt developed, and links among those targeted.[7] I also examine when Xi's attack on high-level corruption began. This is important because corruption did not suddenly worsen in the years just before Xi Jinping started hunting tigers. On the contrary, available evidence suggests that high-level corruption worsened in the decade before Xi Jinping became general secretary, that most of the tigers became corrupt while they were mid-level officials, and that corruption at the top became worse because corrupt officials were promoted into the leadership.

My research suggests that Xi Jinping's crackdown is a political purge but not a factional purge or political witch-hunt. It is *political* because it seeks to tighten Xi's grip on the party. Xi Jinping has clearly targeted networks linked to members of the senior leadership, but these networks more closely resemble gangs of bandits than political factions. The crackdown is a *purge* because it seeks to cleanse the party-state of corrupt officials, cadres, and managers. It may have achieved other goals as well, but the crackdown has enabled Xi Jinping to secure his position as paramount leader and has rid the party of many corrupt officials. It is much less clear whether the crackdown has actually reduced the amount of corruption.

Assessing Xi's Anticorruption Campaign

As the anticorruption crackdown launched in early 2013 enters its sixth year and Xi Jinping begins his second five-year term, it is appropriate to assess the impact on systemic corruption and whether the campaign will continue indefinitely. Wang Qishan, the head of the party's internal police force and the former head of the Central Discipline Inspection Commission (CDIC), has described the intensified anticorruption effort as the "new normal," and the party has pledged that the crackdown will continue.[8] In January 2018, Xi Jinping declared, "As soon as a 'tiger' rears his head, we will strike at once; as soon as a 'fly' flies in disorder, we will swat."[9] Such statements suggest that top leaders expect the problem to persist, as does the recent creation of the National Supervisory Commission system.[10]

After six years of a much hyped crackdown, it is not clear that the effort has yielded major gains. There is no way to measure the "actual rate of corruption" (i.e., the percentage of party cadres, state officials, and managers of state-owned enterprises [SOE] who are corrupt), or to determine whether changes in the "revealed rate of corruption" (the percentage of all officials charged with corruption) result from changes in intensity of enforcement or changes in the severity of corruption. This makes it impossible to determine if corruption is less severe in early 2019 than it was in late 2012. However, it is possible to compare Xi Jinping's attack on corruption to previous crackdowns by examining the extent to which they targeted rank-and-file, mid-level, and high-level corruption.

Despite all the fanfare, Xi Jinping's crackdown may not have changed dramatically the overall tempo of the war on corruption. On the surface the raw numbers are impressive. According to official reports, between 2013 and 2018 the CDIC has investigated 2,300,000 disciplinary cases and sanctioned 2,313,000 party members.[11] Given that the party had a total membership of approximately 90 million in 2017, this implies that slightly more than 2.5 percent of the party membership has been punished.[12] The number of party members investigated each year also suggests dramatic increases since the beginning of the crackdown, with the number of investigations increasing from 155,000 in 2012 to 638,000 in 2018, a fourfold increase.[13]

Data from the Procuratorate, the judicial agency charged with conducting criminal investigations and prosecutions, suggest less dramatic increases, with the number of individuals charged with corruption-related offenses rising from 47,000 in 2012 to a peak of 55,000 in 2014 and then falling 14 percent to 47,500 in 2016. The number of indictments fell again in 2018, dropping to 44,151, which is 5 percent less that the number of indictments in 2012.[14] The number of court cases involving corruption doubled between 2013 and 2017 but dropped substantially in 2018.[15] Because trials are held at the end of the investigation and prosecution process, the "peak" in 2017 likely resulted from the trial of officials placed under investigation in previous years (Figure 3.1).

The gap between the steep increases in party disciplinary investigations and the more flat-line trend in the number of individuals indicted on criminal charges can be explained, in part, by the adoption of the "Eight-point Regulation" ("*Ba Xiang Guiding,*" 八项规定) banning official extravagance,

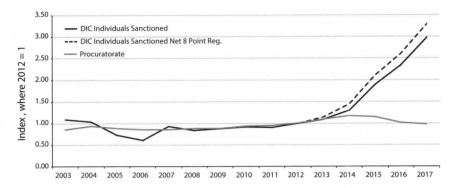

FIGURE 3.1. Investigations by the CCP Discipline Inspection Commission and the Supreme People's Procuratorate 2003–2017

NOTE: Estimate based on five-year totals in 2018 work report

SOURCE: "Work Report of the Central Discipline Inspection Commission" ("Zhongyang jiwei quanhui gongbao," 中央纪委全会公报),various years, http://www.ccdi.gov.cn/xxgk/hyzl/; "Yearbook of the People's Republic of China" ("Zhonghua renmin gongheguo nianjian," 中华人民共和国年鉴), various years (Beijing: Yearbook of the People's Republic of China Publishers); "Work Report of the Supreme People's Procuratorate" ("Zuigao renmin jianchayuan gongzuo baogao," 最高人民检察院工作报告), various years, http://www.spp.gov.cn/gzbg/; and "Work Report of the Supreme People's Court" ("Zuigao renmin fayuan gongzuo baogao," 最高人民法院工作报告), various years, http://gongbao.court .gov.cn/ArticleList.html?serial_no=wx.

including banqueting at public expense, improper use of public funds to pay for travel, improper use of official vehicles, the granting of improper reimbursements and subsidies, accepting improper gifts, and staging extravagant weddings and funerals.[16] Xi Jinping decreed that official banquets be limited to "four dishes and one soup" and banned alcohol.[17] The regulation broadened the definition of what the party considered corrupt but only marginally. The activities banned by the regulation were already proscribed, but the offenses covered by the Eight-point Regulation are not criminal offenses.[18]

Assessing the impact of the "Eight-point Regulation" is further complicated by the lack of clarity about what the number of violations means. According to the CDIC, it investigated 372,137 party members for official extravagance between 2013 and the end of 2018, with 223,197 sanctioned. The party reportedly sanctioned a total of 2,313,000 party members during those years. In theory, if the number of party members sanctioned had remained at the 2012 level of approximately 160,000, the CDIC would have sanctioned about 960,000 party members between 2013 and 2018. Hypothetically the crackdown led to an increase in individuals punished of perhaps 1,353,000. If that were roughly correct, the Eight-point Regulation would have accounted for about 28 percent of the increase. But it is unclear whether the data on violations of the Eight-point Regulation include party members who were sanctioned for violating the regulation alone or were found to have violated the Eight-point Regulation and also to have committed more serious infractions.[19]

The flat trend line for the total number of individuals indicted for corruption by the Procuratorate masks the true impact of Xi Jinping's anticorruption crackdown. The Procuratorate subdivides its data on indictments into four levels: rank-and-file personnel, individuals holding leadership positions at the county and departmental levels, leaders at the prefectural and bureau levels, and individuals holding leadership positions at or above provincial and ministerial levels. As Table 3.1 shows, the number of rank-and-file-level indictments increased 8.4 percent in 2013 and another 4.7 percent in 2014. Indictments at that level fell in both 2015 and 2016, with the result that the number of indictments in 2016 (44,299) was roughly the same as the number of indictments in 2012 (44,453). In the first half of 2017, the number of rank-and-file indictments reportedly jumped 30 percent, a sharp increase that, if maintained for the entire year, would imply total indictments slightly in excess of 61,000.[20] The 2018 Procuratorial Work Report, however, suggested that for 2017 as a whole the total number of rank-and-file indictments was down 2.1 percent.[21] The number of indictments at the other three levels, in contrast, increased substantially during the five-year crackdown, with the number of indictments at the county-department level increasing 91 percent between 2012 and 2016. The number of indictments at the prefectural-bureau level rose over fourfold in that same period, and those at the provincial-ministerial level shot up from 5 in 2012 to 41 in 2015. After 2015 the number of indictments at the county, prefecture, and provincial levels fell to perhaps 2,273, 338, and 18 respectively in 2017. This would have approximated precampaign levels except for the number of high-level officials.[22]

The data clearly show a change in the targets of the crackdowns. Whereas earlier crackdowns focused on rank-and-file (in 1982, 1986, and 1989) and

TABLE 3.1   Indictment for corruption-related crimes by the Supreme People's
Procuratorate, 2003–18

Year	Rank-and-file Indictments	Change (%)	County/department Indictments	Change (%)	Prefectural bureau Indictments	Change (%)	Provincial-ministerial Indictments	Change (%)
2003	37,664		2,363		163		5	
2004	40,588	7.8	2,960	25.3	198	21.5	11	120.0
2005	38,444	−5.3	2,799	−5.4	196	−1.0	8	−27.3
2006	37,097	−3.5	2,736	−2.3	202	3.1	6	−25.0
2007	37,995	2.4	2,203	−19.5	177	−12.4	6	0.0
2008	38,307	0.8	2,687	22.0	181	2.3	4	−33.3
2009	38,649	0.9	2,670	−0.63	204	12.7	8	100.0
2010	41,362	7.0	2,723	−5.2	186	−9.2	6	−25.0
2011	41,777	1.0	2,524	−7.3	198	5.3	7	16.7
2012	44,453	6.4	2,390	−5.3	179	−9.6	5	−28.6
2013	48,174	8.4	2,871	20.1	253	41.3	8	60.0
2014	50,444	4.7	4,040	40.7	589	132.8	28	250.0
2015	48,871	−3.1	4,568	13.1	769	30.6	41	46.4
2016	44,299	−9.4	2,884	−36.9	446	−42.0	21	−48.8
2017 (est.)	43,484	−1.8	2,273	−21.2	338	−24.2	18	−14.3

SOURCE: *Procuratorial Yearbook of China* (*Zhongguo jiancha nianjian*, 中国检察年鉴) (Beijing: China Procuratorial Publishers, various years); "Work Report of the Supreme People's Procuratorate" ("Zuigao renmin jianchayuan gongzuo baogao," 最高人民检察院工作报告), various years, http://www.spp.gov.cn/gzbg/.

mid-level corruption (1993), Xi Jinping shifted the focus to high-level corruption in 2013. The focus on high-level corruption (tigers) distinguishes the current crackdown from earlier campaigns.

Genesis of the Tiger Hunt

Although Xi Jinping was not elected general secretary until November 2012 and did not announce the new anticorruption campaign until early 2013, the starting point can reasonably be set at the detention and subsequent convictions of Liu Zhijun, former minister for railways, and Gu Junshan, lieutenant general and deputy director of the PLA General Logistics Department, in 2011–12. Liu Zhijun was convicted of accepting RMB 64,500,000 in bribes while he oversaw the development of China's high-speed rail system. According to the investigators, Liu Zhijun had begun accepting bribes in 1986, when he headed the Wuhan Railway Sub-bureau, and continued to do so as he rose through the ranks to become vice minister of railways in 1996 and then minister in 2003. Liu Zhijun was at the center of a network of railway officials and contractors, including major state-owned companies that had been skimming huge sums from contracts. He was rumored to have told some of his confederates that he planned to "buy" a seat on the Politburo. Liu Zhijun was given a suspended death sentence in 2013.

According to the charges against Gu Junshan, he bought his way back into the army after being demobilized in the 1980s for lackluster performance, rising ultimately to the rank of lieutenant general. To build close personalistic ties (*guanxi*), Gu Junshan allegedly distributed scores, perhaps hundreds, of luxury villas built using funds for the military. Gu Junshan was said to have received RMB 600 million in bribes. When investigators raided his luxury home in Puyang, Hunan, they allegedly seized four truckloads of evidence, including twenty crates of high-priced mao-tai, 400 kilograms of gold, and a gold statue of Mao Zedong. Scores of senior officers, including General Xu Caihou, a vice chairman of the Central Military Commission and a member of the Politburo, and General Guo Boxiong, also a vice chairman of the Central Military Commission and member of the Politburo, were apparently implicated by Gu Junshan.[23] Gu Junshan was convicted and given a suspended death sentence in August 2015. Although the amounts of money involved in the Gu Junshan case were huge, it might be more significant that the military appears to have been reluctant to investigate him. General Liu Yuan, the son of deceased President Liu Shaoqi, is said to have first accused Gu Junshan of corruption in 2011. The military reportedly stonewalled, and Gu Junshan was not arrested until early 2012.

Two additional developments in early 2012 likely helped set Xi Jinping's anticorruption crackdown in motion. One was the Bo Xilai case that erupted when Wang Lijun, the recently demoted director of the Chongqing Public Security Bureau, fled to Chengdu and asked the American consulate for political asylum after a confrontation with Bo in which Wang Lijun threatened to expose Gu Kailai as the murderer of Neil Heywood. After being told that political asylum was not possible, Wang Lijun contracted allies in Beijing, who flew to Chengdu and escorted him past police officers from Chongqing who had surrounded the US consulate. Bo Xilai and Gu Kailai were detained in April 2012. She pled guilty to murder and was given a suspended death sentence in August 2013. Bo Xilai was sentenced to life in prison in September 2013 after being convicted of accepting bribes totaling RMB 22.4 million.

The second development was the March 18, 2012, crash of a Ferrari sports car driven by Ling Gu, the son of Ling Jihua (the director of the party's General Office and widely seen as General Secretary Hu Jintao's right-hand man). Ling Gu was killed and two women were critically injured. Despite a hastily organized attempt to cover up the accident, word quickly leaked out and went viral on social media (see Chapter 5 by Xueguang Zhou, this volume). Ling Jihua, who many believed would be elected to the Politburo where he would act as Hu Jintao's eyes and ears after Hu Jintao retired at the upcoming 18th Party Congress, managed to hang on politically and was elected a member of the 18th Central Committee in November 2012, but he was demoted to head of the United Front Department. Over the next two years, rumors circulated that Ling Jihua, his wife Gu Liping, and brothers Ling Zhengce, a senior official in Shanxi, and Ling Wancheng, a business-man, were at the center of a network of corrupt officials. They allegedly belonged to a so-called West Hill Club whose members all hailed from the Lings' home province of Shanxi. Ling Zhengce was detained in June 2014 and charged with accepting RMB 16 million in bribes. In December 2016, Ling Zhengce was sentenced to twelve years and six months in prison. Gu Liping was convicted of accepting RMB 8.81 million in bribes and sen-tenced to eleven years in prison in April 2017. Ling Jihua was detained in December 2014 and sentenced to life in prison in July 2016 after being convicted of accepting RMB 77 million in bribes. Ling Wancheng fled to the United States and disappeared.

These examples suggest that Xi Jinping was confronted with evidence of serious high-level corruption as he prepared to succeed Hu Jintao as general secretary. In addition, there was evidence that Bo Xilai had the backing of Zhou Yongkang, a member of the Politburo Standing Committee and the chairman of the party's Politics and Law Committee, the body that oversees China's internal security apparatus. Although Zhou Yongkang was due to retire at the 18th Party Congress, it was widely assumed that he would back the selection of Bo Xilai as a member of the Politburo Standing Committee. After Bo Xilai's arrest, wild and unsubstantiated rumors of a coup plot involving Zhou Yongkang, Bo Xilai, Ling Jihua, Xu Caihou, Guo Boxiong, and others began to circulate.[24]

In theory, the crackdown on corruption gave Xi an opportunity to take out potential political rivals. However, it is not clear that Zhou Yongkang, Ling Jihua, Sun Zhengcai, or the other "big tigers" posed a real political threat to Xi Jinping. Instead, these actions might better be seen as a warning to any potential foes. Taking down "big tigers" would help Xi Jinping to create an environment in which other members of the leadership would have strong incentives to cleave closely to the new general secretary and eschew taking positions that might bring unwanted attention from Wang Qishan and the Discipline Inspection Commission.

Development of the Tiger Hunt

The first tiger to be taken down after Xi Jinping became general secretary was Li Chuncheng. Li Chuncheng had been a deputy mayor of Chengdu, the capital of Sichuan, when Zhou Yongkang served as Sichuan party secretary (1999–2002). Li Chuncheng subsequently become deputy party secretary of Sichuan in 2003, after Zhou Yongkang was transferred to Beijing, where he became minister of public security and, in 2007, secretary of the party's Politics and Law Committee. At the time of his transfer to Beijing in 2002, Zhou Yongkang became a member of the Politburo of the 16th Central Committee. Five years later, Zhou Yongkang was promoted to the Politburo Standing Committee. Because Li Chuncheng had been promoted while Zhou Yongkang was party secretary in Sichuan, a number of sources described him as a Zhou Yongkang protégé. Li Chuncheng's alleged crimes, however, were linked to real estate deals in Chengdu and involved the chair of a state-owned investment company and may have been unrelated to Zhou Yongkang's crimes.

Over the next few months, several senior officials were reported to be under investigation, including Ni Fake, a vice governor of Anhui accused of illegal dealings with mine operators, and Yang Kun, a vice president of the Agricultural Bank of China. Yang Kun was suspected of having ties to Xu Ming, a Dalian-based businessman who allegedly had acted as the "white gloves" for Bo Xilai by providing his family with funds. In June 2013 a second figure linked to Zhou Yongkang, Guo Yongxiang, was detained. At the time, Guo Yongxiang was chair of the Sichuan Provincial Federation of Arts and Literature, typically an innocuous position. Guo, however, had been one of Zhou Yongkang's secretaries when Zhou Yongkang was an executive in the petroleum sector. Guo Yongxiang was also linked to Jiang Jiemin, the director of the State-owned Assets Supervision and Administration Commission (SASAC) and former president of PetroChina. By the time Guo was detained, Jiang Jiemin was rumored to be under suspicion of having attempted to cover up the death of Ling Jihua's son Ling Gu. Prior to being named president of PetroChina, Jiang Jiemin had been a senior executive of the China National Petroleum Corporation (CNPC), the company of which Zhou Yongkang had been general manager before he became the minister of state land and resources in 1998. Jiang Jiemin was also said to have business ties to Zhou Yongkang's son Zhou Bin, who was involved in ventures involving contracts with CNPC. By the spring and summer of 2013, there were reports that Zhou Yongkang and his family were under investigation. In late 2013, Zhou Yongkang, his wife, son, and other members of his family reportedly were detained.

By the summer of 2013, the tiger hunt had moved into high gear (Figure 3.2). As the hunt unfolded, it became increasingly clear that China's official tigers hunted in packs and that five particularly big tigers were at the center of networks that included other tigers and nontigers. The big tigers were: Zhou Yongkang, Ling Jihua, Yang Weize (party secretary of Nanjing), Bai Enpei (former party secretary of Yunnan), and Su Rong (former party secretary of Jiangxi). Each of these big tigers was linked to a core group of other senior officials and either directly or through henchmen to a wide range of corrupt officials and accomplices. Zhou Yongkang, for example, appeared to be the center of a circle of onetime colleagues, subordinates, and henchmen that included:

Guo Yongxiang, the chair of the Sichuan Arts and Literature Association but also former governor of Sichuan;

Ji Wenlin, vice governor of Hainan who had formerly served as deputy director of the Sichuan Party Committee;

Jiang Jiemin, the head of the State-owned Assets Supervision and Administration Commission (SASAC) and the former chair of the Chinese National Petroleum Corporation (CNPC);

Li Chongxi, deputy director of the Sichuan Provincial People's Political Consultative Conference (PPPCC) and a former deputy party secretary of Sichuan;

Li Chuncheng, deputy party secretary of Sichuan;

Li Dongsheng, vice minister for public security and a former senior manager at China Central Television;

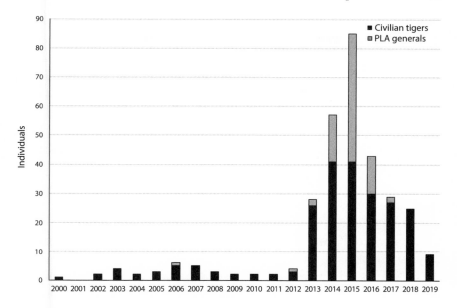

FIGURE 3.2. The tiger hunt.
SOURCE: Created by the author.

Liu Tienan, director of the National Energy Administration;

Ran Xinquan, vice president of CNPC; and

Tan Li, vice governor of Hainan and a former member of the Sichuan Provincial Party Committee.

From this core, Zhou Yongkang's connections spread out across China and included individuals who had served with him at CNPC, in Sichuan, in the Ministries of Land and Resources and Public Security, and the party's Politics and Law Committee. Ling Jihua's inner circle of tigers was smaller and included his brother Ling Zhengce (vice chair of the Shanxi Provincial People's Political Conference), Nie Chunyu (secretary general of the Shanxi Party Committee), and Chen Chuanping (secretary of the Taiyuan Municipal Party Committee). Through his brother Ling Zhengce, his wife Gu Liping, and others, Ling Jihua had extensive ties to individuals in Shanxi. Yang Weize was in the center of a network of corruption in Jiangsu. Bai Enpei was at the center of a corrupt network in Yunnan. Su Rong was at the center of a corrupt network in Jiangxi.

The centrality of these five individuals is obvious from a mapping of the network of individuals identified in the press as being connected to either one of these five big tigers or to other tigers linked to them. Figure 3.3, a network map, reveals a complex structure in which the big tigers were connected in a web of relationships that linked them to 463 smaller tigers, lower-ranking party cadres, state officials, SOE managers, managers of private companies, and gangsters. Still others were linked to spouses, children, and other relatives. Not all of the so-called tigers were connected to these networks, however. In all, 69 of the 203 civilian tigers were "free ranging" in that they were not tied to other senior officials or the confederates of other tigers.

Having a "connection" did not necessarily mean that the parties were coconspirators or partners in crime. In some cases, of course, the parties may have been jointly involved in corruption. But in many other instances, the connection may have been a career connection. Thus, for example, an individual might be described as a "protégé," with the implication that they were either promoted by their patron because they had curried their favor, perhaps by giving cash, valuable gifts, or other property, or that the corruption of the protégé had been covered up by the patron. In other instances, the parties were inferred to have developed bonds of friendship and *guanxi* as a result of having worked or attended school together. In still other cases, the link was a family connection, as when the spouse, child, or relative was accused of acting as an accomplice (e.g., a wife or son who collected bribes on behalf an official or who was given a job or business opportunity to thank a cadre for favors rendered). The existence of connections cannot be equated with evidence that the tigers were engaged in a vast corrupt conspiracy or series of interconnected conspiracies.

All five of the big tigers had held important posts over the course of their careers. Zhou Yongkang had been a senior executive at a major state-owned company, party secretary of one of China's largest provinces, minister of two powerful ministries (Land and Resources and Public Security), and head of China's internal security apparatus. It is thus hardly surprising that he had connections across a wide swath of the party-state. Similarly, Ling Jihua had served as a senior official in the Central Committee's General Office and the party's Organization Department, been a member of the Politburo's Secretariat, and had been Hu Jintao's chief of staff from 2007 to 2012. As such, Ling Jihua was positioned to act as Hu Jintao's gatekeeper,

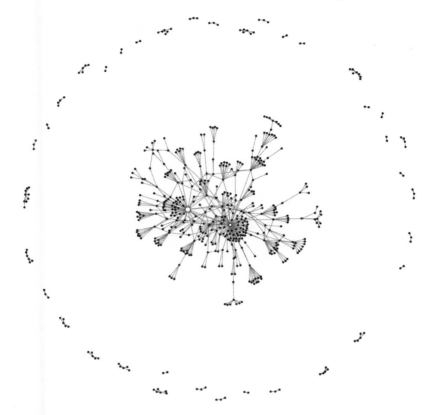

FIGURE 3.3. Tiger net.
SOURCE: Created by the author.

and it is hardly surprising that he developed ties to a wide range of people. Yang Weize, Bai Enpei, and Su Rong had all been powerful officials in their respective provinces.

Factions or Bands of Bandits

The existence of interlinked networks does not imply that Zhou Yongkang, Ling Jihua, Yang Weize, Bei Enpei, and Su Rong were part of a larger faction or were forming factions to seek political power. As scholar Alice Miller has argued, although popular, the concept of "faction" is fraught with problems.[25] The fact that two individuals have a connection does not mean that they possess shared political aspirations or interests. If anything, the presence of a rather dense network of ties linking two-thirds of the tigers to one another and to a wide range of others suggests a "culture of corruption" wherein patrons, protégés, colleagues, friends, and families shared a common belief that it was acceptable and normal to use their offices and authority for personal advantage. As such, the network of ties among tigers might better be taken as evidence that Zhou Yongkang, Ling Jihua, and the other big tigers were, in effect, the leaders of bands of bandits. In theory, Zhou Yongkang, Ling Jihua, and others might have tried to rally their henchmen to resist Xi Jinping's crackdown. But if there were efforts to resist, they failed, and it appears that once in the hands of the Discipline Inspection Commission (DIC), many of the tigers and their cronies were quick to turn state's evidence and help investigators take down others.

It is difficult to construe the networks arrayed around Zhou Yongkang, Ling Jihua, and the other big tigers as conspiratorial political "factions." Bai Enpei, Su Rong, and Yang Weize were provincial-level players. Bai Enpei had served as party secretary of Yunnan for ten years but retired in 2011. However, he remained a delegate to the National People's Congress and vice chair of the Congress's Environment and Resources Committee. Su Rong had served as party secretary of Jiangxi from 2007 to 2013 after having been party secretary of Jilin (2001–2002) and Gansu (2002–2006). In 2013, when he reached the age of sixty-five, Su Rong moved to the less powerful position of chair of the Jiangxi Provincial People's Congress, a fairly common segue to full retirement. Yang Weize was younger and appears to have been on an upward career trajectory, but he was party secretary of Nanjing, a major city, but not on a par with the provincial-level cities of Beijing, Tianjin, Shanghai, and Chongqing that often provide stepping-stones to more senior positions.

Like Bai Enpei and Su Rong, Zhou Yongkang had reached the end of his active career. When the early rumbling of the anticorruption crackdown began in 2012, he was due to retire from the Politburo Standing Committee. Some have claimed that Zhou Yongkang saw Bo Xilai as a possible contender for power, but by 2012 Bo Xilai had been politically crippled and essentially removed from the game. Aside from Bo Xilai, most of those said to have been Zhou Yongkang's key henchmen were second-tier players at best. Jiang Jiemin, the head of SASAC, and Liu Tienan, director of the National Energy Administration, were senior state officials, but several other members of the network were clearly at the end of their careers. Others had yet to enter the senior ranks. Ji Wenlin and Tan Li were provincial vice governors. Li Dongsheng was a vice minister, Li Chuncheng a deputy provincial party secretary. Ran Xinquan was a vice president of a state-owned company, albeit a major one. Despite their connections to Zhou Yongkang, none of these men seemed poised to become part of the core leadership. Ling Jihua, however, did seem to be a candidate for elevation to the Politburo, but his prospects were greatly diminished by the circumstances of his son's death in early 2012, well before such a promotion might have occurred at the 18th Party Congress.

The dense network of connections linking many of the tigers notwithstanding, the evidence that they were part of an organized political opposition to Xi Jinping is not compelling. What the evidence more likely reveals is that networks of corruption linked a substantial number of senior state and party officials. That being the case, it is more likely that a primary objective of the tiger hunt was to attack serious corruption at the core of the party-state and extending down to the provincial level and beyond. The record of investigations and convictions suggest that the "peak" of the hunt was late 2014 through early 2015, when investigators were rolling up these networks and working systematically to trace corruption by one official to their accomplices and confederates.[26]

Some have claimed that Xi Jinping has used corruption as justification for what is actually a political purge. As evidence, they point to Bo Xilai's Maoist revival movement, which they describe as a challenge to Xi, and to the crackdown on senior officials and party leaders. There is little doubt that the crackdown has helped Xi Jinping to consolidate his own power and to move loyalists into positions of power and authority. It is also possible that some of Xi Jinping's loyalists who have been involved in corruption may have escaped punishment. The breadth, scale, and duration of the crackdown, however, have been such that if there were a political purge, it would account for only a small part of the crackdown.

Attacking Deep Corruption

Earlier I argued that the attack on high-level corruption was triggered by the series of cases in 2011 and 2012 that signaled to Xi Jinping and others within the leadership that corruption had spread into the senior ranks of the party, state, military, and state-owned companies. These early cases not only revealed corruption at the senior level, they also suggested that corruption ran deep and that those implicated had been corrupt for some time. Lieutenant General Gu Junshan, for example, appears to have been involved in corruption as far back as the mid-1980s.[27] Gu Junshan joined the PLA in 1971 and served for fourteen years. He reportedly was given unsatisfactory performance ratings but survived by marrying the daughter of a superior officer, Zhang Longhai, and by cultivating friendships with his superiors. He was demobilized in 1985, when the PLA was downsized, and returned to his hometown of Puyang, Hunan.

Gu Junshan, however, remained in the PLA, apparently with the help of Zhang Longhai. He was assigned to serve as a military liaison with Sinopec's Zhongyuan oil field. Promoted to major, Gu arranged for Sinopec to support a number of PLA-controlled factories. He became involved in the selling of raw materials that were bought from Sinopec at low prices and then resold for a considerable profit. Having impressed his superiors with his commercial abilities—and apparently ample "gifts"—Gu Junshan was reassigned to the Jinan Military Region in 1994, where he was once again assigned to logistics and the operation of money earning military-controlled businesses. In 2001, Gu Junshan was promoted to general and transferred to the PLA General Logistics Department in Beijing, where he was named deputy director of the Barracks and Housing Division. At the time, the PLA had begun a major base realignment and reconstruction program that would ultimately involve expenditures of RMB 3 billion and the sale of land-use rights for PLA properties, including valuable properties in Shanghai and other major cities that netted RMB 30 billion. In 2009, Gu Junshan was named deputy director of the PLA General Logistics Department and was promoted to lieutenant general in 2011.

Gu Junshan profited from the realignment by demanding kickbacks from developers, which he used to pay bribes to his superiors, including General Xu Caihou, who was the political commissar of the Jinan Military Region when Gu Junshan began his series of rapid promotions. Xu Caihou was clearly not the only officer to have benefitted from Gu Junshan's bribes. Gu Junshan didn't even try to hide the fact that he had far more money than he ought to have had given his official military pay. He and his brother built lavish mansions in his hometown, and he was said to own numerous properties in Beijing and elsewhere. Nevertheless, Gu Junshan does not appear to have come under suspicion until 2011, when General Liu Yuan, who had served as political commissar of the PLA General Logistics Department with Gu Junshan from 2003 to 2005, accused him of corruption.

Bo Xilai had also been corrupt for an extended period during which he was promoted numerous times. Officially, Bo Xilai was convicted of accepting RMB 21.79 million between 1999 and 2012, when he served as mayor and then party secretary of Dalian, governor of Liaoning, minister of commerce, and party secretary of Chongqing.[28] Of the total, Bo Xilai accepted RMB 1,109,446 in three payments from Tang Xiaolin, general manager of the Dalian International Corporation. One of the bribes was paid to Bo Xilai while he was governor of Liaoning and the other two when he was minister of commerce. Between 1999 and 2012, Bo Xilai and his wife, Gu Kailai, or son (Bo Guagua) allegedly accepted RMB 20.6 million from Xu Ming, chair of the Dalian-based Shide Group. Xu Ming apparently provided money whenever he was asked to do so by Gu Kailai or Bo Guagua. Bo Xilai also arranged for RMB 5 million of government funds "left over" from the renovation of "a confidential location pertaining to a higher authority" to be deposited in the account of a Beijing law firm, which was instructed that the funds were for the use of Bo Xilai's family.

Although he was charged with accepting bribes beginning in 1999, it seems likely that Bo was involved in corruption before then. Xu Ming reportedly got his start doing contract work for the Dalian municipal government in the early 1990s, after first working for a seafood export company and establishing his own company, Dalian Shide, in 1992. Dalian Shide quickly expanded into a conglomerate with ventures in plastics, chemicals, building materials, appliances, and real estate development.[29] Xu Ming also had business ties to Gu Kailai dating back to the mid-1990s. In 1995, Gu Kailai established the Kailai Law Firm that was initially based in Dalian but later moved to Beijing.[30] She developed a thriving law practice, working with Larry Cheng, a Chinese American businessman alleged to have had business ties to former premier Wen Jiabao's daughter Wen Ruchun. Larry Cheng, in turn, partnered with Xu Ming in a variety of ventures.[31] Given that Dalian Shide got its start by winning a contract to provide landfill for the construction of a large urban plaza and grew rapidly in the years when Bo Xilai was a deputy mayor and then mayor of Dalian (1989–99), it would seem plausible that Xu Ming was doing favors for Bo Xilai and giving him and his family "gifts" well before 1999.[32] Regardless of precisely when Bo

Xilai began accepting bribes, the fact remains that he was promoted repeatedly while he was involved in corruption, rising from mayor and then party secretary of Dalian, to governor of Liaoning, minister of commerce, and then party secretary of Chongqing, as well as gaining a seat on the Politburo in 2007.

The public verdict on Zhou Yongkang did not specify the years during which he took bribes.[33] It appears, however, that his involvement in corruption might date from the mid-1980s, when he was an employee of the China National Petroleum Corporation and mayor of Panjin city in Liaoning. No dates were given to indicate when Ling Jihua became involved in corruption, but given the extent of his corrupt connections, it is reasonable to assume that he too had been corrupt for a long time.[34]

Analysis of the dates given for when the various tigers were charged with taking bribes indicates that the high-level corruption exposed by the crackdown began long before Xi Jinping came to power. On average, the tigers had been corrupt for thirteen years before they were put under investigation. A quarter, in fact, had begun accepting bribes before 1998, and half had turned corrupt before 2001 (Figure 3.4). All but 5 of the 139 tigers for which start dates were available were corrupt before 2008, five years before the start of the current crackdown. The data are normally distributed and suggest that two-thirds of the tigers started taking bribes or otherwise abusing their authority in the period 1997–2005, a time when the economy grew very rapidly.

In addition to showing that the corruption Xi Jinping faced in 2012 was not new, data on when the tigers became corrupt suggest that most of the tigers did so before they entered the senior ranks, not after. Based on the thirteen-year average duration for their corruption, most would have been mid-level officials when they began taking bribes. As a result, if high-level corruption worsened during the years before Xi Jinping launched the current crackdown, it seems likely that it did so because corrupt mid-level officials were promoted into the senior ranks. The fact that the tigers turned corrupt in the late 1990s and early 2000s further suggests that earlier crackdowns did not have a significant deterrent effect or weed out corruption. In 1993–94, Jiang Zemin ordered an attack on mid-level corruption that saw the number of officials at the county and department levels indicted for corruption-related offenses increase from a running average of about 900 between 1990 and 1993 to nearly 1,700 in 1994 and then over 2,100 in

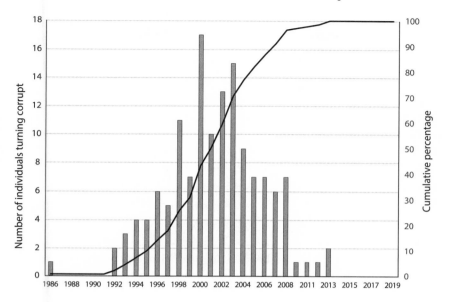

FIGURE 3.4. Date tigers turned corrupt.

SOURCE: Created by the author.

NOTE: In some instances, start dates are not available because in general they are not announced until a verdict has been handed down. Thus start dates for senior officials still undergoing investigation or awaiting trial are not often available. This potentially biases the data by undercounting the number of officials who may have turned corrupt more recently. A comparison of the mean start year by tigers bagged in 2013, 2014, 2015, and 2016, however, shows that the average start year was 2001, with the exception of 2013, when it was 2002.

1995. Thereafter, the number of mid-level officials charged with corruption averaged around 2,200. Jiang Zemin's stepped-up drive against mid-level corruption thus does not appear to have prevented the tigers-to-be from starting to take bribes.[35] Nor did it seem to have prevented them from moving up through the ranks.

Institutional Restructuring

Although it is likely impossible to know if the anticorruption crackdown has reduced corruption significantly by culling corrupt officials and deterring those who have not given in to temptation, a number of institutional changes may enhance the party's ability to deal with corruption. In a move designed to penetrate the "protective umbrellas" that corrupt officials had built, Xi Jinping and Wang Qishan dispatched Central Inspection Groups (*Zhongyang Xunshi Zu,* 中央巡视组) in repeated waves beginning in 2013.[36] As of the fall of 2017, the CDIC had completed twelve rounds of inspections during which central inspectors visited 277 state agencies, party organs, provincial governments and party organizations, state-owned companies, banks, mass organizations, and universities.[37]

Xi Jinping also ordered a restructuring of the anticorruption agencies. In 2017 new supervisory commissions (*jiandu weiyuanhui,* 监督委员会) were set up in Beijing, Shanxi, and Zhejiang. In March 2018 the National People's Congress amended the constitution and established the National Supervisory Commission (*Zhongguo Guojia Jiandu Weiyuanhui,* 中国国家监督委员会) directly under the National People's Congress and hence formally on a bureaucratic par with the State Council, Supreme People's Procuratorate, and the Supreme People's Court.[38] The commissions assumed paramount authority over all corruption-related investigations. Under the previous system that authority was shared by the Procuratorate's Anti-Corruption Bureau, the Ministry of Supervision, and the party's Discipline Inspection Commission.[39] The Procuratorate had judicial authority and was tasked with prosecuting individuals for corruption. The ministry had administrative authority over state officials and public employees. The DIC had political authority over party members. Because many state officials were also party members, the ministry and the commission were merged in 1993. The DIC claimed primacy of jurisdiction over cases involving senior party members and the right to decide when and if a suspect would be remanded to the Procuratorate. Jurisdictions were never clearly mapped out, and party inspectors and prosecutors often worked at cross-purposes.[40] Moreover, because the DIC had no legal authority, evidence it gathered, including confessions, was not legally admissible in court.[41] The merger therefore resolved a variety of jurisdictional complications and vested the lead investigatory agency with judicial authority.

The merger also addressed a long-standing problem with accountability. Because they were under the dual leadership of the local party committee and CDIC, the old DICs found themselves in a difficult position because they depended on the local governments that were de facto under the control of the local party committee for budgets and opportunities for upward career progression. In other words, the DICs were dependent on the people they were supposed to be watching. In 2004 the leadership sought to extract the DICs from the "dual leadership trap" by reducing their dependence on the local party committees and strengthening the authority of the CDIC but with limited success.[42]

In 2017 the leadership merged the CDIC, the Procuratorate's Anti-Corruption Bureau, Anti-dereliction of Duty Department, and Corruption Prevention Department with the Ministry of Supervision and the State Council's National Corruption Prevention Bureau (*Guojia Yufang Fubai Ju*, 国家预防腐败局) to form the National Supervisory Commission (*Guojia Jiancha Weiyuanhui* 国家监察委员会).[43] Local offices of these institutions were ordered to merge with local DICs to form local supervisory commissions.[44] The writ of the new commissions was broadened, covering all party members, state officials, senior employees of public agencies (including village committees), state-owned enterprises, schools, universities, research institutes, and cultural and sports organizations.[45] In theory, by pooling the staff and resources of these multiple agencies, the new supervision commissions helped reduce problems of chronic understaffing and underfunding that reportedly had plagued the anticorruption effort for years.[46]

The law also made materials gathered by supervisory investigators admissible as evidence and eliminated *shuanggui* (双规), a party provision that translates as "double regulation" and gave party investigators the power to detain a suspect indefinitely, incognito, and without recourse to legal protections.[47] *Shuanggui* was replaced by new provisions for "retention in custody" (*liuzhi,* 留置) that allowed investigators to hold a suspect for three to six months.[48] The new law also stipulated that suspects be fed, allowed to rest, and provided with medical care, and that interrogations be limited in frequency and length. These changes at least nominally banned the use of sleep deprivation, hunger, and all-night browbeating techniques allegedly used by party interrogators.[49] The law, however, retained the Procuratorate as the prosecuting authority.

The near- and mid-term impact of restructuring the supervision commissions remains uncertain. Personnel appointments, however, suggest that the CDIC will remain the leading anticorruption agency. At the 19th Party Congress newly elected Politburo Standing Committee member Zhao Leji was named secretary of the CDIC, replacing Wang Qishan. Yang Xiaodu, deputy secretary of the CDIC, was appointed concurrent director of the National Supervisory Commission at the 13th National People's Congress. Yang Xiaodu joined the CDIC in 2014 and served as minister of supervision and director of the National Bureau for Corruption Prevention from 2016 to 2018. The director of the commission thus remains subordinate to the CDIC secretary. Zhang Jun, the former vice minister and minister of justice (2003–18), was named Supreme Procurator. Although both Yang Xiaodu and Zhang Jun are members of the 19th Central Committee, only Yang Xiaodu is a member of the Politburo. Yang Xiaodu would thus be superior politically to Zhang Jun, indicating that the CDIC remains the paramount institution, with the Supervisory Commission ranking second and the Procuratorate playing the subordinate role. As such, the investigatory system would be largely unchanged, except to the extent to which the Supervisory Commission has enhanced judicial powers and greater access to the resources and staff of the Procuratorate.

If party investigators dominate the leadership of the merged supervisory commissions, that could affect how the new investigatory system operates. According to insiders, the party's evaluation system for disciplinary investigators incentivizes maximizing the number of investigations opened while the Procuratorate stress the number of high-level indictments. This suggests that supervisory investigators will have incentives to focus on straightforward low-level cases that can be quickly concluded rather than high-level cases that often require long, complicated investigations. Whereas the formation of the Supervisory Commission in and of itself may be a minor institutional realignment, new regulations promulgated in 2017 gave the commission the right to audit the disclosure forms that senior officials must submit each year. The form requires a detailed accounting of specified topics.[50] Officials must report:

All income, including salaries, bonuses, fees, and honoraria;

All real property, stocks, savings deposits, insurance policies, and other funds held by the official and his family members;

Any foreign bank accounts;

Any previous spouses, children born out of wedlock, and adopted children;

All passports and travel permits, all overseas travel, including visits to Hong Kong and Macau;

Any children married to foreigners;

Dates of any foreign residence by the official or family members;

The current whereabouts of all family members; and

All ties to the private sector or foreign companies, including any employment by the official's spouse, children, and in-laws.[51]

When the disclosure requirement was introduced in 2010, few officials took it seriously because the forms were not rigorously audited. Under the new rules the Supervisory Commission can audit up to 20 percent of the forms each year. Advances in the use of big data reportedly make it considerably easier for auditors to check the accuracy of the reported information. It is too early to assess the impact of the new procedures, but it is worth noting that announcements of disciplinary actions by the Supervisory Commission now frequently charge that that the accused "failed to faithfully disclose personal information in accordance with regulations" ("*bu an guiding rushi baogao geren youguan shixiang,*" 不按规定如实报告个人有关事项), a possible reference to lying on the disclosure form.

Conclusion

Over the past six years, Xi Jinping has centralized and reorganized the anticorruption apparatus. On paper, this restructuring should increase the regime's ability to battle corruption. The new system, however, remains subject to political controls that limit its independence and potentially restrict how, when, and how vigorously the Supervisory Commission's powers are applied. As such, the new system is much like the one it replaced. Corruption was and remains a serious problem in China. Indeed, it is arguably an intrinsic component of modernization, economic growth, and governance "with Chinese characteristics"—as practiced by the party-state regime that has ruled China since 1949. Top leaders recognize and worry about the problem because it has the potential to erode public confidence in the regime and the legitimacy of party rule, but also because it tarnishes China's image abroad and sometimes distorts and impedes efforts to meet critical challenges. Wishing or decreeing an end to corrupt behavior will continue to be inadequate as long as people remain subject to temptation, and conditions and incentives make it possible and profitable to ignore regulations, accept bribes to expedite projects, or in other ways pursue acceptable goals through unsanctioned means.

The current campaign is but the latest in a very long string of high-profile, low-impact attempts to control a problem that seemingly cannot be ended by campaigns that target a few in order to change the behavior of the many. It probably is not the case that the Chinese people and members of the Chinese Communist Party are inherently more corrupt than citizens and officials in other countries, but there are many reasons to judge that incentives to act in ways susceptible to post-hoc charges of corruption are both strong and an inherent part of the contemporary Chinese system of governance, growth, and social control. That being the case, efforts to gauge the success of Xi Jinping's anticorruption campaign and prospects for its duration and impact must conclude that success is likely to be partial and temporary, and that the effort to contain corruption will continue.

Corruption may be an intractable problem, but Xi Jinping's effort to manage it should not be dismissed as mere political theater or intended primarily to eliminate or intimidate political rivals. His approach and statistical results strongly resemble those of previous top leaders, including Deng Xiaoping, but available data do not allow us to make judgments about whether the system and those serving in it are more or less corrupt than their predecessors, or whether the current crackdown on tigers and flies will have more of a deterrent effect than did past campaigns. There certainly is more money in the system than there was in the past, but there are also more decision points and opportunities (and incentives) to cut corners, accelerate "progress," and use questionable means to satisfy rising expectations and escalating demands from the public.

Corruption will persist, as will efforts to contain it. But the important question is not whether it will continue or even whether current or future leaders will be more successful in limiting its scope and magnitude. Rather, for the purposes of understanding China's possible futures, a more important question regarding corruption is whether and how it will affect the ability of the regime to manage the critical challenges discussed by other contributors in this volume. Will corruption facilitate or impede efforts to improve the quality of rural education or extend social benefits to new urban residents? Will it affect trade-offs among health care, elder care, and military expenditure? China must deal with many complex and resource-demanding challenges. This will create and expand opportunities for corrupt behavior. The adoption of new regulations and the restructuring of the anticorruption institutions suggest that the leadership recognizes the problem, but the findings of this chapter provide scant evidence that these initiatives will be significantly more effective than those of the past.

CHAPTER 4

Future of Central–Local Relations

Jean C. Oi

Even a strong one-party Communist state must depend on its agents at the local levels to implement policy. The fate of reform depends on those charged with implementation. The challenge is striking the right balance between central control and local discretion. China would likely not be the economic superpower that it is today had it retained the Maoist methods that relied on political pressure to mobilize citizens and local officials to implement policies sent from upper-level authorities. Instead of relying on control and central planning, China's reform growth story has been one of decentralization and incentives that aligned central–local interests in economic development.

Beginning with the 1980 fiscal reforms, the center instituted a revenue-sharing system to incentivize local officials, especially party cadres, to spearhead economic growth according to local conditions. The center granted localities the right to keep and use increased revenues from development as the carrot to generate growth. Entrepreneurship was rewarded; cadres who successfully grew their local economies benefitted financially, both administratively, through larger budgets for the provision of public goods, and personally, through official bonuses from increased revenues that localities were allowed to keep. Implementing rather than blocking reforms improved prospects for promotion.

When the center realized that it had allowed the pendulum to swing too far toward the localities (i.e., allowing too large a proportion of revenues to be left in the localities during the economic boom in the 1980s into the early 1990s), it swung the balance back in the center's favor with the 1994 fiscal reforms. Beijing took back a substantial portion of the revenues that were going to the localities by redesigning the tax system and specifying which belonged entirely to the center, which were to be retained by the localities, and which were to be shared. The reforms eliminated the extra-budgetary funds given to localities in the 1980 reforms, which had outpaced the within-budget revenues by the 1990s. However, even with the 1994 recentralization of revenues, the center continued to rely on a model of decentralized development, albeit a veiled version, the details of which have only recently become clearer. New research has revealed that Zhu Rongji brokered deals with localities that gave them new incentives and tools to continue generating growth in exchange for supporting the 1994 fiscal reforms.[1]

These details allow us to understand more clearly why localities continued to pursue the local state-led development model after the 1994 reforms. Zhu granted localities the right to operate local state banks, separate from the "Big 4," that allowed localities much more control over the allocation of credit and became a source for local government borrowing.[2] These concessions allowed localities to keep generating and benefitting from development, even if the center took a larger portion of the tax revenue after 1994. It remained legal for local officials to receive bonuses for promoting development, including by attracting outside investment (*zhaoshang yinzi*, 招商引资).

Zhu Rongji's deal with the localities is particularly relevant for understanding the rise of local government debt. The local state banks established as part of Zhu's deal undergird the local government financial platforms that were used to circumvent restrictions against local government borrowing. Ironically, Zhu's concessions to the localities to ensure continued growth opened the door to strategies and behaviors that since 2012 have been deemed unacceptable and dangerous. Such problems have prompted Xi to swing the pendulum back toward the center to reassert control.

One worry is that Xi's sweeping recentralization and reliance on punishment of local-level officials will hinder China's ability to achieve its ambitious goals of becoming a moderately prosperous society (*xiaokang shehui*, 小康社会) by 2020. Xi's policies are the first real test of whether increased centralization is compatible with the growth model China has followed for the past four decades. The overarching question is whether Beijing can maintain sufficient local enthusiasm to generate local state-led growth or will adopt a new model of development.

To gain insights into the current dynamics of central–local relations this chapter examines the challenges Beijing faces in trying to solve the rapidly rising local government debt problem. The division of fiscal revenues between the center and the localities has been at the heart of incentives that have spurred China's economic miracle, but that same fiscal system is at the root of local government debt. The deep institutional flaws in the fiscal system require deep reform to effectively and sustainably control local government debt but Xi's policies have targeted the manifestations of the problem rather than fix the underlying causes. The implications of this may have consequences for China's possible future because some of those policies have dampened the incentive of local state agents, putting the entire system at further risk with even slower economic growth.

Fiscal Reforms Generate Growth and Local Government Debt

Growth and debt have been conjoined twins in China's development since the 1980s. China's local state-led growth model relied on cadre entrepreneurship but generated debt. Cadres engaged in activities that were neither "legal" nor "illegal." Instead, localities operated in the gray area, relying on creative strategies to get around formal constraints or took advantage of loopholes to meet quotas and growth targets. What has been prosecuted under Xi as corruption was previously considered routine and condoned if not encouraged behavior. Indeed, rising local government debt is a direct consequence of the increased autonomy granted to localities as part of a behind the scenes deal with central leaders in the 1990s. Localities were given the right to establish local banks that then led to local government financing platforms.

Debt has been part of China's growth model, but the fiscal system that allocates resources and responsibilities to each level of government is the root problem. In the pre-reform period the center was able to control localities through the allocation of budgetary funds. Like state-owned enterprises (SOEs), localities were not responsible for losses nor did they benefit from profits (i.e., surplus revenues). Localities had no debt but also little incentive to be entrepreneurial. Below I first discuss how the 1980 fiscal reform radically changed the system to provide a powerful fiscal incentive for localities to pursue rapid economic growth but also created incentives for borrowing to develop. While providing safety nets for the poorer, less developed localities by continuing to pay subsidies or not collect taxes, Beijing declared that if localities generated growth, they could keep over-quota amounts as specified in the formula for sharing revenue with the center. Moreover, there was a separate category of extra-budgetary funds (EBF) that localities could keep in their entirety.[3] Incentives for development were firmly entrenched, for rich and poor localities. Second, I explain why the incentives for growth and debt continued, even after the 1994 fiscal reforms were adopted. I stress that it was the 1994 reforms that made it impossible for local governments to meet routine expenditures with the formally allowed within budget tax revenues. Local governments increasingly had to rely on off budget revenues and borrowing.

1980 FISCAL REFORMS

The 1980 revenue-sharing policy, dubbed shifting from "eating from one big pot" to "eating in separate kitchens," was the key driver of the local state development model. Localities kept all extra-budgetary revenues in addition to within budget revenues above the state-set quota. Localities had the right and the autonomy to use the extra revenues for both governmental expenditures and to reward cadres for promoting development. More revenue allowed cadres to provide more public goods and demand less from their constituents. Most important, and perhaps the key reason this incentive was so powerful, was that the center allowed these extra revenues to be used for bonuses to local officials. Doing so was completely legal. Such incentives promoted the rise of township and village enterprises (TVEs), which provided a major source of extra-budgetary revenues. In the 1980s they became the initial engine of China's economic miracle.

These centrally granted incentives motivated local officials, including party cadres, to spearhead local economic growth. The precise role of local governments varied across different regions. Some local officials, like those in Jiangsu, where collectively owned village and township enterprises dominated, were the actual entrepreneurs. But in Fujian and Wenzhou, local cadres helped privately owned firms to prosper. One way they did so was to offer protection and preferential treatment by giving them a "red hat" fig leaf that allowed them to masquerade as collectively owned. Regardless of whether the local state played a direct or indirect role, the result was what I have called "local state corporatism," in which local officials used their information, connections, and effort to mobilize resources for rapid development.[4]

In the late 1980s there was a shakeout after markets became saturated and TVEs started facing stiffer competition. This coincided with the center's decision that local state-led growth, especially TVEs, was overheating the economy. Beijing instituted retrenchment policies that froze state credit to the banks. In response, townships created semiofficial financial institutions to circumvent the centrally imposed retrenchment by offering high rates of interest to attract local deposits. This raised the cost of loans to unsustainable levels for firms, especially when the markets were weakening. By the end of the 1980s and into the 1990s, TVEs started to fail and produced the first big tranche of local government debt. Failed township and village enterprises became the biggest source of early local government debt.[5] Township officials signed for village enterprises based on a guarantor system without collateral. Banks and the semiofficial local financial institutions were left with nonperforming loans, and villages and townships were stuck with abandoned factories. Locals lost their savings and localities were left with substantial debt, some of which required upper-level intervention to stave off political unrest.[6]

1994 FISCAL REFORMS

At approximately the same time that localities were hit by the collapse of TVEs, the central state instituted the 1994 fiscal reforms that reclaimed categories of revenues it had ceded to localities in 1980. From the perspective of the center, the 1980 policy disproportionately left the fruits of development at local levels—the center was capturing less than a quarter of total revenues. By the end of the 1980s, extra-budgetary revenues in some localities started to overtake budgeted amounts. The 1994 fiscal reforms ended the ballooning of extra-budgetary revenues in the localities. Commonly known as the system of tax-assignment reform (*fenshuizhi*, 分税制), the 1994 fiscal reforms eliminated the category of extra-budgetary funds and recategorized all local revenues as taxes that (1) belong exclusively to the central authorities; (2) belong exclusively to the localities; or (3) shared between the central government and the localities. These changes recentralized control of tax revenues and shrank local revenues significantly by eliminating extra-budgetary funds previously allotted exclusively to local governments.

The 1994 recentralization gave Beijing control of more tax revenues, but left localities with insufficient returns to pay for routine administration and government responsibilities assigned by higher administrative levels. The fiscal gap—that is, the difference between official government revenues and expenditures—grew. Some localities had struggled with debt before the 1994 reforms, but fiscal recentralization created new institutional problems that made debt much more widespread. The tools granted by Zhu Rongji to win support for the 1994 reforms gave localities new ways to borrow.

THE RISE OF LOCAL GOVERNMENT DEBT

Statistics on local debt in the 1990s and the early 2000s are scant. In 2000 the Ministry of Finance ruled that local governments at all levels must report the volume of both direct and contingent debt to higher administrative levels.[7] As of 2003, 974 of 2,938 county-level units lacked sufficient fiscal revenue to cover their expenditures.[8] Of these, 653 lacked the funds needed to meet basic operational costs.[9] Furthermore, 291 of these 653 units had insufficient revenue to cover expenditures even for personnel wages (food money). The fiscal predicament led to wage arrears, poor administrative services, and the accumulation of local debt.

As Table 4.1 shows, all regions of China sustained heavy debt in the early 2000s. The eastern area, which is the most developed part of the country, accounted for about 40 percent of the total. The central area, the second most developed region, had about 33 percent. The western area was responsible for only 26 percent of total local debt, but its local debt constituted a much higher percentage of total revenue. This suggests that less developed areas faced more severe fiscal conditions than more developed ones. However, because the western region, especially the northwestern area, depends on fiscal transfers from upper-level governments, the provincial or central

TABLE 4.1 The debt accumulation of the county and township in 2002 by region (in RMB billion)

Region	Total (RMB billion)
All areas	728.5
Eastern area	290.0
Central area	244.6
Western area	193.9

SOURCE: Zhiyong Yang and Zhigang Yang, *30 Years of Chinese Public System Reform* (Shanghai: Gezhi chubanshe, 2008).

NOTE: The eastern area includes Beijing, Fujian, Guangdong, Guangxi, Hebei, Heilongjiang, Jiangsu, Jilin, Liaoning, Shandong, Tianjin, and Zhejiang. The central area includes Anhui, Henan, Hubei, Hunan, Jiangxi, and Shanxi. Other provinces belong to the western area.

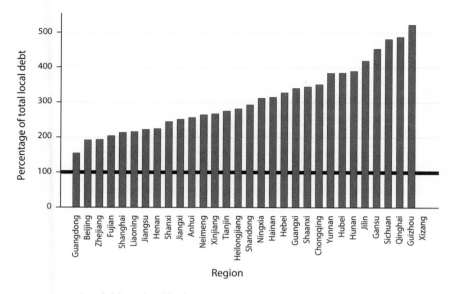

FIGURE 4.1. Local debt to local budgetary revenue, 2013.

SOURCE: Adam Liu and Jean Oi, "The Institutional Foundations of Local Government Debt in China," unpublished manuscript, 2019. Data is from the National Audit Office (NAO), the People's Bank of China (PBOC), and the National Bureau of Statistics of China.

government eventually will assume the potential fiscal risk and fiscal burden for that debt.

As Figure 4.1 shows, the situation has not changed much in the intervening decade. In Xi's first full year in power, 2013, every province had local government debt.

Institutional Sources of Local Government Debt

Xi has instituted policies, including the anticorruption campaign, to stem the growth of local government debt. But do those measures address the actual sources of local government debt (LGD)? Although some stem from efforts by local officials to improve their GDP numbers, many are for the cost of routine administrative duties and implementation of state policies that localities must cover. Below I examine two of the most burdensome: (1) unfunded mandates assigned to localities by higher levels of government; and (2) matching funds required from localities in order to receive fiscal transfers designed to relieve budget shortfalls.

UNFUNDED MANDATES

The 1994 reforms took more revenues out of the localities and assigned more fiscal responsibilities to local governments. The center sent down unfunded mandates, which set targets and launched projects, but "let the localities pay the bill" ("*zhongyang qingke, difang maidan,*" 中央请客, 地方买单). For example, localities were ordered to repair schools and build public works projects. Such projects may improve the well-being of citizens in these localities, but Beijing did not provide the funds needed for what it had mandated. The center was not the only source of unfunded mandates. There was a cascade effect in which provincial governments would delegate a responsibility to municipal governments, which would assign the responsibility to subordinate levels. Responsibility for expenditures was pushed down the administrative hierarchy. Government officials at the bottom—the county level and below—had to find ways to pay for mandated activities.

Earlier studies have focused on how much revenue was taken from local governments by the 1994 reforms, but that is only half of the story because localities also had more expenditures to cover. The 1994 fiscal reforms did not specify the allocation of responsibilities at subprovincial levels of government. Provincial authorities retained the ability to determine the amount of tax revenue that subprovincial levels could keep *and* the expenses they would bear.[10] In other words, higher levels of local government had the power to delegate the responsibility and costs of providing public goods and services (*shiquan,* 事权) to lower-level units. Ultimately this meant that township governments (and eventually villages) incurred greater fiscal responsibility as revenue was increasingly centralized at higher levels of government. For example, China has a costly nine-year compulsory education funded by localities (see chapter 8 by Hongbin Li et al., this volume). Provinces have the authority to shift the costs of compulsory education to prefectural governments, which push it further down the hierarchy.[11] This led to unfunded mandates.[12] The result is that China's subnational governments bear the highest fiscal burden in the world as a percentage of total public expenditure.[13] Moreover, according to a recent IMF report, counties bear the largest share of these burdens as a percentage of GDP.[14]

The fiscal burden and the challenges localities face are evident in the gap between revenues and expenditures. Figure 4.2 shows the national difference in revenues and expenditures of local governments after the 1994 reforms, when the central government controlled more than 50 percent of

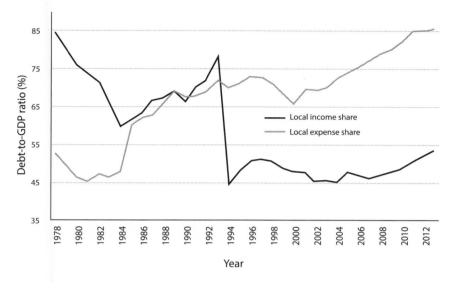

FIGURE 4.2. Local share of total revenue and expenditure.

SOURCE: National Statistics Bureau, 2013.

the total within-budget revenues, and local governments were responsible for 80 percent of expenditures—a gap of 30 percent.[15]

MATCHING FUNDS

China's 2008 stimulus package has been widely blamed for the rise in local government debt. Figure 4.3 shows that debt did increase greatly after the stimulus package. Why and how did the stimulus create so much debt? If the central state was simply sending money down to the localities, doing so should not have generated such a large debt. Part of the answer to this puzzle is that strings were attached to some of the stimulus money—local governments had to provide matching funds to obtain earmarked fiscal transfers (*zhuanxiang zhuanyi zhifu,* 专项转移支付). The 2008 stimulus package was not the first time this requirement was imposed, but the size of the stimulus aggravated problems that began with the 1994 reforms.

The stimulus package nominally provided RMB 4 trillion, but the center provided only a portion (30 percent); local governments were expected to find the rest. For example, in 2008–2009 the central government provided RMB 588 billion in incremental funding for investment but expected local

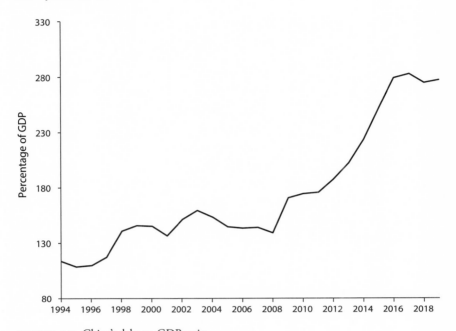

FIGURE 4.3. China's debt-to-GDP ratio.

SOURCE: Goldman Sachs/Investment Strategy Group, *Walled In: China's Great Dilemma* (2016), p. 22. https://www
.goldmansachs.com/what-we-do/investment-management/private-wealth-management/intellectual-capital/isg-china
-insight-2016.pdf.

governments to contribute more than RMB 600 billion, even though it
was clear that localities had only about half that amount. The matching
fund requirement aggravated the rapid growth of local government debt
after 2009. Much of the stimulus was used for infrastructural development.
Research has shown that local government debt tracks infrastructural investment rather than GDP.[16]

The sharp rise of local government debt in the aftermath of the global
financial crisis revealed the dangers inherent in how localities obtained
funding needed to grow their economies after the 1994 fiscal reforms. This
was especially the case with infrastructural development needed for the
provision of public goods and further economic growth. If the localities
didn't have enough money, the center created opportunities for localities
to borrow. Localities could also get help from higher levels through fiscal
transfers earmarked for infrastructural development. The problem is that
"aid" from the upper levels also created more debt for the localities. Ear-

marked fiscal transfers created a catch-22 situation—localities had to have money in order to get the allocations.

The Tools for Growing the Economy and Local Government Debt

Since 1994, the central government's solution to the problem of insufficient local revenues, whether to pay for unfunded mandates or secure sufficient matching funds, was to allow localities to raise their own revenue. However, that the center would allow localities to do so is not evident if one looks only at the official 1994 fiscal reform policy. That the 1994 reforms took revenues away from the localities is well known; but only recently has the backstory become public of what Beijing had to do to get localities to agree. These heretofore unknown details are particularly relevant in light of attacks on local officials in the current anticorruption campaign. The center claims to have been unaware of the magnitude of local government debt until the last few years. That may be true but it was not entirely the result of localities hiding debt and engaging in illegal fundraising activities. Zhu Rongji offered localities the means and incentives to develop as long as they were willing to give the center its share of taxes from the growth. Zhu assured localities that they would have "autonomy over local spending, the center will not intervene."[17] These concessions help explain why the center had only limited knowledge of how much debt was being accumulated: the lack of transparency was deliberate. The center gave localities the tools and means to develop in spite of taking away more of the tax revenues. Over time, this set in motion a process that resulted in mounting local government debt.

LOCAL BANKS AND GOVERNMENT FINANCING VEHICLES

The deal made by Zhu to secure local-level buy-in for the 1994 fiscal reforms gave localities the right to run local state banks.[18] But local governments were prohibited from directly borrowing from any bank, local or otherwise. Localities thus needed an indirect way to borrow from banks because they could not do so directly. The solution was for local governments to create local government financing vehicles/financial platforms (*rongzi pingtai,* 融资平台). These local government financing vehicles (LGFVs) were created by local governments as an intermediary institution, as a middleman, to legally obtain loans from banks on behalf of local government needs and instructions. LGFVs were staffed by cadres from existing local agencies and bureaus, including local finance bureaus, and should be considered an arm of the local state, even though they are categorized as a state-owned enterprise.

LAND FINANCING

The operation of the LGFVs required local governments to have collateral for the bank loans. The most readily available collateral was land because the right of alienation (i.e., sale of land) was never given to household but kept by the collective. Land was thus an accessible source of capital that localities could control, either directly or through land taking from rural households.

As China's growth continued and urbanization took off, land became an increasingly valuable source of collateral, especially in the wake of the collapse of TVEs as a source of income. These two core elements of "land financing" allowed the rise of local government debt.[19] The loans obtained by the LGFVs on behalf of local governments were used to finance various needs, including the unfunded mandates that localities had to implement and the matching funds needed to secure earmarked fiscal transfers from the center. The LGFVs became both the conduit and the instrument through which local governments were able to profit from the sale of land assume local debt. This solution was viable because Zhu Rongji had given localities autonomy to develop nontax sources of revenues and the tools to facilitate that development.

The value and the accessibility of land led local governments to secure as much land as possible by conducting what has come to be known as "land takings." These land appropriations have caused much discontent and protest in China's countryside.[20] The appropriated land could either be sold to earn revenue or used as collateral by the LGFV (also see chapter 7 by Mary E. Gallagher, this volume). Xun Wu has shown that land sales increased greatly after the stimulus package was launched, finding on average that 40 percent of local government loans are backed by land sales.[21]

Land deals are often opaque and easily subject to corruption and abuse of power, so it is not surprising that they have become a target of public ire. But land financing has been in use since the mid-1990s, and until recently little was done to stop the practice—such strategies conformed to the deal made by Zhu with the localities. The claim that the center did not know the total local government debt until 2010, and did not have provincial estimates until 2013, seems implausible until one factors in Zhu's vow not to intervene in local financial affairs. Honoring Zhu's deal made in the mid-

1990s tied the center's hands. The decision not to know was expedient, but over time it meant that Beijing was less able to penetrate and control local government financial transactions, both borrowing and debt. It also led to a situation where local governments' increasing reliance on land finance meant that it was in the interest of localities to have land prices increase. But this created problems for citizens facing escalating housing prices, which created yet another source of instability.

Can Xi Control Local Government Debt without Stifling Growth?

In the wake of the 19th Party Congress, the party-state has made controlling local government debt a major priority. To do so, it utilized the anticorruption campaign and made organizational changes to close banking and insurance loopholes. The principal organizational change was to merge the China Banking Regulatory Commission (CRBC), the banking regulator, with the China Insurance Regulatory Commission (CIRC), the insurance regulator, to form the more powerful and comprehensive China Banking and Insurance Regulatory Commission (CBIRC). The current methods are decidedly centralized, with the center instituting tighter controls and using threats of punishment. Beginning in 2013, the center incorporated a "debt" element into cadre evaluation criteria. Starting January 1, 2015, as part of the New Budget Law, local governments were ordered to sever their ties with the LGFVs, which are now depicted by the center as the major culprit generating local debt. As SOEs, LGFVs must repay the debt they have incurred. But this has not worked, and debt continues to rise. Local government will have to find other ways to borrow if they cannot do it through the LGFVs.

The assumption in many of Beijing's new control measures is that local government debt happens because of "bad individuals engaging in bad behavior." However, while there have been cases of corruption (see chapter 3 by Andrew Wedeman, this volume), the sources of local government debt are largely systemic. If our analysis is correct, policies formulated to rectify systemic ills by tightening controls or using the anticorruption campaign as a substitute for institutional reform are futile. Moreover, this is not just an analytical question. Getting the diagnosis right will be crucial to China's future growth prospects. Applying the wrong medicine could be lethal to China's growth model. While detailed post-2013 data on local government debt is lacking, and what we have is likely to be incomplete, all signs suggest that the success of current strategies is dubious at best. Some recent estimates, citing a report to the National People's Congress in 2015 by former Minister of Finance Luo Jiwei, indicate that local indebtedness has more than doubled in the past five years.[22] Moreover, given how Chinese statistics can be manipulated, numbers on local debt must be taken with many grains of salt.[23]

More recent reports suggest that the debt problem remains significant despite the new regulations and efforts to make local governments sever ties with the LGFVs. According to reports from the National Audit Bureau, local government debt continued to grow in the first half of 2017. As of March 2017, the National Audit Bureau reported that while the risk from debt in sixteen provinces, sixteen municipalities, and fourteen counties was basically under control, the amount of debt that local governments were committed to repay had gone up by 87 percent compared with the end of June 2013. Furthermore, at the district and county levels, and in the western areas of China, the increases more than doubled.[24] In addition, the quota for local government debt specified in the budget assumes that debt will continue to increase. The Ministry of Finance set the 2017 local government debt quota at RMB 18.8 trillion (*wanyi,* 万亿), which is significantly higher than the 2016 figure of only RMB 14.7 trillion.[25] Thus, rather than reducing local government debt, it increased by RMB 4.1 trillion. Based on the quota/plan, local government debt is estimated to increase by 27.8 percent, which suggests that local government debt is expected to grow substantially.[26]

If the underlying cause is institutional, no matter how hard and how long the center attempts to solve the debt problem through stronger regulation, the problems will continue. The anticorruption and tighter regulation strategies assume that LGD is the result of localities borrowing to spend lavishly, wasting, or simply pocketing money. While some of those assumptions may hold in some cases, they cannot account for the widespread local government debt that has existed in China since the mid-1990s. Perhaps most important, there is a presumption that localities can control their expenditures and their borrowing, but as shown earlier, a good portion of local government expenditures are mandated from above. Deep institutional reforms are needed to address the problem.

The 13th National People's Congress in 2018 announced new agencies to control banking and insurance and close loopholes that have allowed risky shadow banking and speculation in the stock markets. The state has also taken steps to reduce/remove local government debt by shifting responsibility for repayment, including the 2015 New Budget Law, which mandates that local governments severe their ties with the LGFVs and disavow responsibility for repaying their debt. A late 2014 revision of the budget law is providing some relief to local governments. In a three-year debt-bond swap program all provincial governments were allowed to convert LGFV debt to local government bonds, subject to a cap established by the National People's Congress.[27] The amount involved in 2014 is reported to have been 22 percent of GDP.[28]

According to an IMF report, between 2014 and 2017 the size of the local government bond market grew from RMB 1.1 trillion to RMB 14.7 trillion. As of 2017, local government bonds account for 20 percent of China's total bond market and exceed the stock of sovereign debt.[29] These local debt–bond swaps help local governments because bonds give localities more breathing room both in terms of when repayment is due and in lower interest payments.[30] This strategy has been dubbed "opening the front door and closing the back door," which means that Beijing is tightening upper-level control and increasing transparency of local government borrowing and debt. However, there is limited demand for these local government bonds, and most are held by banks with limited trading.[31] In addition, while the issuance of bonds has eliminated some forms of off–balance sheet borrowing, localities still need money for infrastructural development. To address that need, the center has approved more special purpose bonds for 2019.[32]

Recent central policy changes may cause local debt numbers to decline or reduce the risks and burden on local government repayments, but unless far-reaching fiscal reforms are made, any relief likely will be temporary. Two big problems remain. The first is that local governments still need sustainable sources of funding. While it is clear that the center seems to disapprove of LGFVs, they are only slowly to be phased out. In the meantime, they are supposed to raise funds. How will this be possible? Local governments underwrote the ability of LGFVs to obtain loans and do business. Without such underwriting, who is going to be part of such operations? Second, isn't the government ultimately responsible for SOE debt? What is going to happen to the debt that these LGFVs already hold? An unexpected announcement by the General Offices of both the Chinese Communist Party and the State Council in fall 2018 cited a document with "guiding opinions" that LGFVs can go bankrupt.[33] Will this actually happen, or is it a signal that the central state will not bailout LGFVs? These questions remain unanswered.

Although the central state has yet to acknowledge that its own institutions cause local debt, it seems to be backing away from putting all blame on the localities. The center has progressively, if still indirectly, admitted that certain policies have to be stopped (i.e., "have been harmful"). Documents from the 18th Party Congress (dated November 15, 2013) called for fiscal reform, specifically calling out the need to "progressively abolish *earmarks* for competitive areas and *local funding supplements*" (emphasis mine). Those unfamiliar with the details of how fiscal transfers work could easily miss the significance of that statement. The 2016 State Council Document 49 explicitly and directly warns against unfunded mandates and the need for matching funds. While never mentioning local government debt, it states that: "For central projects, the center will spend; central departments must NOT ask for local matching funds (*shuyu zhongyang de caizheng shiquan, yingdang you zhongyang caizheng anpai jingfei, zhongyang ge zhineng bumen he zhishu jigou bude yaoqiu difang anpai peitao zijin. Zhongyang de caizheng shiquan ru weituo difang xingshi, yao tongguo zhongyang zhuanxiang zhuanyi zhifu anpai xiangying jingfei,*" 属于中央的财政事权, 应当由中央财政安排经费, 中央各职能部门和直属机构不得要求地方安排配套资金。中央的财政事权如委托地方行使, 要通过中央专项转移支付安排相应经费)。"[34] The practice of pushing costs down the administrative hierarchy (*shiquan*) is to be stopped. But those efforts have just begun.[35] The 2016 State Council announcement (SC 2016 No. 49) is the most significant signal to date that explicitly addresses the need for an intergovernmental fiscal reform and misalignments of revenues and expenditures, but the actual reforms are not expected to be completed until 2020.[36] If these policies are implemented, the local debt problem should ease, but these reforms do not address the question of whether Beijing can revitalize local entrepreneurial activity.

Adverse Reaction to Wrong Medicine

Simply tightening controls and instituting more regulations may have severe consequences beyond failing to solve the local government debt problem.

The political fallout from the impact of the anticorruption campaign on cadres may well affect China's future. The attitude of local state agents is crucial for assessing whether the local state-led model, which hinges on strong incentives for local cadres to pursue development, is still viable. Although we lack hard evidence that China's slower growth is linked to the anticorruption campaign, there is consensus that local officials have taken a more cautious approach to being entrepreneurial and prefer to "sit on their hands." Such allegations are given credence by new regulations that punish "lazy officials" for not doing their job, being too passive, including not spending the funds that they have.[37] Such reports support the judgment that growth rates would likely be higher if local officials were still working to bring in business and spearheading growth as vigorously as they did in the past.

Other evidence allows us to see just how cadre incentives have been dampened by recent policy changes. For example, regulations issued in the past few years as part of the anticorruption campaign have severely restricted cadre perks and now prohibit bonuses to officials for bringing in investment and development. Table 4.2 summarizes some of the change in national policies adopted since 2012.

Another sign of waning enthusiasm among local officials is the fact that many are leaving their positions. Data from the Ministry of Human Resources and Social Welfare shows that approximately twelve thousand civil servants resigned in 2015.[38] According to online news reports, between the 18th Party Congress in 2012 and September of 2015, at least thirty-four officials above section level (*keji,* 科级) voluntarily left their positions. We don't know why they have left, but these departures coincide with the grumblings of officials at all levels and sectors, who say they have had it with the multiyear anticorruption campaign and the enforcement of stringent policies that have taken away perquisites of being an official. Not only are officials leaving, interest in working for the government reportedly is declining. The evidence is very preliminary, and we don't have information for all levels of government. But there is a statistically significant drop in the ratio of test takers for each central-level civil service job.[39] The ratio declined from 55:1 to 43:1, meaning that whereas fifty-five people competed for each job before Xi came to power, now only forty-three people compete for the same job.[40] One might look at the numbers of those quitting and the drop in the test takers as perhaps what Xi wants—to get rid of all but those who really

TABLE 4.2 Dampening cadre incentives

Former incentive/policy	Change	Time of change	Enforcing bureau/ organization
Local cadres could get bonus/ material compensation by bringing in investment or infrastructure projects	Prohibit all such bonus/ compensation	September 25, 2013	Central Discipline Inspection Commission
Local cadres could hire professionals from companies or social organizations for part-time or temporary jobs in the government (*gua zhi*, 挂职)	Prohibit all such temporary jobs to people in business or social organizations	September 25, 2013	Central Discipline Inspection Commission
Local cadres in the government, state-owned enterprises, and universities could receive prize or aid from international organizations or domestic civic organizations without reporting to the party	Require all cadres at or above vice division level (*fu chu ji*, 副处级) to report all past prizes, aid, or scholarships received from international or civic organizations	September 15, 2017	Central Organization Department

SOURCE: "Clean Bureau: Prohibition on Violations against Rules on Part-time Jobs and Paid Broker Jobs" ("Lianzheng zhunze guanyu weifan guiding jianzhi he congshi youchang zhongjie huodong de jinzhi xing guiding," 廉政准则关于违反规定兼职和从事有偿中介活动的禁止性规定), Central Discipline Inspection Commission, September 2013, http://www.ccdi.gov.cn/djfg/fgsy/201309/t20130924_46357.html; and "Mandatory Reporting of Receipt of International and Civic Prizes by Cadres" (Guanyu dui lingdao ganbu jieshou guoji he minjian jiangli de youguan qingkuang jinxing tongji bing kaizhan diaoyan de tongzhi, 关于对领导干部接受国际和民间奖励的有关情况进行统计并开展调研的通知), Organization Department at Baotou Municipality, September 2017, http://www.btdj.gov.cn/c/2017-09-07/1080405.html.

are willing to "serve the people." But the cream of the crop may be going elsewhere. The thirty-four officials above section level who voluntarily left their positions between 2012 and September of 2015 seem to include some that the government presumably would want to have leading the localities. They are young, were in the most dynamic areas of the country, and had business skills.[41]

An Alternative Future or a Return to the Past

The balance and swings in central–local relations have determined the success of China's economic growth model. Had the center not loosened control and used powerful economic incentives to spur entrepreneurial activity at the local levels, China's economic miracle likely would not have happened. The current regime has swung the pendulum back toward recentralization, attacking activities that were critical to economic growth, and using control and punishment rather than positive incentives to align the interests of its agents at the local levels to those of the center. The previous model had its problems, including corruption and inefficient use of resources. Xi has good reason to try to clean up the system. The question is whether he is using the right medicine and attacking the actual source of the problems.

We have used the center's handling of local government debt as a window into the dilemmas facing the regime and an opportunity to assess the effectiveness of the solutions that have been proposed by Xi Jinping. With regard to the debt problem itself, we find that China continues to face the twin dilemmas of growth and fiscal discipline. Until now, the need to generate growth always trumped the debt problem. But now debt has grown at such a rapid rate and is such a large percentage of GDP that more stringent means are needed. Xi has made control of local government debt a top priority and instituted measures to achieve that goal. Action is necessary, but the anticorruption campaign and arrests are unlikely to solve the problem in the longer term and may be inadequate even in the short term. Much of the local debt problem is rooted in China's flawed institutions, specifically the fiscal system itself, which Xi has already identified as a target of reform.

This examination of the local debt problem brings to the surface the deeper dilemma that Xi faces—effective fiscal reforms would involve a much more complicated and interconnected reform of the entire political and economic system. As has already been evident in the reform of SOEs, one cannot fix a firm simply by changing what goes on inside that firm. Institutional complementarities require changing the much larger economic and political system.[42] The current solutions suggest that party leaders may not be ready to risk making such changes. The result is that the current solutions continue to ignore the true sources of local debt and instead seek short-term answers that are unlikely to yield long-term success.

China has long operated with flawed institutions. One of the most impressive feats of China is how successfully it has been able to grow while using institutions and methods created to operate in the planned economy of the Mao period. These institutions worked surprisingly well with tweaking and adaptation to accommodate the reforms and operation in a market economy. But whether those institutions can be tweaked yet again or have become an impediment to sustained growth and continuous modernization is far from certain. It may no longer be possible to meet looming challenges by tweaking legacy institutions. China may have reached the limits of what is possible without deep system reform. One of many questions raised by this study of local government debt is how long China can afford to avoid making fundamental changes to the system. Asked another way, can China buy time by reverting to tighter centralization and control while hoping that conditions will become more propitious for deep reform in the future? There is both a chance and a danger that this strategy will make it harder and more destabilizing to achieve Beijing's ambitious goals.

Ultimately, however, the greater danger is not the growing debt, but what may be happening to those who will facilitate growth—local authorities. Some may argue that Xi is preparing China to adopt a new model, that the past local state-led growth model is something that can be abandoned. Perhaps incentives have purposefully been dampened in the localities, signaling that China wants to employ a novel development strategy, with fresh drivers and engineers to steer an updated model. There is evidence that the state is turning to and working closely with private companies like the highly successful Internet company Alibaba.[43] There is also evidence that the center is using Alibaba as a way to circumvent some of the problems of center-local relations and to provide new sources of development through the "*taobao* villages," where rural households can engage in building businesses and prosper without heavy dependence on local officials.

While the state may use private actors like Alibaba to get around local authorities, the dilemma of center–local relations/principal-agent remains. It does not negate the question of how the state will control its agents. Moreover, even if we take Alibaba as a surrogate state agent, many of the questions raised above are still relevant. What incentives can be offered for their cooperation? What will be the costs? Perhaps most important, what controls will the party-state have over such agents, to ensure that they are "safe" allies to preserve CCP rule? The recent example of the state clipping the wings of some of the biggest private firms suggests that the state has not yet solved this problem. Finally, even if Alibaba and its *taobao* villages allow small individual entrepreneurs to bypass the local state for inputs, the response of local authorities and local governments, where both the companies and the producers live and operate, will still matter. Will they be supportive, obstructionist, or rent-seekers? These questions are of paramount importance.

The 19th Party Congress and the 13th National People's Congress endorsed ambitious development. In the wake of these goals, and despite actions that suggest recentralization, there are signs that Xi, like all his predecessors, will accord higher priority to growth than to fiscal discipline in order to achieve the ambitious goals of achieving a moderately prosperous society and advanced economic system by 2049. Recent state documents suggest that the regime is not yet ready to abandon the model of development that made it the world's second largest economy; and that the center isn't ready to forgo its reliance on the local state. The 2016 State Council Document 49 signaled that the center might have decided to return to an earlier equilibrium in center–local relations—that is, moving away from strict control and intervention in local fiscal affairs.[44]

These directives signal that the center is again granting leeway and autonomy and may finally reform the fiscal system. Perhaps most important, such directives acknowledge and emphasize the use of incentives. This is reminiscent of what Zhu Rongji acknowledged when he gave concessions to the localities in order to obtain buy-in for the 1994 reforms. Zhu and then minister of finance Xiang Huaicheng agreed that the center "must win the hearts and minds of the localities" to preserve incentives for growth. It is difficult to see how Beijing can achieve its ambitious goals without rekindling the entrepreneurial spirit of its local agents. Recent directives might signal renewed recognition that this is the case, but it remains highly uncertain that putting old wine into even older bottles will be as successful as it was in the past.

CHAPTER 5

Social Media and Governance in China

Xueguang Zhou

Ideology and organization have been redefined and repurposed many times in the past seventy years but remain central features of the authoritarian state in China.[1] The modalities and content have changed over time, but tight political control of media, press, education, and other channels of information by party and state organizations has been one of the few near-constants in the history of the People's Republic, except for a few dramatic episodes. The Internet and social media expand mechanisms for shaping and monitoring the dissemination of information and ideas, but they also create unprecedented challenges to regime control. They are—and are recognized to be—a double-edged sword with the potential to both reinforce and undermine the political regime. How—and how effectively—the party manages the challenges inherent in these new communications mechanisms will have a profound influence on China's future.

The Internet and spread of social media provide an infrastructure for the transmission of multiple channels of information that facilitate forums for netizens to share information and opinion and the rise of interest and opinion groups.[2] All of these capabilities pose significant challenges to the traditional mode of governance in China. The opportunities inherent in social media are at odds with core features of an authoritarian state that strives to monopolize information in order to mobilize its citizens to pursue regime-determined goals and priorities and to minimize dissenting voices that undermine the authority of the ruling party. However, social media also provide channels that enable the regime to monitor public concerns and transmit official positions and guidance in a more efficient and timely manner than is possible through other avenues. These capabilities have conflicting implications for state control, and the central authority's still evolving policies toward social media reflect the challenges of trying to reconcile inherent contradictions by pursuing inconsistent goals.

What are the significance and consequences of social media for China's governance? How has the authoritarian state responded to these challenges? What are the implications of these challenges and responses for China's future evolution? These are complicated and consequential questions that can be answered only with speculative judgments based on limited information from the short but turbulent history of social media in China. What follows is more illustrative than definitive and is based largely on my own observations and efforts to understand social interactions, mobilization, and state responses in the realm of social media. Given the broad reach of the Internet and the scope of social media, the variety of participation by people from all walks of life, and the diversity of what is discussed on social media, what is presented and discussed in this chapter is necessarily highly selective and focuses on high-profile opinion leaders and salient episodes and political events. Although this is only a small slice of what is going on, the examples used here reveal important undercurrents in the changing landscape of state-society relationships with the potential to have far-reaching influence on China's future.

Official censorship, especially the removal of individual postings and comment strings, poses special challenges for scholars attempting to follow developments and present the empirical evidence undergirding judgments. Indeed, some of the postings discussed in this chapter are no longer discoverable on the Internet. Experience has taught me to take screen shots of particularly interesting postings, but that is an imperfect system that makes it inconvenient for others to review my analyses. I identify the sources used, but some of them are no longer available on the Internet.

A short history of social media in China illustrates its scope, how quickly it has spread, and its increasing importance as a source of information. The principal point makes clear why social media are troublesome for a regime that has made the control of information a pillar of its legitimacy and control. I then examine tensions between the logic of governance and the logic of social media. Conflicts and challenges to official control are illustrated with examples that highlight interactions between public opinion and government responses. The chapter ends with a brief assessment of recent efforts to impose greater control and speculation about the role social media might play in shaping China's future.

A Short History of Social Media in China

Use of the Internet in China has grown tremendously since its introduction in the 1990s. According to the 2016 report of the China Internet Network Information Center (*Zhongguo hulian wangluo xinxi zhongxin,*中国互联网络信息中心, officially abbreviated CNNIC), there were more than seven hundred million Internet users in China as of mid-2016.[3] This equals about 52 percent of the entire population (Figure 5.1). The majority of users are twenty to forty years old, with education levels between junior high and high school (Figures 5.2 and 5.3). The Internet provides the infrastructure that enables netizens from different localities and walks of life to form active but invisible social networks of people with shared interests and concerns.

For the purpose of this chapter, I am especially interested in the subset of Internet users who are active participants on social media. The rise of social media in China has closely followed and paralleled major Internet-enabled developments in the United States. Sina-blog, the Chinese equivalent to blog websites in the United States, first emerged on the Internet in China in 2005. Its introduction enabled individuals to express views on their own websites; some popular blogs attracted thousands or even hun-

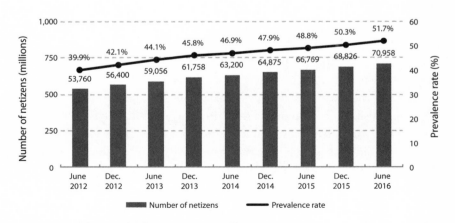

FIGURE 5.1. The growth of Internet users in China, 2012–16.
SOURCE: China Internet Network Information Center, "China Internet Development Survey," June 2016.

dreds of thousands of readers. Weibo, the Chinese equivalent to Twitter, appeared on the scene in 2009 and quickly became an active and dynamic forum for netizens to share views and form opinion groups by following, reposting, and commenting on the postings of others. The process created a significant number of popular opinion leaders. WeChat, the Chinese equivalent to WhatsApp, was launched in 2011 and became the most popular vehicle for netizens to form social circles on the basis of workplace, interests, friends, or task groups. Both Weibo and WeChat provide the infrastructure for multiple types of social media in China.

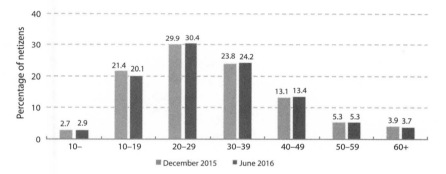

FIGURE 5.2. The age distribution of netizens in China, December 2015–June 2016.
SOURCE: China Internet Network Information Center, "China Internet Development Survey," June 2016.

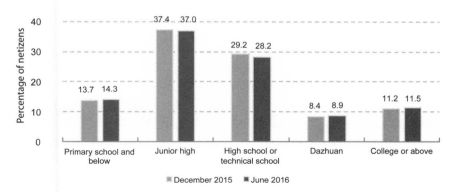

FIGURE 5.3. The distribution of educational levels of netizens in China, December 2015–June 2016.
SOURCE: China Internet Network Information Center, "China Internet Development Survey," June 2016.

In little more than a decade, social media in China have experienced explosive growth. The case of Weibo is particularly striking. It now serves as a public space where netizens post messages, report local events, voice opinions, and respond to the views of others. Postings can reach millions of readers through networks organized around social media. Although initially limited to just 140 words, Chinese characters can transmit much richer information than an equivalent number of English words. In recent years, Weibo has lifted word limits and allowed the attachment of longer documents. Many individuals, such as public intellectuals from different positions along the ideological spectrum, have emerged as opinion leaders whose social media posts are followed by tens of thousands or even tens of millions of people. These opinion leaders reach reader groups much larger than the readership of popular newspapers.

Between 2008 and 2012 the expansion of social media occurred with relatively little regulation as the authorities experimented with a variety of response strategies. As of 2015, Weibo had more than 236 million monthly active users (MAU) and 100 million daily active users (DAU).[4] WeChat had 1 billion accounts, with 650 million active users, of which 70 million were outside of China. The largest group of active users on Weibo is between seventeen and thirty-three years old. The majority are located in large cities, and 76 percent have a college education or above.[5] Active users of social media tend to be better educated and have more work experience than average users of the Internet. The "self-initiated media" (*zi meiti,* 自媒体) on Weibo and WeChat reach up to 10 million people, a figure ten times larger than are reached by traditional media organizations.[6]

During the period of limited regulation, China's top leaders showed a positive attitude toward the Internet, urged government agencies to make greater use of its capabilities, and called for greater transparency of government affairs.[7] Governments at lower levels also embraced social media, describing it as an effective means of communication and signaling. "Administrative Weibo" (Zhengwu Weibo, 政务微博), the outlet used by a number of local government offices, such as the Bureau of Public Security, became a preferred mechanism for linkage between those offices and local residents. Many government officials established personal accounts on social media and sometimes encouraged nonofficial media to participate in the investigation of significant social events. Social media were depicted as playing an important role in social justice and checking the abuse of power by local authorities.[8]

Social media also became primary channels for sharing information and forums where netizens could share ideas, debate issues, and form opinion groups. According to one survey reported on the Internet, the amount of time Chinese adults devoted to digital media as a percentage of time spent on all media increased from 36 percent in 2011 to 50 percent in 2015. The second largest percentage was devoted to television, which declined from 56 percent to 44 percent in the same period (Table 5.1).

What is shared via social media is both broad in scope and diverse in its origins. Official media (e.g., Xinhua News and CCTV) have regular postings on Weibo, and so do other content producers, including foreign media outlets from Japan, Russia, and the United Kingdom. The early 2010s saw the emergence of freelance investigative reporters who posted their findings on social media. Such reports have exposed corruption, abuse of power, and distortions in policy implementation. Some public intellectuals have become major voices on social media, interpreting and analyzing political undercurrents, economic situations, and social events. In doing so, they became opinion leaders able to mobilize and shape public opinions.[9]

The content of information on social media is as significant as its reach. Postings, often from previously obscure sources, revealed embarrassing or astonishing secrets that previously would have been carefully guarded or suppressed by the authorities. Indeed, photos, documents, and other materials posted on the Internet offer people unprecedented glimpses into dark episodes in China's past. Examples include a letter written by a grandparent to his children before he starved to death in the midst of the Great Leap Forward, the official record of cannibalism during the 1959–61 period, pictures of the cruel treatments of top officials and intellectuals during the Cultural Revolution, and the violent eviction of residents by agents of the government during land seizures. Other postings contrast the lifestyles of the rich and powerful to scenes of extreme poverty. Information and expressions along the wide ideological spectrum previously confined to small geographic locations and networks of family friends now reach audiences in distant administrative jurisdictions and social groups. It is not an exaggeration to say that freedom of expression on the Internet in the early 2010s was greater than it was (or has been) in any other period in the history of the People's Republic.

TABLE 5.1   Share of average time spent per day with major media by adults in China, 2011–15 (percentage of total)

	2011 (%)	2012 (%)	2013 (%)	2014 (%)	2015 (%)
Digital	**35.8**	**40.5**	**45.4**	**48.5**	**50.4**
Mobile (nonvoice)	15.4	21.0	26.9	30.7	32.9
—Smartphone	7.3	12.5	16.3	18.8	20.3
—Tablet	1.7	3.4	6.5	8.4	9.5
—Feature phone	6.4	5.1	4.1	3.5	3.1
Desktop/laptop*	20.4	19.4	18.6	17.8	17.4
TV**	**55.5**	**51.7**	**47.6**	**45.1**	**43.6**
Radio**	**3.7**	**3.6**	**3.4**	**3.2**	**3.1**
Print**	**4.9**	**4.3**	**3.6**	**3.2**	**2.9**
—Newspapers	4.4	3.9	3.2	2.8	2.6
—Magazines	0.5	0.5	0.4	0.4	0.3

SOURCE: eMarketer, June 2015.

NOTE: Ages 18+; time spent with each medium includes all time spent with that medium, regardless of multitasking—for example, 1 hour of multitasking on desktop/laptop; numbers may not add up to 100% due to rounding; * includes all internet activities on desktop and laptop computers; ** excludes digital.

Social media have quickly become a primary locus of social interaction in China. A large proportion of Chinese citizens now obtain much—even most—of their news through social media. This is also a primary mechanism to establish and maintain links to others with similar interests, and to coordinate collective action. Indeed, social media have reshaped and reconfigured the political dynamics and mechanisms through which China is governed.

Governance Meets the Internet

The institutional logic of governance in China is fundamentally incompatible with the distributive logic of the Internet. In contrast to the conventional hierarchical links of organizing that is vulnerable to disruptions in the chain of command, the distributive logic of organizing takes the form of multiple, dense, and redundant connections among nodes in a network, which is multicentered and hence resilient to disruptions or removal of any particular ties in the network. This inherent incompatibility already has triggered recurring waves of tension and reaction and is certain to spawn renewed regime efforts to impose control and netizen efforts to find new ways to bypass regime restrictions.

To understand the implications of social media for China's authoritarian state, it is useful to review the institutional logic (i.e., the stable, recurrent institutional arrangements of political control, problem solving, and response to crises) of governance in the People's Republic. As I have argued elsewhere, there is a fundamental tension between the centralization of authority and the effectiveness of governance in China.[10] The vast size and regional diversity of the country warrant—even require—devolution of decision rights to local levels of the system so that resource allocation and policy implementation can be adapted to suit local conditions and solve local problems. However, China's political system has the tendency to centralize decision rights in policymaking and resource allocation at the top of the system, where an elaborate bureaucratic apparatus is responsible for the allocation of economic and human resources. The resultant system tensions have produced distinctive institutional arrangements and strategies.

One such institutional arrangement is the form of government organizations at local levels. Historically and today, China has been governed through bureaucratic organizations based on territorially defined administrative jurisdictions at the levels of province, prefecture, county/district, and township. Residents are further organized into workplaces, residential areas, or villages that are subordinate to the authority of the administrative jurisdiction in which they are located. Political control and patronage ties are the most important organizing mechanisms.[11] Within this institutional arrangement local issues are attended to and dealt with by local authorities using both formal and informal means to insulate and resolve conflicts, or to sweep them under the rug, so to speak, within the local administrative boundary. When an event cannot be contained within the local boundary, it draws the attention of higher authorities and forces their intervention, thereby inducing shocks at a larger scale with broader impacts at the macro-level.

Such "divide and govern" institutional arrangements lead to several defining characteristics of governance in China. One is the fragmented authoritarian structure of formal governance in which power is dispersed among multiple government organizations.[12] This results in a "honeycomb" structure at the local level with strong social closure and boundaries resistant to intervention by officials at higher levels.[13] These institutional arrangements also give rise to the "divide and diffuse" character of governance in China. Local conflicts are confined and diffused within local administrative boundaries, thereby preventing local problems from spreading beyond that locality, becoming linked to other issues, or being referred to the next higher level. For example, social protests triggered by large-scale layoffs from state firms in urban areas, land seizures in rural areas, or abuse of power at local levels were rampant in the past two decades, but most were confined to a single locality and seldom spilled over to other administrative jurisdictions.[14] Such institutional arrangements have in effect produced variable coupling between centralized authority and local adaptation. Sometimes the coupling is tight, but at other times it is loose, an arrangement that alleviates fundamental tensions in the system through political cycles of alternation between centralization and decentralization over time.[15]

This system of governance has been used in China for centuries. The Internet poses challenges to the existing system, but it also creates opportunities to transform the traditional mode of administration and control into a modern legal-rational institution of governance. For example, contemporary communication technologies, such as social media, permit more effective communication between the modern state and its citizens, and can provide a check on the actions of intermediate bureaucratic organizations. As a reviewer of this chapter observed, social media facilitate direct communication between ordinary people and central government officials, bypassing intermediary bureaucratic layers. He likened the role of social media to "what the Protestant Reformation did to the Catholic Church by obviating the need for intermediation by priests and saints."

In the early 2010s local governments made considerable effort to use social media to communicate and interact with local residents.[16] Forums on social media provided a public space for communication, discussion, and open debate, thereby greatly expanding possibilities for freedom of expression. Nascent self-regulatory mechanisms appeared to be emerging in these forums to settle disputes or accusations of misinformation. In 2012, for example, Sina-Weibo established Weibo Community Regulations and the Weibo Community Council to review and adjudicate complaints filed by its users.[17] These examples suggest the possibility that over time and with enough experimentation, social media might provide a gateway toward greater freedom of expression, association, and political participation that would gradually erode and transform the authoritarian state.

For this possibility to be realized, the traditional institutional logic of governance must change in ways that central authorities have not yet been willing to allow. Social media technologies provide multiple channels as well as diverse sources of information, allow netizens to voice their opinions, and form interest groups by following and echoing individuals who become opinion leaders. Thanks to the existence of social media, events and informal activities now can and often do transcend local boundaries, sometimes becoming national events that shock the political arena and create heretofore unprecedented pressures on the central government. Social media provide multiple venues for netizen participation and offer alternative sources of information and interpretation of "facts" regarding incidents and episodes reported via the Internet. A recent study found distinct differences in the way news is covered by official and unofficial media.[18] For example, 75 percent of the "facts" reported in stories appearing in government outlets were attributed to official sources. In contrast, only 42 percent of the information used by opinion leaders was derived from official sources. Similarly, when interpreting and discussing what had caused the problem being reported, official media blamed government actions or officials 43 percent of the time, but opinion leaders on social media ascribed responsibility to government 72 percent of the time.

Another characteristic of social media is the structure of its distributional network, which consists of multiple links among netizens. Those joined together in the resultant networks constitute invisible but cohesive groups. Traditionally, social movement organizations tended to be hierarchically structured with recognizable leadership that could be controlled or crushed by attacking key leaders and their organizational structures. Online opinion groups, in contrast, are multicentered, multichanneled, and resilient. This makes them better able to escape traditional modes of political control and repression. Even if the authorities remove a key figure (i.e., a node) from this structure, the network can rewire and repair itself by channeling information through other links. In this sense, networks formed on social media are robust, resilient, and able to resist government interference.

WeChat (unlike Weibo) allows the formation of social circles comprised of family members, friends, colleagues, or task groups. Circles of people with shared characteristics (classmates, workplace colleagues, task group members, etc.) resemble "gated communities" in that they are more closed and segmented than open forums on Weibo. This makes WeChat groups more resilient but less threatening to the authorities. Though using different mechanisms, both Weibo and WeChat have facilitated exchanges and

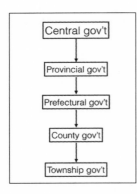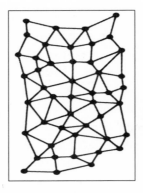

FIGURE 5.4. Comparison of different logics of governance for government and social media (left to right): hierarchical (government); distributed (Weibo); social circle (WeChat).
SOURCE: Made by author.

mobilization of public opinion that are at odds with the traditional logic of governance in China (Figure 5.4).

The significance of social mobilization on the Internet is aptly captured by Benedict Anderson's concept of "imagined communities."[19] The rise of opinion leaders with thousands or even millions of followers and dense networks of connections constitute imagined communities in which netizens become aware of, and echo and reinforce, one another's emotions, opinions, and attitudes. The existence of such imagined communities has important implications for social mobilization and collective action on the Internet. The awareness of such a community greatly increases one's willingness to give voice to opinions, concerns, and resentments. This, in turn, lowers the political risks of participation. Easy access to social media and the existence of multiple channels has had a profound effect on the opportunity structure for mobilization. Any local incident—be it abuse of power, official corruption, or deviation in policy implementation—can trigger waves of public comment and outrage that transcend administrative boundaries. The impacts can be enormous. Because social media are not confined to a specific location, information about developments anywhere can spread across the country and national borders at lightning speed.

The capabilities and inherent characteristics of social media constitute fundamental challenges to the traditional ways of governance and resistance in China by providing new vehicles for social mobilization and collective action.[20] Under traditional, fragmented authoritarianism, interests that are not officially recognized tend to be unorganized. It is still possible for collective action based on unorganized interests to occur because government actions often trigger spontaneous responses by large numbers of individuals with similar experiences and complaints. Social media technologies make it much easier for netizens to self-organize into opinion groups, coordinate their behavior (i.e., voices), articulate their interests, and create waves of collective action on the Internet. Indeed, news about local developments posted on Weibo often prompt opinion leaders to mobilize collective action by reposting, commenting on, and echoing one another. Such mobilization and collective action can put enormous pressure on Chinese governments, as is illustrated by the examples below.

SOCIAL MOBILIZATION IN WUKAN, GUANGDONG

An early attempt to use social media as a tool of social protest occurred during the so-called Wukan incident in 2009. Wukan is an administrative village in Guangdong. For several years in the 2000s it was the center of a large-scale social mobilization to protest the abuse of power by local authorities. Social media played a critical and sustained role in mobilizing and maintaining pressure on local government authorities. In April 2009 an anonymous flyer circulated among the villagers. The flyer accused village cadres of corrupt behavior and triggered waves of discussion and mobilization. During the period of contention that lasted for several years, local authorities tried repeatedly to prevent local leaders from mobilizing collective action by cutting off channels of communication and arresting and stigmatizing protest organizers. Both sides refused to yield and the situation became explosive.

During the prolonged confrontation, protest organizers skillfully used social media to initiate and self-organize collective action. They operated out of sight but maintained contact with the outside world. In the past, information about local disputes like that in Wukan rarely reached the outside world, allowing local authorities to suppress resistance with impunity and confine the impact within local boundaries. In the Wukan case, however, protest leaders used social media to draw the attention of people from across the country and even outside China, as well as from higher authorities. By doing so, they kept pressure on the local authorities and made the protest a national event that could not be handled by using traditional repressive methods. Their tactics, including use of social media, eventually forced authorities to negotiate an agreement that satisfied the protesting villagers. This was one of the few, early instances in which government authorities publically yielded in the face of large-scale social protests.[21]

In retrospect, social media played a critical role in this process. According to one study, during the Wukan incident period, there were more than four million items on this episode (news, commentaries, reposts, etc.) on Weibo, 250 times the number of the news items on this episode carried by formal media outlets. In other words, social media kept the Wukan incident alive, restrained local officials from cracking down, and forced the intervention from higher authorities. The process eventually led to a negotiated solution that met villager demands.[22]

THE GITHUB ACCESS EPISODE

GitHub is an open source platform for engineers to share freeware and other engineering/programing tools. For a long time, engineers in China routinely used this website when doing their own professional work. In early January 2013, Chinese authorities blocked access to GitHub, reportedly because of political information that had been posted on the platform. At 9 p.m. on January 22, Li Kaifu, then an opinion leader on Weibo, posted a complaint message on his Weibo account:

> [Strong protest of the blockade of GitHub] GitHub is the largest website globally for social network programing and codes. In recent days, domestic access to it has been completely blocked. China is the fourth largest country among the 3 million members of GitHub. GitHub is the first choice of tools for programmers to learn and to connect with the rest of the world. It is ideologically neutral, and does not have antigovernment content. There is no reason to block access to GitHub. Blocking access will cause programmers in China to lose touch with the rest of the world, undermine their competitiveness and forward-looking capacities. Repost!

Li probably never anticipated that his brief message would trigger a storm of reaction and a huge wave of collective action. In three hours his message was reposted thirty-two thousand times, which vibrated across ten levels of reposts, reached millions of netizens, and led to a nationwide wave of protests. Reactions were especially intense among netizens in large cities such as Beijing, Guangzhou, and Shanghai. This large-scale and fast-evolving protest on the Internet caught government authorities off guard and forced them to react haphazardly. Within eighteen hours the government reversed its decision and quietly reopened access to GitHub. This might have been the fastest reversal of an administrative decree in the history of the People's Republic of China.

THE "BIAOGE" ("WATCH BROTHER") EPISODE

On August 26, 2012, a photo taken at the site of a major traffic accident involving thirty-six deaths appeared on Weibo. In the picture Yang Dacai, head of the Safety Inspection Bureau of Shaanxi Province, appeared to be smiling. Yang said later that his smile was an effort to relax tensions at the site. Netizens were outraged by his unprofessional manner and launched a web search to find negative information about him. Within a few days dozens of pictures of him wearing different expensive watches were posted online. The pictures were characterized as evidence of a lifestyle beyond the means of his official salary, which further enflamed public opinion on the Internet. The public uproar forced the government to open an official investigation of the evidence that Yang was corrupt. Less than a month later, Yang was removed from his position. He was eventually sentenced to a ten-year prison term for corruption.[23]

THE REN ZHIQIANG (任志强) EPISODE

The case of Ren Zhiqiang, a real estate tycoon, who was a major voice on social media with close to thirty million followers at the beginning of 2016, illustrates how difficult it is for the traditional, locality-based system of governance to cope with social mobilization that transcends jurisdictions. On February 24, 2016, he criticized central government efforts to impose political control over the content on social media. Shortly thereafter, his Weibo account was closed, effectively silencing his voice. Imposing additional penalties was constrained by the contradiction between local jurisdictions and national reach in the age of the Internet. Although Ren had expressed his views on social media, which had national impact, any disciplinary penalty had to be imposed, at least formally, by the party office in the Beijing district where he resided. There is no appropriate political and legal apparatus at the national level to deal with social media.

In a related episode, Professor Ge Jianxiong, a respected historian, commented on the way in which Ren Zhiqiang had been treated. His comment was (mis)interpreted as an endorsement of the government action. A flood of critical commentary and reposted criticisms appeared almost immediately after his initial posting on March 1, 2016. Within ten hours his "clarification" was reposted five thousand times, with more than three thousand commentaries, mostly criticizing his alleged siding with the government. Social media criticism of Ge was a low-risk way for netizens to vent their anger at the way the government had treated Ren Zhiqiang.

These illustrative episodes, and many others, reveal both the ability of social media to mobilize political pressure, and the inability of existing political institutions to cope with new modes of collective action. Such mobilization of public opinion could help central authorities to combat corruption and abuse of power at local levels, but viewed from the top of the system, the threat to authoritarian power from independent voices and forces on the Internet is unacceptably high. The boundaryless flow of information on the Internet defies the traditional institutional "divide and govern" arrangements, with the tendency to turn local events into national ones. In all these cases the rapid spread of nonofficial opinion caught the authorities off guard, paralyzed their responses, forced them to react in embarrassing and haphazard ways, and exposed the arbitrariness and ineffectiveness of political institutions.

To be sure, information on the Internet is full of noise and vulnerable to manipulation. However, because official media remain subject to tight control, social media are often able to provide more current information, at a faster speed, and with a higher degree of credibility, especially when reporting sensitive social and political developments. Indeed, social media opinion leaders often have more credibility and greater impact in mobilizing public opinion than do the official media. Public knowledge of government-sponsored posts by the so-called "50 cent party" further undermines the credibility of official voices on the Internet.[24] The logic of the Internet is so incompatible with the traditional way China is governed that the authoritarian state had to respond by either changing its old mode of governance or by making social media more compatible with traditional instruments of governance. In the early 2010s the central government oscillated between crackdown/censorship and tolerance/adaptation. The balance varied from case to case, but in general the atmosphere was relaxed and tolerant, reflecting the larger trend of openness in China's reform era. Observers saw this trend as a possible sign of movement toward Chinese-style democracy.[25] But the trajectory has changed significantly in recent years.

Recent Trends in the Political Control of Social Media

Significant changes during the past few years reflect the authoritarian state's renewed effort to rein in social media and make it subject to the state's traditional institutional logic of governance. Beijing has adopted a series of measures to impose political control over public opinion on the Internet. The means used range from enlisting an army of hired hands to support messages from the official media (the 50 Cent Party), to intensified use of intimidation, harassment, and arrest of public intellectuals to silence their voices on social media.

An early sign of the change to greater control and repression was the so-called Xue Manzi (薛蛮子) episode. Xue was an opinion leader on Weibo with ten million followers. Xue often expressed views at odds with government positions and critical of government policies. In August 2013 he was arrested for soliciting a prostitute and forced to make a confession on national television. Humiliated and defamed, he withdrew from the public arena and ceased to be an active voice on political issues. Subsequently, the government silenced many other opinion leaders on social media. Social news websites also have been shut down and dissenting voices have been muted. This has had a chilling effect on social media. During the following year, netizen participation (comments and "like" postings) on social media declined from 34 percent in 2013 to 20 percent, according to one report on the Internet.

Another signal of the changing trend was the reduction of the role played by social media in transmitting news and interpreting government policies. For many years in the post-Mao era, state policies and government directives became increasingly transparent and were often transmitted through mass media, including social media. Ordinary citizens often used these policies to challenge the abuse of power by local officials. In my fieldwork in rural China in the 2010s, I often witnessed or heard stories about villagers who had quoted government rules and regulations to challenge the actions of local officials accused of manipulating village elections or seizing land in illegal ways. Top leaders could use such challenges from grassroots citizens to rein in the abuse of power by local officials. I also heard local officials complain that state policies were being transmitted directly to the residents of their jurisdictions through media (e.g., TV reports and printed media) rather than through bureaucratic channels. They complained that this made it difficult for local officials to control policy implementation.

The use of social media and the Internet to communicate directly with ordinary citizens, however, has proven short-lived. Top leaders have reasserted that administrative directives are to be transmitted through bureaucratic channels and tightened controls on the use of social media for conveying news and investigative reporting. When a cruise ship sank in the Yangtze River, causing 442 deaths on June 1, 2015, the government blocked all reporting on social media. Only the official Xinhua news agency was allowed to provide information about the incident and the rescue effort.[26]

In 2016 the government took additional steps to control the Internet and closed down hundreds of websites that allegedly spread false information about the history of the Communist Party or the People's Republic. The National People's Congress passed the Internet Security Law, which stipulates netizen rights and responsibilities, and tightens control over freedom of expression. By explicating legal consequences for behaviors on the Internet, the main effect of the legislation is to deter netizens from voicing opinions that are seen as offensive or posting information that may turn out not to be fact-based. Local authorities are reported to have detained persons who complained about their misconduct. One telling statistic is that participation in opinion forums declined 9.1 percent between December 2015 and June 2016, while other use of the Internet (shopping, personal finance, or education) increased significantly.[27]

A recent study by political scientists Gary King, Jennifer Pan, and Margaret Roberts corroborates these developments.[28] Their study reveals an astonishing degree of political manipulation by local offices of the authoritarian state. Using leaked information from official documents on political manipulation of the Internet in one local area, the authors found that local officials had hired a large number of henchmen to fabricate information, distract attention from inconvenient truths, and manipulate public opinion in subtle ways. The scope and scale of what they uncovered indicates the extent of manipulation and distortion. Political suppression also has intensified in recent years, resulting in significant changes on the Internet in China. A recent report on Internet opinion analysis in the 2017 *Blue Book on China's Society* observed:

A noticeable change in the domestic Internet opinion field on the Internet in 2016 is the further strengthening of governmental control. As a result, complaints about government decision-making and public affairs have declined drastically. In contrast, pro-government opinion groups emerged, and showed strong patriotic enthusiasm and defense of government. At the same time, web-based individual broadcasts of entertainment became popular, signaling the decline of political participation among the new generation of Netizens, and the turn toward self-expression and entertainment.[29]

Although social media in China has been tamed considerably by these new restrictions, there is still room for dissenting voices, information about local controversies (such as the public critique of government policies toward North Korea), on ethnic relations (especially with Muslims), and of course on the abuse of power by local authorities. Suppression has been far from total. Eruptions of public opinion still occur occasionally when the government is uncertain how to respond or unable to respond quickly and effectively. For example, in the so-called Leiyang (雷阳) episode in 2016, a college graduate turned government official died while in the hands of local police in Beijing. Netizens reacted with shock and outrage that spread across the country on social media (both Weibo and WeChat). People all over the country posted their own informed or speculative analyses and interpretations of what had happened. Many signed petitions. This episode lasted for several days before official censorship decisions kicked in.[30]

Criticism and challenges on social media continue, albeit in more subtle ways. In December 2017 official media boasted that half a billion Chinese now have family doctors in the national health system (see chapter 6 by Karen Eggleston, this volume). It did not take long before a netizen posted a message on Weibo declaring that their parents were forced to join the local community-based family doctor network, even though they had never used its service in the past three years. They were forced to participate in order for the local authorities to show off their administrative achievement. Otherwise, their parents could not get reimbursement of their medical expenses incurred elsewhere.[31] This message triggered a flood of responses reporting similar situations and exposing the absurdity of official claims. In another episode in late 2017, when the Beijing government evicted a large number of migrant workers from slums in the suburbs despite bitter cold, scenes of plight and cruelty were exposed online, which led to another wave of public uproar.[32]

As the barometer of political tensions and the mood of public opinion, social media in China have already experienced significant twists and turns in its short history. Social media have expanded windows into the undercurrents, open voices, and tacit resistance in Chinese society, albeit in a selective and transient manner. They also provide insight into new modes and dynamics of social mobilization, as well as the tactics of political control in the Internet era.[33] This window allows researchers to explore the ideological spectrum revealed by online opinion surveys.[34] Social media have become a new and active arena in which tensions between the traditional, institutional logic of governance and the logic of the Internet era are being played out.

The Future of Social Media in China

What is the future of social media and of the Internet in the shadow of tightened political control? What are the implications of social media for governance in China's future? In recent years the central government has made tremendous efforts to reassert political control over the Internet and to reshape social media to fit into its hierarchical authority structure by silencing opinion leaders, censoring dissenting voices, and imposing tight control on the flow of information. The extensive and effective efforts have enabled the state to gain the upper hand, at least in the short run. In this sense the authoritarian state is indeed resilient.[35] Social media have been used by the authoritarian state for its own purposes, such as when it engineers political persecution by transmitting damaging information, as happened in the case of Wang Lijun's (王立军) defection in the Bo Xilai episode.[36] Top leaders also use social media to gather needed information about, and put a check on, the behavior of local officials.

Despite extensive manipulation by government authorities, the distributive network of social media is resilient and able to resist manipulation.[37] New forms of social media appear and adapt to the changing political environment. Even if the government tightens control in the political arena, issues and problems in other realms are likely to become political issues because of state dominance and the interconnectedness of all types of social interaction. The very nature of the Internet and social media, characteristic of distributed networks, defies efforts to achieve monopoly in a top-down process—unless and until the entire Internet is shut down, but that would also end the state's efforts to leverage the Internet for its own development purposes under the "Internet+" policy. Several new trends are already beginning to appear.

First, netizens are self-selective in choosing their sources of information and following those with whom they identify. Unlike the pre-Internet age, when authoritarian states could aspire to total control of all sources of information, the likelihood of achieving that goal now is much smaller and declining. As noted earlier, a large share of the population obtains news and information through access to social media, which provides the infrastructure for multiple sources and different voices. Second, as open expression of opinions on Weibo was tamed, the popularity of WeChat soared. WeChat is more conducive to the formation of small groups and coordinating activities and to the formation of social circles that allow for differential treatment/discrimination among friends. It may also provide forums to voice opinions and commentaries among the members, which tend to be confined within the small social circles of friends or "gated communities," which seems less threatening to the state. WeChat fits the Chinese cultural characteristic of "differential mode of association" that ranges from close kin ties, to intimate social circles, to distant groups.[38] As opinion groups become segmented and multiply, the impact of social media becomes less widespread, but it also becomes less visible to official monitors.

As the sociologist Charles Tilly observed: "We shall know that a new era has begun not when a new elite holds power or a new constitution appears, but when ordinary people begin contending for their interests in new ways."[39] Seen in this light, the fate of social media in China indicates an uncertain period of muddling through, with constant negotiation of territories and boundaries among myriad players and the central government. Government manipulation clearly plays a significant role in shaping the views expressed on the Internet today, but resistance has not ceased to exist. Rather, resistance on the Internet continues to evolve, often in subtle ways—such as hidden transcripts, coded expressions, pictures, poems, satire, storytelling, metaphors, and analogies of historical episodes—that evade official censorship. For example, the rhetoric of top leaders is used to expose the hypocrisy of official claims. Even reported accidents abroad are used as an occasion for netizens to criticize their own government. Thus the accidental sinking of a ferry in South Korea, which led to the resignation of top officials, was used by netizens to draw comparisons with a similar accident on the Yangtze River, voicing their critique of the poor performance as well as the lack of accountability of the Chinese authorities in this episode. These small, subtle forms of resistance remind us of those familiar instances of resistance using the weapons of the weak that eventually led to the wave of social protests against authoritarian states in the Soviet Union and Eastern Europe.[40]

A recent example illustrates the subtle form of resistance on social media in China today. In December 2017 the official media launched a wave of propaganda criticizing and discouraging the celebration of Western holidays, such as Christmas. On January 2 a video clip appeared on Weibo of a children's choir in a foreign (Western) country singing a "Happy New Year!" song. In the middle of the performance the conductor escorted a small Chinese girl into the choir, and the entire choir sang the Happy New Year song in both English and Chinese. Many netizens responded to this clip by reposting, sometimes with pointed commentaries: "//Happiness with tears running down my face//Best wishes from abroad//Those objecting to the Christmas holiday, take a look at the foreigners singing 'Happy New Year' in Chinese, this is what cultural self-confidence is really about// All those that resist beautiful things are bad guys, no matter whether they are potbellied or pretend to be on the moral high ground."

PART II

Domestic Policy Choices and Constraints

CHAPTER 6

Demographic and Health Care Challenges

Karen Eggleston

Demography does not determine destiny, but it does constrain, drive, and shape choices. Historically, large populations have often been considered a source of national strength, but keeping pace with growing numbers and rising expectations is a major challenge for any society and political system. In China multiple dimensions of demographic transition further compound the challenges. How—and how well—Beijing manages these challenges will have a profound impact on what the country will be like and what it can and will do in the decades ahead. To examine all facets of China's demographic challenges is beyond the scope of this chapter, but their complexity and importance can be illustrated by focusing on challenges and choices related to health care and the country's rapidly aging population.

China has already experienced demographic transition to relatively low mortality and low fertility, with its population now rapidly aging and coping with chronic diseases. Two generations of strict family planning policies contributed to this demographic reality, but so have an array of forces that accompany socioeconomic development and urbanization. These demographic shifts reflect the success of earlier investments in infectious disease control, public health measures, and other contributors to mortality reduction, as well as the lingering effects of family planning policies interacting with son preference and rapid economic development. Together, they have produced a shrinking working-age population, growing number of elderly, imbalance of men to women, and challenges of assuring inclusive urbanization that constrain China's future (see chapter 7 by Mary E. Gallagher, this volume).

Economic growth in the future must be achieved without the so-called demographic dividend from the large bulge in the working-age population that contributed to China's growth for four decades. Future growth will require education-based improvements in the quality of the workforce (see chapter 8 by Hongbin Li and colleagues, this volume). Moreover, a smaller workforce will have to support China's large and rapidly growing cohort of retirees. These and other demographic developments will require effective and expensive measures to address the nonmedical determinants of health and promote healthy aging. Among other challenges, the health system should be reengineered to emphasize prevention (as called for in the "Healthy China 2030" strategy), provide coordinated health care for people with multiple chronic diseases, assure equitable access to rapidly changing medical technologies, and ensure long-term care for frail elderly, all without unsustainable increases in opportunity costs for China's future generations.[1]

Meeting these challenges is not simply a matter of money. They involve problems of coordination between levels of government and managing an increasingly complex range of choices for both treatments and insurance plans for more mobile individuals and families. Additional problems result from the division of regulatory and administrative authority. Like many countries, China would benefit from improved coordination across multiple agencies and structure incentives to avoid or mitigate unintended consequences that undermine the goals of China's health system. Recent governance reforms, such as the creation of the National Healthcare Security Administration, aim to address these challenges. China's current policies seek to balance individual responsibility, community support, and taxpayer redistribution through safety-net coverage funded by central and local governments. This balance is changing. To adapt to an aging society, policies call for building a "sustainable, multilevel social protection system," but how well Chinese officials, firms, and localities are able to manage the country's changing demographics and resultant challenges to social and economic governance is unclear. Any stumbles in doing so will contribute to and magnify the effects of already slowing economic growth.[2]

Over the past decade health expenditures have increased rapidly as China has developed its system of universal health coverage (Figure 6.1a), growing at a double-digit rate surpassing the rate of economic growth. As a result, health spending absorbs a larger and larger share of the total economy (Figure 6.1b). China can little afford a likely scenario where the approximately

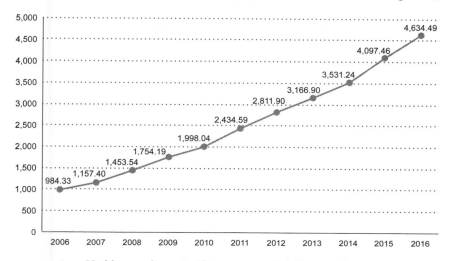

FIGURE 6.1A. Health expenditures in China, 2007–17 (in billion yuan).

SOURCE: National Bureau of Statistics of China, October 31, 2018, Statista, accessed August 22, 2019, https://www.statista.com/statistics/279400/health-expenditures-in-china/.

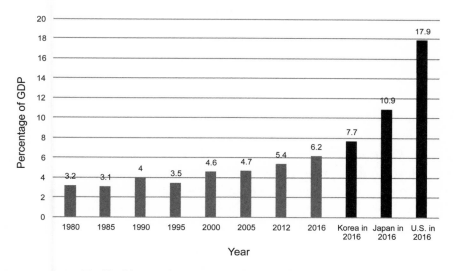

FIGURE 6.1B. Total health expenditures as a percentage of GDP, China 1980–2016, compared with the Republic of Korea, Japan, and the United States in 2016.

SOURCE: OECD Health Data, World Health Organization, People's Republic of China Health System Review, Health Systems in Transition 5, no. 7 (Asia Pacific Observatory on Health Systems and Policies, 2015); National Bureau of Statistics of China (n.d.); and "Health Expenditure in China as a Proportion of GDP from 2006 to 2016," in Statista, accessed April 26, 2018, https://www.statista.com/statistics/279402/health-expenditure-in-china-as-a-proportion-of-gdp/; and Micah Hartman, Anne B. Martin, Nathan Espinosa, Aaron Catlin, and The National Health Expenditure Accounts Team, "National Health Care Spending in 2016: Spending and Enrollment Growth Slow after Initial Coverage Expansions," *Health Affairs* 37, no. 1 (2018): 150–60.

6 percent of GDP spent on health and elderly care almost doubles, unless that spending delivers high returns in terms of longer, healthier lives.

Population Aging, Gender Imbalance, and Urbanization

"Demographic transition" refers to the historical process of moving from short and uncertain lifespans with large families, to longer lives and fewer children. This transition began in the 1800s in Europe and transpired much more quickly in the developing world in the twentieth century.[3] Mortality declined first with improvements in nutrition, better sanitation and safe water, control of communicable diseases, and basic medical care (e.g., vaccines and antibiotics). Mortality has been further reduced by better treatment of heart disease, cancer, and other chronic illnesses. In China this demographic transition from high mortality and fertility to low mortality and fertility occurred largely in the decades since the 1960s.

China's total fertility rate declined from approximately 6 in 1950–55 to around 2 in 1990–95. It has been below replacement level for about a generation.[4] The most rapid decline was in the 1970s, prior to adoption of the one-child policy. The dependency ratio declined by more than a third during the past three decades, primarily because of the reduction in youth dependency. Large cohorts in the working ages have contributed substantially to economic growth but are now moving toward retirement. China's population in the age category of fifteen through sixty-four has begun to decline and is projected to decrease to a little more than eight hundred million by the one hundredth anniversary of the People's Republic of China in 2049. Over the same period, the sixty-five and older population will likely reach about three hundred and fifty million (Figure 6.2). By 2050, China's "oldest old"—those eighty years and older—will represent the same share as the sixty and older population did in the 1960s and an absolute number greater than the current population of France. The proportion of China's population age sixty and older is projected to more than double over the next three decades, reaching 33 percent in 2050.[5]

By midcentury China's population of children younger than fifteen is projected to be around two hundred million. Together, older adults and children will constitute a dependent population so large that it will act as a demographic headwind for China's continued rise as formidable as the demographic tailwind it enjoyed for a quarter century. Figure 6.3 displays

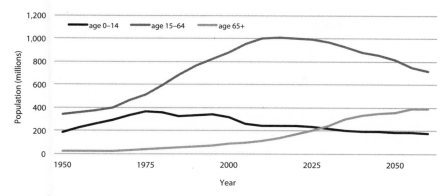

FIGURE 6.2. The population age structure of China, 1950 to present, and projected to 2060.

SOURCE: United Nations, Department of Economic and Social Affairs, Population Division, "World Population Prospects: The 2017 Revision," 2017.

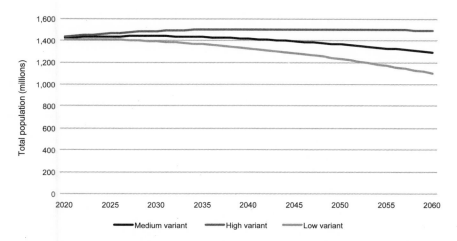

FIGURE 6.3. Total population of China as projected by the United Nations: low, medium, and high variants, 2020–2060.

SOURCE: United Nations, Department of Economic and Social Affairs, Population Division, "World Population Prospects: The 2017 Revision," 2017.

the range of estimates for China's total population in 2050 (and beyond) produced by the UN Population Division. In contrast to the widely cited "medium variant" (which I use for all other figures in this chapter), the "high variant" shows China's population continuing to increase past 1.5 billion, and the "low variant" suggests an even greater decline in population, to substantially less than the current 1.4 billion by 2050. Experts differ on how China's recent relaxation of family planning policies may impact long-run fertility. But most agree that total fertility will rebound to no more than replacement levels.[6] The new births will *increase* the total dependency ratio in the intermediate term but eventually make filial piety to China's elderly less of a burden on the young.

Demographic change involves more than population aging. China's large gender imbalance portends unknown macroeconomic and social impacts in the future. The sex ratio at birth (SRB)—the number of boys born per 100 girls—has long been abnormal, with the excess of boys to girls much higher in rural than urban areas despite policies allowing a second child if the first was a girl. Sex-selective abortion is illegal, but it has contributed to the imbalance. According to the 2010 census, 118 boys were born for every 100 girls. Beijing is aware of potential problems and launched the "Care for Girls" campaign in 2006 to address gender imbalance issues.[7] The government also has implemented a number of policies regarding female employment and caregiving roles.[8]

Such a large gender imbalance in a rapidly aging and urbanizing population is unprecedented, and its impact uncertain.[9] The recent relaxation of family planning policies might ameliorate the son-favoring sex ratio at birth, but the existing imbalance will create tens of millions of "forced bachelors." According to demographer Christophe Guilmoto, even if the sex ratio at birth returns to normalcy by 2020—and it is unclear that it will—*the proportion of men in China unmarried at age fifty is expected to rise to 15 percent by 2055.*[10] The impact and societal (and political) challenges of having more than 100 million unmarried men are uncertain but likely to be significant. Studies document how the quality of life of unmarried men, especially rural unmarried men in their late twenties and older, tends to be worse than for both younger unmarried men and married men of similar ages.[11] Projecting into the future, households and society will confront a "marriage squeeze" that will contribute to the domestic policy challenges China must confront in tandem with population aging and reduced economic growth.[12] The longer life expectancy of women compared to men makes "population aging an important women's issue."[13] China will have a dearth of marriage-eligible young women and a surplus of older women, who because of deprivations in childhood, such as lack of education, suffer from more problems of cognitive decline and poor health. This means that China's demographic destiny includes strains on family patterns and gender roles.

Rapid urbanization in China provides impetus for economic growth and human capital resources for urban industrial and service-sector development. Although the exact pace and character of household registration (*hukou* status) reform remain unresolved (see chapter 7 by Mary Gallagher, this volume), existing trends indicate that about three-quarters of Chinese will reside in urban areas by 2050.[14] For urbanization to help fuel continued economic growth, localities will need fiscal incentives to provide access to local social benefits for new residents as well as for the original registered *huji* population (such as access to urban schools for migrant workers' children, portable health insurance, and affordable housing with room to accommodate multigeneration families).[15]

Urbanization and gender imbalance will interact with population aging to present policymakers with opportunities and constraints different from those of other countries and China's own past. Figure 6.4 shows the median age in China and several other countries for the century since 1960. The median age in China increases from twenty years old in 1965 to more than fifty by 2050. Although Korea's pace of aging is much faster—from younger than India in 1960 to older than Japan by 2050—China's aging arguably presents the greater policy challenge because the population is much larger and has a much lower per capita income. As this is being written, China's median age is crossing that of the United States (thirty-eight years). India's median age is ten years younger.[16]

THE DEMOGRAPHIC TRANSITION AND ECONOMIC GROWTH

China's ongoing demographic, epidemiological, and nutritional transitions have been both the cause and effect of rising living standards. In later decades of the twentieth century, China (like most countries in East Asia) benefitted from the "demographic dividend" of a growing working-age population. Estimates suggest that roughly one-third of East Asia's economic "miracle" can be attributed to the demographic dividend. In China the demographic dividend is estimated to have accounted for no less than 15 percent of economic growth between 1982 and 2000.[17]

Demographic changes impact economic growth through several interlinked mechanisms. A "first demographic dividend" arises from a higher ratio of workers per capita, which raises total output for any

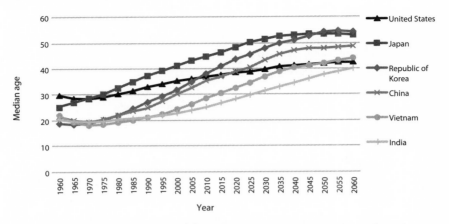

FIGURE 6.4. Median age in Asia and the U.S. in comparative perspective, 1960–2060.

SOURCE: United Nations, Department of Economic and Social Affairs, Population Division, "World Population Prospects: The 2017 Revision," Medium Variant, 2017.

given amount of output per worker. "The cumulated effect of the first dividend raises per capita income by 30% or 40% spread over at least four decades and often longer."[18] Because China's output per worker was also increasing rapidly—from growth of industry and services, catchup in technology, and transformation into a market-based economy—this pure demographic effect provided strong tailwinds for robust increases in living standards. Aggregate savings increase during the demographic transition as working-age people tend to save more (currently as well as in anticipation of future needs). During this transition China achieved high savings rates and the investment that such savings enable. Moreover, the presence of relatively fewer children in the population meant that some spending that would otherwise have supported dependent children was available for investments in physical and human capital that helped fuel economic growth.[19] Here we see the effects of the demographic change described above. China's age structure is rapidly shifting toward older ages. With smaller families, each child must shoulder greater responsibility for parental care. The size of the workforce is decreasing. In addition, older people have greater health and long-term care needs, leading to increased expenditure that can impose an economic burden on families and society.[20]

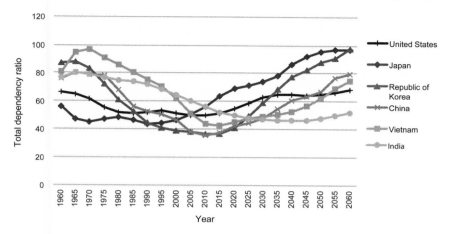

FIGURE 6.5. Total dependency ratios in Asia and the U.S. in comparative perspective, 1960–2060.

SOURCE: United Nations, Department of Economic and Social Affairs, Population Division, "World Population Prospects: The 2017 Revision," Medium Variant, 2017.

Figure 6.5 depicts the total dependency ratios—ratio of youth and elderly compared to the working-age population, a rough age-based approximation of consumers to producers in an economy—for China and several other countries from 1960 through 2060. The relatively flat line for the United States underscores that demographic changes are occurring much more quickly in China. With projections of eighty dependents per one hundred working-age individuals by 2060, China will face a dependency ratio similar to that of the 1970s, when the dependents were predominantly children rather than the oldest-old.

China is catching up to high-income countries in terms of the survival gains that accrue in the traditional retirement years (i.e., after age sixty-five).[21] The share was only about 50 percent for China at the end of the twentieth century but is destined to increase significantly in the next twenty years, reaching almost two-thirds. The increase in share of survival gains realized late in life has important economic and social consequences. The macroeconomic implications depend on behavioral and policy responses. Foreseeing longer lives, individuals might choose to work longer and save more, or consume less per year in retirement, or extract more transfers from younger generations, within the household, through public policies, or from some combination. China has an opportunity to establish sustainable institutions and avoid dysfunctional incentives—such as policies that discourage working past age sixty or sixty-five—but to realize that opportunity, it will have to revise the social compact governing retirement ages and encourage healthy lifestyles and longer working lives.

LABOR FORCE PARTICIPATION

Health and demography influence the population engaged in formal and informal employment, and thus China's transition toward a modern, urban, service sector–dominated market economy.[22] Although a detailed discussion of China's labor markets and pension policies falls outside the scope of this chapter, this section briefly highlights recent trends to underscore the importance of investing in healthy aging and how health policies at central and local levels interact in complex ways with household decisions about work.

Figure 6.6 depicts China's labor force participation rates over the past quarter century. Among males and females age fifteen and older, labor force participation rates have declined gradually from the comparatively high rates during the Mao era. Such a decline would be expected given the relative aging of the population, the ongoing shift from agricultural to industrial and service-sector employment, and the increased investment in education for adolescents and young adults. Pressures to reduce work-life as a share of life expectancy include more years of schooling, increased demand for leisure as incomes rise, the shift away from artificially high labor force participation under central planning and efforts to decrease the workforce in state-owned enterprises, and pension policies designed for an earlier era of shorter lives.[23] Labor supply is also strongly shaped by the intergenerational systems of support, with co-residence allowing sharing of household "public goods" and childcare provided by grandparents that enables both parents to work in the formal sector and/or migrate for work.[24]

China is transitioning to a new model of growth and development with new patterns of age-specific labor force participation predicated on longer working lives for both men and women. In navigating and steering this transition, Chinese officials and society must contend with numerous and sometimes contradictory forces. Urbanization tends to reduce labor force participation because in lower-income and agricultural-based economies people tend to work longer. However, elderly rural workers have relatively low productivity, compared with healthier younger cohorts with more education. Policymakers must develop ways to encourage increased labor sup-

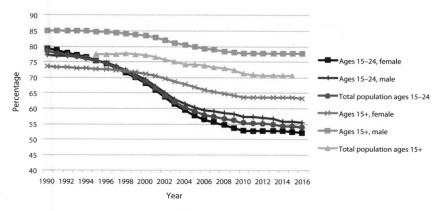

FIGURE 6.6. Labor force participation rates in China, 1990–2016.

SOURCE: World Development Indicators, World Bank, based on International Labour Organization, ILOSTAT database.

ply at older ages. In the West there was a dramatic decline in labor supply at older ages that is now beginning to reverse. China has an opportunity to prevent such a decline and to create expectations among both workers and employers of continuing to work for as long as one is healthy and capable.

Yin Weimin, the minister of Human Resources and Social Security, recently floated the idea of raising the retirement age.[25] He is not the first official to do so. Past proposals were scuttled by fears of exacerbating unemployment.[26] "Nudging" Chinese to embrace longer work-lives for both men and women will not be easy. But the need to extend working lives is urgent. The triumph of longevity threatens the fiscal integrity of pension systems and other social support programs disproportionately used by older adults. Policies are also needed in rural China to ease the transition of families strained by migration and work pressures, and to support the adult children who wish to fulfill roles of filial piety for parents left behind in rural areas or those already relocated to the city with them.

THE IMPORTANCE OF HEALTHY AGING

Longer working lives are possible because older adults are generally healthier than counterparts in previous generations. Although many observers argue that the primary benefit of healthy aging is that it saves money—"an ounce of prevention is worth a pound of cure"—cost control is *not* necessarily the most important reason to emphasize prevention. In fact, prevention often leads to more spending rather than less, because healthy people live longer. Investments in healthy aging will be critical if China is to meet public expectations for fuller, longer lives. It is not clear whether China's future elderly will benefit from a substantial compression of morbidity into the later years of life.[27] David Bloom and coauthors estimate that the cost of China's five main chronic diseases will total about $23 trillion between 2012 and 2030.[28] Cardiovascular disease is the most expensive and makes the greatest contribution to lost output in China.

Another policy challenge centers on the need to tailor policies to fit changes in healthy lifespan and to promote healthy aging with inclusiveness rather than exacerbating inequalities. Healthy aging may extend years of vitality, with the aid of better lifestyles and enabling technologies and rising living standards, postponing the onset of disability and chronic diseases, and enabling people to work longer before reaching their frail years. However, longer lives may mean more years with disability and frailty. According to the China Health and Retirement Longitudinal Study 2011 national baseline data, Chinese older than sixty face many health challenges: 38 percent report a disability, 24 percent require assistance with basic daily activities, and 54 percent had hypertension, with a large minority undiagnosed and untreated.[29] The prevalence of diabetes is now similar to that in the United States. A recent study has documented substantial cognitive impairments among the oldest-old in China, consistent with trends also evident in other studies of mainland China, Hong Kong, and Taiwan.[30] Additional investments to control chronic disease could enhance the working capabilities and quality of life of China's elderly as well as prepare society for supporting dignity for those generations that have contributed much to the country's current stage of prosperity. There are several challenges in reaching that goal, however. For example, designing and implementing effective policies for healthy aging is more difficult than continuing current policies and requires a substantial fiscal commitment when it might be easier to assume households must internalize the costs of caring for the sick and elderly without expecting state-financed support.

INEQUALITIES IN HEALTH AND HEALTH CARE

Many studies document the disparities in health between rural and urban Chinese, correlated with and in some respects perpetuated by distinctions in education, lifestyles, and livelihoods. These disparities begin with prenatal exposure and nutrition that shape life-long outcomes. For example, a study of trends in China's maternal and child health outcomes from 2000 to 2013 found that the urban–rural disparity in maternal mortality rates, under-five mortality rates, and neonatal mortality rates improved over the study period, but the gaps remained substantial. Indeed, the documented reductions in disparity of maternal and child health outcomes fell short of China's own goals as articulated in the "Healthy China 2030" strategy.[31] The difference in height between urban boys in east and west China actually increased during 1985 through 2010.[32]

Rural residents who migrate for work may suffer disproportionately from injury in hazardous occupations. For example, data for 2004 suggest that migrant workers accounted for 85 percent of construction industry deaths.[33] Partly as a result of these early life and occupational differences, inequalities in health are also evident at the other end of the life course. In the China Health and Retirement Longitudinal Study (CHARLS) baseline survey, controlling for per capita expenditures and other economic and location variables, economists Xiaoyan Lei et al. document strong educational gradients in self-assessed health, presence of any disability (ADL), and in survival expectations (respondents' self-report of possibility of surviving to age seventy-five).[34] Estimates of average life expectancy across different regions suggest gaps of 11.8 years for men and 12.8 years for women in 2013.[35]

Poorer Chinese are increasingly afflicted by "diseases of affluence" such as hypertension, diabetes, and other chronic illnesses. Diagnosing and managing chronic disease to prevent morbidity and premature mortality across the entire population will require significant changes to the health-care system. For example, according to nationally representative data from 2010 through 2011, 44 percent of hypertensives with rural *hukou* were undiagnosed, compared to 36 percent of hypertensives with urban *hukou*.[36] Rural, less educated individuals may be increasingly at a disadvantage in understanding the importance of adherence to medication regimens, dietary adjustments, regular check-ups, and other factors.[37] Analysis of the 2000 census shows that Chinese men and women of the 1940 birth cohort (i.e., at age sixty) with a college education were expected to live, respectively, 6.5 years and 7.6 years longer than their counterparts with no formal schooling. In comparison, the 1985 birth cohort (i.e., at age fifteen) who would go on to get a college education were expected to live 12.5 years longer than those with no formal schooling.[38]

Controlling for demographic differences, GDP per capita, and other factors, a one standard deviation increase in average years of schooling among residents in a county was associated with an increase of 0.38 standard deviations—about 1.4 years—in life expectancy for residents of that county.[39] Progress has been made since then, but rural residents continue to be disadvantaged in terms of both education and health care, a critical consideration for China's future workforce productivity (see chapter 8, this volume).

Health Care for 1.4 Billion: Health System Reform Challenges

China has made significant progress toward universal health coverage that meets the reasonable expectations of the population and addresses the perennial patient complaint of "*kan bing nan, kan bing gui*, 看病难，看病贵" ("obtaining health care is difficult and expensive"). Yet many challenges remain.[40]

ACHIEVING UNIVERSAL HEALTH COVERAGE

Before the twenty-first century, China's health system was relatively decentralized, with health-care financing and access linked to an individual's place of residence and employment (*danwei*), and with small risk pools that linked local benefits to local government resources. This system began to change with the introduction of urban reforms in the 1990s and subsidized rural insurance pilots in the early 2000s. National health reforms introduced in 2009 put in place a new system to finance medical care that has achieved universal health coverage, albeit at a relatively low level of coverage. These reforms were linked to a mechanism for fiscal redistribution that partially alleviates the disparities inherent to locality of birth (see chapter 4 by Jean C. Oi, this volume).

Five overarching goals guided the national health reforms adopted in and since 2009: extending basic government-subsidized health insurance to achieve universal coverage, expanding health benefits, strengthening primary care, implementing an essential drug list (and removing the profit margin from drug dispensing that distorts treatment and prescribing), and reform of government-owned hospitals. Extending basic health insurance coverage to over 95 percent of the population is a major achievement even though separate health insurance systems for urban and rural residents offer only modest financial protection from catastrophic medical spending and imperfectly cover the vast migrant population (see chapter 7, this volume).

The 13th Five-Year Plan for deepening health system reform issued by the State Council acknowledged that reforms have entered a difficult "high water phase," with goals that include establishing effective referral systems and expanding family doctor contracting systems to promote trustworthy first-contact care in the community rather than at crowded hospital out-patient departments. China's health spending has grown even more rap-idly than overall economic growth for more than a decade (see Figure 6.1). Health care's share of the economy now equals more than 6 percent of GDP (totaling approximately RMB 4634.5 billion in 2016) and continues to grow. The 6 percent of GDP figure does not include what households spend on care for their elderly members and other community-based or government-funded long-term care expenditures.

China must find an appropriate balance between household financial responsibility for health and elderly services, and social protection provided through tax-based, government-designed programs. Transition from the former to the latter is already occurring and will continue in conjunction with urbanization and efforts to address disparities through social pro-grams. China's urban residents have long enjoyed a more comprehensive "welfare state" than do rural residents. Social programs with pooled fi-nancing are key to addressing inequalities, but the extent of this transition will depend on policy decisions apportioning risk and financial burdens among households, local governments (taxpayers in a given locality), and the central government (all taxpayers). The spectrum ranges from the great-est inequality (taxing the sick by having them pay for their own care) to the greatest pooling of risk and loss of "skin in the game" to constrain the ten-dency to buy all the services that someone else is paying for (moral hazard).

PROBLEMS OF COORDINATION AND STANDARDIZATION

The vast array of stakeholders, government regulatory and administrative oversight bodies, and multiple fiscal flows compound the intertwined chal-lenges of demographic change and health system reform. The health-care dimensions of China's future will be shaped by the choices of myriad house-hold, community, and state decision-makers with competing interests and priorities.

The March 2018 13th National People's Congress changed the institutional responsibilities in the health sector. Previously, the National Health and Family Planning Commission (NHFPC), which was subordinate to the State Council Health Reform Leading Group, played a primary role, in conjunction with the generally more powerful Ministry of Finance (MOF), National Development and Reform Commission (NDRC), and Ministry of Human Resources and Social Security (MHRSS). The reorganization abolished the Health and Family Planning Commission, replacing it with the National Health Commission (*Guojia Weisheng Jiankang Weiyuanhui*, 国家卫生委员会). The National Health Commission (NHC) combines the responsibilities previously managed by the Office of the Leading Group for Deepening Reform of the Medical and Health Care System, the China National Committee on Aging, responsibilities for implementation of the "Framework Convention on Tobacco Control" formerly under the Ministry of Industry and Information Technology, and the State Administration of Work Safety, to name a few.[41] The NHC is now the primary central agency for coordinating health policies, including implementing "Healthy China 2030." Other NHC objectives include implementing the universal two-child policy and interlinking with promotion of maternal and child health and efforts to promote healthy aging.

The institutional structure has been changed but the dispersion of central government functions in the health sector persists. The health insurance (purchaser) functions fall under the new National Healthcare Security Administration (*Guojia Yiliao Baozhang Ju*, 国家医疗保障局); the NHC remains the central government agency overseeing government-owned hospitals and clinics (provider) as well as overseeing the broad range of health and aging policies. The Ministry of Finance and the NDRC continue to play key roles in most policies related to health and demographic change.

For nursing homes and other forms of long-term care for the elderly and disabled, the Ministry of Civil Affairs is the primary policymaking authority. Other important regulatory bodies include the Ministry of Housing and Urban–Rural Development, the Insurance Regulatory Commission, and the Ministry of Commerce (for foreign investment), and other agencies. There are multiple areas of gray jurisdiction and overlap of functions. For example, elderly individuals often need coordinated medical care and long-term care services; regulations stipulate that long-term care providers cannot provide medical care services, just assistance with activities of daily living.

The State Council has called for increasing the number of facilities that integrate medical and long-term care for the elderly, but implementation has been uneven and slow. Other key actors in health policy include provincial and local governments, government-owned and nongovernment health providers, from village doctors to specialists and CEOs of large urban hospitals, medical schools, key professional and scientific bodies, and corporations involved in pharmaceutical and medical device development and distribution.

Each administrative layer has different roles, and some policies require close coordination among overlapping jurisdictions. For example, family planning policies are national but implemented at different speeds by different provinces, and local enforcement often creates within-province variation.[42] Each county develops its own New Cooperative Medical Scheme (NCMS) program, and each municipality has responsibility for health sector planning, merger of NCMS with urban resident insurance, pace of introducing catastrophic insurance coverage, and many other policies. Localities take initiative to meet central government articulated goals, but a recent report suggests that jurisdictional problems inhibit progress in assessing the health impact of urban policies. The report recommends that the Patriotic Health Campaign Committee be transferred to the mayor's office rather than subsumed under the National Health Committee because the latter lacks the authority to coordinate across different agencies.[43]

Similarly, each firm determines benefits for its workers within legal guidelines, as mediated by local government decisions. For example, social insurance contributions by firms (i.e., for pensions, unemployment, injury, maternity, and health insurance) generally are expected to be about 40 percent of worker wages. This is a sizable proportion, especially so as real wages have doubled in the 2006–16 period. However, a pioneering 2016 survey of firms and employees discovered that the surveyed manufacturing firms in Guangdong and Hubei actually contributed only 17 percent of wages to social insurance contributions, accounting for less than 3 percent of total costs of those firms. This lower rate was "due to lower effective contribution rates set by cities, including use of reference wages below actual wages to determine required contributions, incomplete social insurance coverage of workers, and other forms of evasion."[44] Thus stakeholders at the local level often have incentive to "work around" directives from higher administrative agencies in ways that compromise the intent of national policies, reduce revenues for redistribution, and/or have other consequences.

Policies decided at multiple levels of government and individual circumstance shape household decisions about life-course issues that reverberate across society and between generations, including migration for work, how much to invest in the health and education of their son(s) and/or daughter(s), which occupations to undertake themselves and/or encourage for their posterity, whether to enroll in social health insurance programs available to them, and whether and from which providers to seek health care. Other decisions include which pension plan to contribute to for the current elderly and for current workers to help support them when they retire, who should live with and/or care for the disabled or frail elderly, and so on. Making decisions on such issues when institutions and possibilities are in transition is both difficult and consequential.

Many issues involve both local and national-level policy decisions. Choices affecting redistribution of amounts large enough to close urban-rural gaps and encourage higher levels of risk pooling for health care and elderly care can be made only at the national level. But local implementation matters tremendously because national "one-size-fits-all" policies are always adapted to fit local circumstances. And local decision-makers may have different approaches to managing issues, such as the appropriate roles of private and government-owned health service providers of primary care, inpatient services, and elderly care services. Some localities have privatized almost all their hospitals; most, however, retain a majority share of government providers. Some localities stipulate that private primary care organizations must be not-for-profit organizations; others strive to assure an "equal playing field" for private for-profit organizations providing services to patients covered by social health insurance. Health-care markets are inherently local. Patients with pressing medical needs cannot go halfway across the country to shop for the best care, and insurance policies reinforce the importance of local policy decisions because insurance typically reimburses patients only for medical care received within that locality, or at a much lower rate for care elsewhere. Therefore local policy decisions are critical.

LONG-TERM SERVICES FOR CHINA'S AGING POPULATION

As noted above, China's approach to health and social support tries to balance individual responsibility, community assistance, and national-level taxpayer redistribution. The same is true of care for frail elderly individuals. Until recently, households were responsible for all long-term care, but small families, changing living arrangements, and a much higher proportion of frail elderly preclude relying exclusively on this traditional model. National policy now envisions a three-way division of responsibility. Family-based care for the elderly and disabled remains the foundation, but it is now supplemented by services in the local community, and, for the most disabled, by institutional care. This three-part plan for elderly care has variously been framed as "9064" or "9073"—90 percent of living at home cared for by family members, 6 or 7 percent receiving services within the community, and 3 or 4 percent institutionalized.

Some localities have experimented with long-term care insurance (LTCI) to cover costs of elder care. Qingdao, in Shandong province, was first to adopt a pilot LTCI program in 2012. Since then, at least fifteen regions have initiated pilot programs that utilize a combination of fiscal resources, including individual contributions (both prepaid premium contributions and copayments for services when used), social insurance (sometimes from the medical insurance funds), and government fiscal support. Different management models are being tried, such as management by local government agencies (as in Qingdao, Shanghai, Changchun, and Guangzhou) or in conjunction with insurance companies (as in Nantong, Ningbo, Anqing, Chongqing, and Chengdu).[45]

China has substantially increased the number of residential facilities for long-term care, especially in urban areas, often by establishing or expanding neighborhood programs. For example, in Beijing the Civil Affairs Bureau required each "street" administrative unit to establish a fifty- (or more) bed nursing home for dementia patients. Despite such local initiatives, it is not clear that supply can keep up with effective demand. By the end of 2016, there were approximately 7.3 million long-term care beds in 140,000 nursing homes, amounting to a total of only 31.6 beds for every 1,000 people age sixty or older. This national total is below China's target ratio and those of many other countries. Moreover, many of those beds are too expensive for the poor or even middle-income households.[46] Relatively low salaries have yielded another key constraint—lack of a qualified and professional long-term care workforce.

FUNDED AND UNFUNDED MANDATES

China did *not* achieve universal health coverage exclusively through unfunded mandates to local governments (e.g., at the county, district, or municipal level). Unfunded mandates on local governments characterized the health system in the 1980s and 1990s, but since at least 2003 when NCMS began, China has had an evolving system that divides responsibility among different layers of government and individual households. The role of central government transfers for specific health programs is growing.

Central government transfers and subsidies to complement provincial-level funds have played a key role in China's health system reforms, providing subsidies to government-managed facilities and to the voluntary insurance programs for rural residents (NCMS since 2003) and urban nonemployed residents (URBMI since 2007). However, local governments continue to bear a large fiscal responsibility for health that can be considered a partially unfunded mandate (see chapter 4 by Jean C. Oi, this volume). The division of public expenditures on health between national, provincial, and city levels (including prefecture-level and county-level expenditures) was approximately 10:20:70 in 2011.[47] Central government spending on health remains low compared with many other middle- and high-income countries (less than 6 percent of total government spending and only 3.2 percent of central government expenditure in 2013) and almost surely will increase in the future.[48]

China's reforms over the past decade or two have tried to redress disparities and raise basic levels of access for all. Financing flows can be fragmented in China's system, with overlap between different agencies or providers. For example, per capita budget allocations for "equalization of basic public health services" include a subcomponent for chronic disease control and management, but that is a separate pot of money from health insurance, which also covers treatment of chronic disease for enrolled patients. As a result, an individual with diabetes may participate in a series of checkups at a community health center funded through the population health budget and also have insurance-covered visits to hospital outpatient departments for similar services.

Localities sometimes have perverse incentives to degrade health coverage to avoid attracting the "wrong" kind of migrants or workers. Shanghai, for example, has a disincentive to advertise its excellent tuberculosis control program because it does not wish to attract patients with complicated cases of TB from other parts of the country. Similarly, employers that provide generous parental leave, childcare support, and other services may place themselves at a competitive disadvantage if there is a "race to the bottom" rather than a virtuous cycle of competition to attract and retain talent.

COLLABORATIVE GOVERNANCE FOR HEALTH AND ELDERLY CARE

Chinese officials are learning from experiences in localities and other countries that actively partner with the private sector to support health and long-term care services. Building upon a foundation of policies to encourage private sector growth to supplement the dominant role of government hospitals, Beijing prescribed that 20 percent of hospital beds should be supplied through the private sector. Most provinces failed to reach that goal.

The private role in long-term care—such as nursing homes and home care assistance for the frail, disabled, and oldest-old—tends to be larger in many countries than the private role in medical services. Beijing has explicitly called for development of the "health industry," which is described as including recreation, physical fitness, and long-term care. Many analysts have recommended a mix of public and private sector initiatives to support services for China's older adults, including mobility aids for people with disabilities, interventions for social and leisure activities, and life-long learning opportunities.[49] China's future health and long-term care systems almost certainly will include a larger share of nongovernment providers and "collaborative governance" with the private sector. This will entail an entirely different set of challenges related to the development of incentive structures to guide entrepreneurial behavior toward the creation of public value while still motivating innovation and investment.[50]

Chinese government documents have repeatedly called for development of private *not-for-profit* providers, but there is no mechanism to require such health service organizations to provide community benefits in exchange for tax-exempt status. This is but one part of a much larger problem—namely, the absence or inadequacy of collaborative governance mechanisms with rewards and penalties that induce private agents to advance public missions.[51]

PERSONALIZED MEDICINE, HEALTH-CARE FINANCING, AND SOCIAL OPPORTUNITY COSTS

Health spending is likely to increase at double-digit rates and crowd out other social investments, while income per capita grows at single-digit rates (see Figure 6.1b). The double-digit growth rate of medical expenditures stems from the changing character of health care. The kinds of institutional innovations that China used effectively in the past, such as barefoot doctors in the Mao era and affordable village doctors providing immunizations and antibiotics, remain critical for healthy aging. But future gains in health are more likely to depend on specialized medical technology and pharmaceuticals.[52]

The technological innovations extending life in the twenty-first century probably will derive more from personalized therapies for cancer and cardiovascular disease than from low-cost public health measures pioneered in shortage economies. New precision medicine technologies such as genomic diagnostic tests and targeted therapies often promise great clinical benefits—substantial gains in survival or even "cures." However, they almost always are extremely expensive. One example is the targeted treatment for HER2-positive breast cancer. Only around half of the women with breast cancer in China were tested to determine whether the patient would respond to this personalized and highly effective treatment, and only about 30 percent of all HER2-positive patients were able to use Herceptin for treatment.[53] This was so, even though the testing had been covered by many insurance programs in China and Roche had started a patient assistance program in 2011.[54] Herceptin was added to the insurance reimbursement list in July 2017 along with several other leading cancer drugs as part of a negotiated reduced-price agreement between pharmaceutical firms and China's Ministry of Human Resources and Social Security.[55]

Constraints, Choices, and Possible Consequences

What do the aforementioned trends in health and health-care disparities—by *hukou*, urban/rural residence, income, education, and other dimensions—imply regarding China's choices and trajectory? The size of China's population is an inescapable constraint; extending any health care, elder care, or other benefits to all citizens engenders huge aggregate demand for funds, facilities, and trained personnel. Under what circumstances should the needs and/or demands for improved health care or elder assistance trump those for education, military equipment, or pension funds? Constraints are more likely to bind as economic growth slows and public expectations rise.

Attempting to narrow existing and future access gaps by helping the most disadvantaged would require covering more of the costs through government-funded social insurance. Raising the per capita health spending for rural residents and urban nonemployed populations to equivalence with the urban employed population could entail a fiscal commitment equal to a few percent of GDP. Addressing the social determinants of health disparities and long-term care access could require another few percent of GDP. This would bring China to a level of health spending (9–10 percent of GDP) equal to the average in high-income countries.

Even with a commitment to closing the "opportunity gap" in China, however, differences by *hukou* and many other dimensions will probably persist for a long time. Changing the investments in health and education for the rural population, especially in the most remote areas of the country, will be difficult, costly, and take years to implement. In the meantime the nutritional and educational disparities afflicting current youth and adults from rural areas will manifest in the health conditions they face in adulthood.[56] Moreover, it is politically infeasible, and certainly not desirable, to degrade health coverage for urban residents merely to reduce the gap with rural residents; the large gap has to be closed by improving coverage in rural areas faster than in cities.

Implementation effectiveness depends on addressing an array of daunting incentive issues. For example, to assure primary care for rural residents China has recruited capable students for medical school from rural areas, who then must serve in the countryside after graduation. This has had the unintended consequence of reducing rural students' motivation to become high-quality doctors. These kinds of incentive challenges are rife within the complicated "social engineering" project of China's health system reforms. Merely increasing funding without careful evaluation of programs and policies won't solve the problem.

Well-being and the realization of *xiaokang* (the China dream) encompasses many dimensions of quality of life that are not necessarily reflected in per capita income and economic growth. Longer and healthier lives can bring great improvements in well-being. Choosing to care for children or elderly at home rather than through institutionalized day care or nursing homes leads to lower formal employment and income, but no less work and service to society and families. Having access to high-quality health services with fewer re-admissions after hospitalization, for example, reduces the volume of output in the health sector but may represent a significant improvement in social value and quality of life. Decision-makers need information to gauge broader social well-being as they guide how China adjusts to small families, an older, more urban population, a growing prevalence of chronic diseases, and the social opportunity cost of closing disparities in access to medical care technologies between the least and most advantaged populations within China.

Perhaps ironically, China's health system has been viewed by many as less adequate and responsive to patients' needs, even as China has completed steps toward universal health coverage and continues to improve access, quality, and risk protection. Improvements in many cases fall short of rising expectations. Indeed, in some respects patient–physician relations have become more strained, as manifest by violent incidents of patients and their family members physically attacking physicians. This tension arises for many reasons and is exacerbated by lack of a transparent system for handling malpractice claims. No health system can be considered well-functioning if doctors discourage their own children from becoming physicians, and young people interested in medicine and nursing are advised to direct their talents elsewhere. China also lacks a system of antitrust enforcement in health care, but as providers compete for patients and purchasers seek ways to rein in spending growth, consolidation among providers and their market power to charge high prices will gain more salience, requiring discussion at the level of system governance. The presumption that government purchasers can count on government-owned hospitals to "do the right thing" cannot be presumed forever, since government hospitals are also under market and administrative pressures to earn net revenue. China needs regulatory and incentive structures to align provider interests with social goals.

Recent efforts to strengthen primary care well illustrate the challenges ahead. A chosen strategy has been linking individual patients to primary care doctors ("general practitioners," or GPs) to encourage patients to seek care outside of hospitals for regular services, including immunizations, colds, and chronic disease management. Starting in mid-2016 a nationwide push was made to implement the "family doctor" system that formalizes a "contract" between a patient and a primary care management team, which promises a set of services in exchange for the patient regularly seeking care with that team. With GPs as "health gatekeepers" (*jiankang shoumenren*, 健康守门人), this initiative seeks to create a system of primary care management with these doctors empowered to deny or discourage referral to specialists to reduce the flow of patients to hospitals for routine services.

The effectiveness of this contract initiative is promising but constrained. First, even with ramped-up training programs, China currently lacks well-trained GPs. As of 2016, there were 209,000 registered GPs, accounting for 6.6 percent of practicing (assistant) physicians and representing only 1.51 GPs per 10,000 population.[57] Second, patients are distrustful of the expertise of physicians outside of hospitals, and unclear what extra value is being offered under a "family doctor contract" in exchange for giving up the freedom to seek care directly at hospitals. Policies are quite heterogeneous and nontransparent, and the logic for patients does not always accord with their expectations, except for those with chronic conditions for whom seeking care and prescription renewals at the local clinic is convenient. Third, physicians and nurses lack clear incentives to work together as an efficient team or to treat each patient as a "valued client," although some localities have experimented with promising models for team-based care.[58]

MACROECONOMIC GROWTH SCENARIOS AND FISCAL COMMITMENTS

If China could achieve robust economic growth, most social adjustment costs, including redistribution toward poorer households and regions, could be shouldered without difficult trade-offs. However, under medium- or low-growth scenarios, which are more likely (see chapter 2 by Barry Naughton and chapter 8 by Hongbin Li et al., this volume), leaders will be tempted to ignore these issues in favor of other pressing social concerns, to China's longer-run peril. Among other consequences, households will face greater burdens of dependent care, and an inefficient health service delivery system will absorb larger shares of GDP and reduce funding available for long-term care, education, and other social determinants of health.

According to the first comprehensive summary of China's health system, in 2012 China spent 5.4 percent of its GDP on health, with more than half from general government expenditure.[59] As in the United States, public funds constitute a little over 50 percent of total health spending, much more than in many low-income countries but significantly below the average for OECD countries.[60] Studies of health expenditure growth in China show that the "raw" impact of population aging is less prominent than the ongoing and relentless pressures from technological change in medical care and increasing spending per patient for a given disease. As China has improved access to a wider range of health services for all citizens, health spending has increased. The link to personalized medicine is readily apparent.[61]

The choice set is constrained in many ways. To state the obvious, controlling health expenditure growth by curtailing medical services, ignoring medical advances, and not spend so much money on access to health care is not a viable option. China, like other countries, must develop institutions that can make difficult decisions about how to provide access to the latest drugs, therapies, and devices, to whom, and with what requirements for households to bear part of the costs. China's policymakers are aware of and are trying to mitigate the fiscal pressures from government commitments to improved health insurance coverage.

China's future will be shaped by choices determining the proportion of total resources devoted to health expenditures. The share of GDP absorbed by the health system almost surely will grow, but whether it ends up closer to those of Singapore or South Korea (i.e., less than one-tenth of the total economy) or balloons to a much larger fraction, such as the extremely high 17 percent of GDP in the United States will make a huge difference for other policy areas (see Figure 6.1b). If China follows Japan, health spending and long-term care spending could approach 10 percent of GDP over the coming two decades. If it follows a scenario of "business as usual" under fee-for-service and uncoordinated care that more resembles the United States, the share of GDP could be even larger.

FERTILITY, LABOR FORCE, AND DEMOGRAPHIC DIVIDEND

Demographic forces of population aging, gender imbalance, and urbanization will constrain and enable China's rise. Losing its "demographic dividend," China faces inevitable adjustments. Either labor supply must increase, or consumption must decrease, to lower the ratio of consumers to workers.[62] Decline of consumption—or even slowing in the growth rate of consumption—is not appealing and could lead to substantial discontent. Increasing the quantity and quality of labor supply is crucial. Given China's age structure, this makes it imperative to promote healthy aging and longer working lives as well as fully supporting female labor force participation.

There is no simple formula for assessing the social and macroeconomic impact of "losing the demographic dividend." The impact depends entirely on the efficacy of adjustments made by society and the economy. For China those adjustments also depend on the interplay with gender imbalance and urbanization. Will young people be more productive than the retiring older generation to a large enough extent to compensate for the macroeconomic effects of a shrinking working-age population and commensurate with the growth of real wages? The answers to those questions depend on investments in the health and education of today's infants and youth, especially those who otherwise may not be productively employed in a more capital-intensive, service and skill-based economy.

One of China's most pressing demographic adjustments hinges on the extent fertility rebounds toward replacement levels and policy support for mothers striving to balance careers and childcare. More births will result in *more* dependents per worker for the next decade or more because the additional children will not join China's labor force for approximately two decades. In the meantime more children may mean some parents—especially mothers—will have to drop out of the formal labor force to provide childcare, exacerbating rather than ameliorating the decrease in working-age population, unless they are supported with quality childcare services. Will China embrace "women hold up half the sky" with a newly realized conviction of its economic necessity as well as ethical appropriateness? Or will social norms continue to see men as providers, and women as primarily responsible for raising children and caring for aging parents and parents-in-law? China's policymakers can either fully support female labor force participation with subsidized quality childcare opportunities, or implicitly assume that employers are justified in discriminating against women because they believe that only men can be simultaneously good parents and good workers. This choice will shape China's fertility, labor markets, gender roles, and family dynamics for decades. China also faces a large gender imbalance with unknown macroeconomic and social implications. Whether rising incomes will dampen or spur son preference in China remains unclear. A recent study found that increases in incomes associated with land reform and introduction of the household responsibility system in agriculture were associated with strong increases in gender imbalance.[63]

More generally, local and national decisions by Chinese policymakers will determine whether the country will build a social protection system that enables inclusive, equitable growth and provides a safety net for those with ill health, disability, or threats to livelihood. Those same decisions will determine if, in its rush to modernize, China goes to the opposite extreme and creates an unsustainable social protection system that forces government officials to renege on promises. Finding the right balance among competing but interconnected policy challenges will be critical and difficult. China's challenges in demographic change, health care, and elder care are not simply a matter of spending more money, or continuing business as usual at a higher level of per capita income. The issues are more complicated than that and will interact with decisions about education, urbanization, and many other policies. A few things are certain, however. China's population aging will continue. China will need to find a way to support households in caring for the burgeoning elderly population as well as additional children born in response to relaxed family planning policies.[64] More people will suffer from chronic diseases. Health spending will increase in real terms and as a share of China's total economy. Health interventions and medical technology will continue to progress, and China's health system will be continually challenged to define what is "basic" and available for everyone and what is "luxury" and available only to those who can afford to buy it.

SMALL STEPS ON A LONG JOURNEY

Recent policy statements reveal considerable continuity with previously announced reforms. Xi Jinping has emphasized that reforms must accelerate in the social sector, including social security and public health. China has articulated a plan for "Healthy China" that includes goals for longer life expectancy, expanding healthy life expectancy (in other words, helping older adults live longer, healthier lives), continuing to reduce infant, maternal, and under-five mortality, and expanding the universal health coverage system to further reduce out-of-pocket payments and to improve convenience, quality, efficiency, and sustainability. Almost everyone now has health insurance, and more Chinese have catastrophic coverage to break the vicious cycle of illness-induced poverty and intergenerational transmission of poverty. Family planning policies have been relaxed to allow more fertility choice. Experiments with long-term care financing promise paths forward for supporting families' care for the elderly, and policy statements advocate revising provider payment and strengthening primary care, but implementation remains problematic and uneven.

Creation of the National Health Commission may enable closer coordination of a life-course approach to healthy aging—from planned fertility and prenatal care, to preventive and curative services for middle-aged and elderly, to integrated health and long-term care services for the oldest-old. Whether the new institutional structure consolidating purchasing under the National Healthcare Security Administration will effectively address the challenges of healthy aging, translate the complex multiple dimensions of policy into effective and concrete enhancement of quality of life, protection from financial risk of ill health, and providing equality of opportunity in human capital by closing large gaps in health and health-care access remains to be seen. It would be naïve to assert that any change in regulatory or organizational structure can "solve" the problems confronting China's health system.

The most recent reorganization of China's central government agencies may represent a "new normal" in which the "top-level design" for health system reform has been largely orchestrated and now policies can revert to the National Health Commission or National Healthcare Security Administration for implementation and refinement. However, multiple central and local government agencies will continue to oversee important aspects of healthy aging, and lack of coordination may undermine best efforts in local experimentation with effective solutions. Moreover, health system reform is not a one-off accomplishment but will periodically require larger incremental changes and will incessantly call for smaller adjustments, because of rapidly changing technologies of treatment with ever-higher price tags and necessity of adjustment to China's changing demographics. The challenges ahead are enormous, as are the implications of policy choices to address them. How effectively and efficiently Beijing meets health- and aging-related challenges will have a major impact on its ability to manage all other challenges discussed in this volume.

CHAPTER 7

Can China Achieve Inclusive Urbanization?

Mary E. Gallagher

One of the most pressing challenges on the Communist Party's agenda is that of achieving inclusive and sustainable urbanization that will provide social security and equal citizenship benefits to the vast number of Chinese rural citizens and migrant workers left out of China's exclusive urban welfare state. With these goals the future of China's urbanization will be quite different from its past. The partial urbanization of the first thirty years of reform was mainly bottom-up. Rural people left their villages in search of work in the cities. They had low expectations about access to urban life and goods, and they returned to their villages and their land when no longer able to work in the city. China's current and future urbanization is more top-down.[1]

The central government encourages urbanization as a solution to the middle-income trap.[2] An urbanized and consuming society is the basis for China's next stage of development, as China weans itself off high rates of government investment and reliance on exports. Local governments, too, have strong incentives to encourage urbanization, as it means more land requisition, real estate development, and revenue. However, just as the government begins to encourage this "new-style urbanization," to use the government's own phrase, many rural residents have grown reluctant to relinquish the security of rural land. Rural *hukou* (household registration), previously seen as quite inferior to urban *hukou*, has important benefits linked to collective land ownership. As urban *hukou* becomes less attractive without the promise of a job and with often meager benefits for the unemployed or informally employed, social conflict over the thorny issues of land security and employment insecurity is likely to intensify.[3]

China's central government has pursued the goals of inclusive urbanization and the dismantling of the household registration system since 2006.[4] While these goals are laudable and demonstrate the government's attention to inequality in contemporary China, they have remained elusive. Localities continue to resist reforms that might boost large-scale migration of rural citizens and increase their own social burden. The linked problems of land, employment, and social welfare have also slowed progress, as there are knock-on effects from one issue area to the other. Despite ambitious targets in the 2014 New Style Urbanization Plan, progress has been slower than anticipated.

Central government efforts have made substantial changes to the rural welfare state and social and legal protections for China's large migrant workforce. But central intentions are only the beginning; local governments implement central goals with their own interests in mind. Whether China can achieve inclusive urbanization encompasses a subset of questions about the diverse processes of urbanization in a large, regionally imbalanced country like China. Is urbanization based on meritocratic criteria like skills and education preferable? Is urbanization based on local territorial rights and the spatial expansion of urban citizenship better? What are the costs and benefits of each? How do diverse patterns of urbanization affect social welfare inclusion and employment opportunities of different types of citizens?

This chapter examines these questions through a comparative analysis of two dominant types of urbanization in China: workplace-based and citizenship-based. Workplace-based urbanization relies on formal employment as the main mechanism to incorporate rural citizens into urban social welfare programs and, eventually, urban residency and citizenship. Workplace-based urbanization functions according to a meritocratic logic, with citizenship linked to one's skills, education, and employment prospects. A rural person from Sichuan, for example, with higher education and permanent employment can become a legal resident of Shanghai through this process. Citizenship-based urbanization, in contrast, targets local rural citizens for inclusion and applies a spatial logic to urbanization, with citizenship linked to one's location. Rural citizens from districts on the outskirts of cities, in their rural districts, are gradually incorporated into the urban *hukou* system, often in exchange for surrendering their land-use rights. This process enables a rural resident of Chongming Island, a formerly rural district of Shanghai municipality, to become an urban resident of Shanghai.[5]

In practice, these two patterns of urbanization are not mutually exclusive. Most localities use variants of both, but with different patterns of emphasis and design. For example, rich, coastal megacities tend to emphasize meritocratic and exclusive workplace-based urbanization. Inland cities, employing variants of early experiments in Chongqing and Chengdu, have tended to favor urbanization schemes that incorporate rural local citizens and people from the same province. Whichever approach is used (i.e., workplace- or citizenship-based) necessarily has a flip side that excludes others. This makes it important to understand how the particular logics of inclusion are constructed because each mode of inclusion for some entails the marginalization and exclusion of others.

This chapter examines the dynamics of both types of inclusion. Workplace-based urbanization has been the dominant urbanization policy of both the Chinese central government and international organizations such as the World Bank.[6] Part of its attraction is the link between employment and social welfare, which accords with the productionist bias of East Asian welfare states.[7] The model's reliance on the workplace is also a legacy of the socialist welfare state utilized in the Maoist period when the work unit (*danwei*) was the key institution delivering public goods and welfare to China's urban citizens.[8] However, relying on formal employment as the linchpin of urbanization tends to marginalize citizens who are not formally employed. Urbanization by spatial expansion of city boundaries is another form of inclusion. This form of citizenship-based urbanization does not require formal employment and is attractive to local governments because linking it to the surrender of land-use rights provides a source of revenue.[9] The central government has also promoted the expansion of new social insurance programs, including pensions and health insurance, that are residency-based as opposed to employment-based. However, rural citizens remain reluctant to surrender their land rights because social welfare based on citizenship pays out meager benefits and can't substitute for either urban employment or rural land.

Implementation of both types of urbanization is slowed and skewed by China's decentralized system of governance. The principal distorting factor in the case of workplace-based urbanization is the "race to the bottom" effect of local competition. Pressures to remain competitive (i.e., profitable) result in lax enforcement of workplace protections and social welfare inclusion that are especially disadvantageous to workers in the informal sectors who tend to have lower skills and education. For citizenship-based urbanization, distortion is often the result of the "enclosure effect" of local government's reliance on land revenue that drives officials to pressure rural citizens to surrender their land rights in exchange for the benefits of urban residence. The result is top-down "forced" urbanization that provides neither urban employment nor adequate social welfare.[10] Central government objectives for both types of urbanization are frustrated or distorted by the localism inherent in the institutions that govern China's political system.

However, rapid technological change and the rise of the gig economy may be making even workplace-based urbanization anachronistic and increasingly unable to solve China's social welfare needs. Citizenship-based urbanization is likely to become more important and the dominant mode of urbanization in the future. Under decentralized governance, however, this will likely entail ever greater localism on the part of officials and the hardening of territorial boundaries, such that the major divide in urbanization politics will not be rural versus urban but rather locals versus nonlocals.

Workplace-based Urbanization

China 2030: Building a Modern, Harmonious, and High-Income Creative Society, released in 2013 by the Development Research Center (DRC) of the State Council and the World Bank, was a bold vision for China's future that proposed programmatic goals for structural change, institutional reform, and a roadmap toward a new development model for China.[11] *China 2030* was a blueprint for the deep reforms that many expected to be undertaken in the Xi Jinping era. This development model was inspired by fears that China would become ensnared in the so-called middle-income trap because of the global instability triggered by the 2008 global financial crisis and its attendant negative effects on US standards of living and consumption and the cohesion and stability of the Eurozone.

China 2030 was quickly followed by an even longer treatise on China's urbanization. *Urban China: Toward Efficient, Inclusive, and Sustainable*

Urbanization presented an equally bold agenda for China's transformation from a country with unbalanced and incomplete urbanization to an idyllic urbanized society.[12] *Urban China* envisions shifting away from the mode of urbanization of the 1990s and early 2000s in which rural migrant workers became long-term residents of cities but almost never achieved permanent legal urban citizenship. It also proposes changes to land use and fiscal policies intended to give local governments the capacity to fund more inclusive social welfare and public goods programs.

Both of these visions for urbanization posit a strong state with the capacity to enact major structural and institutional reforms to China's famously decentralized system of governance. The envisioned reforms include gradual abolition of the household registration system (*hukou*) to enable rural citizens to obtain the public goods and social welfare benefits that have been enjoyed by urban citizens for decades, and changes to the system of social insurance that would finally pool fund management at higher levels of government and increase the portability of benefits. These visions promised greater labor market integration, increased labor mobility and flexibility, and fiscal reforms to give local governments the capacity to expand protection of and accountability to new urban residents from the countryside.

The role envisioned for the workplace in China's ambitious plan for inclusive urbanization was as important as that of the state. Although often only implicitly articulated in China's ambitious plan for inclusive urbanization, the workplace is the linchpin connecting urbanizing rural citizens to the services, benefits, and welfare of urban life. But the workplace is also a major stumbling block for China's urbanization strategy. This model of urbanization assumes that the workplace can continue to serve as one of the most important links between the state and its increasingly diverse, mobile, and demanding population. That is a huge and consequential assumption because hundreds of millions of rural citizens have migrated to cities in search of work and the benefits of urban life. During the first three decades of the reform era, workplace institutions were bifurcated and workers were subdivided on the basis of their *hukou* status.[13]

Since 1958, Chinese citizens have been categorized as urban (nonagricultural) or rural (agricultural) on the basis of the household registration system. The *hukou* system was used to restrict internal mobility, especially rural-to-urban migration, by tying state welfare to a specific locality. Labor migration increased dramatically when the effectiveness of the *hukou* system as a control mechanism was undermined and eventually relaxed in the early reform period. However, *hukou* continued to play a critical role in China's system of differential citizenship rights. Urban citizens received social benefits and welfare through their places of work, but these benefits were dependent on their possession of urban, local *hukou*. Rural migrant workers were excluded from these social benefits, even if they were long-term residents in an urban area and employed by an urban firm.[14] However, by virtue of their rural status, they were granted user rights to collectively owned rural land where their *hukou* was registered. Granting different benefits to workers with local urban residence permits and to migrant workers from rural areas created a pattern of urbanization that was partial and inadequate. In addition to its failure to provide some of the basic needs of migrants, it also severely curtailed labor mobility, exacerbated inequality, and encouraged social discrimination and mistreatment of rural citizens in cities.[15]

China's central government began to acknowledge the problems resulting from this pattern of urbanization in 2006 with the first of several documents on the treatment of migrant rural labor and the *hukou* system, and advocated moving toward a more inclusive, equitable, and sustainable development model.[16] The new approach called for replacing the system of bifurcated workplace and spatially determined, differential citizenship rights with a new process of urbanization in which access to formal (urban) employment for rural migrants would serve as the pathway to participation in the urban welfare state. However, the new approach assumes that urbanizing rural citizens will be willing to surrender their land-use rights in exchange for new rights of urban citizenship and employment.

Rising expectations for security through state-sponsored social welfare may be a natural consequence of urbanization, but in the Chinese context this expectation is compounded by the complex nature of property rights involving rural land. Ownership remains with the collective, but use and management rights are given to households with village household registration. When peasants leave the countryside for urban employment, they still have the right to the use of their allocated plot of collectively owned land. Migrants will not willingly give up rural land-based security unless they are confident that they will receive the social welfare benefits the Chinese state provides to urban residents through their workplace, which makes effective and reliable protection via the workplace the key to urbanization.[17] In 2014 the Central Committee of the CCP and the State Council jointly issued a plan for a "National New Type of Urbanization, 2014–2020" (*guojia xinxing chengzhenhua guihua*). This six-year plan for "state-led urbanization" proposes to increase the de facto urban population from 54 percent of the total population to 60 percent while increasing the number of permanent urban residents with urban *hukou* from 35 percent of the total population to 45 percent.[18]

This is an increase in the number of people who de facto reside in cities, but also narrows the gap between the actual urban population and the urban population with legal residency. Under this plan more than one hundred million rural residents would be given legal status to reside in urban areas permanently and have full access to urban social welfare benefits.[19] However, the plan assumes that these migrants will enter into formal labor contracts with their urban employers. Without formal employment these urbanizing rural citizens will continue to be excluded from the most consequential urban social welfare, such as pensions, medical insurance, unemployment insurance, and occupational injury and disease insurance.[20] The central government's 2006 decision to adopt policies of inclusive urbanization was made in anticipation of changes to China's labor and employment laws adopted between 2008 and 2012 that were both more *protective* and more *inclusive*. The new laws increased both the scope of worker rights and the proportion of workers legally entitled to those rights.[21] Specific laws include the 2008 Labor Contract Law (LCL) (and its 2012 revision), the 2008 Labor Dispute Mediation and Arbitration Law, the 2008 Employment Promotion Law, and the 2011 Social Insurance Law.[22]

In addition to enacting legislation to provide greater social protection, the government also mandated a series of information campaigns to foster greater awareness of legal rights and protections. As a key part of the model, it delegated responsibility for enforcement to workers themselves, encouraging individuals to lodge arbitration claims (and then litigation claims if arbitration was unsuccessful) against employers.[23] Encouraging and authorizing citizens to file claims as individuals was favored by the party because the legal system was constructed to minimize the collective action by workers.[24] Legal resolution of complaints was attractive because it appeared formal and modern, but it was also highly atomized and therefore less threatening to leaders obsessed with the dangers of social instability.[25]

Encouraging workers to pursue satisfaction through the legal system was successful, but it did not do as much to reduce extra-legal modes of contestation, as some officials had expected.[26] Indeed, the number of both legal challenges and strikes triggered by labor disputes increased during this period, spiking each time new protections were enshrined in law.[27]

These legal changes produced modest improvements in rural migrants access to labor contracts and social insurance. In the 2016 China Urban Labor Force Survey (CULS) the percentage of local workers working without labor contracts declined from 26 percent in 2010 to 23 percent in 2016. The decline among migrant workers was similar, dropping from 49 percent to 44.6 percent.[28] Greater use of written labor contracts also led to somewhat better firm compliance with social insurance obligations. Migrant and urban workers' participation in the most important forms of social insurance, pensions, and medical insurance increased after the LCL took effect, as shown both by the CULS and other surveys.[29] In the 2016 CULS, migrant workers without access to social insurance decreased from 61 percent to 47 percent. In contrast, only 16.4 percent of local workers lacked acess.[30]

Despite the improvements in compliance and greater ability of workplace-based inclusion to improve migrant workers' access to social benefits, China still has a long way to go. Utilizing a strategy of inclusion that relied heavily on the use of formal employment contracts and self-enforcement of the new protective laws was only partially effective. The proportion of migrant rural workers with labor contracts expanded during this period.[31] Social insurance participation also improved but at a slower rate because many migrant workers were unwilling to contribute to programs that lacked portability. Migrant workers who pay into the pension system, for example, are only able to withdraw their individual contributions if they move out of the locality. The larger portion, funded by the employer, remains in the local social pool to be paid out to local retirees. This system creates strong disincentives on the employer and the migrant employee to pay into the system. Urban residents have far higher protection and inclusion into social safety nets because local governments are more likely to require that employers pay into social insurance systems founded on the tripartite model of government, employer, and individual contributions. Urban residents can also be far more confident that they can access those funds when they retire.

Most important, access to labor contracts and, by extension, access to social insurance, and the ability to transfer rural *hukou* to urban *hukou*, are all still highly correlated with skills and education. Workers with these attributes have far more bargaining power with employers, which they can use to demand a labor contract. Earning the right to a labor contract vastly improves the chances for inclusion into social insurance. Moreover, inclusion into formal employment and social insurance is absolutely essential for permanent urban residency through *hukou* transfer. For rural migrants in major cities, the ability to qualify for *hukou* transfer is through a restrictive point system, which generally requires several years of both formal employment and participation in social insurance.[32] For example, the point system in Guangzhou mandates age between twenty and forty-five, education above middle-school level, legal residency in the city, four years of payment into the social insurance system, and no criminal record.[33] Thus employment-based opportunities for inclusion into urban social services and eventually local legal citizenship are limited to the few who qualify.

As scholars Zhiming Cheng, Russell Smyth, and Fei Guo argue, this is to be expected in a highly segmented labor market with strong institutional barriers to labor mobility.[34] The institutional discrimination of the *hukou* system has also been attributed to large gaps in wages and barriers to certain jobs and preferential employment of locals.[35] Migrant workers also bear the brunt of egregious violations of workplace standards. For example, migrant workers are far more likely to experience wage arrears, especially in sectors like construction.[36] Migrant workers are also more likely to suffer from occupational diseases, such as silicosis and black lung, and to experience occupational injury and death.

The continuing gap between urban and rural migrant workers exposes the limitations of a workplace-based inclusivity that relies heavily on formal employment. This model of inclusion tends to reinforce existing inequalities rather than serve as a lever to ratchet up standards for more marginalized populations. Despite the new protections and the real legislative efforts to improve the inclusivity of China's labor laws, enforcement by local governments and firm compliance are weak and uneven. With weak government enforcement and lackluster firm compliance, improvements after the 2008 LCL have tended to help those who already have advantages in the labor market, such as workers with higher levels of education, skills, and urban residency.[37]

Citizenship-based Urbanization

Another type of urbanization promoted by the central government through pilot experiments in select cities is based on citizenship criteria, with less or no emphasis on employment status or skill/education level. Citizenship-based urbanization is based on a spatial logic in which a city expands to incorporate local citizens that reside in its outlying rural districts. In some cases, this mode of urbanization also entails inclusion of citizens who reside outside the city but in the same province. Citizenship-based urbanization has been championed by proponents of the Chengdu-Chongqing "coordinated development model," which was piloted in Chengdu in 2003.[38] In 2007 the southwestern cities of Chengdu and Chongqing were designated National Comprehensive Reform Pilot Regions for Coordinated Urban–Rural Development. Since that time, other provinces have adopted elements of this model to increase urbanization, especially of periurban and suburban areas. The goals of this model are coordinated development, including reducing barriers for rural residents to become urbanized, equalization of social welfare between urban and rural residents of the same locality, and more efficient and large-scale agricultural production made possible by the consolidation of landholdings surrendered by rural citizens in exchange for urban benefits.

This coordinated development model is attractive for several reasons. First, its main principle is "rural–urban harmonization," which is the erasure of differential citizenship rights for citizens of the same locality.[39] Labor mobility and prospects for social mobility increase by reducing the differences between rural and urban citizens of the same administrative region. Second, as the crux of the government's "new-style urbanization," creating new urban citizens is key to a model of consumption-driven development. The transformation of rural and suburban districts on the outskirts of cities should improve the public infrastructure, especially public schools, roads, and public transportation. This reduces congestion and related problems in urban centers, providing China's rising middle class with new residential opportunities in outlying areas, which further boosts growth. Rapid improvements in high-speed rail and subway development also improves the quality of life and enhances employment opportunities by reducing travel time within and between cities.

Greater labor mobility and employment opportunities for rural citizens should also alleviate labor shortages resulting from the end of China's demographic dividend (see chapter 6 by Karen Eggleston, this volume). But restrictions on good urban jobs are common in many cities, where nonlocal rural workers are prevented from filling them. An option is opening up the labor market to *local* rural workers. For example, in Shanghai many taxi drivers are citizens of Chongming Island, a Shanghai rural county until 2017. Possession of a Shanghai *hukou* allowed them to be employed in jobs denied to rural residents of other places. Finally, citizenship-based urbanization, and its logic of spatial expansion, maximizes the cultural and linguistic overlap between existing urban residents and new urbanizing citizens. This may reduce social conflict and discrimination of the kind that has been common in Chinese cities with large migrant populations. Local rural citizens will have less trouble overcoming dialect differences and unfamiliar cultural practices.[40]

Citizenship-based urbanization, nonetheless, faces a number of significant obstacles and challenges. Perhaps the most important challenge is to resolve contradictions and uncertainties in the relationship between land security and citizenship. Under China's differential citizenship policy, rural citizens have access to collective land rights; urban citizens do not. In previous decades, when land values were low and urban social welfare was dramatically better than what existed in rural areas, a rural *hukou* was far less valuable than an urban one. However, with the rapid increase in land values and expanded access to social welfare through employment or through the residential pension/health-care systems, rural citizens are no longer necessarily willing to give up their land-use rights in exchange for urban citizenship. In some cases, rural–urban harmonization equalizes the residential pension system so that rural residents of the locality receive the same amount as an urban resident without giving up their land. When urban citizenship does not come with an employment guarantee, when residential welfare programs have been harmonized between urban and rural citizens of the same locality, and when rural *hukou* still allows access to land, the value of an urban *hukou* becomes far less clear.

Rural citizens are now more invested in their collective land rights (and their rising value) and are reluctant to surrender these rights without adequate compensation even when they are offered urban *hukou*. At the same time, local governments, under fiscal strain and heavy debt, are eager to gain control over rural land to generate revenue to boost income and foster development.[41] This is a perfect storm. Urbanization, based on the spatial logic of ever-expanding urban boundaries with *hukou* transfer tied to land requisition, exacerbates social tensions and erodes trust between citizens and the local state. Violent clashes between local officials and resistant rural residents are commonplace.[42] In response, cities like Chengdu allow access to the benefits of urban citizenship without requiring rural citizens to relinquish land. However, this solution may not work in other areas where local governments have fewer resources, less capacity, and have become addicted to land requisition as a source of revenue.

Citizenship-based urbanization is very narrowly focused on harmonization between urban and local residents of a single locality. For coastal megacities, like Shanghai, spatial urbanization is nearly complete. For many provinces, however, expansion of spatial urbanization beyond the boundaries of a single city requires multilevel government coordination and cooperation. It also requires more centralized pooling of key social welfare funds, such as pensions, so that citizens have portable insurance and can move freely to take advantage of employment opportunities. Achieving such cooperation and coordination has been extremely difficult, even within provinces, because richer, often younger, municipalities are loath to share resources with poorer counterparts.

Finally, citizenship-based urbanization cannot address the needs of interprovincial migrants, which is estimated to be about half of the total migratory workforce of approximately 170 million people.[43] In some coastal areas nonlocal migrants outnumber locals by four, five, or six to one. Highly skilled and educated migrants can attempt to qualify for *hukou* transfer through the points system, but many migrants in key industries like construction, services, and domestic work are at risk of long-term marginalization and exclusion.[44]

Barriers to Inclusive Urbanization

Under the best of conditions the challenges of urbanization are many, complex, and expensive. They are even more demanding at a time when China is burdened by slowing growth and heavy debt. China's system of decentralized governance is ill-suited for the demands that urbanization presents. Decentralized governance is defined as a system that devolves significant fiscal and policymaking autonomy to subprovincial governments, especially cities.[45] In China's nondemocratic system local officials are accountable to higher levels of government and are expected to meet key central goals, but their access to fiscal resources is constrained by central control over most tax revenues (see chapter 4 by Jean C. Oi, this volume). Unfunded mandates, especially to improve local social security, education, and welfare, are common. Officials at the very top of the locality are motivated by the chance of promotion and generally stay in a single place for only three to five years.[46] With a plethora of goals and targets to meet, they behave strategically. The most important goal is to boost local economic growth and development, often through large infrastructure projects. Another goal is to raise revenue outside of the regular tax system.

Decentralized governance creates at least two barriers to inclusive urbanization. One, the race-to-the-bottom effect constrains effective workplace-based urbanization. Decentralized governance, with its heavy emphasis on top-down economic goals, encourages race-to-the-bottom competition between localities. Implementing and enforcing environmental and labor protections are often seen as obstacles to local economic development, especially when officials have short-term time horizons and very limited downward accountability.[47] The other barrier, the enclosure effect, constrains citizenship-based urbanization. Urbanization policies that encourage rural land requisition and increase the potential for large development projects are welcomed. But the burdens of compensating rural citizens fairly for the value of their land and providing these urbanizing rural citizens with the benefits of urban life (e.g., better public schools, health care, and employment) are not.[48] Like the enclosure movement that began in sixteenth-century England, land requisition in contemporary China strips rural citizens of their land security and puts their struggle for livelihood in direct conflict with the economic and political interests of local officials.[49]

RACE TO THE BOTTOM

The weak and uneven enforcement of labor laws are in large part a consequence of China's decentralized authoritarianism that grants local governments significant autonomy and responsibility for the local economy.[50] As has been well documented, in the post-Mao era, China's decentralized system was combined with a cadre evaluation system that strongly prioritizes economic growth. Local governments were motivated to attract investment, especially foreign investment, to boost the economy, increase employment, and raise revenue.[51] The resultant near-exclusive focus on the economy encouraged local regulatory agencies to look the other way when enterprises violated laws and regulations, such as environmental regulations, labor laws, and occupational health and safety standards, which are often viewed as obstacles to rapid growth. In what effectively became a race to the bottom, social concerns, including better treatment and inclusion of migrant workers, were deferred.[52]

During the Hu Jintao period the criteria used in the cadre evaluation system became more complex, with a less myopic focus on economic growth. There were multiple attempts to incorporate new goals that reflected society's growing concerns about environmental degradation, inequality, social security, and working conditions, and in some policy areas, such as air pollution and mine safety, the government centralized regulatory enforcement with harsher penalties for violations and accidents.[53] However, the decentralized governance system maintained its strong focus on economic goals, partly because they are easier to calculate than many of the newer objectives and partly because economic growth creates personal enrichment opportunities for local cadres and their families.

Decentralized governance makes local government accountability for inclusion difficult to achieve. Local officials often lack the capacity or desire to take on new goals and enforce the protections and inclusivity mandated by the recent labor laws. This structural reality adds to the importance and difficulty of giving workers primary responsibility for securing their rights. Unless individual workers demand enforcement of their new rights, these laws would not achieve their desired effects. However, the enforcement model is far too heavily dependent on the actions of individual workers.[54]

Restrictions on organization for collective action and selective repression of civil society limit the efficacy of enforcement dependent on workers' own agency and impede the party-state's inclusive urbanization goals. Mobilization is fragmented and individualized. Disputes that begin as large collective disputes are apportioned into individual complaints. The official trade union, the All-China Federation of Trade Unions (ACFTU), is unable to represent workers adequately as a junior partner of the government in resolving labor disputes.[55] Labor nongovernmental organizations (NGOs) and "rights defense" lawyers are constrained by the political environment. The system and political environment have become more restrictive in the Xi Jinping era. Since 2014, arrests of labor activists and rights defense law-

yers, and the closure of many labor NGOs, have stymied the rise of a collective movement to improve conditions.[56]

THE ENCLOSURE EFFECT

After the 1994 centralizing tax reforms, the combination of decentralized
governance and a centralized fiscal system produced many unfunded mandates for local governments (see chapter 4 by Jean C. Oi, this volume). As
growth continued, however, local governments found new opportunities
to raise revenue through land requisition and real estate speculation. This
funding model creates strong disincentives for local officials to implement
policies that encourage long-term inclusion of migrant workers. In Chinese
cities there is a clear hierarchy of citizenship, with urban local residents at
the top, rural local residents in the middle, and rural nonlocal residents at
the bottom. Local rural citizens, who generally are not as well off as their
urban compatriots, have one important asset: use rights on collectively
owned land. These rural local residents are often enriched by their ability
to earn income by renting their land to nonlocal rural migrants. Rural local
residents serve as low-cost landlords for migrant populations that in some
places outnumber local residents by as much as twelve to one.[57] These "villages in a city" (*cheng zhong cun,* 城中村) further complicate the system of
decentralized governance by requiring rural governance structures to colo-
cate with urban district governments. Urban officials are often in conflict
with these collections of rural local residents because of the value of their
land and the need for land requisition to fund local budgets and real estate
development.[58]

As local governments have become more dependent on revenue from
land requisition, a kind of enclosure effect has occurred where rural local
citizens are moved off their land, compensated for their loss of land, and
then transformed, bureaucratically at least, from rural citizens with collective land rights into urban citizens without such rights. This process
disenfranchises two populations. Rural local residents have lost their land
security and usually face uncertain employment prospects in the city, but
they also have lost their ability to live off the rental income that came with
land-use rights. At the same time, nonlocal rural migrant workers lose their
access to cheap housing and are driven elsewhere, usually further outside
the city. The enclosure effect—through which the collectively owned land
of villagers-within-cities is confiscated and villagers are moved elsewhere—

is ongoing amid rapid urbanization and land requisition.[59] Urban governments gain revenue from such a land exchange and, in theory, they become responsible for providing public goods to their new urban local residents. However, in practice, for these new urban residents, without formal employment, urban public goods, such as the residency-based pension program, urban governments offer only modest support, usually only a few hundred RMB per month. This is far below the minimum wage level and the average employment-based pension program.[60]

Local urban governments are extremely reluctant to take on the additional burden of rural nonlocal residents, as they are already fully engaged in the process of stripping land rights away from their own rural population and ostensibly providing urban citizenship and public goods in return. Reluctance to be more inclusive extends to local citizens as well. Within this hierarchy of citizenship, urban local residents, even those who have only recently become urban via the loss of their land, are opposed to sharing scarce resources with outsiders. This is particularly the case when the presence of a large number of nonlocal rural residents creates the perception of lower-quality resources, such as public schools, lack of safety and rising crime, and unfair competition in the labor market. Rural migrants are disparaged as willing to work harder for less money.

Decentralized governance has made inclusive urbanization more difficult. The race-to-the-bottom effect was particularly pronounced when China's competitive advantage was low-cost production and there were large supplies of surplus labor in the countryside. Workplace protections were simply not that important in the drive to develop the economy and attract outside investment. Local governments were even more likely to turn a blind eye when the harshest working conditions and problems affected nonlocals. The enclosure effect is more recent but no less important as it demonstrates the complex connections between land security (and its loss) and employment security. Land security facilitated China's reliance on cheap rural labor to fuel its industrialization, as migrant workers left their families in the villages and returned there when they became ill or too old to continue to work. But collective land ownership also enriched rural residents of China's cities, as they became landlords to the millions of rural nonlocals in their midst. Both sets of rural citizens stand to lose out as China's urbanization drive continues. Local rural residents are often ill-suited for urban labor markets, and urban citizenship does not guarantee a substitute for the loss of land-based security. Only a stable and formal job will do so. Nonlocal rural residents also face other challenges if they do not enjoy formal employment. They may be driven from their unauthorized homes in a campaign to clean up the city, or they may lose access to affordable housing as urban development drives the disappearance of "villages in the city." [61]

Whither the Workplace? Urbanization and the Gig Economy

It is a truism that Chinese society is full of contradictions. Mao Zedong, of course, emphasized the role of contradictions in structuring Communist Party thought and action. Xi Jinping did the same during the 19th Party Congress. Setting out a broad and ambitious agenda for China domestically and externally, Xi proclaimed that the principal contradiction facing Chinese society is now "the contradiction between unbalanced and inadequate development and the people's ever-growing needs for a better life."[62] China's challenge, put simply, is to manage rising expectations at a time of slowing growth and persistent inequality.

Both models of urbanization are constrained and shaped by the challenges of decentralized governance. Workplace-based urbanization also faces an important new complication: the rise of the gig economy and the decline of traditional work. This phenomenon is not unique to China; it is global and ubiquitous. Wikipedia defines the gig economy as "a labor market that is distinguished by the prevalence of short-term contracts or freelance work rather than permanent jobs. In place of regular salaries, gig employees are paid in return for the 'gigs' they perform."[63] This type of employment includes independent contractors, part-time workers with multiple employers, outsourced work, and subcontracted work.

To one degree or another, these new modes of employment fall outside the parameters of China's current labor law system, creating complex problems for the protection of workers in this new economy and their inclusion into social security institutions tied to traditional labor relations. Current systems rely on the traditional notion of employment defined by a formal relationship between a single employer and an employee, formalized by a written labor contract, which can be either open-ended or term limited. The written labor contract then becomes the basis for a tripartite arrangement for the provision of social insurance. The parties to this arrangement are the government, the employer, and the employee. Each pays a set amount into social pooled funds that pay for social insurance, including pensions, medical insurance, unemployment insurance, and occupational injury and disease.

Informal, casual, and precarious work is not new to China. Recent research finds that nearly 50 percent of migrant rural workers are still employed informally, without a formal labor contract or access to social insurance.[64] Informal work is endemic in certain sectors, such as construction and services. The 2008 Labor Contract Law and its 2012 revision addressed the issue of informality and precarity directly. However, the rise of the gig economy presents a different challenge. The challenge is not noncompliance with the existing law, or simply a question of improving enforcement. It is, instead, a more fundamental problem that new forms of employment are becoming increasingly common and the current legal system does not adequately regulate them. The labor law system and the system of social insurance must change if workers in this new economy are to be included in China's developing welfare state.

A recent report by the State Information Center (*Guojia Xinxi Zhongxin,* 国家信息中心) finds that in 2016, there were sixty million people engaged in the sharing economy, including about six million people employed full-time. Estimating about 40 percent growth from one year to the next, by 2020 more than one hundred million people will be providing services in the sharing economy, with twenty million people working full-time in the sector.[65] Recent news reports express anxiety about how social insurance systems will remain solvent as this new economy expands.[66] The expansion of these new employment patterns further calls into question the long-term sustainability of China's current system of social security, which is so closely tied to employment and is rigidly defined as a relationship between a single employer and an employee.[67] If inclusive urbanization is based on the assumption that urbanizing rural citizens receive state benefits via formal employment, it is likely to lead to more exclusion, more informality, and narrow access to urban welfare.

High-ranking leaders, economists, and many businesspeople have criticized the 2008 Labor Contract Law as too inflexible.[68] This creates an opportunity for the central government to pass fresh legislation that offers basic protections and covers a range of employment types, including part-time work, multiple employers, and independent contractors. Like other

East Asian development states, China's evolving welfare state is a *productive* one, with most social benefits tied to work.[69] If China wishes to develop the gig economy as a source of entrepreneurship, technical innovation, and social mobility, it must redefine the relationship between citizens, workplaces, and the state. A flexible and dynamic labor market requires strong safety nets.[70] But the complexities and challenges are multifacted, requiring institutional reforms in more than just welfare benefits.

If the gig economy is undermining workplace-based inclusion as the dominant mode of urbanization, urbanization based on citizenship and territorial location is likely to become ever more important, despite the difficulty of land requisition and adequate compensation for the loss of land security. Other trends may improve the conditions for urbanization that is inclusive but more localized. The rate of interprovincial migration is slowing as wages rise in inland China and the working population ages and declines in absolute number. Economic development in inland China provides new incentives for migrant workers to stay closer to home, to integrate their productive and reproductive lives.[71] If municipalities and provinces focus on inclusive policies for all residents, the divide between urban and rural citizens would diminish. This would require greater coordination at the provincial level, social pooling of pensions at the provincial level, and changes to center-local fiscal relations. China's inclusive urbanization may be possible initially only at the subnational level.

If provincial-level inclusive urbanization is possible, there are likely to be stark differences between provinces, with poorer inland provinces unable to match the social welfare capacity of rich coastal provinces like Guangdong, Shanghai, and Zhejiang. Regional inequality may increase and provincial differences in social welfare could reduce labor mobility. The central government should be the setter of minimal standards. Basic labor rights should be mandated in a minimum standards law that would cover diverse types of employment. This should include working hours, the minimum wage, and health and safety protections. Social insurance should be restructured to encourage participation by those in nonstandard employment relationships and the self-employed. If this is done through the residency-based social insurance systems that have been widely expanded in rural and urban areas, they should be improved so that benefits guarantee a basic livelihood.[72] Stark differences between provinces should be mitigated through central revenue transfers to less developed areas. As long as local governments are myopically focused on the dynamics of local citizenship, it will be up to the central government to bear the burden of inclusive urbanization.

Inclusive urbanization is both a goal and a critical component of Beijing's modernization agenda, but the challenges of urbanization involve far more than building housing, workplaces, and supporting infrastructure. Indeed, that is the easy part. It will be far more difficult, costly, and contentious to reduce inequality by providing access to social benefits linked to urban residence and formal employment in an era of slower growth, rising expectations, and perceptions of zero-sum competition between those who have and those who want the full benefits of urban residency.

CHAPTER 8

Human Capital and China's Future

Hongbin Li, James Liang, Scott Rozelle, and Binzhen Wu

Decades of rapid economic growth have transformed China in manifold and fundamental ways, but rates of growth are declining as China exhausts the principal sources of past growth and confronts challenges of transition to more advanced and more demanding stages of development. Historically, two main forces have driven the growth of China's economy: a "demographic dividend" (which occurs when the working-age population has increased as a proportion of the total population) and increases in labor productivity (due to increases in physical capital and the reallocation of labor to more efficient sectors). In recent years, however, many of the forces that drove China's economic growth are fading (see chapters 2, 4, 6, and 7, respectively, by Barry Naughton, Jean C. Oi, Karen Eggleston, and Mary E. Gallagher). The size of the working-age population (individuals aged fifteen to sixty-four) as a proportion of the total population reached its peak in 2010 and is now declining.[1] In addition, the movement of labor between sectors (that is, from rural to urban sectors or state to private sectors) has slowed, and there is little room for further reallocation.[2]

Improvements in human capital have contributed significantly to China's economic growth in recent decades and will be even more important for growth in the future.[3] Research using a cross-country correlation between average years of schooling and per capita income found a quite stable relationship between human capital and economic growth in most parts of the world since 1990.[4] China, prior to 2010, was an exception to the general pattern. China's growth was driven primarily by more efficient *use* of human capital, including the transfer of labor to more efficient sectors, and using it more efficiently in the current sector. Since 2010, however, China has exhibited the same general relationship between average years of schooling and per capita income, as does the rest of the world. The implication is that China's ability to sustain economic growth will depend primarily on improvements to the stock of human capital because the potential for gains from more efficient use of human capital is now also limited. An obvious and essential next step is for China to increase productivity by upgrading the country's human capital, principally through improvements in education.[5]

That general observation can be made more specific by assuming that China will henceforth exhibit the world-average relationship between education and economic growth, and that this relationship can be used to estimate future economic growth rates in China. Doing so, and assuming that China's human capital stock increases at a reasonable rate and that other growth-augmenting factors increase at world-average levels, yields a projected economic growth rate of about 3 percent to 4 percent over the next two decades.[6] This growth estimate is similar to those produced by the Organization of Economic Cooperation and Development (OECD) (4 percent growth during 2010–60) and PricewaterhouseCoopers (3 percent during 2016–50).[7] These findings imply that the 6.5 percent annual growth rate target specified in the Chinese government's 13th Five-Year Plan cannot be sustained in the longer run.

To explore how investments in education could drive or constrain China's future, we used international data to examine the relationship between human capital and economic growth in other countries to see how developments in China compare to those in the rest of the world. Our analysis indicates that while China is unlikely to maintain growth rates above 6 percent over the next several decades, increased investment in human capital and global-average levels of physical capital investment could enable China to grow at a rate of 4–6 percent over the short run (up to 2025) and 3–4 percent over the medium- and long-term (up to 2035 and 2055, respectively). However, for China to achieve these rates, the regime must make commitments that will allow it to overcome the serious impediments and shortcomings that currently constrain the ability of China's education system to meet future human capital requirements.

The proportion of individuals having at least a high school education or at least a college education will be increasingly important for China's economic growth as the country experiences additional technological change. For example, having skills taught at high school and college levels will be increasingly necessary to be competitive in the higher value-added industries currently emerging in China.[8] Improving educational outcomes in China, particularly in poor rural areas of the country, however, will be difficult because doing so will require meeting the challenges of a complex set of interconnected problems. Meeting those challenges will be expensive, but money alone will not solve problems involving teacher quality, incentives to leave school, and nutritional and health impediments to learning.

To meet future needs for human capital, China must raise the education level of its youth, especially in the countryside, where the level of education is far below that in the urban areas. According to China's 2010 national census, only 28.8 percent of the working-age population (i.e., individuals between the ages of twenty-five and sixty-four) had attended high school, and only 12.5 percent had attended college. These figures are far lower than the average high school and college attendance rates of the working-age population in OECD countries (80 percent and 36 percent) and many other emerging economies, such as Mexico (36 percent and 16 percent), Brazil (47 percent and 14 percent), and South Africa (42 percent and 15 percent).[9]

China's low high school and college attendance rates result primarily from the fact that compulsory education extends only through the ninth grade. Data from the 2010 census regarding China's entire labor force reveal that in 2007 the vast majority of children living in both urban and rural areas of the country had attended school only through ninth grade (97 percent and 89 percent, respectively). Very few rural individuals attended high school and college (only about 40 percent and 9 percent). This fact is important because school-age children living in rural China today will soon comprise most of China's labor force.[10] Indeed, China's future economic growth will likely be shaped primarily by the pace of increase in the *number of years* that students in rural areas attend high school and college as well as on the *quality* of the education these students receive. China must overcome both of these challenges if China is to continue to grow at even the 3–4 percent rate.

Having more students in high school and college will require increasing budgets for education, but the cost of adding classrooms, teachers, and teaching materials would require relatively small increases in direct spending on education. We estimate that the additional annual cost of expanding education would be approximately 0.5 percent of total national government educational expenditure in 2007. But just expanding budgets for the type of teachers who are teaching currently in rural areas, for example, probably is an imperfect and inadequate indicator of future expenses. China must also improve the quality of teachers and teaching to meet the demands of an increasingly sophisticated economy. The requisite funds are likely to be available, at least in theory for all these expenses, but whether they will be allocated to education or to other purposes, such as health care or infrastructure will depend on policy priorities.

Sufficient budgetary priority is only a necessary, not sufficient, condition for increasing enrollment in high school and college programs. Additional actions and outlays will be required to overcome financial and systemic conditions that impede learning and disincentivize students from remaining in school. Central government expenditures for education are only a fraction of the total. Local governments and the families of students provide most of the money for education so any increase would come at the expense of other priorities. Improving human capital by providing better education to more people will also require reducing the financial burdens on students and their families, improving nutrition and health conditions in rural schools, and improving educational quality. Implementing measures of this sort will be costly, require many people with specialized expertise, and have to overcome significant behavioral obstacles.

This chapter is organized as follows. First, we use our econometric model to show that China has reached the limit of income growth from making better use of existing human capital (e.g., from rural to urban transfers) and to predict possible growth from improvements to China's human capital. We examine the effect on growth rates of increasing levels of educational attainment, without consideration of the quality of education. Building on the insights from the model and worldwide trends, we develop different scenarios to estimate China's education attainment and economic growth rates over the short- (2025), medium- (2035), and long-terms (2055). We then evaluate the direct costs and challenges of increasing average years of schooling and addressing associated challenges such as improving the quality of education and providing incentives to remain in school.

Human Capital and Income

To establish a baseline for comparing and predicting returns from improvements to human capital in China, we used cross-country data from the

UNESCO Institute of Statistics (UIS) and the World Bank Education Statistics (EdStats), respectively, to estimate the correlation between per capita income and human capital. To examine how the relationship between human capital and per capita income has varied over time, we ran regressions for the years 2000, 2005, 2010, and 2015.[11] There is data for between 85 and 150 countries in each of these four years.[12]

Our measure of human capital is the average number of years of schooling attained by adults (defined as individuals aged twenty-five years and over). We also considered the average educational attainment of individuals in the labor force (i.e., individuals aged twenty-five to sixty-four) as well as two other measures of educational attainment: the proportion of adults with at least a high school education and the proportion of adults with at least a college education. Average years of schooling of individuals in the labor force is probably a more accurate representation of human capital stock as it relates to income and growth, but unfortunately most non-OECD countries do not provide the necessary education data and little information of this type was available before 2005. As a result, the sample size when evaluating the average years of schooling of the labor force is small (forty countries in 2015).

To estimate the correlation between per capita income and years of schooling, we first estimated a simple income equation with measures of education as the main explanatory variables.[13] After running cross-country regressions to determine the correlation between education and income around the world, we compared the relationship between these two factors in China to the global average. Examining the cross-country correlations over multiple years enabled us to determine how this correlation changed over time. Finding the relationship to be generally stable across years and around the globe, we used the current data in China to estimate the relationship between education and income in future years for China.

Table 8.1 presents the baseline correlation between education and income across all sample countries and years without controlling for other growth-augmenting factors. It shows a strong and positive correlation between income and education across all sample years when we use GDP weights (columns 1–4).[14] The relationship between education and income has remained relatively stable over time, meaning that we can use fitted models based on current data (i.e., 2015 data) to estimate future income in China.

TABLE 8.1 OLS regressions estimating the effect of education on income for a cross-section of countries

Year	Baseline (using GDP as the weight)				Do not consider weight			
	2000 (1)	2005 (2)	2010 (3)	2015 (4)	2000 (5)	2005 (6)	2010 (7)	2015 (8)
Years of schooling	0.250***	0.267***	0.249***	0.262***	0.275***	0.287***	0.285***	0.295***
	(0.0287)	(0.0247)	(0.0215)	(0.0194)	(0.0215)	(0.0181)	(0.0168)	(0.0167)
Constant	7.351***	7.261***	7.438***	7.331***	6.686***	6.719***	6.784***	6.705***
	(0.313)	(0.280)	(0.256)	(0.239)	(0.161)	(0.152)	(0.150)	(0.151)
Observations	139	144	150	148	139	144	150	148
R-squared	0.676	0.733	0.740	0.783	0.509	0.576	0.604	0.633

SOURCE: China Population Census (2000, 2005, 2010); UNESCO Institute of Statistics (UIS); and Education Statistics in the World Bank (EdStats).

NOTE: Robust standard errors in parentheses. * significant at 10%; ** significant at 5%; *** significant at 1%. We exclude China for these regressions. We also exclude countries with population in the bottom 3 percentile or GDP per capita ranking in the top 3 percentile.

To check whether our results were sensitive to the GDP weights, we presented the results of the unweighted regressions in columns 5–8. The results are similar to those from the weighted specification, as income per capita remains strongly correlated to years of schooling.[15] The coefficient estimates are similar to those in the weighted regression for the same years. In addition, the R-squared for each year is still relatively high (≥0.504), although all are lower than those from the weighted specification. Given that the estimates are not sensitive to weight choice and using GDP weights produces better-fitted results (higher R-squared), our analyses use the weighted specification. To ensure that our results were not sensitive to the measure of human capital used or controls for other growth-augmenting factors, we performed additional analyses that can be considered a robustness check.

The data presented in Figure 8.1 allow us to examine how the relationship between years of schooling and per capita income in China compares to those in other countries. The figure presents years of schooling on the x-axis and income per capita on the y-axis. The fitted line represents the average relationship between these two variables. The figure shows that China's economic growth can be decomposed into two parts: growth resulting from improving the efficiency of utilizing human capital (i.e., moving up toward the fitted line) and from increasing the level of human capital (i.e., moving along the fitted line).

These data show that China has been moving steadily closer to the fitted line over the past several decades, meaning that the efficiency of the

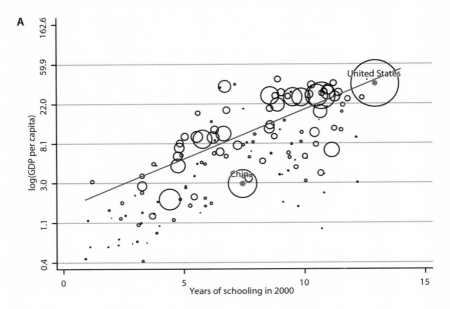

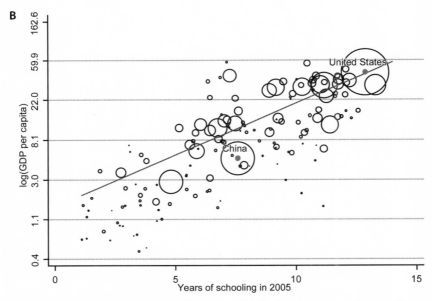

FIGURE 8.1A–D. Income per capita (thousands of dollars) and education: Scatter plots and fitted lines 2000, 2005, 2010, 2015.

SOURCE: China Population Census (2000, 2005, 2010); UNESCO Institute of Statistics (UIS); and Education Statistics in the World Bank (EdStats).

NOTE: Education is measured by years of schooling of all adults above age twenty-five. We exclude China for the fitted lines. We also exclude countries with population in the bottom 3 percentile or GDP per capita ranking in the top 3 percentile. The vertical axis is labeled with actual dollar amounts (in thousands), but the regressions are fitted with log income. Income per capita is measured using the current (each of the five years) PPP dollars.

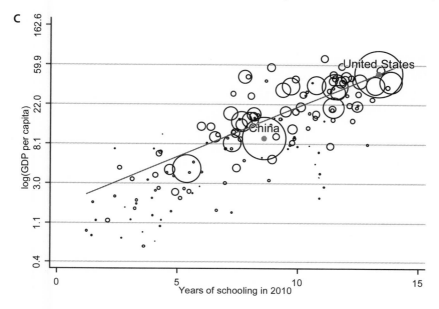

C

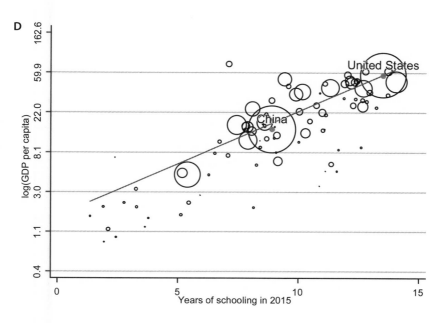

D

utilization of human capital was initially lower than, but has been moving toward, the global average. This process of moving closer to the fitted line reflects the fundamental changes in China's labor market separate from increases in human capital that led to improved labor productivity, such as reallocation of labor to more efficient sectors and increased investment in physical capital. The figure also shows not only that China moved toward the fitted line between 2000 and 2015, but also that it has moved along the fitted line. This suggests that modest increases in educational attainment also contributed to economic growth.

Figure 8.1 also demonstrates that China was very close to the fitted line in 2015, suggesting that the relationship between education and income in China is now similar to that in other countries. This indicates that the efficiency of the Chinese labor market is now close to the world average. As a result, it is now more difficult to increase economic growth through efficiency improvements. This finding is consistent with recent labor market trends—namely that there is little room for gains from labor reallocation, that the marginal gains from labor reallocation have been decreasing over time, and that the return to physical capital has been declining.[16] This indicates that China must rely primarily on increases in human capital to maintain economic growth going into the future.

China's Possible Future Human Capital Development and Growth

Let us now consider how investments in human and physical capital might change in the future. For the purposes of this discussion, we consider "human capital" to be education and skills that can improve labor productivity. Our primary measure of human capital is the average years of schooling attained by individuals aged twenty-five years and over. When we refer to physical capital (or simply "capital"), we mean the material inputs (such as machinery, infrastructure, and technology) used in production processes. For physical capital we follow the perpetual inventory method used by Vikram Nehru and Ashok Dhareshwar and use data on capital formation (i.e., investment) from the World Development Indicators of the World Bank.[17]

DIFFERENT HUMAN GROWTH SCENARIOS

We have used three different scenarios, which we refer to as an "optimistic scenario," "normal scenario I," and "normal scenario II," to predict human capital growth.

Under the *optimistic scenario*, college admission quotas increase at an annual rate of 5 percent and universal high school education (that is, 100 percent enrollment in high school) is achieved by 2020 (requiring high school enrollment to increase at 9.5 percentage points a year for rural students and 2.8 percentage points a year for urban students between 2015 and 2020).[18] To achieve universal high school enrollment (twelfth grade) by 2020, rural high-school enrollment rates must increase by 9.6 percent a year and urban enrollment must increase 2.8 percent per year.

Under *normal scenario I*, high school and college enrollment rates continue to increase at the average rate for the years between 2010 and 2015 (meaning that college admission quotas increase at an annual rate of 2.2 percent, and high school enrollment rate increases at 0 percentage points for rural students and 1.3 percentage points a year for urban students between 2015 and 2020).[19]

Under *normal scenario II*, they increase at the average rate of growth in 2005–2007 (the most recent reliable enrollment information based on the 2010 population census, implying that college enrollment increases at 0.9 percentage points a year for rural students and 2.7 percentage points a year for urban students, and high school enrollment increases at 1.2 percentage points a year for rural students and 2.5 percentage points a year for urban students, starting from 2007). Given the large differences in enrollment rates between students in urban and rural China, we calculate enrollment growth rates separately for each type of student.[20]

Estimates of average educational attainment until 2055 are presented in Figure 8.2. From this figure we can see that average years of schooling are similar under all three scenarios over the medium-run (that is, until 2035). After 2035, however, average years of schooling begin to increase more quickly under the optimistic scenario than under the two normal scenarios. Due to this increase, we find that by 2055 the average years of schooling under the optimistic scenario is 13.1 years. Under normal scenarios I and II, it is 12.3 years.[21]

IMPACT ON GROWTH RATES

Table 8.2 displays our short-term (2025), medium-term (2035), and long-term (2055) estimated economic growth rates under each of the three human capital development scenarios. From these estimates we conclude that China is highly unlikely to sustain 6.5 percent economic growth (stated

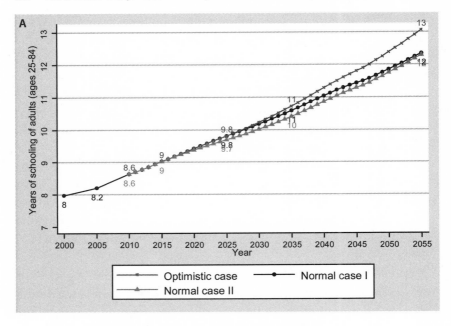

FIGURE 8.2A–C. Education attainment of the adults: Different scenarios.

SOURCE: China Population Census (2000, 2005, 2010); UNESCO Institute of Statistics (UIS); and Education Statistics in the World Bank (EdStats).

in the short-run five-year plan) over either the medium- or long-term. This is due, in part, to the fact that it becomes more difficult to achieve efficiency gains in the utilization of human capital. In addition, because improving labor force human capital requires investment in education over the course of several decades, it is not possible to achieve rapid increases in human capital.

Although the short-run growth rate (2015–25) is more sensitive to model specification and can be as high as 7.3 percent, we find that the predictions for models that do not control for capital stock (columns 1–4) are always less than 4.4 percent per year in the medium-run (2015–35) and long-run (2015–55). The growth rates are around 3 percent in our baseline model, which considers only education attainment of all adults (column 1). When we consider human capital of the labor force (ages twenty-five through sixty-four) rather than of all adults, the growth rates are about 1 percentage point higher (column 2). When we use the alternate human capital specifi-

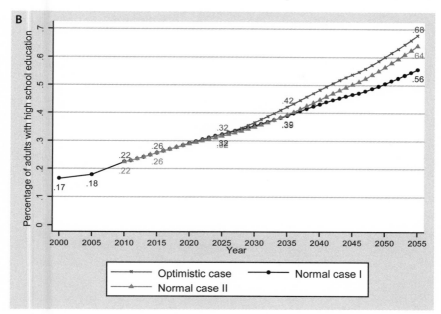

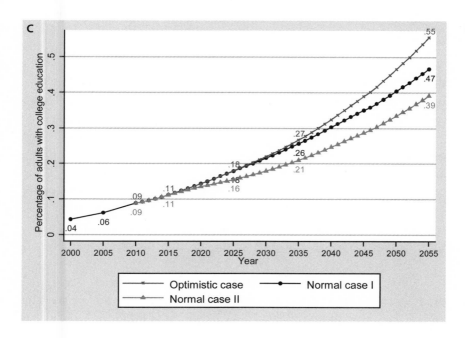

TABLE 8.2   Predicted annual economic growth rate (relative to 2015) under different scenarios

Year	Baseline (1)	Model 2: Education attainment for labor force (25–64) (2)	Model 3: Alternative measure of human capital (3)	Model 4: Control for population (4)	Model 5: Control for capital stock (5)	Model 6: Pessimistic growth of capital stock (6)
			Optimistic Case			
2025	0.033	0.050	–0.009	0.016	0.082	0.040
2035	0.029	0.040	0.006	0.010	0.066	0.026
2055	0.030	0.038	0.016	0.017	0.069	0.030
			Normal Case I			
2025	0.033	0.050	–0.009	0.016	0.081	0.040
2035	0.027	0.037	0.002	0.007	0.063	0.025
2055	0.025	0.031	0.010	0.012	0.065	0.028
			Normal Case II			
2025	0.030	0.047	-0.009	0.014	0.080	0.039
2035	0.025	0.035	0.003	0.006	0.062	0.024
2055	0.026	0.032	0.015	0.013	0.066	0.028

SOURCE: China Population Census (2000, 2005, 2010); UNESCO Institute of Statistics (UIS); Education at a Glance (2016); and Education Statistics in the World Bank (EdStats).

NOTE: See Table A3 for the detailed explanation for different cases.

cations in column 3 or the controls for population size and population share of the labor force in column 4, the estimated growth rates are smaller than those determined using model 1. Notably, there are only small differences in magnitude between the growth rates determined under our three human capital development scenarios.

Changes in capital stock can have substantial impacts on our growth predictions. In column 5 we estimate using a predicted capital stock growth rate based on the historical rate between 2005 and 2015 (14 percent). If the capital stock grows at 14 percent a year, the annual economic growth rates would be 5.2 percent over the medium run and 5.8 percent over the long run under the optimistic scenario. Even under normal scenarios I and II, this rate reaches 5.0–5.1 percent over the medium run and 5.5–5.6 percent for the long run, respectively. However, this rate of capital stock growth is unlikely to continue in the future because of the decreasing marginal productivity of physical capital. Therefore, if we consider a more realistic capital stock growth rate of about 7.6 percent per year (which is the global average between 2005 and 2015), the rate of income growth decreases substantially to between 2.2 percent and 2.4 percent over the medium run and between 2.8 percent and 3.0 percent over the long run.

In summary, our predictions show that the growth rates in the medium run (2035) and the long run (2055) are likely to be only 3 percent to 4 percent, assuming that physical capital stock grows at the world average rate of 7.6 percent a year. This would mean that even with the modest growth predicted by our model, China's GDP per capita could be comparable to the current level of high-income countries by 2035.

Costs and Challenges to Improving China's Human Capital

Although we have demonstrated the clear benefits that educational expansion can provide to China's economic growth, achieving the required improvements and expansion will require government decisions to alleviate the wide range of existing impediments that will directly affect whether its human capital will improve. The costs will involve more than just those required to increase the number of enrolled students. All of the models and scenarios discussed above simplify the actual situation by omitting consideration of complex challenges associated with increasing human capital in China, especially in the rural areas. Benefits from additional spending cannot be realized unless government expenditures on education keep pace with escalating demands and requirements to improve the quality of education. This means that the problem is more than just allocating funds for more schools. Perhaps equally important, students must be incentivized to stay in school and to master the more demanding skills required for success in the more complex, technologically sophisticated, and rapidly changing work environments of the future.

First we consider the costs of simply expanding educational opportunities based on the different scenarios examined above (i.e., percentage increase in the number of students), without considering whether it is realistic to assume that rural children will want to stay in school or that increased enrollment will be accompanied by improvements in the quality of education. Later we consider the more complex challenges of the associated costs of improving human capital by looking at how much more it would cost to solve those systemic, institutional problems that are keeping students, especially in rural areas, from staying in school.

DIRECT COSTS OF INCREASING EDUCATION

Over the past two decades the central government has increased educational expenditures to expand high school and college enrollment rates across the country. Across all levels of government educational expenditures as a share of GDP increased from 2.3 percent in 1995 to 4.3 percent in 2015. The actual increase was from RMB 141 billion to RMB 2,922 billion (or about $22 billion to $469 billion). Over this period the average years of schooling achieved by Chinese adults increased by 2.5 years (from 6.5 to 9 years). In addition, the proportion of adults in the labor force with at least a high school education increased from 13 percent to 26 percent, and the share of individuals in the labor force with at least a college education increased from 3 percent to 11 percent.[22]

To examine how much additional funding is required to expand education in the coming decades, we calculated the additional costs the government would incur if education continued to expand under our optimistic scenario and normal scenario II. In 2015 the average government educational expenditure (by all levels of government) per high school student in China was approximately $2,420.[23]

Under normal scenario II, the enrollment rate of fifteen-year-old children (who would typically be in their first year of high school) in rural China (about eight million students in 2015) would increase by 2.5 percentage points annually (or by two hundred thousand students). Enrollment rates for fifteen-year-old students with urban *hukou* living in cities (about 6.5 million students in 2015) would increase by 1.2 percentage points annually (or by seventy-eight thousand students per year).[24] Taken together, expansion in high school enrollment would cost the Chinese government approximately $673 million per year, which is about 1.4 percent of the total government expenditure on high school education and 0.14 percent of total government educational expenditure in 2015.[25]

The rural or urban status in the population census is determined by the current residence location, which means that migrant kids living in the urban areas are counted as urban kids in the census. The upper bound estimates for the size of these fifteen-year-old migrant kids is 1.7 million in 2015. To increase their high school enrollment rate at 2.5 rather than 1.2 percentage points annually would require an additional $53 million a year. That would bring the total cost to about 1.5 percent of total government expenditure on high school education and 0.15 percent of total government educational expenditure in 2015.[26] This amount is an annual incremental expenditure, which means that until the enrollment rate reaches 100 percent, the annual expenditure after n years of expansion will be higher than the current level by about $n*0.15$ percent of current total government education expenditure.

Under the optimistic scenario the enrollment rate of fifteen-year-old children living in rural areas would increase by 9.6 percent annually and that of fifteen-year-old students living in urban areas would increase by 2.8 percent. Given the number of fifteen-year-old children enrolled in high school in 2015, these rates of annual increase mean that 770,000 more rural students and 180,000 more urban students would enroll in high school each year. Therefore, according to our estimates, expanding high school education would cost an additional $2.3 billion dollars a year. The total increase needed would be about 5.0 percent of the total government expenditure on high school education and 0.51 percent of total government educational expenditures in 2015.

A similar approach can be used to calculate the cost of increasing college enrollment. The average educational expenditure for each college student was $4,732 in 2015. Under normal scenario II the admission rate increases at 0.9 percent a year for rural kids and 2.7 percent a year for urban students, which implies about 256,000 more students would be able to enroll in college annually (based on the population at age eighteen in 2015). Therefore the college expansion under normal scenario II would cost about $1.2 billion a year, or about 1.0 percent of total government educational expenditure on colleges and 0.24 percent of total educational expenditure in 2015. Under the optimistic scenario admission quotas would increase at 5 percent a year, which implies 370,000 more college enrollments each year (based on 2015 college enrollment quotas). The college expansion would thus cost about $1.8 billion a year, about 1.4 percent of the total educational expenditure on colleges in 2015.

ADDITIONAL COSTS AND INSTITUTIONAL CHALLENGES IN IMPROVING HUMAN CAPITAL

Although average education levels improved over the past two decades and we believe there is sufficient fiscal space to continue to expand education enrollment rates, improving the human capital stock in China will require successful resolution of issues related to urban-rural educational disparities and the incentives provided to students, educators, and local governments—all of which may be more difficult than simply finding the money to increase enrollment numbers. Above we noted the educational disparities between urban and rural areas. Here we want to highlight the widened gap during the past twenty years even as average enrollment rates improved.

Between 1995 and 2015 the gap in average years of schooling of adults living in rural and urban areas increased only slightly from 2.4 years to 2.6 years (6.6 years in rural areas and 9.0 years in cities to 7.7 years and 10.3 years, respectively). However, we find larger differences in the proportions of the rural and urban populations that have attended high school and college. In 1995 the gap was 23 percentage points (6 percent in rural areas versus 29 percent in urban areas). Twenty years later, the gap had increased to 31 percentage points (10 percent in rural areas versus 41 percent in urban areas). The gap in college education rates increased from 10 percentage points to 17 (from 0.6 percent in rural areas and 10 percent in cities to 2 percent and 19 percent).[27] So why are there these differences? Students generally choose to continue their education when the returns to schooling are higher than the cost of attendance. Returns to education rely heavily on educational quality and, in China, the educational quality in rural schools is typically much lower than in urban schools.[28] This is partly a function of lower per capita spending on facilities and programs in rural schools and partly the result of difficulty retaining high-quality teachers.[29]

URBAN–RURAL GAP IN GOVERNMENT EXPENDITURE

Closing the rural–urban gap in government expenditure on students would be costly. In 2015 the government expenditure in rural areas was $1,591 per person for primary schools, $2,100 for middle schools, and $1,950 for high schools. These totals were lower than the level in urban areas: $1,720 for primary $2,370 for middle schools, and $2,436 for high schools.[30] If we raise the expenditure level in rural areas to the level in urban areas, it will cost about $6 billion a year for the current number of students in schools (30 million primary school students, 7 million middle school students, and 0.8 million high school students in rural areas). If the high school enrollment expansion for rural areas entails such higher educational expenditure level ($2,436 rather than $2,420, the level we used before), the cost of enrollment expansion increases only slightly, by about $5.1 million a year under the normal case II and $17 million under the optimistic case.

TEACHER INCENTIVES

The quality of the education students receive depends heavily on the quality of teachers. However, rural schools often have difficulty recruiting and retaining high-quality instructors. One reason is that life in rural communities is less comfortable and attractive than life in urban areas.[31] Long commutes and the many demands imposed on rural teachers are additional disincentives to work in the countryside and might contribute to stress and fatigue that make teachers less effective. As a result, teachers are often from rural areas themselves and have lower levels of education.

Another factor affecting performance in the classroom is the relatively low teacher salaries, which are often tied to education and experience. In 2015 the public expenditure on salary and compensation payment to teachers and other supporting staffs was about 41 percent of the total expenditure, much lower than the world average of 68 percent.[32] Moreover, the average salary and compensation for rural teachers are significantly lower than those for urban teachers.[33] Increasing the salaries of rural teachers is one potential solution but inevitably puts additional demands on local budgets.[34] There are relatively inexpensive interventions to improve teaching quality. For example, teacher performance pay, especially "pay-for-percentile" incentives that provide monetary rewards to teachers based on the educational gains of individual students have been tested and proven to be an effective and affordable way to improve the quality of rural instruction in China.[35]

Costs to Students and Families

Estimates for improving human capital that look only at the costs of increasing the number of seats in schools at different levels are incomplete. The assumption is that students will fill those seats. No consideration is given to the question of whether students and their families have incentive to fill them. Thus, to get a full picture of the costs of improving human capital, we need to consider the costs of education for potential students and their families. If the cost of going to school exceeds the expected benefit to students, to increase student enrollments, either students need to be convinced that they will have a greater benefit or governments must lower the cost.

Students and their families must shoulder two types of costs: out-of-pocket expenses (such as tuition fees and the cost of school supplies) and opportunity costs (i.e., the wages a student would earn in the labor market). The average tuition cost was $309 for high school and $1,149 for college, which represented 16 percent and 58 percent of the average household income in rural areas of China in 2015.[36] Both rates are quite high compared with the corresponding tuition levels globally.[37] Moreover, as wages continue to rise in China, students will have greater incentives to drop out of school and enter the labor force.[38] Policies to incentivize high school age students to continue their education through high school and college must consider both the returns to and the costs of education.

One option is for the government to make high school free, as in the majority of the countries in the Global Tuition Survey. But that would cost about $7.4 billion a year for the current number of high school students (twenty-four million in 2015) and about $14 billion a year if all individuals at high school age (forty-four million in 2015) attend high school. For the high school enrollment expansion, waiving tuition reduces government revenue from tuition by $98 million under the normal case II and $329 million under the optimistic case. If we reduce the college tuition by half and get close to the United States and OECD level (about 14 percent of GDP per capita), it will cost about $16 billion for the current enrollment of college students (twenty-eight million in 2015).

Another possible approach would be to keep tuition but reduce the financial burden assumed by students and their families by providing financial aid or tuition assistance at both the high school and college levels. Research has demonstrated that properly designed financial aid programs improve college attendance and completion in many countries, including China.[39] China has tried to use financial aid. However, research has shown that college financial aid in China is insufficient and poorly targeted.[40] According to Hongbin Li, Lingsheng Meng, Xinzheng Shi, and Binzhen Wu, most aid goes to the higher-quality universities, where students are relatively well-off. In addition, returns to higher-quality universities also means that families are willing to finance the education of their children. Currently, opportunities to receive financial aid at the high school level are very limited in China.[41]

A third option would be to provide conditional cash transfers (CCTs) to incentivize students to remain in school. Studies confirm that CCTs can substantially reduce dropout rates and improve student academic achievement significantly.[42] More than twenty developing countries have used

CCT programs to increase enrollments but China is not one of them.[43] While research has shown conditional cash transfers work in China to improve enrollment, discussions with education officials seems to suggest that giving families cash (in addition to making schooling free) is something that is against the norms that govern schooling policy.

Health Impediments to Learning

Improving human capital by improving education will also require alleviating nutritional and health-related impediments to learning. Children living in rural areas of China often suffer from anemia, intestinal worms, and myopia—all of which have been shown to have a negative impact on student learning.[44] In fact, the problems can be reduced substantially by using relatively inexpensive interventions to improve health and nutrition. Specific forms of intervention include providing children with vitamins and/or nutritious lunches, eyeglasses for the nearsighted, deworming medicines, and providing early childhood development resources.[45] Per pupil costs are low, but the number of students is large and poor school districts lack the necessary funds to undertake these steps without shortchanging other measures to expand enrollment and improve quality. However, in most rural schools there are no systematic efforts to address these conditions.

In addition, an abnormally large share of children in poor rural areas of China have been shown to have delayed cognitive development.[46] One study shows rural primary students who were cognitively delayed scored systematically lower on standardized math scores.[47] To solve this problem, investments in early childhood education are needed in terms of parental training and nutrition interventions.

TOTAL COSTS OF IMPROVING EDUCATION

Even this brief discussion underscores the need to restructure the way money is raised and allocated for public goods like education. Under current arrangements, schools generally lack funding for the types of measures discussed above. Improving educational outcomes in China depends heavily on infusions of money from outside the locality and/or incentives for local governments to reduce allocations for other purposes to increase spending on education. In 2015 about 67 percent of the funds spent on education was dispersed by local governments.[48] However, given that most local government officials serve terms of five years or less, they have little incentive to make investments whose benefits will only be realized over the long-term, as is the case with expenditures on education or health.[49] This has a clear and negative impact on the quality of schools in rural areas.[50] Among the many difficult and consequential decisions that China's leaders must make are whether (and how) to transfer greater direct responsibility for education outcomes to the central government. Transferring greater responsibility to Beijing might improve the quality of education and reduce regional disparities, but it would put education in direct competition with health expenditures, environmental cleanup and protection, and myriad other priority spending categories.[51]

In our model, we adjust the estimated costs of improving human capital to encompass the associated costs and institutional challenges. It is generally difficult to calculate the full costs, including both direct costs and opportunity costs of education, but we can calculate the outlays of education expansion with the improvement of the quality of rural education. To close the urban-rural gap in pre-tertiary education will cost the government $29 billion annually.[52] This also makes education expansion more expensive, by approximately $0.6 billion a year under the optimistic scenario, or pushing the total costs of education expansion up to $5.4 billion a year. Thus the total incremental costs of expanding education, with the rural pre-tertiary education up to the urban standard, will be $34.4 billion, or about 7 percent of the total education expenditures. This is doable if education budgets can increase by 5 percent a year. Of course, the opportunity costs of going to school could be very high for rural children. The full opportunity costs of a rural child remaining in school is the lost wage, which is about $6,000 annually, implying that the total opportunity cost of keeping twenty-four million (eight million in a cohort) rural children in high school would be $144 billion. Even one-tenth of this would be a formidable number.

Investment Choices and the Future of Human Capital

China has reached the world-average relationship between years of schooling (human capital) and per capita income (economic growth). Future economic growth in China will be determined primarily by the rate and character of increases in human capital achieved by increasing access to and the quality of high school and college education. Using models employing data on many countries compiled by the World Bank and what we consider reasonable assumptions about physical capital growth, we consider it highly unlikely that China will be able to maintain economic growth above 6 percent per year over the medium run or long run (over the next twenty and forty years, respectively). China has been very successful at allocating and utilizing human capital more efficiently during the first decades of reform and opening with relatively limited spending on education, but it will be difficult to achieve similar efficiency gains in the future.

Achieving a growth rate of about 3 percent to 4 percent is a realistic target for China in the coming decades. But to reach even this rate of growth, China must continue to invest in physical capital at a rate of around 7.6 percent (close to the global average rate between 2005 and 2015) and to invest heavily in human capital development and to manage a plethora of difficult budgetary, institutional, and attitudinal challenges. Our estimates suggest that developing human capital by increasing high school and college enrollment is expensive but is likely doable financially. However, expenditures that merely increase the number of seats in high schools and colleges will be insufficient to achieve rapid improvement of human capital, especially in the rural areas where the levels of educational attainment are substantially lower than in cities. One cannot assume that having more schools and more teachers will incentivize youth to stay in school. The quality of education is lower in the rural areas and the incentives to leave are stronger than they are to stay in school. This is critical because, as we have stressed, the majority of children in China still live in rural areas and will comprise the majority of China's labor force in the coming decades. Substantial improvement of China's human capital will require incentivizing more students to enroll in and complete high school, particularly in rural areas of the country. That is unlikely to happen unless China increases the priority of education relative to other activities demanding attention and revenue.

PART III

External Ambitions and Constraints

CHAPTER 9

Sources and Shapers of China's Foreign Policy

Thomas Fingar

China's foreign policy, like that of all countries, is shaped by opportunities, threats, and possibilities in its external environment; the resources and requirements of its domestic situation; and the perceptions and priorities of political leaders. What political leaders would like to do must be tempered by judgments about what is necessary and what is possible. Bold visions and grand strategies are constrained by hard realities, and what actually happens is shaped by the aspirations and actions of other players. No nation's foreign policies succeed completely; reality is always a mix of wins, losses, and unanticipated consequences. Political will and diplomatic skill are important, but so too are luck and serendipity. This makes confident prediction of China's future foreign policy goals and prospects difficult, but understanding what shaped past behavior usually provides a better guide to future actions than do soaring rhetoric or worst-case jeremiads.

Goals, Priorities, and Key Assumptions

Since the dawn of Reform and Opening, the primary objectives of China's foreign policy have been to minimize and manage threats to national security and to maximize opportunities for economic growth and modernization.[1] These goals were not new, are unlikely to change for the foreseeable future, and are not unique to China. What has changed and will change again are the means used to pursue them. At the founding of the People's Republic of China (PRC) in 1949, Mao Zedong calculated that aligning with the Soviet Union was the best way to counterbalance the perceived threat from the United States and other "imperialist" nations, and to secure the assistance needed to rebuild China's backward and war-torn economy.[2]

This was a fateful decision. Leaning toward the Soviet Union during the Cold War made China the enemy of the United States and a target of US containment policies.[3] Being cut off from access to US markets, capital, and technology seemed a small price to pay for access to developmental assistance from the Soviet Union. Mao doubtless chaffed at China's dependence on Moscow, but Stalin's "multiple autarky" model of development offered the prospect of rapid modernization and an early return to the high degree of economic independence that was a hallmark of China's imperial system.[4] The break with Moscow and the Soviet economic model in the late 1950s ushered in a period of strategic vulnerability (soon mitigated by the acquisition of nuclear weapons) made worse by the Great Leap Forward and the Cultural Revolution. Political choices and failed economic experimentation left China almost as poor and vulnerable in the late 1970s as it was in 1949.[5] After Mao died in 1976, his successors abandoned the search for a revolutionary path to modernity in favor of following the model of export-led growth pioneered by Japan and Taiwan.[6] That decision shaped, and to a considerable extent determined, the contours and content of Chinese foreign policy for the next four decades.[7]

Foreign Policy Requisites and Implications of Reform and Opening (1979–1989)

China's strategy of Reform and Opening was and is predicated on foreign policy choices that were as consequential as Mao's decision to align with the Soviet Union in 1950. The decision to follow the export-led growth model was characterized by Chinese leaders as a choice to accept limited and temporary dependence on the US-led "free world" economic order to jumpstart China's economy and attain sufficient wealth and power to reduce the constraints of dependency. The strategy envisioned taking advantage of the free world system and competition among capitalist economies without becoming a member of or being enmeshed in that system. The decision to pursue modernization and national power by working through the liberal order was also, in effect, a choice to tie China's future to the US–China relationship. China needed American acquiescence and assistance. Not only was the United States the biggest market and source of capital, technology, and training, it was also the gatekeeper of the liberal order. Security and economic dependence on the United States made American allies wary of incurring Washington's displeasure. They were not going to get too far ahead of the United States with respect to engagement with China.[8]

Accepting the risks of even limited dependence on the United States was difficult for Chinese leaders, but they ultimately did so. Four factors appear to have influenced that outcome. One was the decision of the Carter administration to assist China's drive for modernization if Beijing adopted reforms that opened China to foreign trade and influence.[9] A second factor was the posited capacity to limit dependence on the United States by using European and Japanese eagerness to access the China market and imputed desire to use China to counterbalance US hegemony.[10] This was, of course, a refurbished version of using one barbarian to control another.[11] The third factor was a shared interest in deterring and constraining the Soviet Union, which had brought Mao and Nixon together earlier in the decade and undergirded Carter's support for China's modernization.[12] Chinese leaders saw this shared strategic interest as a constraint on actions by Washington to impose unacceptable demands that might undermine Beijing's willingness to maintain the tacit partnership.

These three factors were important and mutually reinforcing but paled in comparison to the fourth one: namely that Chinese leaders saw no viable alternative. China was dangerously weak, party legitimacy was fragile, the Soviet Union was unlikely to provide the kinds of assistance China needed, and PRC leaders were unwilling to risk another failed attempt to discover a new path to modernity. They were convinced that China had to modernize quickly, that the best way to do this was through export-led growth, and that the only way to accomplish that was by casting their lot, temporarily, with the United States.[13]

Derivative Goals and Priorities of China's Foreign Policy

China's foreign policy was, is, and will be shaped by the content and consequences of the developmental strategy that resulted from choices made in 1977 and 1978. Implementation of that strategy required postponing (through deterrence and diplomacy) the still "inevitable" attack by imperialist forces determined to thwart China's rise. Success also required the cooperation of countries with the markets, technology, and capital needed to jumpstart China's economy.[14] PRC security and foreign policies were and are calibrated to achieve these instrumental objectives.

Beijing adopted a multifaceted strategy to manage real and imagined threats. The nature of the international system was described in a way that rationalized the reallocation of resources from the military to higher domestic and developmental priorities.[15] Deng achieved this by declaring that the danger of war had been reduced by the success of Mao's diplomatic strategy (a clever and irrefutable political assertion) and that contention between the superpowers deterred both from attacking China. Both the United States and the USSR were still perceived to harbor aggressive designs, but skillful diplomacy would enable China to defer inevitable conflict for "two decades."[16]

The diplomatic strategy that derived from this assessment centered on manipulation of the PRC–US–USSR strategic triangle. This was an extension of what Mao and Nixon set out to do earlier in the decade but with a very important difference. Deng's strategy required far more assistance from the United States and maintenance of a qualitatively different relationship with Washington. Achieving the economic and developmental goals of the Reform and Opening strategy required maintaining at least minimally good relations with the United States. Unless Washington endorsed engagement, American firms and those of its allies would not provide the access and assistance required for the strategy to work. By mid-1978, Washington was willing, even eager, to support Deng Xiaoping's self-strengthening strategy to make China a stronger partner in the seemingly endless struggle with the Soviet Union.[17] But willingness to assist China's modernization came with a price; the PRC would have to abandon its long-standing insistence that Washington sever all ties to Taiwan. Beijing had to choose between standing on principle and making pragmatic accommodation. Deng chose pragmatism.[18]

Chinese leaders recognized that pursuit of Deng's strategy would make China highly dependent on the United States and American goodwill, and that this in turn would make China vulnerable to US pressure. They rationalized acceptance of this vulnerability by arguing that the period of dependency would be short-lived. Deng and others conveyed the impression that China's problems could be "fixed" with a one-shot injection of more advanced technology and foreign capital, and that China's system would have to change very little to obtain and exploit inputs from the capitalist world. In other words, the risks of vulnerability would be limited in both scope and duration.[19]

Party leaders knew better than anyone how much the economy, the country, and regime legitimacy had been weakened by the break with Moscow, the Great Leap Forward, and the Cultural Revolution. They also judged that Washington's willingness to assist China's drive to modernize was likely to be fragile and fleeting. This made it imperative to pursue export-led growth before the window of opportunity closed. It also made it prudent for Beijing to keep the window open by acceding to US demands. Economic blandishments and other instruments of diplomacy were utilized to maintain the US counterbalance to China's adversaries and willingness to assist the drive for wealth and power.[20] These same instruments were used to mitigate economic dependence on the United States and expand China's access to and support of developed countries.[21]

The decision to pursue modernization by working with and through the US-led rules-based order was a third critical driver and shaper of China's foreign policy. In retrospect, senior leaders clearly underestimated the cohesion of the order and overestimated the extent to which "capitalist greed" would enable China to exploit competition and evade rules that it found burdensome. In the early years, acquiescence to the rules of the liberal order was grudging at best, but pragmatic accommodation became more common as maintaining access and relationships became ever more critical for China's sustained growth. China's aspiration to limit the magnitude and duration of its participation in the liberal order shaped several dimensions of its foreign policy. For example, at the start of Reform and Opening, Beijing insisted that China would not be bound by any international arrangements that it had not helped to create.[22] There were of course exceptions, notably Beijing's accession to the permanent seat on the United Nations Security Council, but Beijing was generally unwilling to accept constraints on China's freedom of action (e.g., control regimes to limit the spread of nuclear weapons and to protect intellectual property).[23]

This was more than just a matter of principle; it was also a manifestation of leadership determination to retain maximum freedom to do what it judged to be in China's interest. This posture proved impossible to maintain because multilateral arrangements, control regimes, and codified rules are fundamental components of the regime from which China sought to benefit.[24] Early in the reform era, Beijing maintained that cooperation with the

US-led order was like a joint venture in which both sides made adjustments to accommodate the practices and priorities of the other. States that had forged and benefitted from the rules-based order rebuffed Chinese efforts to bend the rules to accommodate a country that wished to benefit without accepting the conditions and constraints of membership. This proved to be another arena in which principle yielded to pragmatism. Beijing never repudiated the principle, but in case after case it grudgingly acceded to the constraints of preexisting rules and multilateral arrangements. Beijing characterized its acceptance of conditions, rules, and norms as either temporary, tactical moves required to obtain urgently needed benefits, and/or as minor adjustments to align Chinese policies with standard international practices. This was an ongoing process that required Chinese diplomats and other negotiators to seek exemption from normal free world practices and, when those efforts failed, to limit China's concessions/acceptance as narrowly as possible.[25]

Enduring Priorities, New Challenges, and Constrained Options (1989–2008)

The interplay of Chinese political and pragmatic judgments about what was necessary to best meet those needs and the nature of the international system set the priorities and parameters of China's reform era foreign policy. The highest priorities in the late 1970s were to prevent attack by the Soviet Union and the United States, to modernize and expand the economy as quickly as possible, and to bolster party legitimacy by improving the lot of the Chinese people. Beijing's foreign policy derived from and reflected those priorities. Mutatis mutandis, it still does.

Much has changed in the decades since Deng launched Reform and Opening. China is more prosperous, more powerful, and more influential. But it is also more deeply enmeshed in and dependent on the rules-based international order, more vulnerable to developments and decisions beyond its borders, and more constrained by citizen expectations and demands. The Soviet Union no longer exists, the rules-based order once largely confined to the free world is now the only game in town, and dozens of countries seek to emulate China's economic success. China and the world are very different than they were when reform and opening began, but China's needs, priorities, and policy choices have remained remarkably constant.

The danger of unprovoked military attack by the Soviet Union or the United States was almost certainly lower than estimated by Chinese leaders, but it was politically necessary and prudent to lower it even further.[26] As noted, one component of Reform and Opening foreign policy was to exploit the PRC–US–USSR strategic triangle. China, like the other two corners of the triangle, exaggerated the leverage it derived from being able to play one partner against the other. Washington's relationship with Beijing may have reduced the direct threat to China and to the United States and its allies, but it may also have increased China's dependence on the United States by stimulating or reinforcing Soviet decisions to align with India, to invade Afghanistan, and to challenge Chinese influence in Southeast Asia. Managing and mitigating these threats required, inter alia, retaining the cooperation of the United States.

China's de facto highest national priority was sustained economic growth and comprehensive modernization; maintaining the cooperation of key countries needed for that growth effectively became the highest foreign policy priority.[27] Managing relations with Washington was both the highest derivative priority and biggest foreign policy challenge. Beijing had to be attentive to US interests and concerns without yielding to American pressure to act in ways inimical to continued party rule or other Chinese interests. In other words, political leaders had to gauge when and how much to yield in response to American demands.

The linked challenges of deterring aggression and maintaining US support for China's modernization became even more challenging with the demise of the Soviet Union. The original pillar undergirding the US–China relationship was shared determination to constrain Moscow's options and ambitions. When the USSR imploded in 1991, Beijing no longer needed Washington to counterbalance its principal adversary, but it still needed US cooperation to reach its developmental objectives. Indeed, in the early 1990s, in the aftermath of Tiananmen, when Chinese Communist Party (CCP) legitimacy was damaged and growth was slowing, it became more imperative and more challenging to restore American willingness to assist China's quest for wealth and power.

PRC leaders recognized that China needed US cooperation as much as it did at the beginning of the reform era. They also recognized that the loss of a common enemy made it prudent for Beijing to be even more attentive to other American concerns because Washington no longer needed

China to deter Moscow. The demise of the Soviet Union not only jeopardized Washington's support for China's development, it also meant that Beijing could not use the USSR to counterbalance the possibly now greater threat from the United States. In the near term, Beijing had to keep the United States on its side through skillful diplomacy. Key manifestations of Beijing's greater responsiveness to US concerns include abandoning its principled refusal to join or abide by international control regimes (e.g., the Treaty on the Non-Proliferation of Nuclear Weapons, the Missile Technology Control Regime, and the Chemical Weapons Convention).[28] In the longer term it would have to build a more modern military.[29]

The end of the Cold War fundamentally changed the international system and China's security situation. Beijing had done virtually nothing to cause or shape these developments beyond aligning China with the United States—and therefore the "free world"—in a way that complicated Moscow's strategic calculus. Chinese leaders were as ill prepared for the demise of the Soviet Union as were political leaders elsewhere. In addition, China's leaders had to grapple with the consequences of reform successes.

By the late 1980s the Reform and Opening strategy was beginning to produce results. Foreign invested factories were coming on line, new and better jobs were being created at an accelerating pace, and "made in China" goods were beginning to flow into lucrative foreign markets. A still small but rapidly growing set of foreign firms and Chinese entities had increasingly important stakes in reform and continuing engagement. Small improvements in living standards were a welcome change from the stagnation, uncertainty, and deprivation of the Maoist era. Fewer restrictions on personal activity and the availability of more consumer goods restored confidence, but it also raised expectations, fueled inflation, and created new opportunities for corruption. The resulting witches brew of dissatisfaction and demands for even faster change led to protests that culminated in the Tiananmen Square demonstrations and June 4, 1989, crackdown.[30]

The drivers and dynamics of what happened in 1989 were largely internal, but iconic symbols, such as the Goddess of Democracy, and persistent discomfort with China's dependence on the capitalist West increased the resolve of party leaders to strengthen control of society, the pace of change, and interaction with foreign actors. This led to a pause in reform and second thoughts about reliance on foreign partners.[31] China slowed the pace of engagement. So too did governments in the democratic countries that previously had responded enthusiastically to China's opening. The reciprocal stand-down lasted about a year and yielded a number of lessons that reshaped China's foreign policy and interaction with other countries.

Some in China argued that the costs and risks of engagement and growing dependence on foreign firms and governments must be scaled back. The counterargument, supported by individuals and entities that were beginning to benefit, was that the risks of engagement could be managed and were less dangerous to the party's performance-based legitimacy than the risks of prolonged economic slowdown. While this was being debated, foreign firms became more cautious and governments in the most developed democracies became less tolerant of noxious Chinese actions and attitudes.

Deng confidently predicted that greedy capitalists would soon return, but the stand-down demonstrated the extent to which China still needed foreign markets, capital, and technology if it was to satisfy the social and economic aspirations of its people sufficiently to deter pressures for political change. Beijing was becoming at least as dependent on engagement as were the firms that invested in China. Companies remained eager to engage, but Western governments (with the notable exception of Japan) were constrained by domestic politics in the wake of the Tiananmen crackdown.[32] Governments in the United States and many European countries became more attentive to human rights and other dimensions of the Chinese system that had been overlooked or downplayed during the early years of engagement.[33]

Beijing responded to the new and more challenging situation created by the end of the Cold War and far more negative perceptions of China in the advanced democracies after Tiananmen by modifying the strategy and methods adopted a decade earlier. To limit the perceived military threat from the United States and its allies and to persuade the advanced democracies to maintain support to China's modernization strategy, Beijing tempered its principled opposition to the rules-based order. Doing so reflected a pragmatic decision to propitiate the countries most important to China's sustained economic growth, but it also resulted from changing judgments about how best to pursue China's increasingly diverse interests in the international arena.

One example of this new thinking that began in the 1990s was Beijing's increased attention to countries that did not threaten and/or could do little to assist its development.[34] One reason for the change was to demonstrate that many countries were still willing to receive Chinese officials who were no longer welcome in Western capitals in the wake of the repression of Tiananmen demonstrators on June 4th. A more substantive geopolitical motivation was to counterbalance the US-led alliance of highly developed countries.[35] But the most important reason was that China's economic successes during the previous decade had made developing countries more important as markets, source of inputs, and investment opportunities.

Beijing's quest for status and substantive engagement was tailored to suit different countries and regions but can be described, in general terms, as a neomercantilist effort to ensure access to specific commodities and markets by relying on government-to-government arrangements. Chinese officials depicted these arrangements as win–win propositions different from the exploitative and condition-laden terms imposed by Washington, Moscow (during the Cold War), and European and Japanese firms and governments.[36] The government-to-government arrangements were sometimes facilitated by side payments to local leaders, but whether or not that was the case, a primary purpose seems to have been to reduce the vulnerability of supply lines to the vicissitudes of the market and disruption by hostile powers.[37]

Beijing's engagement with countries in the Middle East illustrates how China's foreign policy priorities and possibilities were shaped by changes in the international system, economic success, and greater dependence on participation in the rules-based order. Until the early 1990s, China's economic stake in the Middle East was extremely small. That being the case, Beijing tended to view regional instability as beneficial to China because it distracted the superpowers. Beijing supported Libyan-backed and Palestinian guerrilla movements and, beginning in 1980, sold arms to almost anyone able to pay for them. Iran was the focus of Chinese diplomacy in the region until the Shah was overthrown in 1979.[38] Beijing's tacit alignment with Tehran to foster and exploit geopolitical rivalries in ways beneficial to China had the inevitable consequence of straining and limiting Chinese relations with the Arab states and Israel. The Iranian revolution forced Beijing to develop new means to pursue its limited goals in the region. The 1980–88 Iran–Iraq War gave them new opportunities and incentives to do so. Among other consequences, it opened arms markets previously monopolized by the superpowers at precisely the time that Beijing was curtailing weapons purchases for the People's Liberation Army (PLA) and encouraging defense (and other) firms to sell anything they could to anyone who would buy it. China almost immediately became a major supplier of conventional arms and began to accrue political influence. More important, it cleared the way for very different relationships with Israel and the Arab states.[39]

These developments increased China's engagement with the region but arguably were not as important as drivers and shapers of Beijing's foreign policy toward the region as was the PRC's growing dependence on oil from the Middle East. China's economic growth outran its ability to meet the escalating demand for oil from domestic production, and the country became a net oil importer in 1993. This development altered Beijing's perspective on and policies toward the Middle East.[40] Increasing dependence on oil shipments from the Persian Gulf region gave China a greater stake in regional stability and made it easier for Beijing to accede to US pressure to support or join control regimes and other multinational and rules-based efforts to enhance regional stability. Incentives to accede to US demands in order to sustain American willingness to support China's modernization were reinforced by recognition that doing so would enhance China's economic security. The concatenation of these developments illustrates a broader pattern of decisions to pursue China's interests by accepting constraints and obligations in the rules-based order it had previously sought to limit.[41] China had become more deeply enmeshed in and dependent on the rules-based international order. However, its leaders continued to see dependence—including interdependence—as a worrisome vulnerability.

More Active, More Assertive, and More Ambitious (2008–Present)

By 2010 many observers had concluded that China's actions in the foreign policy arena had become more assertive and more worrisome.[42] What should have been a tentative judgment or hypothesis about Chinese foreign policy based on a small number of cases has instead become a Procrustean bed to which developments are fitted in order to prove, despite evidence to the contrary, that China has abandoned the goals, priorities, and approach adopted in 1978.[43]

The cumulative impact of these judgments is widespread conviction that China has become a revisionist power determined to change fundamentally the liberal order from which it has benefitted and to challenge the United

States in ways that make conflict inevitable.[44] I do not share the judgments that China has abandoned the basic foreign policy approach adopted four decades ago or that China's foreign policy actions should be viewed as inherently antithetical to US interests.[45] That said, Chinese foreign policy has changed in the past decade, and it is important to analyze key changes to establish both a baseline and a framework for anticipating how China's international engagement might evolve in the future.[46]

The previous section argued that the scope and modalities of Chinese foreign policy changed in the early 1990s in response to changed external conditions (the end of the Cold War and Organization for Economic Cooperation and Development [OECD] nation reactions to Tiananmen) and internal developments (economic growth-driven requirements for energy and other resources). Proximate causes of policy change in the 2010s are more obscure, but I agree with those who ascribe shifts in foreign policy to the ironic combination of overconfidence and greater insecurity.[47] Before the great recession of 2008, China's booming economy was on the verge of overtaking Japan's as the second largest in the world, and foreign commentators regularly described it as a major engine of global growth. As the recession began, many speculated that China's economy would be little affected by broader developments because it could be "decoupled" from the portions of the global economy most affected by the financial meltdown.[48] That ultimately proved not to be the case, but for a time China's limited exposure to risky financial practices and adoption of massive stimulus packages enabled the PRC to escape the sharp contractions experienced elsewhere.[49]

These developments interacted in a way that seems to have convinced Beijing that China had become much less dependent on the United States and its allies than it was in the 1980s or 1990s, and that the world had become more dependent on China than China was on the liberal international order. Official media paeans to the country's achievements created an echo chamber effect that transformed assertions and exaggerations into "facts" that were readily accepted by the majority of China's population that had known only rapid growth and steady increases in China's capabilities. Well-deserved pride in China's achievements was reinforced by contrasts to the "Century of Humiliation" and claims that the United States and others feared China's rise and were acting to contain the People's Republic.[50]

Internal assessments of China's reduced dependence on external good-will and assistance were further reinforced by external speculation and assertions that China had achieved a degree of self-sufficiency that insulated it from normal economic perturbations and attempts by other countries to stifle China's rise. Extreme forms of this argument depicted China as an economic—and political—juggernaut destined to displace the United States atop the global system and determined to remake the international order in ways that protected and advanced Beijing's interests.[51] For a time such judgments seemed to be validated by China's escape from the first-order effects of the 2008 global financial crisis.[52]

The "made in America" financial crisis convinced many Chinese (and many inside and outside the region) that the United States was clearly and irretrievably in decline.[53] While that made it less necessary for Beijing to heed advice from Washington or be attentive to American concerns in the international arena, according to the logic of the "power shift" theory embraced by many Chinese, it also made the United States more dangerous. The so-called Thucydides Trap that compels a fading power to take extreme measures to thwart the ascent of a rising challenger before it can displace the waning hegemon was widely discussed in China.[54] Many consequences follow from acceptance of this inaccurate and inappropriate reconstruction of history, including a perceived need to thwart imputed American efforts to surround and contain China, enhanced measures to deter American aggression, and efforts to separate the United States from its regional allies.[55]

The concatenation of these developments probably changed attitudes and predispositions more than it changed China's foreign policy. Tracing the impact of specific developments is always difficult and especially so given the opaque nature of decision-making in China, but the list of resultant actions probably includes the more assertive posture China has taken toward Japan since 2010, construction of artificial islands and other actions in the South China Sea, and Beijing's threats to European nations that planned to send officials to the Nobel Peace Prize ceremony for Liu Xiaobo.[56]

Some in Beijing doubtless continue to judge that China no longer needs to worry overly much about keeping the United States on board, but the idea that China had developed to a point at which it was no longer highly dependent on the international system for investment, technology, and access to markets was quickly disproven by events. China did not escape the effects of the global economic slowdown because its economy was and still is heavily dependent on exports to North America, Japan, and Europe. Economic contraction elsewhere compounded the consequences of the normal slowdown that occurred in China as the economy matured. Beijing's efforts to maintain high rates of growth by injecting large amounts of money produced nonperforming loans, lower productivity, and excess capacity. The latter led to what other countries perceived to be large-scale dumping of Chinese products and retaliatory actions by important trading partners.[57] The decline in Chinese demand for energy, metals, minerals, and other commodities depressed the economies of supplier countries and made it difficult for developing countries to repay loans from Chinese entities.[58] In many countries China's image changed from benevolent savior to greedy Shylock.[59]

The combination of China's need for new markets to soak up excess production and sustain levels of economic growth necessary to provide jobs, housing, health care, and other benefits expected and demanded by the two-thirds of the population that has known only rapid growth revealed multiple structural and policy problems. Building infrastructure in other countries is one way to alleviate such problems; Xi's Belt and Road Initiative is clearly intended, in part, to preserve Chinese jobs (see chapter 10 by Ho-fung Hung and chapter 12 by David M. Lampton, this volume). Another motivation is to defeat putative US efforts to surround and contain China by providing funds, markets, and investment that tie recipients to China.[60] China's Belt and Road Initiative has taken on geopolitical and military as well as economic significance.[61]

What proved to be excessive confidence in the independence of China's economy was accompanied by increased concern that the United States would more actively seek to thwart China's rise, engineer a "color revolution" to achieve regime change, and/or use military force to prevent the otherwise inevitable "power transition" to a China-led world.[62] Concern about what the United States might do was fueled by commentary about American decline.[63] Developments that Chinese analysts interpreted as indications of hostile American intent include President Obama's "pivot" to Asia and negotiations for the Trans-Pacific Partnership.[64] The combination of excessive exuberance about the Chinese economy and exaggerated fear of American hostility may have contributed to behavior inconsistent with past practices designed to avoid alienating advanced democracies in general and the United States in particular. More muscular displays of Chinese military power may have been intended to dissuade neighboring countries from lending support to imputed US military planning, but they seriously undercut efforts to reassure other countries that they had no reason to fear China's "peaceful rise."

Exhibit "A" for many who contend that China has embarked on a more assertive and aggressive foreign policy is the construction and militarization of reefs in the South China Sea and Beijing's rejection of the Permanent Court of Arbitration ruling on China's claims.[65] China's actions and attitude with respect to its claims in the South China Sea are difficult to reconcile with the logic undergirding the Reform and Opening strategy, but thus far they are anomalous and almost unique. This does not make them unimportant, but it is reason for caution in extrapolating trends and inferring broad intent from this single case.

Analysts of Chinese foreign policy behavior continue to add examples to the list of actions that "prove" Beijing has abandoned Deng's "24 character" injunction to hide capacity, bide time, and eschew leadership, but the number pales in comparison to the number of instances in which Beijing continues to act within the parameters established in the late 1970s and adapted to changing internal and external circumstances in the years since.[66] For example, although Chinese firms and governments continue to press the envelop or flat out violate rules and commitments to which they have agreed, its dismissal and disparagement of the tribunal ruling on its South China Sea claims remains the only such instance of outright rejection. Moreover, evidence suggests that Beijing is quietly complying with a number of the tribunal's judgments.[67]

Oft-cited examples of challenges to US primacy and the rules-based liberal order include establishment of the Asian Infrastructure Investment Bank (AIIB) and the Belt and Road Initiative (BRI) (see chapters by Ho-fung Hung, Christine Wong, and David M. Lampton, this volume). Characterizing them in this way is an example of the fitting evidence to a preconceived judgment problem noted above. But rather than view them as breaking with the existing order and past Chinese practice, I believe they should be seen as evolutionary extensions of what China has been doing for the past four decades. The AIIB supplements Bretton Woods international financial institutions (IFIs) and makes additional funding available; it is not in zero-sum competition for money or projects. Contrary to the concerns of the Obama administration, it does not utilize standards or procedures very different from those of the older IFIs. Indeed, I judge that one of the reasons Beijing established the bank was to provide multinational cover for curtailing the "no conditions" loans it had trumpeted as a key difference between Chinese developmental assistance and that offered by the United States and other nations. Like those who ventured into this arena previously, China learned that loans without conditions to problematic borrowers might not be used as intended or repaid when due. The AIIB (and the New Development Bank) provide a graceful way for China to apply conditions and spread the risk of future loans.[68]

Moreover, other motivations for both AIIB-funded projects and the Belt and Road Initiative include job preservation in industries where China has substantial overcapacity, use of China's economic power to strengthen ties with neighboring countries imputed to be targets of US efforts to contain China, and ensuring access to energy and other resources needed to sustain Chinese growth and prosperity. These motivations extend practices employed in earlier phases of Reform and Opening and are likely to persist into the future because they are part of China's long-standing approach to geopolitics. Three decades of Mao's reckless experimentation had made his successors understandably wary of "revolutionary" change with the potential to disrupt the economy and alienate the public. The resultant cautious approach to change contributed to policy stability, including in the foreign policy arena. Other reasons for the high degree of continuity include the absence of fundamental changes in the international system since the end of the Cold War and clear evidence that the approach was working. The United States remained supportive, its allies were contributing to China's growth and modernization, and the consequences of China's dependence on the United States were judged to have been held in check by a foreign policy that used real and exaggerated rivalries to constrain Washington's ability to exert pressure on Beijing.[69]

With benefit of hindsight, it appears that at least some of China's actions from 2009 through 2017 were responses to particular events rather than harbingers of a new approach to foreign policy. If one omits relations with Japan, the ham-handed use of economic pressure on South Korea to protest its decision to deploy THAAD missiles and radars, and the South China Sea from the equation, it is clear that China's overall foreign policy has changed much less than its rhetoric and the characterizations of many commentators suggest.[70] China continues to broaden and deepen its engagement in multilateral groupings and control regimes and increasingly sees them as instruments to protect and promote Beijing's interests.[71] It also remains heavily dependent on foreign sources of technology—which it continues to steal or demand as the price of being allowed to operate in China—and markets. Beijing might wish to escape from the constraints of participation in the rules-based liberal order, but it has not yet done so.

Lessons and Implications of Trump's Trade War

Deviations from the approach advocated by Deng Xiaoping and pursued for the first three decades of reform can be explained as anomalous responses to specific developments, the result of erroneous Chinese assessments and wishful thinking, and/or mistaken expectations based on the past behavior of the United States and other countries. Whatever the reasons, deviant actions became more common and more egregious after Xi Jinping assumed the helm.[72] Whether he and other senior leaders acted out of desperation to maximize China's national power before the United States and its allies closed the window of opportunity opened in 1978, or out of arrogance about the relative strength of China's economy and putative dependence of other countries on trade with the PRC, they continued and escalated practices that violated World Trade Organization (WTO) and other treaty commitments, bilateral agreements, commercial contracts, and unilateral pledges.[73]

President George W. Bush intended to confront China on violations that began before he took office but was soon diverted by the events and aftermath of 9/11. President Obama was pressured by the American business community to compel Beijing to honor its commitments and halt illicit actions, but the US economy and other foreign policy problems commanded higher priority. When Donald Trump entered the White House, problems had festered for more than a decade, economic losses were mounting, and both the business community and bureaucrats had grown weary of Chinese promises that were never honored.[74] Trump has a unique style and can be faulted for the way in which he sought redress, but the problems had become too serious, the losses too great, and business pressure too intense to ignore. His imposition of tariffs and threats to impose more caught Beijing (and many American allies) by surprise and raised serious questions in

China about the vulnerability of China's economy and the ability of Xi to manage the still important relationship with the United States.

The so-called trade war initiated by the Trump administration underscored the extent to which China's integration into and dependence on the liberal order constrain its choices, and that the choices it makes in response to pressure from the United States have significant consequences for Chinese firms, local governments, and ordinary citizens. Continuing or recurring trade and foreign policy friction will have at least a short-term adverse effect on the Chinese economy and make it harder to manage the myriad domestic challenges discussed elsewhere in this volume.

Drivers and Shapers of China's Foreign Policy for the Foreseeable Future

Every nation's foreign policies are shaped by the personalities and priorities of its leaders and developments in the external environment, but the broad outlines of China's future international behavior will be determined primarily by whether Beijing judges that it can best—or only—meet party and nationalist objectives by working within or withdrawing from the rules-based international order. When Deng and his colleagues launched Reform and Opening, they anticipated—or at least claimed—that China could take advantage of a probably short-lived opportunity to jumpstart and modernize China's economy, and that accepting short-term dependence and vulnerability would quickly pave the way for long-term prosperity, power, and independence.

The foreign policy component of the strategy adopted in 1978 was designed to reduce and manage threats to China's security; gain and sustain access to urgently needed capital, technology, training, and markets; and mitigate vulnerabilities resulting from temporary dependence on the United States and its allies. A key objective of China's external policies was to concede as little as possible and to make concessions only when absolutely necessary to move to the next higher stage of economic development. In all matters, China was to retain as much freedom of action as possible by avoiding long-term commitments and entrapment in multilateral arrangements and control regimes. In other words, China would remain a detached free rider until it had the ability to achieve sustained growth and greater power without dependence on external actors or conditions. At that point, it was posited, China could and would withdraw as much as possible from the constraints of operating in accordance with the liberal order.

This approach was fully consistent with the proclaimed—and possibly genuine—conviction that China could take advantage of the liberal order without being transformed by participation, and that exiting from arrangements that had strengthened China could be achieved at acceptable cost. Many American officials and international relations scholars viewed the situation differently. They—we, because I certainly put myself in this category as both a former official and a scholar—were content to let Beijing proclaim and even believe it possible to dip in, get rich, and get out without incurring long-term interdependency. We did not think that would be possible, or that Beijing would ever get to a point at which it judged prospects for sustained "independent" growth were as good as or better than the perceived advantages for China of continuing to work with and within the rules-based order.

After four decades of interaction, integration, and growing interdependence, there is little likelihood that China's leaders think—or will think—that China could or should attempt to disengage from or disrupt the rules-based order from which it has benefitted and in which the country, key institutions and individuals, and even the party have an enormous stake. China seems to have judged that China's success, the size of its economy, and imputed American decline made it both possible and even necessary to reduce its dependence on and vulnerability to the United States. Beijing seems to have decided that the best way to protect China's growing interests and to address the challenges described in this volume is to work within the existing order.[75]

China's renewed decision to pursue its interests by working within the system did not mean, however, that it would remain a largely passive and reluctant participant coerced (in Beijing's eyes) to accept rules and join institutions that would restrain Beijing's freedom of action. Four decades of Chinese success and changes in the global system made it possible and necessary for China to take a more active role in reshaping old and building new institutions to protect China's interests and to meet twenty-first-century challenges. Illustrative examples of China's new and still current approach to managing its external relationships include the leading role it has taken in the East Asia Summit and negotiation of bilateral and regional trade agreements, formation of the Asian Infrastructure Investment Bank and leading role in the New Development Bank (formerly known as the BRICS Bank), and the highly ambitious Belt and Road Initiative to expand infrastructure in South, Southeast, and Central Asia (see chapter 10 by Ho-fung Hung, chapter 11 by Christine Wong, and chapter 12 by David M. Lampton, this volume).[76]

These and similar initiatives launched or endorsed by China are more accurately viewed as supplements to post–World War II arrangements developed to manage global problems. For the most part, the organizations are inclusive and operate in accordance with the rules-based approach of the liberal order. Some of these initiatives will falter or fail, and Chinese diplomacy has not always proved up to the job of persuading prospective partners to meet China's preferred conditions, but most Chinese initiatives thus far are best seen as new elements of (rather than challenges to) the international order that China entered, reluctantly, in 1979. What does the analysis of factors driving and shaping Beijing's foreign policy and international behavior over the past forty years tell us about how China is likely to act in coming decades? While it is far too simplistic to assert without elaboration that the future is likely to look a lot like the past, extrapolating from past foreign policy behavior is usually the best starting point for anticipating the future.[77] One reason for basic continuity is that geography does not change. China will continue to be located where it is in Northeast Asia, and will be bordered by states with essentially the same factor endowments and historical legacies as exist today.

Technology has made distant regions more relevant to China's security and economy, but in the age of globalization, nuclear weapons, and intercontinental missiles, the countries perceived and treated as most important by Beijing fifteen to twenty years from now are likely to be the same ones accorded that priority today. Geography and geopolitics shape mind-sets as well as the structure of the external environment, and together these factors make continuity more likely than sudden or dramatic shifts in international behavior. Most of the time geopolitics can be treated as a constant, but the nature of regional and international systems can change, as they did in the early 1990s. Although it is difficult to imagine changes to the international system as significant as the end of the Cold War, efforts to project China's future foreign policy behavior must consider how developments in the external arena would affect China and how Beijing might attempt to ameliorate or exploit the consequences. Given China's size and strength, the external shock to the system would have to be very large to change the basic trajectory of Chinese foreign policy. If the United States really were to descend into irreversible decline and/or extreme isolationism, China could and would have to respond, but such an eventuality is unlikely and it is difficult to imagine other developments that would be as consequential.

A second factor that has driven and will continue to shape China's foreign policy is the importance of sustained economic growth. The analysis summarized in this chapter underscored the importance of this factor throughout the first four decades of Reform and Opening. That, too, is unlikely to change in the next few decades. As other chapters in this volume make clear, growth is slowing; needs, demands, and expectations are rising; and China still has a long way to go to attain developed-country status. Ill-founded and delusional judgments about China's economy and ability to disengage from the liberal order that flourished for a short time at the end of the 2000s were quickly and firmly disproved by reality and Chinese foreign policy returned to more-or-less the same trajectory it had been on before the 2008 financial crisis. The priority and requisites of modernization and the continuing importance of economic performance to regime legitimacy are further arguments for basic foreign policy continuity. China continues to need access to a well-functioning liberal international order. It wants to and will play a larger role in maintaining that order, but it will likely do so as a cautious and deeply invested stakeholder.[78]

A third factor that will shape China's foreign policy is the way other nations respond to Chinese actions. Beijing proclaims its desire for harmony, mutual benefit, and respect for the core interests of all nations, but its foreign policies, like those of every country, serve its own interests. Sometimes China's interests coincide or are compatible with those of its neighbors and economic partners, but that is not always the case. Other states want things from China, often turn to third countries for leverage to support their policies, and must contend with their own internal challenges. Chinese leaders surely are drawing lessons from developments during the past decade, when its more muscular displays of military power and assertions of economic clout have proven to be at least partially counterproductive. If, as seems likely, a primary objective of such policies was to dissuade countries from aligning more closely with the United States, the policies have not only failed, they have achieved the opposite result. The jury is still out on the efficacy of the BRI and AIIB initiatives to buy friendship and tie the prosperity of others to the Chinese economy, but it is worth noting that many of the deals struck and projects launched are of questionable economic viability and were approved by unpopular autocratic regimes. To an as yet unclear extent, China has tied the success of these foreign policies to individuals and regimes that might not endure.

To sum up, there is always a high degree of inertia and stability in any nation's foreign policies, and there is no reason to think that China is fundamentally different. Moreover, the priorities and logic of China's self-strengthening strategy are unlikely to change because they respond to public demands for greater opportunities and prosperity and regime perceptions of what is necessary to maintain domestic tranquility and party legitimacy. Unless there is dramatic—and unlikely—change in the international system or equally unlikely collapse of the regime in Beijing and its replacement by one that is far more jingoistic and revisionist than what we have seen for the past forty years, the priorities, objectives, and basic parameters of China's foreign policy are likely to continue on essentially the same trajectory they have followed since the late 1970s.

Beijing has not announced its vision for the future world order but it has made clear, at least unofficially, that while it expects China to play a more influential role in shaping the global order, it does not (yet) aspire to lead it.[79] This could change in the future, but that future will not arrive for many years and probably many decades. The requirements and modalities of China's foreign policy will continue to evolve, but for the foreseeable future, China's actions on the world stage will be variants of what we have seen for the past four decades.

CHAPTER 10

China and the Global South

Ho-fung Hung

Solidarity with the developing world has been a staple of Chinese political rhetoric since the earliest days of the People's Republic, but substantive engagement with the Global South was minimal during the first decades of Reform and Opening. The reasons, described in chapter 9 by Thomas Fingar, were that developing countries did not threaten China's security and were unable to provide the capital, technologies, training, and markets needed to jumpstart modernization through export-led growth. The situation began to change in the 1990s in ways that made countries in the Global South more important to the success of Beijing's quest for sustained growth. This chapter examines why and how Chinese actors engaged with the developing world to obtain energy and other inputs needed to satisfy escalating domestic demand, consequences of this engagement, and challenges and choices that will shape China's future policies and prospects.

Commentary on China's engagement with the Global South generally asserts that it is highly beneficial to both parties or, conversely, that it constitutes a familiar and exploitative form of neocolonialism.[1] Whether lauding or condemning Chinese actions, most commentators assert that they both reflect and contribute to China's growing international influence and imputed quest to displace the United States as regional or global hegemon. This chapter argues that the motivations for and modalities of China's engagement with developing countries are shaped more by China's immediate needs and perceived opportunities and by decisions made outside Beijing than by grand strategy or geopolitical ambition. It also argues that much about China's engagement with the Global South is driven and shaped by challenges and choices similar to those of earlier modernizers, which will propel and constrain China's future international behavior in familiar and predictable ways.

China's rise has been achieved through export-led growth facilitated by participation in the rules-based economic order pioneered and promoted by the United States and its closest allies. Participation enabled China to take advantage of opportunities previously limited to members of the "free world," but it also shaped and constrained Beijing's choices in ways germane to understanding China's engagement with the Global South. The key to China's economic dynamism is the nature and performance of its export sector. That sector is dominated by private enterprises (domestic and foreign) and is closely integrated into the production and supply networks and other mechanisms of the global trading system.[2] Relatively unprofitable state-owned enterprises have played a much less significant role as exporters of high-value products, magnet to attract foreign investment and technologies, and sources of funding to meet the daunting and expensive challenges described elsewhere in this volume. Among other consequences, the critical importance of export industries dominated by private firms integrated into the rules-based globalized economy has enabled and required the central government to tolerate and facilitate economic ties that constrain its own freedom of action.

Reengaging with the Global South

During the first fifteen years of the reform era, Chinese officials and firms looked primarily to the highly developed countries of Europe, North America, and Japan for the investment, technology, and markets needed to implement the strategy of export-led growth. Africa, the Middle East, South America, and South, Central, and Southeast Asia did not figure prominently in Beijing's diplomacy or economic strategy because developing countries had little that China needed to launch its quest for rapid modernization and sustained economic growth. This situation changed in the 1990s because the success of China's policies and changes in information technology and the international system made it possible and necessary to seek lower-cost labor, energy, and other resources as well as new markets for Chinese goods and capital.

China's economic engagement with the developing world has been shaped more by the decisions of players in different arenas than by conscious design or strategic plan. One set of decisions was made—and continues to be made—by multinational firms, most based outside China, seeking to take advantage of opportunities to increase profits by relocating nodes in production and supply chains. Rising wages in China were only one of many considerations. Others include IT and other technical advances that made it possible to disaggregate production, tax, and other incentives that made it attractive to relocate specific activities and use of relocation to open new markets. Many of the production chains continue to rely on final assembly in China, but subcomponents can be manufactured in more distributed ways than was possible before advances in digital technology.[3]

A second development driving and shaping China's reengagement with developing countries was the growing need for energy and other raw materials to sustain economic growth and meet the demands of China's more prosperous citizens. Oil was among the first and most important shapers of Chinese foreign engagement in the second and subsequent decades of Reform and Opening (see chapter 9 by Thomas Fingar, this volume). Simply stated, China's quest for reliable sources of oil compelled Beijing to engage with oil-producing countries. Third, the growth of indigenous Chinese manufacturing capabilities created incentives to seek external markets, particularly for lower-quality goods that could not be sold in more developed countries. Markets for lower-quality Chinese goods exist primarily in the Global South. As with the search for resources, Chinese firms and Beijing sought markets for lower-quality goods within the developing world.[4] Over time, exports of Chinese-manufactured products increased in quality as well as volume and posed greater challenges to indigenous industries in more industrialized developing countries.

A fourth factor driving and shaping China's engagement with the developing world was the need and opportunity to export capital and alleviate the consequences of excess capacity and overproduction. The long boom of China's export-led growth hit a wall in 2008 and 2009, when the global financial crisis dealt a severe blow to US and European consumption markets. In response, the Chinese government rolled out an aggressive stimulus program that produced a strong economic rebound driven by debt-financed fixed-asset investment. During the pre-2008 boom years China's exports, together with the influx of export-oriented manufacturing capital, accounted for a large part of the growth of China's foreign exchange reserves, mostly in the form of US dollar assets. Without this expanding reserve, Beijing would not have been able to increase the growth of money supply through lax state bank lending. But the export sector and the increasing reserves it generated enabled the regime to undertake a debt-financed investment spree between approximately 2000 and 2008 without incurring the economic malaise experienced by many Southeast Asian economies on eve of the 1997–98 Asian financial crisis, which erupted because years of debt-fueled investment without adequate growth in foreign exchange reserves had debased their currencies and unleashed capital flight.[5]

China's situation changed after 2008. The weakening of the export engine and the reckless investment expansion resulting from government stimulus during the rebound of 2009 and 2010 created a gigantic debt bubble that is no longer offset by commensurate expansion of foreign exchange reserves. Between 2008 and late 2017 outstanding debt in China skyrocketed from 148 percent of gross domestic product (GDP) to more than 300 percent. This exceeds the level in the United States and most other developing countries.[6] The long fast rise of China's foreign exchange reserves ended and began to stagnate or shrink in 2014. Beijing imposed draconian measures to restrict capital outflow after 2015, but the amount of debt constitutes a ticking time bomb. The export sector has not rebounded to the pre-2008 level, and China has run out of room for growth through fixed-asset investment (see chapter 8 by Hongbin Li et al., this volume).[7]

The loss of momentum suffered by the Chinese economy after the 2009–10 rebound is illustrated by changes in the manufacturing purchasing manager index (PMI), an indicator used to measure the state of the manufacturing sector. A PMI higher than 50 signals expansion of manufacturing, whereas values lower than 50 show contraction. PMI, unlike GDP growth data, is not subject to inaccuracies caused by exaggeration of local growth performance. PMI data indicate steady decline after the rebound of 2009–10.[8] The index now fluctuates around the stagnation line of 50, which is a significant change from the continuous expansion that occurred before 2008. The slight rebound of the index that occurred after 2015 was mostly the result of a surge in bank lending. Comparing the two series in Figure 10.1, we can see that the most recent lending surge resulted in only meager economic expansion, while the lending surge in 2009–10 fostered an impressive economic rebound. This reveals that that lending is much less effective in stimulating growth now than it was in the previous decade.

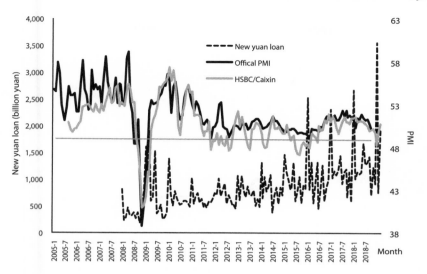

FIGURE 10.1. China manufacturing purchasing manager index (PMI) and new yuan loan, 2005–19.

SOURCE: National Bureau of Statistics of China, HSBC, Caixin, and People's Bank of China.

The many redundant construction and infrastructure projects begun during the debt-fueled economic rebound may never be profitable, and repayment and servicing of the debt are problematic. The manufacturing capacity and infrastructure, apartments, coalmines, steel mills, and so on that expanded rapidly during the boom time and the post-2008 rebound have become excess capacity with falling profit rates. China is now experiencing a typical overaccumulation crisis epitomized by the high number of ghost towns and shuttered factories across the country.[9] This crisis of overaccumulation is driving China to export capital and capital goods to seek profits overseas to countervail declining profitability at home. China's capital exports have soared since the early 2000s, increasing from a total of $28 billion in 2000 to $1,300 billion in 2016. This total is impressive, but it is still small in comparison to smaller advanced capitalist economies like Singapore.[10]

State-owned corporations, mostly energy firms and infrastructure construction firms backed by the large foreign exchange reserves generated by the export sector, have been at the forefront of Chinese outward investment in the Global South, most notably in Africa and Southeast Asia. Chinese

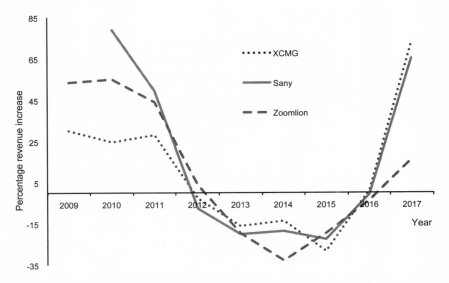

FIGURE 10.2. Percentage revenue increase of three big construction machine makers in China, 2008–17.

SOURCE: Statistica.

manufacturing also has been relocating to lower-wage countries like Tanzania and Vietnam. The same drive to export surplus capital and products fuels China's recent ambitious efforts to create a "One Belt, One Road" network of ports, railroads, and highways linking China to Europe across Central Asia and the Indian Ocean (see chapter 11 by Christine Wong and chapter 12 by David M. Lampton). For example, as Figure 10.2 shows, revenue growth of the three major construction machine makers in China plunged from their high point amid the 2009–10 stimulus into negative territory, only to rebound after 2013 when the Belt and Road Initiative (BRI) started. Annual reports of these companies explicitly divulged how important orders from Belt and Road projects, financed by Chinese lending, were to their revenue growth, as domestic markets for their products had been contracting since the tapering off of the 2008–2009 stimulus.

Unlike Japan and other postwar capitalist exporters of capital, China cannot rely on the US geopolitical and military umbrella to manage the rising security and political risks of its overseas investments. This vulnerability impels Beijing to increase its own political influence and military capabilities (see chapter 13 by Karl Eikenberry, this volume).

The Contour of China's Capital Export

Journalistic reports on China's economic engagement with developing countries often exaggerate or misrepresent the magnitude and modalities of what is actually taking place. Many of these reports and estimates of Chinese activity and impact on specific countries are based on pledges and memoranda of understanding announced by Chinese firms or government officials. This is misleading because only a small fraction of such pledges become real projects. According to the American Enterprise Institute's China Global Investment Tracking Database, which tracks pledged and announced Chinese direct investment, China's investment in Africa totaled $306 billion (as of the first quarter of 2016). But official data released by China's Ministry of Commerce report that China's direct investment in Africa totaled only $35 billion at the end of 2015.[11] The same phenomenon exists with respect to Chinese grants and loans. One oft-cited estimate of China's aid commitments to Africa based on media reporting calculated that the amount totaled $189.3 billion in 2011.[12] An alternative estimate using a more rigorous methodology came up with a more modest total of $4.5 billion for the same year.[13]

To assess the real extent and coverage of Chinese outward investment, either as direct investment (FDI) or in the form of grants and loans, is difficult because the Chinese government does not release detailed breakdowns of its foreign economic engagement. All we have are broad-stroke data released once every few years. Nevertheless, this intermittent data allows rough estimates of China's capital exports. Table 10.1 shows that China had become the only developing country among the world's top ten capital exporters by the end of 2015, but its total stock of exported capital is still much smaller than those of other leading capital exporters, most notably the United States. However, in 2015, China was the second largest source of outward FDI flow.

The top destinations of China's outward investment are Hong Kong and Caribbean tax havens, followed by a host of developed countries. This finding is in marked contrast to the impression conveyed by journalistic accounts that China's outward investment is concentrated in developing countries. Categorization of China's worldwide outward FDI shows that the leasing and business services sector accounts for the largest share. This sector covers a broad range of businesses, and Chinese investments are judged to be concentrated in holding companies for merger and acquisition operations. It is reasonable to speculate that investment in this sector

TABLE 10.1   Top ten countries (regions) as sources of global outward foreign direct investment (FDI) stock and annual flow by the end of 2015

Ranking	Country/ region	Stock (US$ billion)	Share of global total (%)	Country/ region	Flow (US$ billion)	Share of global total (%)
1	United States	5,982.8	23.9	United States	300.0	20.4
2	UK	1,538.1	6.2	China	145.7	9.9
3	Germany	1,812.5	7.2	Japan	128.7	8.8
4	Hong Kong	1,485.7	5.9	Netherlands	113.4	7.7
5	France	1,314.2	5.3	Ireland	101.6	6.9
6	Japan	1,226.6	4.9	Germany	94.3	6.4
7	Switzerland	1,138.2	4.5	Canada	67.2	4.6
8	China	1,097.9	4.4	UK	61.4	4.2
9	Canada	1,078.3	4.3	Hong Kong	55.1	3.7
10	Netherlands	1,074.3	4.3	Singapore	35.5	2.4
	TOTAL	17,748.4	70.9	TOTAL	1,102.9	75.0

SOURCE: Ministry of Commerce, China.

TABLE 10.2   Top twenty countries (regions) as destinations of China's outward foreign direct investment (FDI) stock and flow, by the end of 2016

Ranking	Country/region	Stock (US$ billion)	Share of global total (%)	Country/region	Flow (US$ billion)	Share of global total (%)
1	Hong Kong	780.7	57.5	Hong Kong	114.2	58.2
2	Cayman Islands	104.2	7.7	United States	17.0	8.7
3	British Virgin Isl.	88.8	6.5	Cayman Islands	13.5	6.9
4	United States	60.6	4.4	British Virgin Isl.	12.3	6.3
5	Singapore	33.4	2.5	Australia	4.2	2.1
6	Australia	33.4	2.5	Singapore	3.2	1.6
7	Netherlands	20.6	1.5	Canada	2.9	1.5
8	United Kingdom	17.6	1.3	Germany	2.4	1.2
9	Russia	13.0	1	Israel	1.8	0.9
10	Canada	12.7	0.9	Malaysia	1.8	0.9
11	Indonesia	9.5	0.7	Luxembourg	1.6	0.8
12	Luxembourg	8.8	0.6	France	1.5	0.8
13	Germany	7.8	0.6	United Kingdom	1.5	0.7
14	Macao	6.8	0.5	Indonesia	1.5	0.7
15	South Africa	6.0	0.4	Russia	1.3	0.7
16	Laos	5.5	0.4	Vietnam	1.3	0.7
17	France	5.1	0.4	Netherlands	1.2	0.6
18	Kazakhstan	5.1	0.4	South Korea	1.2	0.6
19	Vietnam	5.0	0.4	Thailand	1.1	0.6
20	United Arab Em.	4.9	0.3	New Zealand	0.9	0.5
	TOTAL	1229.5	90.5	TOTAL	186.3	95.0

SOURCE: National Development and Reform Commission, China.

is more about capital flight from China than productive investment seeking profits. This speculation is supported by the sectorial distribution of China's capital exports across different regions. Table 10.3 shows that investments in the leasing and business services sector constitute the largest share of Chinese investment in Asia (including Hong Kong) and Latin America (including Caribbean tax havens).

Excluding the plausible cases of capital flight suggested by the large share of investment in the leasing and business service sector and in financial services, Table 10.3 shows that the mining, construction, and wholesale and retail trade sectors receive the most Chinese investment in developing regions. The data also show that manufacturing investment accounts for a large share of China's capital exports to North America and Europe. This distribution supports the assessment that China's outgoing investment has been driven by Beijing's desire to lock in access to energy and raw materials supplies, and to export China's excess capacity in infrastructure construction (and sectors connected to construction like steel making) to the developing world, while its investment to the developed world is driven by the aspiration to acquire patents owned by established Western manufacturers (Chinese car-maker Geely's acquisition of Volvo in 2010 being a case in point). Chinese investment in wholesale and retail trade is likely intended to facilitate importing raw materials from and exporting manufactured products to other developing countries.

China's capital export to other developing countries is not restricted to outward FDI. It also takes the form of foreign aid, including grants and loans offered by China's official financial institutions. Many of the loans China has offered to countries in the Global South were intended to elicit diplomatic support and/or preferential access to energy and raw materials. Others pave the way for the export of China's spare capacity. Countries receiving the loans use most of the funds to hire Chinese companies and procure Chinese supplies for local construction projects. Examples include China's loan to Ethiopia for construction of electricity distribution lines, cement factories, roads connecting the landlocked country to ports, and other projects.[14] In other cases, loans are made to energy or raw materials exporting countries with the terms of loans set in a way that the debtors would repay the loan with specified amounts of commodities. The best-known example of this type of loan is China's $63 billion in loans to Venezuela in 2007–14 to be repaid with deliveries of oil.[15]

TABLE 10.3   Top five industries of China's outward foreign direct investment
(FDI) stock in different regions by the end of 2015

Region	Industry	Stock (US$ billion)	Share of global total (%)
Asia	Leasing and business services	331.31	43.1
	Financial services	103.09	13.4
	Wholesale and retail trade	100.43	13.1
	Mining	71.46	9.3
	Manufacturing	40.71	5.3
	SUBTOTAL	647.00	84.2
Africa	Mining	9.54	27.5
	Construction	9.51	27.4
	Manufacturing	4.63	13.3
	Financial services	3.42	9.9
	Scientific research and technical services	1.46	4.2
	SUBTOTAL	28.56	82.3
Europe	Mining	24.18	28.9
	Manufacturing	16.08	19.2
	Financial services	15.34	18.3
	Leasing and business services	8.00	9.6
	Wholesale and retail trade	5.86	7.0
	SUBTOTAL	69.46	83.0
Latin America	Leasing and business services	60.25	47.7
	Financial services	23.07	18.3
	Mining	12.15	9.6
	Wholesale and retail trade	9.62	7.6
	Transportation, storage and postal services	4.55	3.6
	SUBTOTAL	109.64	86.8
North America	Manufacturing	12.19	23.4
	Financial services	12.17	23.3
	Leasing and business services	6.57	12.6
	Mining	6.48	12.4
	Real estate	3.76	7.2
	SUBTOTAL	41.17	78.9
Oceania	Mining	18.57	57.9
	Real estate	2.99	9.3
	Financial services	2.56	8.0
	Leasing and business services	2.34	7.3
	Manufacturing	1.33	4.1
	SUBTOTAL	27.79	86.6

SOURCE: Ministry of Commerce, China.

TABLE 10.4 Outward loan versus outward foreign direct investment
(FDI) as the main channels of China's influence in the
developing world (stock in US$ billion)

Region	Foreign aid by the end of 2012	Outward FDI by the end of 2012	Outward FDI by the end of 2015
Asia	18.0	364.4	768.4
Africa	26.4	21.7	34.7
Europe	0.4	37.0	83.7
Latin America and Caribbean	6.5	68.2	126.3
North America	0.0	25.5	52.2
Oceania	2.3	15.1	32.1
Others	2.3		
TOTAL	55.7	531.9	1097.9

SOURCE: Ministry of Finance, Ministry of Commerce, China.

China's export of capital in the form of loans has been growing rapidly
in comparison to the value of outward FDI. In the case of Africa, loans
have surpassed outward FDI as the main form of China's capital export
(Table 10.4).

Although most of China's capital outflow is to tax havens and developed
countries and probably represents capital flight, outward FDI and aid to
other developing countries is rising rapidly. China is becoming a new major
source of capital in the Global South. The form and size of China's capital export varies from place to place, depending on China's needs and the
destination country's geopolitical and economic relationship with China.
Most of this capital export is supposed to be instrumental to China's effort
to secure commodities and export its excess capacity. The impact of China's
capital exports on the receiving countries is highly variegated.

China's Impact on the Global South

China's growing presence in other developing countries has triggered debate
and polemical writing on the character and impact of China's engagement.
Some depict China as a beneficent savior who treats developing countries
with respect and equality and eschews conditionality and moralizing interference in their internal affairs. Other commentators present a more malign
assessment of Chinese engagement, effectively or explicitly depicting China

as a neocolonial power interested only in extracting what it needs from other developing countries to achieve its own developmental and political objectives.[16] Most such assessments, whether laudatory or critical, extrapolate from limited anecdotal evidence, accept Chinese and developing country rhetoric at face value, and/or impute motivations based on preconceived notions of "China's" objectives and decision-making procedures. Recent and more rigorous academic research presents a more complex picture of China's engagement and impacts in the Global South.[17]

The development studies literature describes "development" as diversification away from heavy reliance on the export of natural resources.[18] Reducing reliance on the export of natural resources and expanding industry have been a long-standing priority of governments in the Global South. They have aimed to achieve these goals either through import-substitution (i.e., blocking imports of foreign manufactures to foster growth of domestic industries) or through export-oriented industrialization (subsidizing and promoting local industrial products sold in the world market). The rise of China has disrupted such endeavors in many developing countries. Escalating Chinese demand for oil, raw materials, agricultural products, and many other commodities drove up prices and produced huge profits for commodity exporters. Some of the profits resulted from sales to China; others from the rise in the price of commodities attributable to China's increased production of manufactures for export.[19]

Increased earnings in commodity exporting countries led to the expansion of mining industries and agribusinesses across the developing world, confounding development policies designed to reduce the share of the commodity exports in many economies. For example, the amount of land used for soybean cultivation in Brazil doubled between 1990 and 2005. This entailed expansion of farmland deep into the environmentally sensitive Amazon frontier. This vast expansion was in response to demand from China, which constituted 42.7 percent of Brazil's soybean export market in the early 2000s. China's share shot up to 80 percent in 2018 amid the US–China trade war that drove more Chinese importers to turn to Brazil.[20] In Argentina, Chinese companies dominated both ends of the soybean commodity chain, skewing the distribution of income in the economy even more than what typically happens when integrated commodity chains serve markets in developed countries.[21]

Thanks to China, the copper-mining industries in Chile and other Latin American countries also expanded significantly during the same period. Exports of copper from Latin America increased by 237.5 percent between 2000 and 2006; most of the increased amount went to China. In 2016, 67 percent of Chile's copper exports and 73 percent of Peru's exports went to China.[22] Much the same phenomenon occurred in Africa, where countries rich in metal ores, such as Zambia, have benefitted from China's high demand, although their raw materials export was also hit by China's recent slowdown.[23]

Although China helps boost the profits of raw material exporters in the developing world, its efficient, low-cost manufacturing sector puts increasing competitive pressure on the manufacturing sectors of many developing countries. Some argue that the genesis of China's export-oriented manufacturing in the 1990s, particularly during the one-off but substantial devaluation of China's currency (the renminbi, or RMB) in 1994 to boost exports, is connected to the economic troubles of other Asian exporters like Malaysia and Thailand, paving the way for the Asian financial crisis of 1997–98.[24] Political economists Kevin Gallagher and Roberto Porzencanski have compiled an index for Latin American industries to assess the threat from Chinese manufactured exports. They found that more than 80 percent of the manufactured exports of all major Latin American countries are directly or partially threatened by Chinese manufactures.[25] Manufactured goods from China occupy a large and growing share of both international and domestic markets for Latin American manufactures.

The combined effect of expanding raw material exporting sectors and increasing competitive pressures on domestic industries resulting from the China boom created conditions that could lead to deindustrialization and the return of dependence on natural resources export in the developing world. However, whether and how much this change will damage or benefit the long-term developmental prospects of individual developing countries depends on each country's internal political economy. Rather than trying to shape the local political economy of its aid and investment partners like many traditional capital exporters, China has been more willing to tailor its requirements and modalities to suit local conditions.

An example of such accommodation that is sometimes construed as a Chinese tendency to deal with governments rather than private firms is the way China has engaged the mining industries in Latin America. In most Latin American countries, mining corporations are owned or heavily regulated by their governments. Naturally, even inevitably, Chinese entities must work with these state-dominated natural resource companies. Prevailing ownership and/or regulatory arrangements give these countries at least some leverage over the pricing and output volume of the materials in demand. Their relationship to national governments give them an advantage when negotiating with China and other customers. Governments can also establish institutions that direct gains from the natural resources bonanza to other uses, including long-term investment, support of economic diversification, and poverty alleviation. The Economic and Social Stability Fund that the Chilean government instituted and Brazil's Bolso Familia conditional cash transfer program are the best-known examples.[26]

In contrast to Latin America, where regional and state-owned companies dominate the resource-extracting sector, many African countries lack competitive homegrown mining corporations and have been reliant on foreign companies to extract their resources. As a result, China's economic engagement with Africa has been marked by extensive direct investment in local natural resource sectors. In many cases Chinese state companies, often in tacit partnership with other transnational mining corporations, own and run the entire commodity chain from mining sites to the ports that ship the raw materials. Under such circumstances the African governments are in a much less favorable position to negotiate with their Chinese partners, who can extract and export the materials they need without much consideration of the long-term impact on the local economy and environment. Whether the practices of Chinese companies are worse or better than those of Western companies operating in African natural resource sectors remains unclear. What is clear is that under prevailing conditions, foreign companies accord higher priority to their own interests than to the long-term developmental prospects of their host countries. The copper industry in Zambia—where Chinese mining corporations expand, casualize labor, and collude with the corrupt local government to maximize short-term gains—is illustrative.[27]

The impact of competition from China's manufactured exports also varies from country to country, depending on the country's place in the value chain of the industry in question. For example, even though most Latin American countries face similar competitive pressure from Chinese manufactures, some are having a more difficult time than others. Mexico has experienced the biggest impact because its manufacturing establishment exports a range of products similar to Chinese manufacturers. Mexico's export industries have taken a bigger hit from China's exports because both rely heavily on the North American market.[28]

Comparing the impact of Chinese manufacturing on other Asian economies and Latin America reveals a more diverse picture. As discussed earlier, after the initial impact of China's rise as an export-manufacturing powerhouse in the form of the Asian financial crisis, many of China's Asian neighbors adjusted their industrial structure to achieve better integration with China. Many of China's neighboring economies have shifted their focus to products either higher or lower in the value chain than what China was producing to avoid head-to-head competition. Much of China's export sector consists of process manufacturing in which China imports components from elsewhere in Asia and assembles them into final products that are exported to ultimate destination markets as "made in China" items. Such goods are, in fact, the products of regional production networks spanning a number of Asian countries. In the network manufacturers supplying China with components and machinery benefit from China's rise as a manufacturing powerhouse. The situation of Asian economies is very different than that of Latin American economies, which enter into Sino-centric global production networks as natural resource providers rather than components suppliers.[29]

As China's economic influence in Asia has increased, it has begun to leverage its greater economic clout to exert regional leadership. The way Beijing acts vis-à-vis its Asian neighbors could be a harbinger of how it will interact with other regions. China was never a political power with global reach, but the Chinese empire did exercise hegemony in Asia until Western imperial powers overturned the premodern Asian order. Some observers see the trajectory of China's rising power in Asia as at least a partial revival of the premodern Sino-centric regional order.[30] Reconstruction of anything approximating the Chinese imperial order is impossible in the twenty-first century, but citizens of former vassal states worry that a stronger China will act like an imperial hegemon.[31] Although I doubt that many Chinese strategic thinkers aspire to re-create the idealized world order of bygone centuries, attitudes of superiority and expectations of deference to China's wishes are a recurring feature of Beijing's engagement with neighboring countries.[32]

Incipient Chinese Hegemony and Its Limits

China's growing centrality in Asia evinces the consequences and contradictions of China's geopolitical ascendancy. China's increasing political influence in neighboring countries is a direct outgrowth of its increasing economic power, but its political influence is constrained by the continuing preeminence of the United States and regional anxiety about overdependence on China. This contradiction is not restricted to Asia; it is also reflected in the response to growing Chinese influence in other world regions. This resistance, backlash, and hedging reveal the limits and challenges to China's rise as a global hegemonic power.

In premodern Asia, China's rulers viewed the world in terms of concentric circles centered on the emperor with directly governed provinces in the first circle and tribute vassals located in more distant ones.[33] The Sino-centric tribute system disintegrated when Western powers colonized Burma (Myanmar), Vietnam, and other Chinese vassals. Japan, which had industrialized and constructed a modern centralized state after the 1868 Meiji restoration, sought to usurp China's centrality by expanding its own empire in Asia. When the Japanese empire collapsed at the end of the Second World War, the bipolar divide of the Cold War replaced this version of the traditional East Asian order. The United States became the new regional hegemon that provided economic and military security to Japan, Korea, Taiwan, Hong Kong, Singapore, and much of Southeast Asia. As that transition was occurring, the Communists won China's civil war, established the People's Republic of China in 1949, and joined the Soviet bloc.

Mao Zedong's decision to align with the Soviet Union brought badly needed military and economic assistance, but at the price of subservience to Moscow. By the end of the 1950s, Mao was looking for ways to regain control of China's destiny. One component of the strategy he adopted was to restore China's influence in Southeast Asia and to forge ties with revolutionary regimes and movements in other developing countries. Beijing's support for indigenous communist parties and guerrilla movements played a central role in this strategy, but it did more to alienate postcolonial regimes than to restore Chinese influence.[34]

China's economic success and the end of the Cold War made it possible to again pursue creation of a new Sino-centric order. As China became the biggest exporter of finished manufactured products, regional production and supply chains shaped by comparative advantage and divisions of labor made possible by the digital revolution created networks that linked states on the periphery to the Middle Kingdom. China's neighbors specialized in exporting capital goods and components to China, where they were assembled into finished products, most of them for export to the developed world. The result was a new type of Sino-centric production network. China is also becoming active in providing investment funds, loans, and other economic assistance to its poorer neighbors for infrastructure and other projects.[35] As both rich and poor Asian countries become more economically dependent on China, many worry that Beijing will use dependence as a source of political leverage. Many in China see this as an opportunity to be exploited, but Beijing denies using manipulation or threatened curtailment of economic ties as a diplomatic weapon. Facts suggest otherwise. For example, China is rarely hesitant to use or threaten to use economic leverage to reinforce its territorial claims in disputes with Southeast Asian nations and Japan.[36]

This new China-centered Asian order is still far from being a reincarnation of the premodern Sino-centric tribute-trade order. The old China-centric order was based on the cultural foundation of Confucianism. This cultural foundation encouraged most Asian nations to acknowledge (if not always accept) China's primacy as a model of government and economy. Today, however, China's increasing centrality in Asia's international order rests almost entirely on economic pragmatism. China's ability to leverage economic arrangements for political purposes is far more a function of economic realism and the exercise of political skill and will than it is the result of cultural affinity or "soft power." Other Asian countries do not consider China's political system a model worthy of emulation. Many have already moved further toward democracy, rule of law, and official accountability. Also, Japan, India, the United States, and multilateral institutions are forces that counterbalance and constrain China's influence.

The absence of a common cultural foundation, limited appeal of the "Chinese model," and competition from the United States are major obstacles to and checks on the expansion of China's geopolitical influence. The extensive and generally beneficial engagement of the United States enables—and encourages—other Asian states to counterbalance Chinese economic leverage and imputed political objectives. Myanmar's partial embrace of democracy, opening to Western countries, and warmer relationship with the United States since about 2011 illustrates the options available to countries seeking to check or contain China's influence.

Myanmar is not the only Asian state to become wary of China's economic and political influence. Singapore, South Korea, the Philippines, Taiwan, Vietnam, and many other Asian states have bolstered their economic and political-military ties with the United States at the same time that they benefit from increasing economic integration with China. Similar dynamics can also be seen in South Asia (and Central Asia). Beijing's Belt and Road Initiative is expanding China's diplomatic and economic ties with South Asia, particularly countries surrounding India. The motivations appear to be geopolitical as well as economic.[37] Many of China's infrastructure projects, like roads and ports in Sri Lanka and Pakistan, were initiated during the past five years (see chapters by Wong and Lampton, this volume). These projects often aggravated preexisting tension between the incumbent elite, who benefitted politically and economically from such projects, and their rivals, whoever they happened to be.

The 2015 presidential election in Sri Lanka provides a concrete illustration. In that election, the challenger, Maithripala Sirisena, ran on an anti-China platform and defeated the two-term incumbent (Mahinda Rajapaksa), who had approved a number of large infrastructure projects to be built and financed by Chinese companies. After the election many Chinese projects were delayed or revised by the new government.[38] In Pakistan many members of regional elites see Chinese projects as enabling the central military elite to tighten its grip on their regions and resources. Such projects, as well as the Chinese personnel involved, became targets of local rebel groups.[39]

In 2017, Pakistan's government canceled the China-financed $14 billion Diamer-Bhasha Dam project, citing harsh loan terms that involved pledging the new dam, as well as an existing dam, as loan security. In the same year, Nepal canceled a $2.5 billion contract with Gezhouba Group, a Chinese company, for the construction of a hydroelectric plant. The government cited irregularities and corruption during the bidding process. Myanmar also backed away from a $3.6 billion hydroelectric contract with a Chinese company.[40] In 2018, Malaysian opposition candidates ran on an anticorruption platform, accusing the incumbent government of collaborating with China through the BRI that damaged Malaysia's national interests. The opposition won the election and renegotiated the major Belt and

Road project with China. China's relation with its Asian neighbors is further complicated by the territorial dispute over the South China Sea, where China and a number of maritime Southeast Asian states have competing sovereignty claims (see chapter 9 by Thomas Fingar, this volume). Beijing's efforts to win political support from other developing nations by providing economic assistance are not confined to Asia. China began to support revolutionary movements and governments in Africa and other developing regions in the 1960s. During that decade these efforts grew mainly from Beijing's competition with the Soviet Union for leadership of the "Third World." A second objective was to win African votes in the United Nations General Assembly to support its bid for the membership seat then held by the Republic of China on Taiwan.[41]

The amount of attention China devoted to Africa abated after the beginning of economic reform in the 1980s because Africa lacked what China needed most to jumpstart its economy and begin the quest to modernize (see chapter by Fingar, this volume). Interest in Africa revived in the 2000s when the needs of China's rapidly growing economy induced Beijing to "return to Africa" to secure oil, metals, minerals, and other raw materials. Beijing's still highly mercantilist orientation made it eager to control its own extractive operations in Africa to make China less vulnerable to supply disruptions in industries dominated by Western powers. China's general approach when dealing with African exporters of natural resources is to befriend whoever is in power by providing loans, economic aid, and infrastructure investment projects. China has not been overly concerned about the character or type of regime and has not favored either democratic or authoritarian governments. If a country has what China needs and is willing to work with China, it is an acceptable partner. This approach follows Deng Xiaoping's observation that whether a cat is white or black is immaterial if it catches mice.

The investments that China has made in Africa are broadly distributed and often have terms that are more generous (from the perspectives of the investment recipients) than those imposed by other countries.[42] As noted earlier, China's growing investment in and trade with Africa has had different socioeconomic impacts, depending on local institutions and politics in the host countries. Although the magnitude of Chinese economic assistance is much smaller than that offered by traditional Western lenders and investors, above all the United States, it has been far from insignificant.[43]

China's assistance has been welcomed by African countries and generally brings new and positive gains to the continent. Among other consequences, the presence of China creates competitive pressure for other developing and developed countries to offer better terms in their dealings with African nations.

Many African states reciprocated China's economic favors by supporting Beijing's position on political issues such as the status of Taiwan and visits by the Dalai Lama. This support was clearly more valuable to Beijing, which bragged about it in domestic media, than it was to the African governments, which generally considered that they had received something of value in exchange for support that cost them nothing. However, as is true in Southeast Asia, where countries are uneasy about their increasing dependence on China, some African leaders have begun to voice concern about "Chinese colonialism." When Western politicians and scholars first raised the issue of "Chinese colonialism" in Africa in the 2000s, it was quickly dismissed as overwrought and hypocritical, evidence of Western anxiety about losing influence over the continent to China. But in the following decade, accusations of Chinese colonialism emerged from within Africa and opposition parties across the continent began to play the China card by attacking incumbent governments for satisfying China at the expense of what was best for the country. For example, in the 2011 election in Zambia the opposition party campaigned on an anti-China platform and successfully ousted the party in power.[44]

China's growing influence in Africa has spawned concern and second thoughts on the part of African officials. For example, in March 2013, right before the BRICS summit in Durban, the then governor of the Central Bank of Nigeria, which has been one of the African countries heavily reliant on Chinese loans, warned in the *Financial Times* that by embracing China, Africa is "opening itself up to a new form of imperialism." He also wrote: "China takes from us primary goods and sells us manufactured ones. This was also the essence of colonialism."[45]

China's capacity to dominate parts of the developing world has been constrained by the backlash generated by its actions and attitude in Asia and Africa. Similar dynamics are at work in Latin America, which is wealthier and politically stronger. The improvement in relations between the United States and Brazil during the Obama administration illustrates this dynamic. Brazil benefitted significantly from a resource bonanza driven by Chinese demand, but at substantial cost to the environment. The backlash against China's alleged mercantilist trade and currency policies has tarnished China's image and checked its influence in Brazil.[46] How Jair Bolsonaro, who accused China of buying up Brazil as a national security threat and won the presidency of Brazil in 2018, would shape the dynamics of Brazil–China relation remains to be seen. Similar dynamics in other developing countries limit China's political influence and will ultimately constrain the expansion of its economic influence.

Even Latin American countries once considered reliable allies of Beijing now sometimes act in ways contrary to Beijing's wishes. Beijing can do little to prevent or punish such actions. Venezuela is a case in point. When the late socialist president Hugo Chavez broke with the United States, the principal consumer of Venezuelan oil, he turned to China to demonstrate to Washington and the world that he had an alternative market and source of political support. Chavez was more interested in political symbolism and support than in finding an alternative market, but he needed money to maintain oil production. Beijing provided money through the loan-for-oil deal discussed earlier. When falling oil prices and bad policy choices caused Venezuela's economy to fall into deep crisis, the government of Chavez's successor, Nicholas Maduro, began to delay shipments of oil that were earmarked to repay the loan. Venezuela informed Beijing that it needed to sell the oil on the international market to obtain cash needed for the purchase of food and other necessities. Many Chinese companies subsequently left Venezuela without finishing their construction projects.[47]

Beijing's Remedies to Geopolitical Risks

Beijing recognizes and has attempted to address the backlash in a number of ways. One way is to establish multilateral institutions to make China's economic expansion into other developing countries less risky and politically sensitive than the bilateral—and "condition free"—arrangements it extolled previously. The creation in Spring 2015 of the Asian Infrastructure Investment Bank (AIIB) to fund infrastructure projects in Central, South, and Southeast Asia is a manifestation of this approach. As of December 2017, the bank had seventy members, forty-four from within and twenty-six from outside the Asian region, including some European countries.[48] The

AIIB capitalization can potentially go up to $100 billion; China's pledged contribution is $50 billion.[49] By mid-2018, however, the total loans the AIIB had extended amounted only to $4 billion, falling far short of the initial expectation of $10 billion to $15 billion per year. In 2014, China also pledged $40 billion to the new, Shanghai-based New Development Bank (formerly known as the BRICS Development Bank), which was also seen as intended to challenge US leadership in development financing.[50]

China's pledges to these new banks are quite small relative to its bilateral commitments. If China's bilateral assistance had been working well, it would not have needed to build new multilateral banks. China definitely has the capability to lend alone, which allows it to maintain total control over the choice of recipients and terms of the loans. Lending through multilateral banks like AIIB and the New Development Bank constrains China's freedom of action because other stakeholders also have a say. Moreover, even though China is the largest contributor to these banks, it will also be subject to existing standards of multilateral lending institutions. Many observe that the AIIB has been emulating the transparency, environmental, and other standards espoused by older multilateral financial institutions like the World Bank. In 2016 the AIIB and the World Bank signed an agreement according to which a large share of AIIB-funded projects will be cofinanced by the World Bank.[51] This will lead to further convergence of institutional forms and practices of the AIIB and the World Bank.

China's effort to build multilateral banks should be seen not as a challenge to the existing system of international finance but as a way to supplement that system that allows China to sacrifice some of its discretionary power to obtain the cover and legitimacy that other participating countries can provide. In a bilateral loan setting, China enjoys much greater autonomy in deciding which countries and which projects to fund, and the terms of the loans are usually determined by China's negotiation with the debtors, which are often much weaker than China. The downside of bilateral lending is that China is quite helpless if its debtors refuse to repay. If loans are made through a China-led multilateral lending institution like the AIIB, any debtor refusing to repay will face collective pressure from all stakeholders in the institution. Any country that defaults on a loan from the multilateral lending institution will risk losing not only future credits from China but also loans from all other countries involved in the institution.

Another challenge to and constraint on aspirations for Chinese hegemony in the Global South is the inherent security risk and cost of greater engagement. As more Chinese funds, personnel, and critical production facilities are distributed among developing countries, many of them unstable with unpopular regimes, Beijing will be under pressure to protect them (see chapter 13 by Karl Eikenberry, this volume). The sabotage of Chinese facilities and kidnapping of Chinese personnel in unstable areas illustrate this phenomenon. Chinese nationals reportedly have become the number-one target of kidnapping by terrorist and rebel groups in Africa, and Chinese facilities are valuable targets for ransom demands.[52]

China's 2013 National Defense White Paper included protecting overseas economic interests as a core responsibility of the People's Liberation Army. This was the first time this requirement was articulated in such a document.[53] The Chinese army still has a long way to go before it will be able to project capability to protect China's wide-ranging overseas interests, but the need to have this capability is now recognized. As an interim step, Beijing has been experimenting with the use of contract forces (international mercenaries) to defend its overseas interests. In 2014, Erik Prince, the founder and former CEO of Blackwater, the security firm that became infamous for its actions in Iraq, was recruited to head Frontier Services Group (FSG), a new Hong Kong–based logistic and risk management firm with close ties to CITIC, China's biggest state-owned conglomerate. Its main business is to provide security services to Chinese companies in Africa through a network of subcontractors on the ground.[54] In late 2016 the company announced that it was to adjust its corporate strategy to "better capitalize on the opportunities available from China's One Belt, One Road (OBOR) development initiative."[55]

The FSG has been operating a large security training center in Beijing since 2017 and started building another one in Xinjiang in early 2019.[56] China's cooperation with Erik Prince to establish the FSG probably is not intended to be a long-term way to protect Beijing's overseas interests, but it addresses an immediate and growing need. It will not be surprising if China eventually develops some homegrown security and mercenary companies without the help of foreigners. It would resemble the trajectory of development of many industries in China that started with joint ventures with foreign companies and matured with totally homegrown companies without foreigners' participation.

Patterns and Prospects

The central finding and argument of this chapter is that China's engagement with the Global South has much in common with the motivations, methods, and trajectories of other countries that have "gone abroad" for economic reasons, and that doing so creates opportunities and problems requiring political engagement and ways to protect investments, citizens, and national reputation. This finding challenges the arguments—and assumptions—of those who see China's patterns of engagement as markedly different from those of other nations that had reached a stage of economic development at which it was attractive—and perceived necessary—to seek resources, cheaper labor, and new markets beyond their borders. The chapter illustrates some of the obstacles and challenges that must be overcome if China is to achieve its imputed objective of regaining regional hegemony in Asia and displacing the United States atop the international system. It argues that China's accomplishments and activities are facilitated by and enmesh China ever more deeply in the neoliberal order. China's successes deepen its integration into and dependence on the existing rules-based order. To be sure, Beijing wants to change specific aspects of the existing system, as do the United States and many other countries, but it neither wants to nor is capable of abandoning or replacing the most important features of the system.

When China's export-oriented growth began to approach its natural limit, especially after the global financial crisis of 2008, Beijing became ever more reliant on debt-financed fixed-asset investment that boosted short-term growth but aggravated the unsustainable overcapacity and indebtedness of the economy. The stock market turmoil, accelerating capital flight, and currency devaluation in the summer of 2015 signal that China is moving toward an overaccumulation crisis characterized by falling profit rates and financial instability. Such a crisis has been brewing for some time, is apparent to many, and has prompted China to export surplus capital in the form of foreign aid, concessionary loans, and foreign direct investment in the developing countries of Asia, Africa, and Latin America. China's creation of the Asian Infrastructure Investment Bank and launching of the One Belt, One Road infrastructure construction initiative (now known as the Belt and Road Initiative) represent efforts to export excess capacity, alleviate financial problems, and manage the risks of lending to countries with limited ability and uncertain will to repay loans from China.

China's rise as a capital exporter follows in the footsteps of other capitalist powers that went abroad for economic reasons but discovered opportunities and requirements to project their political influence. What China is doing is not novel, but it fuels growing anxiety in neighboring countries that see Chinese actions and attitudes as indicators of intention to achieve regional hegemony or more. This leads to worry not only about China's aspirations but also about how China's actions will affect US engagement in the region and the possibility that competition with the United States will intensify in ways adverse to their own interests. In response, countries hedge against uncertainty by seeking ways to counterbalance and constrain China.

China's economic influence in many countries in the Global South has been rising. This rise has brought China a set of challenges including loan delinquencies and increasing security risks to its personnel and property overseas. Beijing has begun to experiment with different solutions to these problems, such as building multilateral financial institutions to mediate its lending and recruiting international mercenaries to protect its overseas interests. But as others have learned, there are no easy solutions to these challenges and there is little reason to judge that China will succeed where others have stumbled. China is still far from becoming a hegemonic power, even in Asia.

CHAPTER II

Bold Strategy or Irrational Exuberance?

Christine Wong

In a hearing before the US–China Economic and Security Review Commission in January 2018, Jonathan Hillman of the Center for Strategic and International Studies described the Belt and Road Initiative (BRI) as the "best-known, least-understood foreign policy effort underway."[1] This characterization seemed apt at the time. Since the program was launched in late 2013, it has emerged as China's most important foreign policy initiative, one that is tirelessly promoted by the government. A two-day gala Belt and Road Forum in May 2017 in Beijing drew twenty-nine foreign heads of state and representatives from more than one-hundred-thirty countries and seventy international organizations. A year on, the program's goals and approach have become somewhat clearer, but the BRI is still evolving, and its final configuration remains a work in progress.

The idea of a new "Silk Road Economic Belt" was first introduced in September 2013 in Kazakhstan, where Xi Jinping called for regional cooperation in building a network of overland road and rail routes, oil and natural gas pipelines, and other infrastructure projects.[2] The following month, in a speech to the Indonesian Parliament, Xi called for building a "Maritime Silk Road," a maritime equivalent of the Silk Road Economic Belt, with a network of ports and other coastal infrastructure projects. To help finance this "road," Xi proposed the creation of an Asian Infrastructure Investment Bank (AIIB). As outlined in Xi's speeches and elaborated in a 2015 document issued jointly by the National Development and Reform Commission, the Ministry of Foreign Affairs, and Ministry of Commerce, the program is of breathtaking scope that aims to build "multidimensional"

272

networks that link more than sixty countries from Asia to Europe, going through Central Asia, the Middle East and Africa. Together, these countries would comprise almost two-thirds of the world's population and some 40 percent of gross world product. The cost of building this Belt and Road would be enormous, with some estimates running as high as $8 trillion.[3]

At the risk of oversimplification, we can divide the BRI into two components. One is a hard-core economic program that comprises a mammoth set of infrastructural investments. The other is an aspirational regional integration program that calls for cooperation and coordination with the participating countries on several levels including customs, trade, investment and financial policies, cultural and people-to-people exchanges, and so on. Fostering multilateralism has been a big part of the BRI strategy from the outset. Although China proposed the BRI and is spearheading the program, Beijing insists that it will be a joint effort undertaken in partnership with participating countries. In support of this strategy, China led numerous efforts to build multilateral cooperation and new institutions. At the November 2014 APEC meeting in Beijing, for example, China threw its weight behind the idea of a Free Trade Area of the Asia Pacific, helping to win approval for a new "APEC Connectivity Blueprint 2015–2025."[4]

China has also been proactive in other multilateral organizations, including the Regional Comprehensive Economic Partnership, a pan-Asia group of sixteen countries (ASEAN + 6) launched in 2013, where it advocated policy coordination on issues of trade and investment, as well as negotiations on areas such as rules of origin, intellectual property, and electronic commerce.[5] At the same time, China has initiated the creation of new multilateral financial institutions, including the Asian Infrastructure Investment Bank (AIIB), the New Development Bank (previously the BRICS bank), and smaller regional funds such as the China–Central Eastern Europe Fund (CEEF), and has provided generous financial commitments to induce others to join.[6]

The Belt and Road has emerged as a key plank in Xi Jinping's grand foreign policy. It was always a key part of the "China Dream"—intended to return China to its rightful place in the world—and serves clear and extremely important geopolitical objectives in China's development strategy. Because of its size and reach, the BRI will have a very large and important economic and financial impact on the world and has rightly attracted great scholarly and policy interest. This chapter is somewhat narrowly focused on the economic and financial implications of the BRI for the Chinese economy, specifically on assessing whether China has the financial wherewithal to implement this grand scheme. This assessment places the BRI in the long arc of fiscal expansion in China that began at the turn of the century, when a long run of double-digit annual growth of the economy brought government coffers to overflowing. To keep up, government spending ramped up from RMB 1.6 trillion in 2000 to RMB 12.6 trillion in 2012. New programs proliferated, each one bigger and more ambitious than the last. The BRI was conceived in that golden era of high economic growth, rising export surpluses, and high foreign reserve accumulation.

This chapter asks whether the BRI is affordable in the current era of the "new normal," when China's growth rate has fallen a long way from those double-digit levels.[7] By placing the BRI within the context of China's economic and financial development, this chapter provides some material context to anchor the often heated debates on the BRI. Aside from looking at the numbers, I argue that recent reforms in China's fiscal institutions are likely to restrain the tendency of local governments to overreach in jumping on the BRI bandwagon, but they provide no protection against hubris from the top.

The Economic Rationale

The Belt and Road Initiative is a key program in China's economic development strategy. It was included in the Decision of the Third Plenum of the 18th Party Congress in November 2013 as a national strategy, endorsed at the Central Economic Work Conference held a month later, and incorporated into the party constitution in October 2017.[8] The BRI is part of the strategy to find new sources of development to replace the transfer of labor from low-productivity agriculture to higher-productivity industry that drove the "miracle" growth in earlier decades. The end of the unlimited supply of labor coming off the farms led to rapidly rising wages and is driving low-end labor-intensive manufacturing to Vietnam, Cambodia, and elsewhere. Exports, which for a long time had grown at a rate of 20 percent to 25 percent per year, have flattened out since the global financial crisis and even shrank in 2015. Finally, while building infrastructure has been a big contributor to—and sometimes served as the main driver of—growth over the past decade, China has reached saturation level for many types of infrastructure, especially housing and transport. Moreover, the high leverage level in the economy is forcing curtailment of domestic investment. To sustain high growth, China must revamp its economic model and find new drivers.

The BRI contributes to this paradigm shift in several ways. First, it is designed to open new markets. Almost immediately, the BRI project will create new demand for transport and construction equipment, know-how, and logistics services, and these will facilitate China's transition to higher-value manufacturing and exports and spur innovation. Indeed, after more than two decades of catch-up investment in transport infrastructure, high-speed rail, ports, and logistics facilities, China has honed a competitive advantage in these industries and is a world leader in high-speed rail technology. The transport infrastructure networks at the heart of the BRI are tailor-made for China's new comparative advantages. Improved connectivity and reduced transport costs from the networks will spur trade. They have already turned China into the leading exporter to many countries in Central Asia and the Middle East, and it is fast gaining ground in Eastern Europe. Rail service to Tehran since 2016 has delivered Chinese-made clothes, bags, and shoes via Kazakhstan and Turkmenistan.[9] At the BRI Forum, Xi Jinping said that total trade between China and the Belt and Road countries exceeded $3 trillion in 2014–16.[10]

The BRI initiative is well timed for China's structural transformation. Just as pressures of rising costs had led Hong Kong, Taiwan, and South Korea to relocate labor-intensive, low-end manufactures offshore to China as they reached upper-middle income levels in the 1980s through 1990s, China is now poised to relocate some labor-intensive and low-end manufacturing to poorer countries in Southeast and Central Asia to maintain cost competitiveness. In addition, as China aims to achieve higher-quality, greener growth in the twenty-first century, officials hope to find markets for plant and equipment from some of its resource- and pollution-intensive industries. Jin Qi, chairwoman of the Silk Road Fund, has argued that moving factories with excess capacity to BRI partner countries helps China reduce the supply glut at home while assisting these less developed countries build their industrial bases, just as China had imported second-hand production lines from unwanted surplus capacity from Germany, Japan, and Taiwan in the 1980s.[11]

The BRI is an integral part of China's regional development strategy. It was adopted at the 2014 Central Economic Work Conference as one of the three prongs of a regional strategy to promote development in China's central and western provinces. Extending highways and rail links to hitherto hard-to-reach regions will turn deep-inland cities into transport hubs and raise their economic potential. For example, the China-Pakistan Economic Corridor will link Kashgar in Xinjiang to the Port of Gwadar, and rail connections to and from Urumqi are already making the city the gateway to Central Asia. Likewise, the economic corridors to South and Southeast Asia will link Yunnan and Guangxi to overseas markets. The BRI will also provide an alternative route for China's energy and raw material supplies, reducing its current heavy reliance on shipping through the Malacca straits and the South China Sea.

This recitation of the economic logic of the Belt and Road for China would be incomplete without a discussion of the genesis of the idea in the particular historical milieu in the early part of the twenty-first century, when China experienced a period of extraordinary economic growth and expansion of government. From 2000 to 2012, GDP grew at a rate of 13.9 percent per annum in real terms, and government revenues grew at a rate of 21.8 percent per annum in nominal terms (and 18.6 percent per annum in constant prices). Figure 11.1 shows the amount of "fiscal space" provided by the rapid revenue growth that accrued to the central government (i.e., the discretionary, unencumbered revenues at the central government's disposal).[12] This amount was RMB 4.39 trillion ($704.4 billion) in 2015. Needless to say, such budget surpluses can be emboldening.

During the administration of Hu Jintao and Wen Jiabao (2002–12), spending on social services increased rapidly under the call to build a Harmonious Society. New programs proliferated, each one bigger and more ambitious—the free basic education program provided schooling for 140 million children, the rural cooperative health insurance scheme covered more than 800 million rural residents, and the urban and rural residents' basic pension schemes provide coverage for everyone not already under workplace programs—completing the framework for a basic social welfare system, albeit at low and uneven levels of provision.

China also undertook massive investments in infrastructure, building expressways, airports, high-speed rail lines, ports, and logistics facilities at unprecedented rates. The rate of investment in infrastructure rose from 5–6 percent of GDP in the mid-1990s to 12–14 percent during the 2000s, averaging 8.5 percent per annum from 1992 to 2011, more than twice the average

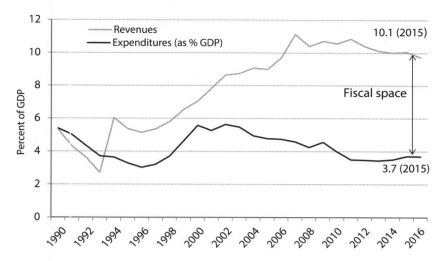

FIGURE 11.1. Central government revenues and expenditures.
SOURCE: National Bureau of Statistics, China Statistical Yearbooks, various years.

for OECD countries.[13] The results can be seen everywhere. From a starting point of only 147 kilometers of expressways in 1988, China had built 68,000 kilometers by 2011, and has added 10,000 kilometers each year since then to reach 130,000 kilometers today.[14] The pace of building high-speed rail lines has been even more astonishing. China has 25,000 kilometers of lines linking twenty-nine of the thirty-one provinces and accounts for two-thirds of the world's high-speed rail lines.[15]

These investments coincided with China's rapid growth and ascent to world-leader status as a manufacturing and exporting power. They also propelled China to a top-tier ranking in the World Bank's logistics performance index (LPI), joining an exclusive group comprised almost entirely of high-income countries.[16] This experience undoubtedly strengthened the belief among Chinese planners in the power of infrastructural investments. In the meantime, strong export growth and persistent current account surpluses after China's accession to the World Trade Organization in 2001 dramatically increased foreign exchange reserves (Figure 11.2). The growth of reserves was partly the result of currency controls which, until they were loosened starting around 2006, required the central bank to purchase dollars to sterilize the effect of the current account surpluses on the

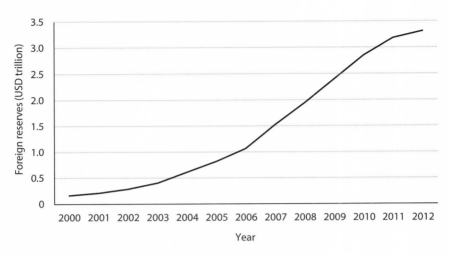

FIGURE 11.2. China's foreign reserves (in US$billion).

SOURCE: People's Bank of China time series data of China's foreign exchange reserves, http://www.safe.gov.cn/.

yuan–dollar exchange rate.[17] The secular increase in foreign reserves gave rise to the "going out" policy that encourages Chinese firms and the government itself to invest outside of China to earn better returns than attainable by holding US Treasury bonds.[18] The "going out" push grew even stronger after the global financial crisis in 2008, when the resultant loose monetary policies in the United States and Europe drove interest rates to near zero, and the People's Bank ran heavy losses on its dollar holdings.

Under conditions of financial repression and given China's high savings rates and the central bank's sterilization operations, banks were flooded with cheap money and eager to lend. As a result, financial conditions at the end of the 2000–12 period were extremely favorable for launching the BRI, providing a strong reinforcement for China's need to find new growth drivers. Add to that the almost-fundamentalist belief in the power of infrastructure among Chinese leaders, and the BRI was not only a natural next step in China's development, but also in this mind-set a bold and innovative foreign policy to win hearts and minds in China's neighborhood.

The Finances

One of the big unknowns about the Belt and Road Initiative is the scale of investment, especially Chinese investment. Headline numbers look huge.

In the course of 2014–15 alone, China committed a quarter-trillion US dollars to creating financial entities dedicated to the BRI. This included $100 billion for the AIIB, another $100 billion for the New Development Bank (NDB), and $40 billion for its Silk Road Fund. During the Belt and Road Forum held in May 2017, Xi pledged to put an additional RMB 100 billion ($14.5 billion) into the Silk Road Fund and said the China Development Bank and Export–Import Bank would be setting up new lending schemes of RMB 250 billion ($36.2 billion) and RMB 130 billion ($18.8 billion), respectively, for Belt and Road projects.[19] Elsewhere, the words "trillion dollars" are frequently mentioned as the government's promised injection.[20]

How large is China's investment in the BRI? The government's statements have been notably restrained in estimating the government's input to date. The 2015 vision statement repeatedly emphasized cooperation and coordination in implementation, with the strong implication that projects should be jointly funded. Elsewhere, the government and its advisers have urged Chinese entities not to get ahead of their partners. The National Development and Reform Commission (NDRC), the lead coordinating agency for the BRI, reported in November 2017 that "more than $50 billion" has been invested since the 2013 launch, with nearly two thousand projects under way.[21] The Ministry of Commerce reported that investments have totalled "almost $30 billion in 2015–2016"—also at a pace of about $15 billion per year. The quarter-trillion-dollar commitments to AIIB, the NDB, and the Silk Road Fund are long-term promises. Paid-in capital has been much more modest—$20 billion for AIIB and $10 billion for the NDB, stretched out over five years or more.[22] These numbers are tiny in the context of China's $13.5 trillion economy and nearly $6 trillion annual investment.

Instead, it has become clear that the massive investments in the BRI will come overwhelmingly from the Chinese financial sector. Under China's preferred model of state-to-state relations, the lending is led by the two policy banks—the China Development Bank and the Chinese Export–Import Bank. Scholars Gregory Chin and Kevin Gallagher describe a two-step coordinated process whereby an agreement is first drawn up between the Chinese and host country political leaders on a list of priority development projects for the host country.[23] Leaning on the model commonly used in China, the Chinese policy banks then provide a sizable loan to cover the core financing for a bundle of projects.[24] In coordination, Chinese commercial banks then encourage the host government to solicit bids for individual projects, often providing cofinancing and using Chinese engineering and construction firms as well as suppliers for materials needed.

Table 11.1 presents available information on the cumulative investments and overseas lending to BRI projects financed by Chinese banks. Together they total $686 billion. These numbers must be interpreted with caution, however. The reports do not make clear when the loans were made and may include projects that predate 2013 and perhaps even only remotely related to the Belt and Road (see chapter 10 by Ho-fung Hung, this volume). Since its inception, the concept of the BRI has been expanded and stretched to draw in even a polar "silk road." Nevertheless, the size of these numbers points to a potential source of risk that merits watching.

Principal Sources of Financial Risks

There are two main sources of financial risk of the BRI for the Chinese economy. First, a program that earlier looked sensible may no longer be affordable in the current, less buoyant economic environment, when the consensus view is that China has reached a phase of development where its growth rate will be much slower. The government has coined the term "new normal" to characterise this era, whose growth rate they peg optimistically at 6 percent to 6.5 percent (see chapter 3 by Barry Naughton and chapter 8 by Hongbin Li et al., this volume). Second, in China's highly fragmented and decentralized economic system, the government has often struggled to rein in investment drives once they have been unleashed, as happened to the 2008 fiscal stimulus program. In that episode the program ballooned from an original target of RMB 4 trillion to more than RMB 10 trillion, and a decade later local governments are still digging out from under the mountain of debt they ran up (see chapter by Jean C. Oi, this volume).[25]

IS THE BRI STILL VIABLE UNDER THE NEW NORMAL?

China's growth rate has been slowing since 2010, when the 2008 fiscal stimulus had run its course. This has had immediate and significant effects on government revenues, as shown in Figure 11.3. Not only has revenue growth fallen, so also has buoyancy, while each percentage growth in GDP had led to an average of 1.35 percent growth in revenue during 2000–12; during 2012–17 revenue growth was just 0.86 percent.[26] In 2016 revenues grew by

TABLE 11.1 Cumulative investment and lending overseas by Chinese banks

Date	Institution	Description	US$ billion
March 2018	China Export–Import Bank	More than 1,200 projects in more than 50 BRI countries.	125.0
2018	China Development Bank	Has built a project pipeline of more than 900 projects in 60 countries with investments totaling more than US$890 billion; completed the planning of 22 major BRI projects and promoted the implementation of major projects including a refinery upgrade in Kazakhstan and a credit line for the Ministry of Finance of Oman in 2017.	274.5
2017	Bank of China	500 overseas projects in 23 BRI countries with total loans amounting to around $100 billion and total investment of $460+ billion, and have provided intent to grant credit support of more than $103 billion.	100.0
2017	Industrial and Commercial Bank of China	Has supported 358 BRI projects.	94.5
end of June 2017	China Construction Bank	Supported 50 projects in 18 countries in the BRI region. Committed to future loans of $110 billion for more than 200 projects in 48 countries.	9.8
end of June 2018	Agricultural Bank of China	Has supported BRI projects in 45 countries with total loans amounting to $12.6 billion.	12.6
end of September 2017	Bank of Communications	Through domestic insurance loans and overseas syndicates, have loaned cumulatively 400 billion yuan to support 37 key projects in the BRI region.	61.5
through May 2017	Silk Road Fund	Has supported 15 BRI projects with total investments amounting to $6 billion. Has invested another $2 billion to set up a China-Kazakhstan production capacity cooperation fund.	8.0
		TOTAL REPORTED LENDING TO DATE	685.9

SOURCE: Author's estimates.

just 4.5 percent when GDP grew by 6.7 percent. In 2018 revenues grew by 6.2 percent in nominal terms, again lagging GDP growth.[27]

The budget is also coming under growing pressure as programs introduced over the past decade require continuing funding, and the government's fiscal space has shrunk. Figure 11.4 shows that expenditure growth lagged behind revenue growth during the first half of the period, with rev-

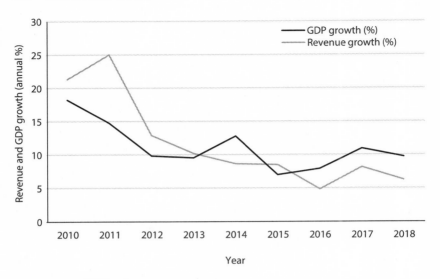

FIGURE 11.3. GDP and revenue growth.
SOURCE: National Bureau of Statistics, China Statistical Yearbooks, various years.

enues growing faster than expenditures in six out of seven years from 2001 to 2007. The reverse was true after 2007, when expenditures grew faster in eight of the eleven years to 2017. In 2019 revenues can be expected to grow even more slowly as the government rolls out big tax cuts to try to reverse the economic slowdown caused by the Trump trade war.

Going forward, China will face intense pressures to further increase many expenditures. For example, even though China raised budgetary spending on education and health at an extraordinary rate of 24 percent per annum during 2000 through 2014, at 4 percent and 6 percent of GDP, China remains below average levels for middle-income countries in both sectors. As China strives to become an innovative economy, it will need to further improve investments in human capital (see chapter by Li et al., this volume). Other expenditure needs include investments in diplomacy and military support to the country's rapidly growing global footprint (see chapter 13 by Karl Eikenberry, this volume). In other words, the large "fiscal space" that existed in the high-growth period is gone—filled up with expenditures from new programs introduced during the Hu-Wen era. In fact, given that expenditures grew by 16.9 percent per annum through the past decade (2007–17), the government will struggle

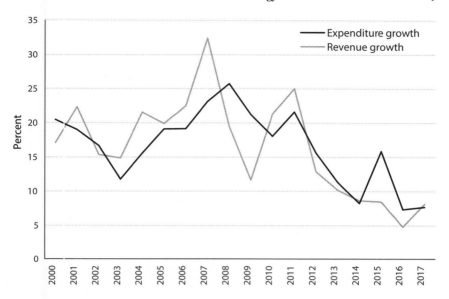

FIGURE 11.4. Revenue and expenditure growth.

SOURCE: National Bureau of Statistics, China Statistical Yearbooks, various years.

to rein them back to the more affordable single-digit rates that the "new normal" will require.

Foreign currency reserves have also come under pressure in recent years. After climbing to $3.8 trillion in 2013–14, they declined by $500 billion in 2015 and another $320 billion in 2016. This trend was stemmed in 2017, but only with the aid of strict capital controls. The changed circumstances point to a need for greater caution in proceeding with the BRI but are far from making the program unaffordable. China is now a $13.5 trillion economy that has $3 trillion in foreign reserves and a healthy current account balance. Its capacity to invest is enormous; the financial sector has assets of more than RMB 300 trillion, and domestic investments are some RMB 35 trillion ($5 trillion) per year.[28] It can easily absorb $10 billion to $15 billion per year investment in the BRI, or even $100 billion.

CAN DECENTRALIZED INVESTMENTS BE CONTAINED?

The Achilles' heel of Chinese macroeconomic management is the tendency toward overinvestment by decentralized agents—not just local governments but also state-owned enterprises (SOEs) and even central government ministries. Throughout the history of the People's Republic, China has struggled to manage its sprawling, fragmented, and decentralized structure of government. Since the 1950s, it has gone through repeated cycles of centralization–decentralization in a search for the right balance between maintaining control and encouraging local initiative. One scholar has called this the "groundhog day" cycle, where "high investment supported by expansionary policy drives growth; inflation follows after [sic] lag; policy is tightened; growth drops away, but inflation is still high; more tightening; inflation falls at last, but growth falls away more than desired at the same time; policy is shifted from tight to expansionary; again, led by investment, growth rebounds," and the whole cycle starts again.[29]

The main source of financial risk for the BRI today is that these decentralized agents can push the program to overextend China's finances. When the government called on all provinces and cities to make plans to support the BRI, some commentators warned that it risked opening the door to a repeat of the fiasco during the 2008 fiscal stimulus program, when local governments responded to the same call with frenzied enthusiasm. In that episode local governments rushed to support the central government's stimulus plan by declaring huge investments of their own. One report noted that within less than a month of the announcement of the stimulus package, provinces had proposed a combined total of RMB 18 trillion in investment projects. By March 2009, *Caijing* estimated the first eighteen provinces to publicize plans had announced investments worth RMB 25 trillion.[30]

In this round every province has reportedly produced a BRI plan, as did many cities, although not all of them are publically available. Among the most ambitious was a sixty-seven-page "Construction Plan for the Transportation Hub and Silk Road Economic Zone for 2016–2030" presented by Xinjiang. The plan calls for the autonomous region to be transformed into a transport hub for the Silk Road, with Urumqi and Kashgar becoming "comprehensive exchange centers for people, logistics, and information between China, Central and West Asia, and Europe." The plan calls for investments of RMB 1.86 trillion, front-loaded to have RMB 1.4 trillion spent during the 13th Five-Year Plan (2016–20).[31] Henan province issued a plan for developing the "Silk Road in the Air" from Zhengzhou to Luxemburg, with each to become a logistics hub for the Asia-Pacific and Europe-America regions, respectively.[32]

These examples are indeed frothy, but they appear to be the exception. Most plans are more modest and vague. For example, Chengdu's plan calls for building ten industrial parks or trade zones in countries along the Belt and Road and participating in one hundred overseas investment projects with a total value of more than $10 billion by 2018, and to double these figures by 2020.[33] Quanzhou (Fujian) called for making the city a "Pioneer Zone for the 21st Century Maritime Silk Road" and set targets for overseas investments worth $2 billion and attracting foreign direct investment of $3.5 billion to Quanzhou by 2020.[34] The restraint shown in these local plans probably reflect local officials' expectation that overly ambitious plans were unlikely to pass the tough vetting process that has been put in place by recent reforms.[35]

Risks of Exuberance

The Belt and Road Initiative is a bold strategy that has sound economic rationale but substantial risks, both geopolitical and economic. In introducing the BRI, China imposed a coherent vision to what had already been taking place in a piecemeal fashion over the past decade, with Chinese firms (often SOEs) investing in and building infrastructure in Southeast and Central Asia. Recasting these activities in a new framework of collaboration fits neatly into Xi's emerging foreign policy framework and may be seen as China's new pledge of improved behavior or, as one author calls it, "Asian Integration 2.0."[36]

At this stage in its development, China has the technical and financial capacity to implement the BRI and wants to export this expertise. The question is whether the government can manage the program prudently. After undertaking reforms and institution-building in public financial management over the past three years, China is better able to manage the risks than it was a decade ago. But the reforms in fiscal institutions are still works in progress, and local governments are still running ahead of regulators. However, with continuing efforts from the Ministry of Finance, the National Audit Office, and the banking regulators, and with strong reinforcement from the anticorruption campaign, prospects are good that

China will finally be able to build frameworks that can curb the ability of local governments to go off budget for resources.

Although recent reforms have introduced safeguards for managing bottom-up risks, they provide little protection against risks introduced from the top—those imposed by central ministries, large SOEs, and hubris. In the 2008 episode central ministries piled on to take advantage of the stimulus program as an opportunity to grow their portfolios. The most egregious was the Ministry of Railroads. Under then Minister Liu Zhijun, the ministry pushed investments up more than tenfold from 2004 to 2010 by adding lines and increasing the speed of trains. The China Development Bank expanded its portfolio of lending overseas far beyond its mandate, as did the China Exim Bank. The biggest risk today is that the Belt and Road program will be pulled into irrational exuberance by an overly ambitious foreign policy agenda.

CHAPTER 12

All (High-Speed Rail) Roads Lead to China

David M. Lampton

Along China's southern border and in Southeast Asia down to Singapore, something very significant is unfolding. The construction of a high- and conventional-speed railway (HSR) system is further along than most Western observers appreciate. China almost certainly will play the dominant role in its development and hopes to be a major beneficiary of its realization. Over the next two to three decades this development (along with connectivity of all sorts) holds the prospect of transforming the pattern of urban and commercial change across the eight immediately involved countries—(southwestern) China, Laos, Vietnam, Myanmar (Burma), Cambodia, Thailand, Malaysia, and Singapore. Such a transformation would reinforce the process of China's emergence as the economic hub of East and Southeast Asia. Such a development would have strategic implications far beyond the region, affecting the interests of India, Japan, and the United States, among many other nations and peoples.

Although by no means foreordained to be either successful or completed, such development could signal that China will play a role in East and Southeast Asia analogous to that of the United States in North and South America. Whether this is characterized by open integration or becomes a sphere of influence is a portentous uncertainty. Beyond the multifaceted and multistage set of projects, which is the topic of this chapter, is Beijing's broader Belt and Road Initiative (BRI), a massive, multimodal infrastructure-building push consisting of six land and maritime transportation corridors all around China's periphery. If even partially realized, these developments would make China the hub for East and Southeast

Asian economic activity. Examining the Southeast Asia railroad piece of the larger BRI enterprise reveals some of the pitfalls and potentialities of this overall undertaking.

Characterizations of the overall BRI project range from laudatory and self-congratulatory praise for the willingness of the People's Republic of China (PRC) to underwrite much of the cost of badly needed infrastructure construction essential for future growth, to darker imputations and fears of intent to foster neocolonialism that will erode the autonomy of China's neighbors, create dependency, promote an inherently inefficient form of state capitalism, and run counter to the post–World War II liberal order. Regardless of where they fall along this spectrum, these expectations and characterizations make assumptions and predictions about the PRC's current and future capabilities and ascribe intentions to a Chinese system with many simultaneous and often competing inclinations. There is fierce debate in China about the tangible and opportunity costs of the overall BRI endeavor, the wisdom of individual projects, and how the high-speed and other railway (HSR) projects of concern in this chapter should fit into Beijing's overall development priorities.[1]

The need for, and projected cost of, building infrastructure projects, including HSR, are enormous. Proposals to construct an interconnected railway network are not new. Earlier efforts dating back more than a hundred years using much more primitive technology either failed to get off the ground or produced fragmented, partial systems that still exist but were (and remain) very inefficient. One important difference this time is the concatenation of factors that has come together in China in the second decade of the twenty-first century. Those factors include:

- Excess capacity in steel, cement, construction equipment, and other industries germane to the construction of infrastructure; and large numbers of PRC construction workers available to work abroad, though rising wages in China are increasing costs.

- The PRC's experience building its own massive HSR rail grid of four north-south and four east-west trunk lines since the early 2000s and its active program of exporting both HSR and conventional railway systems abroad.

- Large amounts of investment capital representing China's gross domestic savings rate of approximately 46.7 percent of GDP (2017) and the accumulation of foreign exchange from trade that the PRC is reluctant to repatriate for fear of inflation.[2]

- The desire of Chinese state and other enterprises to stash resources and assets outside the country.

- Xi Jinping's endorsement of, and commitment to HSR as evidenced by the incorporation of the BRI into the Party Constitution, as well as his push for a strong state role in forging key industries for the future. HSR is seen as a mechanism for boosting domestic development and forging new, strong export industries.

- China's middle class has become more affluent and cosmopolitan and, like earlier generations of Germans, Japanese, and Americans, appetite for travel has surged. Southeast Asia is a major destination.

Another relevant factor is that Southeast Asia is now much more economically and technologically capable and increasingly urbanized. Its hunger for Chinese tourist revenues is going up, even as its concerns about cultural dilution and economic domination increase. And finally, the West has been, for the most part, less energetically involved in infrastructure building in Southeast Asia in recent decades, with Japan being the principal exception and the United States belatedly showing more interest and commitment to becoming involved.

Should even a portion of the contemplated projects in this railway vision be completed, this development will create opportunities and challenges. Among the challenges will be maintaining regional economic and security balance as well as assuring that the West benefits from the regional growth that likely will be unleashed. Ever-deepening integration between China and its neighbors carries with it not only the possibilities of growth and stability fostered by interdependence, but it also entails risks of cultural, economic, and strategic domination by the PRC. At the same time, we should never underestimate the capacities of small countries to push back against larger neighbors.

The Plan in Detail and Context

An early harbinger of this strategy of regional economic integration was unveiled by Cui Liru, then president of the China Institutes of

Contemporary International Relations (CICIR), an intelligence arm of the Chinese state and party, two years before Xi Jinping announced in 2013 his vision of what is now the BRI. Cui called for the following:

> For China, as an Asian nation, an Asian strategy should be the top priority and centerpiece of its diplomacy. As this vast continent is now fast becoming the nascent geopolitical and geo-economic center, we should make vigorous efforts to usher in a new China-Asia epoch, displaying fully the nation's development advantages and tapping the potential of its surrounding regions. We need to match the functioning of the state with that of the market and boost natural cooperation between the economies of our border regions and those of neighboring states.[3]

The BRI, initially called One Belt, One Road (OBOR), is an animating, albeit "fuzzy" vision that places China at the hub of several economic and transportation corridors linking the PRC to Europe, Russia, Central Asia, South Asia, and Southeast Asia.[4] The vision includes power plants, electricity grids, energy pipelines, aviation and port facilities, and communications pathways of many kinds. Constructing the constituent projects is projected to fuel China's continued growth because the PRC will supply much of the labor, materials, and equipment. The projects may or may not make money initially, but China's state-owned enterprises (SOEs) will win market share and gain strength by competing with the best international firms in Canada, France, Germany, Italy, Japan, the Republic of Korea, and the United States. In the long run, the PRC is projected to become a supplier of choice, if not necessity. Such projections are reinforced by pressure from the fact that China's excess metallurgical and building materials production capacity creates enormous incentives to export overproduction (even if below "true" production costs—that is "dumping"). The "China price" reflected in the price of consumer goods at Walmart is also a factor in the prices of China's export of infrastructure, as when an arguably private firm like Huawei offers telecommunications infrastructure systems at 70 percent less than Western competitors.[5]

Fleshing out this fuzzy vision is to be achieved through the dynamic interplay of China's provinces, economic entities, and central bureaucracies, with periodic positive or negative intervention by China's highest authorities, usually in the form of cash, policy, and diplomatic backing. To some extent, the geostrategic and economic goals of the central government are supplemented by the desire of cash-rich firms, agencies, and individuals to use outward investment as a way to productively stash money abroad as a hedge against uncertainty at home.[6]

China's massive BRI effort to build infrastructure around the world is well under way. Among the numerous global projects that Beijing is contemplating and already undertaking under the BRI signboard are projects that would link Singapore to Southwest China's Yunnan province—Kunming Municipality. Once completed, Singapore and the Southeast Asian countries to its north would feed into the PRC's already extensive HSR system—-25,000 kilometers of track in 2017 (anticipated to be 30,000 kilometers by 2025).[7] The PRC's HSR track mileage as of 2017 already was more than the rest of the world's combined. The overall vision embraces three different lines running from Kunming to Bangkok, Thailand, whereupon they would connect to a single line shooting down the Malay Peninsula to Singapore via Kuala Lumpur. The Central Line is well under way in Laos, and construction is beginning in Thailand.[8]

Note that this rail network vision was not China's, much less Chinese leader Xi Jinping's. Rather, it had its origins in the dreams and constructions of earlier colonialists (the French and British), invaders (the Japanese), still later independent governments in the region (Malaysia), and particularly the Association of Southeast Asian Nations (ASEAN) and the Asian Development Bank (ADB)—a Pan Asian railway system was the enduring core idea.[9] Rather, than create a new vision, Beijing has incorporated a preexisting idea for rail interconnectivity into its BRI rubric. More than a rhetorical hunting license for China's state, quasi-state, and arguably private firms to go in search of foreign contracts, the BRI, including the PRC's overall infrastructure and rail-building effort in Southeast Asia, became institutionalized in the Chinese Communist Party Constitution as a signature initiative of Xi Jinping ("We should pursue the Belt and Road Initiative as a priority").[10] This initiative was further undergirded by a powerful domestic coalition of local, provincial, and national-level entities as a long-term program with economic and geostrategic rationales.

The full weight of the PRC's policy banks and new financial institutions such as the Asian Infrastructure Investment Bank (AIIB), which opened for business in January 2016, have been put behind this effort. State firms are supporters who see enormous growth opportunities beyond China's borders (as China's domestic growth rate slows) and look to Beijing's coffers to finance substantial chunks of project costs abroad, thereby helping state-owned enterprise balance sheets even if they pile up mountains of debt elsewhere in China's already stressed financial system.

Beijing's goal is to make PRC firms and state enterprises dominant in both winning contracts and in the underlying technologies and industries themselves. Beijing seeks to make SOEs and consortia of them strong, leading, and permanent competitors in the global economy. General Secretary and President Xi Jinping called for strengthening China's SOEs ("We will support state capital becoming stronger") and wrote the BRI into the party constitution at China's 19th Party Congress in October 2017 as the foundation of his own legitimacy.[11]

A powerful coalition of actors was eager to line up behind HSR: Chinese provinces (often inland, border areas desperate to escape their isolation in a globalizing economy); state-owned enterprises in high-technology fields (such as the China Rail Corporation), large equipment manufacturers, and materials industries; planning agencies such as the National Development and Reform Commission (NDRC); and state policy banks, not least the China Import–Export Bank (China Exim) and the China Development Bank (CDB). Even China's diplomatic establishment is supportive inasmuch as the Ministry of Foreign Affairs (MOFA) system plays an indispensable role in connecting domestic players to counterparts abroad. The BRI, HSR in particular, are tangible symbols of China's global role. China's neighbors salivate over projects offering the prospect of escaping poverty, particularly if the PRC picks up an outsize share of the costs. The BRI and the specific projects discussed in this chapter have powerful champions but also skeptics and outright opponents.

A Grand Debate

The HSR project has powerful champions, but critics (within and outside China) continue to raise questions that underscore risks and tough choices. One set of core issues centers on the fact that the PRC still has enormous domestic needs and confronts significant systemic risks. According to the International Monetary Fund (IMF), for example, the PRC's domestic debt to GDP ratio is reaching worrisome levels, particularly corporate debt. A December 2017 Fund report noted: "Credit growth has outpaced GDP growth, leading to a large credit overhang. The credit-to-GDP ratio is now about 25% above the long-term trend, very high by international standards and consistent with a high probability of financial distress."[12]

Awareness of this situation has sparked considerable domestic concern about how far Beijing can and should go in financing hugely expensive projects abroad that would have long payback periods, indeed might never be repaid. Where should the BRI fit on the national priority list, which includes the needs of an aging population and associated issues of retirement financing and health care, domestic poverty reduction, and environmental and climate change issues, not to mention national defense—or just plain fiscal prudence (see chapter 6 by Karen Eggleston and chapter 13 by Karl Eikenberry, this volume)?

A second set of risks and line of criticism stems from the fact that these infrastructure projects require huge upfront outlays of capital by China to partner states generally considered of moderate to high financial and political risk. Should, indeed can, China shoulder these risks? Will the PRC's slowing (but still substantial) domestic economic expansion and the need to shift to a new growth model driven by domestic consumption rather than exports (as Barry Naughton and Andrew G. Walder explain in chapters 2 and 14, respectively) soon make such massive external commitments look unwise? Specific risks in partner countries include insufficient revenues to service the debt (e.g., Venezuela in the wake of the death of Hugo Chavez in 2013); government instability and unforeseen changes in political leadership or foreign policy orientation (e.g., Myanmar, when it turned toward Washington during the Obama administration, or Malaysia when Mahathir was elected and called into question previously agreed upon rail projects in mid-2018); opposition to a single project (e.g., the Myitsone Dam in Myanmar and violence directed at Chinese projects in Pakistan); and mass, popular opposition to China's methods of conducting business, as occurred in Zambia with Michael Sata's election in 2011 (see chapter 10 by Ho-fung Hung, this volume).

Moreover, the PRC's overall effort could trigger backlash elsewhere in the international system among those who perceive an attempt by Beijing to construct an economic network that places itself at the center. China risks being viewed as an actual or aspiring regional hegemon, in effect an updated version of nineteenth- and twentieth-century colonial powers. Such perceptions have, for instance, been voiced in both Laos and Thailand when Beijing asked for breathtaking development rights and right-of-ways in initial railway negotiations. Finally, there is the danger that partners' needs for PRC financing cannot be met by Beijing and spark resentment—appetites aroused that cannot be satisfied. In late 2017 a delegation of which I was a member met with a very senior Chinese economic leader. I asked about China's BRI financing capacity. He replied: "Well, after BRI was announced, it was very welcome by many because it is a global public good and to promote something of this magnitude much financing is needed. For many projects we studied, technology and economics are viable. But, how to ensure sustainable finance? China will think [twice] about entering these projects. To be frank, some proposed projects by some countries are not viable. We are working with them to bring down the risks and make projects sustainable—based on China's own developmental experience."[13]

For the moment, Xi Jinping and his state-sector allies have prevailed in the debate over whether and how to proceed, but the fact that there is debate attests to a clash between two quite different perspectives. One is embraced by those advocating a "long-term point of view." The core idea is: Yes, if one adopts a short-term, cash-flow perspective with market costs attached to capital, many of these infrastructure projects probably will not pay for themselves in the foreseeable future—if ever. But if one considers the future growth this infrastructure catalyzes, China's building of frontier industries for its competitive future, and the geostrategic gains China makes in power projection and transportation diversification (not to mention positive externalities such as fewer cars on roads and the efficient use of executive travel hours), then these BRI projects could be viewed as sound—indeed visionary. Elaboration of this position almost always ends with the Chinese aphorism, "If you want to get rich, build a road." According to this line of reasoning, infrastructure causes growth; construction should not await growth. As one PRC interlocutor put it: "Implementation of those projects over the next three-to five years will be challenging, but if we look at the next twenty to thirty years, implementation will not be an issue. Look at Opening and Reform. If you look at the last forty years, many of those challenges were resolved."[14] I call this the field-of-dreams approach: "build it, and they will come."

From a political-economy perspective, the BRI could take the PRC economy farther from the objective of having the market play a "decisive role in allocating resources" proclaimed at the late 2013 Third Plenum of the 18th Party Congress, though this seems to be a commitment substantially weakened by the subsequent 19th Party Congress in late 2017 and the March 2018 National People's Congress.[15] To those of market-economy bent, the BRI has the smell of "picking technological and economic winners and losers" and ending up with "bridges to nowhere." This is "China's big gamble." Naugthon (chapter 2, this volume) discusses this "gamble" in an economy-wide framework. This is the "grand steerage" that he believes is "deeply problematic." Walder (chapter 14, this volume) explains: "In this context the Belt and Road initiative, hailed within China as a major strategic foray, does not address these core problems, and in some respects, is yet another way to delay reform. However impressive as geopolitical strategy, the initiative is mobilizing capital for projects with little prospect for financial returns in the near-term, and in fact appears to be motivated in part by desire to absorb excess capacity in loss-making state corporations. Further extending the credit boom into financially risky projects, the initiative delays state-sector reform by propping up overcapacity sectors that are already the most in need of restructuring."

Nonetheless, assessing this vision and its constituent projects is difficult. For example, the Asian Development Bank Institute has written that it is challenging to assess the precise growth and other effects of infrastructure projects in general, much less the effects of a very large set of interacting, diverse projects spanning eight countries at quite divergent stages of development, with varied governance challenges.[16] Economic analysis often is insufficient to resolve whether a given project, or set of projects, is wise, feasible, or viable. How is the analyst to define and measure costs and gains, much less balance among them? The underlying decisions are profoundly political.

The contours of the politics underlying the BRI in general, and the rail undertakings specifically, have become progressively clearer after extensive interviews in China with economic planners, companies, banks, academics, nongovernmental organizations (NGOs), government and legislative personnel, and with counterpart agencies and personalities throughout Southeast Asia. The politics of infrastructure in China derives from the interaction of two clusters of actors. Some actors, such as the NDRC, policy banks (e.g., the CDB and China Exim Bank) and officials of heretofore isolated provinces, tend to want central decision-makers to take the long view. They argue that over time everyone is better off with the resulting urbanization, growth in high value-added exports, more energy conservation, and more efficient supply chains born of faster transportation, not to mention the development of tourism.

More commercial, market-driven banks, financial entities, and market-oriented economic reformers stand on the other side of the argument. Those taking this view include competitors for limited infrastructure investment, rising civil society organizations that worry about negative externalities from big projects, and media that thrive on exposing corruption (see Andrew Wedeman's chapter 3, this volume). There is also a nativist "China First" versus internationalist dimension to this debate, with domestically oriented critics asking, "Why build railways in Laos that are subsidized by us when Chinese citizens have great, unmet needs at home?"

There also is another class of actors who are the project suppliers (e.g., Changchun Railway Rolling-Stock Corporation) that don't concern themselves with project consequences, long-term viability, or development success. They want to be assured of getting paid for what they produce and want to produce more of it. With "markets" and "sales" as their energizing goals, these suppliers are probably indifferent as to whether the project is at home or abroad. They will support, indeed lobby for, any project for which they are guaranteed payment. For them, project politics revolve around the willingness of China's central government to guarantee payment and/or subsidize potentially loss-making contracts. Beijing seeks to keep national growth going at a rapid clip and develop industries of the future (e.g., HSR). Considering that raw materials suppliers (steel, aluminum, and cement) have a surfeit of domestic production and are desperate to sell their stockpiles, and that local politicians try to keep employment levels up and break their geographic isolation, one sees a powerful coalition that favors taking the long view. Milton and Rose Friedman's 1979 classic, *Free to Choose*, identifies the characteristics of responsible and reckless spenders.[17] One who spends one's own money on oneself tends to be most careful. One who spends other people's money on other people tends to be least prudent. These actors in China who spend from central coffers are in the latter category.

HSR Projects in Southeast Asia

The somewhat more advanced status of HSR and other projects in Southeast Asia has revealed a number of challenges that make them useful to examine in some detail. Anticipating what could happen with respect to other BRI undertakings and lessons learned in Southeast Asia might influence thinking in China and partners elsewhere. This chapter examines current and potential construction of three interlinked, relatively high-speed, modern, standard-gauge (1.435 meter) railways radiating from a hub in Kunming, China, and ending in Singapore. The lines traverse three different (not yet entirely fixed) routes (Map 12.1).

Notionally the Western Line would go through Myanmar (via Mandalay) to Bangkok. The Central Line, originating in Kunming, runs through Laos, going from Boten (on the Lao side of the Chinese border with Yunnan province), via Luang Prabang, to Vientiane (Thanaleng). After crossing the Mekong River at Nong Khai, it would continue on to Bangkok. The Eastern Line would go through Vietnam (Hanoi and Ho Chi Minh City) and Cambodia (via Phnom Penh) before reaching Bangkok and heading south to Singapore along a common trunk shared by all three lines south of Bangkok. I focus on the Central Line here because it already is under construction and because Chinese discussions with Vietnam, Cambodia, and Myanmar are less advanced and more problematic. Among other reasons progress has been slower on the Western and Eastern pathways is that these three prospective partner countries are waiting to see how things develop along the Central Line and with respect to other projects they already are undertaking (or may undertake) with Beijing.

All three lines are nearing completion on the Chinese side of the border and will connect to China's nationwide HSR system. As of 2017, the Central Line segment from Boten to Vientiane (Thanaleng), Laos, was well under way, with multiple Chinese construction brigades working at multiple sites simultaneously. This segment almost certainly will reach the Thai border by 2022.[18] About 70 percent of the line will be through tunnels burrowed in karst formations and on bridges spanning many canyons, rivers, and streams.[19] Discussions with Thailand about construction of a standard-gauge (1.435-meter) line between Bangkok and the Thai–Laotian border at Nong Khai are well advanced. A formal groundbreaking ceremony for the overall project occurred on Christmas Day 2017.[20] The potential route of the 250 kilometers per hour HSR train already had been reserved within the preexisting rail right-of-way owned by the State Railway of Thailand and a 3.5 kilometer-long test segment has been completed. As of 2017, Thailand was also double-tracking its preexisting 1-meter gauge, single-track line

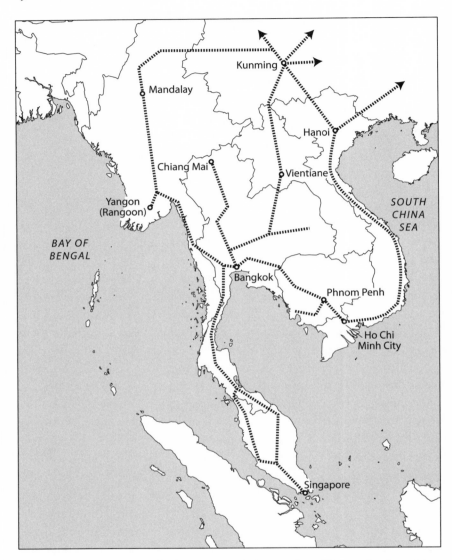

MAP 12.1. The broad vision of rail connectivity linking southern China to Southeast Asia.

SOURCE: Patricia Leong, "China to Build High Speed Railway to Southeast Asia—Asia Briefing," January 23, 2014, http://www.asiabriefing.com/news/2014/01/china-build-high-speed-railway-southeast-asia/.

along the entire route to be used for slower passenger traffic and freight. And Singapore and Malaysia had agreed upon a standard-gauge (1.435-meter) line from Singapore to Kuala Lumpur at the other end of the line(s) from China, with Kuala Lumpur and Singapore having issued a joint tender on December 20, 2017, just five days before Thailand had its groundbreaking.[21] I say "had agreed" because the unanticipated outcome of the Malaysian election of mid-2018 produced a new government under Tun Dr. Mahathir Mohamad, who suspended railway and other projects pending renegotiation with Beijing. Beyond this, significant questions remain. What will happen from Kuala Lumpur north to the Thai border, and what is to happen in southern Thailand, an area currently rife with unrest?

Although there are many obstacles to overcome and details to be worked out concerning these interlinked projects on the Central Line, and the prospects for the Eastern and Western Lines are more uncertain than those for the Central Line, I believe that observers will be surprised by the speed of progress. The completion of each segment makes the next segment more valuable; the Laos segment (to be completed first) was the most financially problematic piece of the entire undertaking. Each of these three Kunming-to-Singapore lines would be longer than the Transcontinental Railway that transformed America, by knitting its coasts together, driving agricultural marketization and urbanization across America's midriff, and making the United States a Pacific power. In his classic study on the building of the Transcontinental Railroad in the United States, Stephen E. Ambrose catalogued the messy, corrupt, problem-plagued, violent process of its construction by concluding that despite all the problems, uncertainties, and missteps during its creation, from the vantage point of a few decades after the project's completion, no one doubted that the undertaking had been transformative.[22] That also must be counted as a field-of-dreams project.

In fact, the PRC's first encounter with the dream of rail connectivity between China and its Southeast Asian neighbors was in the 1990s, when Mahathir, in his first stint as Malaysian prime minister, proposed a rail connectivity vision to Zhu Rongji, China's premier. In December 1995 the Fifth ASEAN Summit called for completion by 2015 of the Singapore–Kunming Rail Line (SKRL), a flagship project that covered "several routes through Singapore-Malaysia, Thailand–Cambodia–Vietnam–China (Kunming) and spur lines in Thailand-Myanmar, and Thailand-Lao PDR

[People's Democratic Republic]."[23] However, China was not in a position to participate in such an effort until well into the 2000s. Until then it lacked the capital, the technology, a suitable vision, or a powerful champion. In June 2016 then former Prime Minister Mahathir recounted: "Zhu Rongji showed interest but China was not that economically capable at that time, not that rich. He was interested, but China could not afford it at that time; now they have the money."[24]

ASEAN in 2010 put forth its own connectivity plan, and the Asian Development Bank Institute recently published *Connecting Asia: Infrastructure for Integrating South and Southeast Asia*. As demonstrated by these proposals, countries beyond China (such as Japan) will play, indeed are playing, a role. Southeast Asian nations already seek to balance north–south dependence on China by east-west connectivity (i.e., linking India to Vietnam, through Myanmar, Thailand, Laos, and Cambodia). Nonetheless, China likely will be the dominant player.

In this set of actual and envisioned rail projects linking China and Southeast Asia, the PRC is aligning itself with a preexisting regional vision and negotiating country-by-country to build segments of what presumably will become an integrated network. This will occur through serial bilateral negotiations with each negotiation framed by those concluded previously. Regime changes and/or other political, economic, and natural calamities are likely to occur as the projects evolve, and they almost certainly will affect the precise routes selected and the order in which they are constructed as well as the distribution of costs and benefits. There is a broad vision, but the precise shape of the eventual system and the process by which it is realized will emerge only gradually from the interplay of events and interests over of the course of innumerable negotiations. China's own political and economic development will be a key determinant of what actually happens. The three railway routes discussed here require negotiations involving eight national-level bargainers at very different levels of socioeconomic development. All have different governing systems, histories, and cultures. Some have unresolved territorial disputes that may complicate negotiations. In addition, each country has a vast and diverse array of self-interested companies, local actors, civic organizations, political parties, and governmental bureaucracies—each of the proposed railway lines must traverse multiple local jurisdictions, some of which are unstable. That there will be a protracted series of negotiations is inevitable.

In China alone, multiple actors (champions) clamor and compete to shape Beijing's approach to the projects. Impetus for many specific projects and the larger vision comes from China's province-level units bordering or near to Southeast Asia (Yunnan, Sichuan, Guizhou, and Guangxi in particular) who seek to escape their geographic, economic, cultural, and trade isolation. It is not the case—as some have argued— that Beijing is coercing provinces bordering Southeast Asia into coughing up resources for grandiose central government plans in which they have no interest. Sometimes, it is precisely the reverse, with desperate localities scrambling to raise enough money to persuade the center to support the locally championed project. They use Xi Jinping's BRI vision to legitimate their parochial efforts and to persuade Beijing to allocate national resources to their pet projects. In some cases, province-level units have made commitments to foreign parties that Beijing then had to rein-in or bail out. Guangdong's relations with Malacca City in Malaysia are a good example of a circumstance in which the city dealt directly with Guangdong, but then "Beijing was not happy to be cut out and [later] forced Guangdong to seek Beijing's blessing afterwards."[25] In the case of ties with Malaysia, for instance, clan organizations and ancestral links to Fujian, Guangdong, and Hainan also play roles. Interest groups, broadly defined, are no small part of the story.

One of the big questions is whether China can successfully conclude a protracted series of negotiations with so many neighbors, all of which want the economic benefits of linkage to China but remain fearful of PRC power and cultural domination. Whatever emerges, it will transform the nature of China–Southeast Asian integration and likely make China progressively more central to the region's economic, political, and diplomatic life.

Strategic Ambivalence

China's neighbors in Southeast Asia have mixed feelings about the rail projects being promoted by Beijing. The nature and degree of ambivalence varies by country, time, and specific project. Vietnam, Laos, and Myanmar in particular face the dilemma of either playing ball with the Chinese or finding that Beijing can make deals with neighbors, leaving them cut off from the presumably expanding economic flows around them. However, their fear of PRC domination dampens their ardor. As Cui Liru of China's CICIR put it in 2011: "In the face of a rising China, Asian nations, especially neighboring nations, are both hopeful of favors and worried about China's intentions."[26]

Hanoi has deferred decision about rail lines down Vietnam's coast by beginning to construct east–west links (highway and rail) that will intersect the Chinese Central Line that will soon cross Laos from north to south.[27] In one conversation with Vietnamese experts, they expressed anxiety about becoming too closely tied into China but acknowledged that they did not wish to become separated from what promised to be the growing economic and human flows that might bypass their country. These experts seemingly concluded that they had no choice but to find a way to connect to the Chinese project. The question is *how*, not *whether*.

The threat of being bypassed was made clear in the case of Laos when the Chinese, in paraphrase, told Vientiane: "If you don't cooperate on the Central Line (from Boten to Luang Prabang and on to Vientiane), we can move to the west of you through Myanmar (or perhaps to the east through Vietnam), leaving you perpetually landlocked, isolated, and poor."[28] Vientiane had to decide whether it wanted to stay poor or run the risks of assuming heavy debt and agreeing to onerous arrangements in the case of loan default. The Lao PDR government chose debt over isolation and perpetual poverty. As one very senior Lao official put it in mid-2017:

> "As you know we are in the middle, a landlocked country. Others have better opportunity. Cambodia has sea; they have railways. Thailand also has good infrastructure. But for us, we don't have good infrastructure. For us, if we don't take the steps [i.e., agree to China's loan terms for the rail line] we will lose the opportunity to connect to China, Vietnam, Thailand, Malaysia, and Singapore." The research indicates that the closest route from China to Southeast Asia is through Laos; but if we are not ready, then we will lose the opportunity. "We need to take the decision, whether we will accept or not to accept. The [Lao] government thinks [that] if we don't accept, then we will lose the opportunity. [If we don't accept] we won't have any debt. But then we will [continue to] be poor like this." "We must try to manage," to leverage on our location. We look at Singapore. They are surrounded by sea; no resources, no land. How do they manage to do that? With a big seaport, the ships have to pass Singapore. So we want to take the opportunity, [to leverage our location]. "Our biggest market is China. Through railways from Singapore, Malaysia, and Thailand, we can benefit from them. We can gain from trade and so on. So this is very crucial. " "We know there will be debt. If we don't know how to manage the debt; it is no good. But if we know how to manage the debt, then OK."[29]

The broad terms of agreement between Laos and China were announced and a call for tenders was published in the summer of 2017. A few days later when our research team went to the northern and central parts of the country, it saw that Chinese tunneling and trestle building had already been under way in earnest for some time. The line almost certainly will reach Vientiane by about 2022.

China was able to leverage the possibility of using alternative routes to win agreement from Vientiane. In the sequence of negotiations needed to extend the line all the way to Singapore, each agreement gives China additional leverage in subsequent negotiations. For example, with the railway to the Laos–Thailand border within sight, the benefits to Thailand from hooking up become greater and more certain, in part accounting for Bangkok's late 2017 agreement to move forward. Of course, the Thais also have some leverage over Beijing because the Chinese already have sunk costs in Laos that cannot be fully recovered without continuation of the line southward beyond the Lao-Thai border. For Beijing's investment to pay off, the Thais must agree to have the railway go on to Bangkok. Once the railway is in Bangkok, Malaysia may well find the project more attractive, particularly if China provides more favorable terms to Kuala Lumpur than initially offered. After all, Malaysia had agreed with Singapore to build the line from Singapore to Kuala Lumpur (along with an east–west spur connecting peninsular Malaysia's east and west coasts) but had postponed soliciting bids for the project.

This is a continuous, progressive game in which prior agreements shape the environment and costs and gains for subsequent negotiations. Beijing is not unconstrained, but on balance it gains leverage and experience as one step leads to the next. Moreover, earlier decisions to purchase Chinese technology and systems and adopt Chinese standards tilt the field of future decisions in Beijing's direction. It is this logic that leads most of Southeast Asia to wish to balance the emerging north–south dependency on the PRC by east–west connectivity (India to Vietnam, through Myanmar, Thailand, Cambodia, and Laos). Japan seeks to play a role in building such balanced interconnectivity, wishing to do so for both commercial and strategic reasons. The Asian Development Bank, based in Manila but an institution in which Japan plays a major role, has studied the prospects and modalities for east-west connectivity and has been working closely with India and Thailand to develop specific projects.

It is possible, at least in theory, for the United States to play roles in both east–west and north–south projects, thereby seeking both commercial gain and regional geoeconomic and geopolitical balance. Southeast Asian nations would welcome this to counterbalance China. But the United States Congress and multilateral development banks and agencies in recent years have been reluctant to back infrastructure projects that displace people and have adverse environmental impacts. American citizens wonder why they should finance and build infrastructure in faraway places when they can't easily travel by train from Washington to New York and their highways are crumbling. These attitudes are beginning to change with the adoption of the BUILD Act of 2018 by the US Congress, but it remains to be seen how much money and attention actually will be devoted to the effort.

The wariness of China's neighboring countries stems not simply from their generally less robust negotiating positions, justified anxiety about excessive debt, and desire to achieve strategic balance and freedom of maneuver. They also worry about Beijing's foreign policy and regional behavior. These anxieties amplify the baseline ambivalence, with worries being more prominent among the maritime Southeast Asian states than among states with fewer (or no) maritime issues with Beijing. Singapore, for example, has sought balancers to offset growing Chinese regional power, particularly in the South China Sea and Indian Ocean littoral. Singapore might well prefer that Japan build the rail line from itself to Kuala Lumpur, but with so little of the route's mileage in Singapore, China probably will build most, if not all, of the track mileage—if Beijing wins Malaysia's support and China renegotiates previously agreed-to terms.

This discussion highlights a crucial question: What foreign policy face will China present to its skittish neighbors over time? The PRC clearly sees itself gaining relative strength globally, not to mention regionally. This attitude is seen in authoritative PRC studies of relative comprehensive national strength and in Beijing's statements. In a study titled "China Road and China Dream," Hu Angang, adviser to senior Chinese leaders and a Tsinghua University professor, concludes that by 2020 China will account for 23.2 percent of global scientific and technical strength, compared to America's 17.8 percent. According to Hu, in 2008 the PRC accounted for 13.14 percent of the world's comprehensive national strength, compared to America's 19.69 percent, with the gap closing rapidly. Japan, China's nearest regional competitor, accounted for only 8.51 percent of global comprehensive national strength in 2008 and was slipping.[30] The point is neither that these calculations are accurate nor that the trends he identifies will persist. Rather, this is how Beijing views its current and likely future circumstance. These perceptions shape Beijing's behavior and fuel anxiety among China's smaller southern neighbors.

More specifically, it is hard for Vietnam to muster the political will to become more integrated with the PRC through infrastructure while Beijing and Hanoi confront each other over claims in the South China Sea.[31] To garner the benefits of rail connectivity without depending on China, Vietnam's executive branch opted in December 2009 to get a bid from Japan to build an HSR linking Hanoi and Ho Chi Minh City. But the Vietnamese National Assembly rejected the resulting plan because of its ($56 billion) cost.[32] Anxiety and ambivalence are further compounded by concern about what one Vietnamese analyst described as "Chinese products pouring in. We always have a huge deficit with China."[33]

Hanoi has only a few options: (1) build transport routes west to Laos and connect there without letting the Chinese directly into Vietnam; (2) have Japan play the lead role, although it would take longer and be far more expensive (Japanese quality is perceived as superior); or (3) go with the Chinese and build a line along Vietnam's coast, the construction of which would be cheaper and faster. This latter option would come at the cost of more dependence on the PRC and against the backdrop of Hanoi's unhappy experience with China's construction of the city's light-rail system. So far, the Vietnamese have chosen the first alternative, building routes westward, not letting China in, although they are aware this may be a suboptimal choice economically.

Learning from Experience

Any balanced assessment of China's development of HSR domestically would rate highly how rapidly China has built its system, overcome problems along the way (such as the Wenzhou collision in 2011 that killed forty passengers), and created an extremely safe network with extensive territorial coverage that is becoming a global standard.[34] Almost every competitor or prospective buyer (of either conventional rail or HSR technology) will tell you that if you want speed of construction and low price, the Chinese are hard to beat. Whatever the reliability and quality of construction differentials with Japan, France, Germany, Canada, or others may be (and there have been significant problems), the PRC is closing gaps steadily.[35]

The speed with which China has moved to the international market has been equally impressive. PRC entities have won an HSR contract (that is experiencing challenges) in Indonesia, won contracts to make subway cars for Boston, Los Angeles, and Chicago (where satisfaction seems high), completed a standard-gauge, more conventional railroad in Kenya running from Nairobi to Mombasa, another 460-mile line from Addis Ababa to Djibouti on the Red Sea, and submitted bids in many other areas, including Eastern and Southern Europe.[36] Despite these notable achievements, the many problems encountered during negotiation and implementation have sparked concern on the part of countries with which Beijing is negotiating to build HSR and other rail lines in Southeast Asia. Some of the problems are technological; others have more to do with Beijing's negotiating stance, corruption, and the pulling and hauling among interests within the PRC. There also have been problems during the construction phases, raising questions about how rapidly China is learning from past experiences.

One very big challenge arises from President Xi Jinping's globetrotting pledges of $30 billion to $50 billion for various projects, including high-speed and conventional rail systems. The Chinese negotiators who follow in Xi's wake must convert pledges into real, feasible projects—this is where Xi's promotion campaign and on-the-ground reality collide. Although China has substantial financial resources, it also has technological, financial, and human resource constraints and many competing domestic demands. One Vietnamese interlocutor said: "We are worried that China's resources now are adequate but not sufficient in the future for all Xi's promises."[37] One Chinese promoter of BRI projects came into my office expressing exasperation that his national leaders were promising more than could be delivered; this person was hoping other countries, public-private partnerships, or multilateral organizations would augment resources and assume some of the risk. Perhaps with some exaggeration, the interlocutor put it this way: "So China's capacity is not sufficient. My understanding after traveling in so many countries is the big difficulty is not because of disagreements, but rather too much support [demand] 'TRUST ME.' This is why Xi Jinping and Premier Li Keqiang say, 'Slow down!' 'Implement one by one—we can't promise so much.' Politics is politics and business is business. Total investment from China into Southeast Asia is up 25 percent in 2015 (over 2014)."[38]

This insufficiency of resources is one reason that China pushed for creation of the Asian Infrastructure Investment Bank with broad international support. The politically aroused desire for projects on favorable terms from potential recipients creates demands on Beijing for concessions that negotiators and more commercially minded financial entities in the PRC find difficult to make. The Chinese tried to drive such a hard bargain with the Thais, for instance, that in 2016 Bangkok decided to fund the capital requirements for the Nakhon Ratchasima rail segment entirely themselves.[39]

Laos offers another example of this dynamic. The central HSR line must cross Laos, which at least initially will derive limited benefits from the railway, to connect to the wealthier countries to its north and south. In Vientiane's view it is being asked to pay (assume a debt burden of) about $5.8 billion for construction of rail mileage traversing difficult and scarcely populated terrain that will bring scant benefits to the country's 6.7 million people.[40] Lao officials and ordinary citizens have resisted being saddled with debt disproportionate to their benefit. Vientiane would have liked the Chinese, multilateral financial institutions, and/or regional organizations to pick up much more of the cost, but Beijing has pressed the Lao very hard. As one well-placed Laotian professional put it: "The benefits here are very small [compared to the benefits of other neighboring countries with larger populations]. The World Bank and the Asian Development Bank should be involved."[41]

There are many other issues to be resolved through negotiation, with Beijing acutely aware that every concession made in earlier negotiations establishes a precedent for equal or better treatment in later rounds. For instance, having agreed with Indonesia to charge a relatively low interest rate for the Jakarta–Bandung HSR, Beijing had to deal with demands from Thailand for similar treatment. Every aspect of a project becomes the subject of hard bargaining: the width of the right-of-way to be used for development; development rights along the right-of-way; loan-grant ratios; interest rates; how debt repayment is to be accomplished if revenues fall below forecast; quality of work; whose labor is to be used in what phases of construction; from whom are materials (e.g., cement, steel, and subsystems) to be procured; and last but not least, land acquisition. The Indonesian Air Force, for example, has held up the rail project from Jakarta to Bandung because the proposed route would infringe on an air base and the military has power to resist.[42]

Another big issue is how to handle customs and immigration at border crossings. Other challenges arise from corruption and access to insider information. Chinese financial interests already have invested in land and development rights at the site of the prospective rail station on the outskirts of Kuala Lumpur–Bandar Malaysia.[43] This aroused public criticism and contributed to the surprise outcome of the May 2018 election in Malaysia.[44] Add to this the challenges resulting from the varied rights of localities, a prominent example being the Sultan of Johor in Malaysia. Malaysia is a federation in which localities control the land as well as water and religion. The Sultan controls the land needed for the HSR link from Singapore to northern destinations, and he apparently has used that leverage for all it is worth.[45]

Challenges and Uncertainties

So what are the implications of all this for China's future and the future of the region of which it is part? This chapter suggests both broad and narrow conclusions and highlights key indicators to monitor as we move into an uncertain future. A first conclusion speaks to how analysts might conceptualize cross-national policy implementation. In this case we have a policy implementation process involving eight national-level, and innumerable local, actors. Prior policy implementation studies considered the challenges of implementation within single national jurisdictions.[46] In the era of globalization, implementation involving several national actors should receive increasing attention.

Second, in terms of how to conceptualize the Chinese domestic political process as it pertains to "going abroad," it is a process similar to the one that observers have noted throughout the past decades in China's domestic reform. The center creates a broad policy thrust, "go out" or Belt and Road, provides state enterprises, localities, and central bureaucracies a broad goal and "policy space," and then a period of untrammeled experimentalism follows. In the ensuing period, actors at multiple levels grasp for central resources and policy endorsement, and only later does the center intervene to curb excess, promote order and more uniformity, and reinforce desired outcomes. This process marries the energy of primitive capitalism with state power, focus, and resources. This process embodies all the contradictions inherent in such a marriage. It is messy, has unanticipated outcomes, and is inefficient, but one must acknowledge its successes. This process should not be underestimated. That Beijing has been able to concentrate research energies, acquire (legitimately and otherwise) foreign technology, provide subsidized financing, and mobilize the engineering and construction talent to build a broad, efficient, and safe domestic HSR rail system in less than two decades—from the ground up—is impressive. The effort is even more impressive because it required reengineering domestic bureaucracies and regulatory frameworks and winning support abroad for the PRC's initiatives.

A third conclusion is that, in the case examined in this chapter, Beijing has embraced as its own a set of projects first conceived by distant powers, southern neighbors, and regional and multilateral organizations over a long germination period. With eight national-level players involved to various degrees a progressive negotiating game is unfolding in which each preceding outcome structures future negotiations, with Chinese money, technology, and human resources driving the process. China's border provinces worked to start rail lines to their boundaries with Vietnam, Laos, and Myanmar, in the process lobbying Beijing to support the effort. With these rail lines a fait accompli on the Chinese side of the border, Laotian leaders felt pressure to connect to escape landlocked isolation. With Laos deciding to initiate construction, the Thai military junta did not want to be left behind (or, put positively, Bangkok saw new opportunities) and jumped on board, thereby leaving Myanmar, Vietnam, and Cambodia to ponder what all this means for them. Moreover, the start at the China, Laos, and Thailand end of the Central Line gave impetus to Singaporeans and Malaysians at the southern terminus to move ahead as well, although the surprise election of Mahathir in mid-2018 has reintroduced uncertainties. In short, each prior round of negotiation changes the context in which all the others must subsequently decide and negotiate.

Fourth, if the PRC maintains domestic stability, manages to accelerate innovation, learns from prior missteps, and keeps its commitments aligned with national capabilities (*each of which is a large assumption*), Beijing will make progress that will alter the face of the broader Asian economy and security relationships. China may be making the kind of far-sighted investments today that America made in the nineteenth and twentieth centuries, investments that opened and developed an entire continent and made the United States globally dominant.

Finally, although individually the smaller nations to China's south are no match for the PRC's comprehensive national power, in an interdependent world of linked policy implementation, they have influence. They can seek influence in numbers through regional and other organizations (e.g., ASEAN and ADB), and sometimes they can just say no. To some extent, they also have the capacity to balance the PRC's north-south thrust with the east-west integrative inclinations of India, Japan, Vietnam, and the United States by building compensating connectivity. Its southern neighbors have the capacity to play the commercial appetites of the Chinese off against those of Japanese, Koreans, North Americans, and Europeans. What we see unfolding is a balance of power game played as much with commercial firms as military forces. Middle powers have options.

Speaking to the risks, uncertainties, challenges, and decisions that loom ahead, I focus on six:

- Will China attract more private sector and foreign and multilateral financial participation into these projects, thereby maximizing the incentives to pick financially and politically feasible projects and reduce PRC risks? Some Chinese clearly see this need: "Our view is that the private sector should play a bigger role."[47]

- Will China's own economic development prove able to support this effort, or will we come to see that Beijing committed extravagantly to unwise projects and was unable to sustain them just as PRC growth slowed, its financial system weakened, and its aging population stretched budgets?

- In terms of political risk, will Beijing learn from past errors (technical, political, and diplomatic in character) in project implementation? Will Beijing avoid being seen as a new colonialist?

- Will the PRC increasingly work with international partners, even economic competitors such as Japan, the United States, Canada, Europe, and the Republic of Korea, to construct a system of interconnectivity in which all have a role and stake, rather than one great power making strategic and economic gains at the perceived expense of others? This question applies equally to the United States.

- Will these HSR projects, and BRI more broadly, transform China and its region as America's transcontinental rail project changed the United States? Or do these endeavors represent the union of the unrealistic aspirations of desperately poor places with the quest for power and legacy of a strongman leader building a cult of personality, reinforced by state enterprises, bureaucracies, and planners soaked in planning ideology and cheap money?

- Finally, will the PRC show the diplomatic dexterity required to construct an integrated, multinational project such as this? So far progress is measurable. This notwithstanding, Beijing's ability to do so sometimes is hampered by Han chauvinism ("China is a big country and other countries are small countries and that's just a fact," proclaimed China's foreign minister in Hanoi in 2010). Beijing's growing foreign policy assertiveness, particularly regarding sovereignty claims, has many Southeast Asians on edge. This, along with PRC efforts to divide and marginalize regional organizations such as ASEAN when they stick up for collective Southeast Asian interests, dampens the ardor many (maritime states in particular) feel to cooperate with the ambitious connectivity vision that Beijing embraces and promotes. As one Malaysian legislator put it: "China needs to get back to the basic issue of 'getting diplomacy right.' You have to get your diplomacy right if all of this is to work."[48] If China can construct the diplomatic foundations for these projects, it will have achieved a political and diplomatic feat more complex than the engineering required to build the rail lines themselves.

CHAPTER 13

China's Military Aspirations

Karl Eikenberry

The People's Republic of China's (PRC) economic growth, global engagement, and national aspirations enable and shape the military dimension of its national security strategy. Modernization and economic success have made China more capable and, in many respects, more confident. But they have also made the PRC more ambitious, more interdependent, and more determined to hedge against and deter potential adversaries. The success of Reform and Opening has expanded the scale, scope, and importance of interests that must be defended and, in some cases, advanced by displays of military capabilities and resolve. The People's Liberation Army (PLA) is far more capable today than it has ever been, but China's leaders want even greater capability to protect the country's growing interests from what they see as a dangerous and hostile international environment.

The evolution of Chinese thinking about the country's military requirements follows a familiar pattern. Having "more" means having more to protect because other nations are assumed or assessed to be envious and/or fearful of China's growing power and influence. Skillful diplomacy and economic leverage are usually the instruments of choice for managing external threats, but the efficacy of both is enhanced when backed by a strong military. Moreover, when it comes to deterrence and defense, having the strongest affordable military is always the preferred option. As China looks to the future, it is making decisions now that will shape its military capabilities for decades to come. Force planners will want more advanced weapons and more funding, but the PLA almost certainly will obtain less than it wants because of budgetary constraints and competition for money to pay for education, health care, elder care, and other high-priority programs discussed in this volume. As PRC growth slows, so too will growth of the budget. Whether the military is able to sustain the relatively large share of the budget that it has enjoyed for the past two decades is uncertain.

PRC military strategy, doctrine, and modernization programs are designed to secure China's land borders and maritime frontiers, to advance its foreign policy aims in Asia, and to secure the country's expanding global economic interests. The ways and means it chooses to do so will be shaped by the strategic ambitions and threat perceptions of top leaders, the amount of resources allocated to the military (both a political and an economic choice), and the ability of the PLA to develop forces capable of deterring or prevailing in potential conflicts. What China does will shape the perceptions and actions of other nations. In turn, the PRC's security opportunities and constraints will in large part be determined by the extent to which major competitors cooperate with, hedge against, or confront Beijing; the decisions made by lesser powers on China's periphery to bandwagon or balance; and the nature of the future security architecture in the Indo-Asia-Pacific Region.

China's military buildup was and will be shaped by its unique geopolitical circumstances, but military modernization with Chinese characteristics has much in common with the perceptions, goals, and methods of other major powers. To establish a baseline for assessing what is typical, predictable, and novel about what China is doing, the first part of this chapter looks briefly at the factors that inform the military strategy and force development of "all" major powers and summarizes the modernization of the PLA since the founding of the PRC.[1] Next the chapter looks at the PRC's current national and military strategy goals, and the factors that will be most important in shaping how Beijing elects to achieve its objectives. Those factors are level of strategic ambition and threat perceptions, resource allocation, and force development processes. The chapter concludes with a discussion of how China's dynamic external geopolitical environment will influence PLA strategy and modernization.

Factors Informing Military Strategy and Requirements

The definition of the term "military strategy" varies across nations. Within the US armed forces, a generally accepted definition is "the art and science of employing the armed forces of a nation to secure the objectives of national policy by the application of force, or the threat of force."[2] The Chinese description is similar: "Subordinate to and serving the national strategic goal, China's military strategy is an overarching guidance for blueprinting and directing the building and employment of the country's armed forces."[3]

A military strategy is one component of a larger national security strategy. The relative importance of the military component (compared to economic, social policy, and other components) changes as actual and perceived conditions change. In time of war or when external conditions are perceived as more dangerous, the military component is accorded higher priority. The military component of national strategy influences policies and other measures designed to achieve strategic objectives. Both strategy and implementing policies must consider the interrelationships among ends (goals), ways (methods), and means (resources). Resources constrain options, but force structures and doctrines guiding their use are designed to achieve strategic goals by using the capabilities available. Multiple interrelated factors shape national military strategies. Politically determined national interests and the perception of threats to those interests play major roles, but geography, history, political ideology and norms, and the relative strength of other components of comprehensive state power (i.e., diplomatic, economic, informational, and cultural) are also important. How these elements and considerations shape national and military strategies is a function of leader preferences and the national security decision-making processes.

The transformation of PLA military strategy over the past twenty-five years has been evolutionary but rapid and in accord with economic and technical advances. China's strong and sustained economic growth and increasing dependence on markets, resources, and supply chains in all parts of the world over the past three decades has created interests and equities in Asia and beyond. China's leaders, unsurprisingly, have decided that the PLA must have the capabilities needed to protect these new interests and are allocating the funds required to generate forces with the ability to achieve that goal.[4]

Chinese perceptions of the world and what is required to protect and advance their national interests are also shaped by a victimization narrative that underscores the dangers of military weakness. A key lesson learned from the so-called Century of Humiliation is that weakness invites predation by stronger states.[5] This narrative fuels nationalistic aspirations to build a strong military capable of defending the nation's sovereignty. President Xi Jinping reflected and played to this aspiration in his speech at the Chinese Communist Party's 19th National Congress: "Our army is the people's army; our defense is national defense. [We must] enhance the education on national defense education, [and] consolidate the unity between the military and civilian in order to achieve the Chinese dream of a strong military."[6]

China's historical legacy is intertwined with its geographic destiny. With the longest land border of any country (22,117 kilometers) and largest number of neighbors sharing these borders (fourteen), China's armed forces have faced a daunting set of security challenges in the modern era. The land frontiers vary widely by climate and topography, posing formidable logistic problems for military planners. Since the founding of the PRC in 1949, the PLA has been involved in ground combat with four contiguous states (Korea, India, Vietnam, and Russia [then the Soviet Union]), and still has unresolved territorial disputes with two (India and Bhutan). Four of its neighbors possess nuclear arsenals (Russia, North Korea, India, and Pakistan), and the actual employment of nuclear weapons in a conflict on the Korean Peninsula or in South Asia cannot be ruled out. Two of China's neighbors are afflicted by high levels of intrastate violence (Myanmar and Afghanistan), and four serve as actual or potential sanctuaries for international militant jihadi organizations that could target China (Afghanistan, Pakistan, Tajikistan, and Kyrgyzstan). The persistence of separatist sentiment in Xinjiang and Tibet has further heightened Beijing's anxiety over cross-border security threats in China's western reaches.

In addition, in recent years the PRC has become increasingly assertive in pressing for recognition of its expansive claims in the Western Pacific, its eastern and only maritime frontier. The mutually reinforcing elements of growing economic interests, history (a state-sponsored narrative of Chinese sovereign control of large bodies of blue water over the millennia and foreign invaders precipitating China's Century of Humiliation by advancing from the sea), and growing military capabilities all contribute to the implementation of a more proactive military maritime strategy than one would have imagined possible just three decades ago. These factors are filtered through and further shaped by the strategic policy preferences of Chinese Communist Party (CCP) leaders. China is not unique in this regard. President Ronald Reagan presided over a massive increase in US defense spending in the 1980s aimed at countering the Soviet Union. Vladimir Putin has placed great emphasis on modernizing the Russian armed forces' conventional and nuclear capabilities. Similarly, President Xi Jinping has devoted time, energy, and (above all) state resources to strengthening the PLA, declaring at a 2017 military parade in Inner Mongolia: "Today, we are closer to the goal of the great rejuvenation of the Chinese nation than at any other time in history, and we need to build a strong people's military more than any other time in history."[7]

PLA Military Strategy and Force Modernization since 1949

Changes in PLA doctrine and force modernization priorities since the establishment of the PRC illustrate how the factors mentioned above have influenced the evolution of Chinese military strategy. The military strategic guideline (*junshi zhanlüe zhidao,* 军事战略指导) promulgated by the Central Military Commission (CMC) serves as both the foundation and the compass for PLA military strategy. The PLA's "Glossary of Military Terms" defines the military strategic guideline as the "core and collected embodiment of military strategy."[8] Nine such guidelines have been issued since 1949, the most recent in 2015. Four of these—the 1956, 1980, 1993, and 2015 versions—are regarded as the most consequential in shaping PLA military modernization; the last three are worth briefly reviewing as they offer useful insights into the drivers of Chinese military modernization over the past four decades.[9]

The CMC promulgated the military strategic guideline of 1980 just prior to Deng Xiaoping's 1981–89 tenure as its chairman but after he had redefined the international situation from one in which war was inevitable and imminent to one in which war, though still inevitable, could be deterred for at least two decades.[10] This guideline offered a clear assessment of what was deemed a relatively benign international environment, with the Soviet Union considered the main, though not existential, threat. The derivative military strategy and doctrine—"people's war under modern conditions"—emphasized forward defense (i.e., stopping attackers before they could reach and destroy critical infrastructure and population centers). Its character also reflected the priority Deng and his leadership team placed on rectifying China's economic backwardness, leading to military modernization being accorded the lowest priority in the "Four Modernizations" campaign.[11] The strategy also refocused the PLA on military tasks, though the charge to generate some of its own resources to compensate for modest defense budgets had the perverse effect of spawning corruption within the officer corps, undermining efforts to professionalize the force.[12]

By 1993, China had recovered from the brief period of post-Tiananmen diplomatic isolation and was again enjoying the double-digit growth generally maintained over the previous decade. Stunned by the decisive performance of the US armed forces and their coalition allies during Operation Desert Storm against Iraq in 1991, the CMC issued a new military strategic guideline in 1993. The new guideline set forth a military doctrine of preparing to "win local wars under high-technology conditions" ("*yingde gao jishu tiaozhan xia jubu zhanzheng*," 赢得高技术条件下局部战争). Local war contingencies no longer focused on fighting defensive wars inside of China but on projecting sufficient capability to prevail in conflicts, limited in both time and space, along its border. With China's leaders now having the economic means to apportion more resources to the PLA, beginning in the mid-1990s, annual defense spending increases surpassed 10 percent. The Taiwan Strait crisis of 1995–96 stimulated PLA strategists and planners to further concentrate on scenarios involving US military intervention in the Western Pacific.[13]

Many of the important factors informing military strategy and force development changed dramatically between 1993 and 2015, when the CMC, under Xi Jinping, issued a new military strategic guideline. By then, China had advanced from the seventh or eighth largest economy in the world to the number two position. It had become the world's leading trading nation with the largest number of merchant ships and had moved globally from eighth in annual military expenditures to second, behind only the United States. The current military strategy instructs the PLA to be prepared to "win informationized local wars" ("*daying xinxihua jubu zhanzheng*" 打赢信息化局部战争). This is a qualitative advance over the 2004 military strategic guideline that emphasized "winning local wars under the conditions of informatization" ("*daying xinxihua tiaozhan xia de jubu zhanzheng*" 打赢信息化条件下的局部战争), reflecting growing confidence in China's technical and material capacity to engage in high-end combat with major powers, including the United States.[14]

The 2015 guideline also reflects China's growing maritime and overseas economic interests. It calls for the PLA Navy (PLAN) to change its emphasis from "near seas defense" ("*jin an fangyu*," 近岸防御) to the combination of "near seas defense" and "far seas protection" ("*yuanhai huwei*," 远海护卫).[15] Likewise, the PLA Air Force (PLAAF) is directed "to shift its focus from territorial air defense to both defense and offense, and to build an air-space defense force structure that can meet the requirements of informationized operations."[16] The need to defend expanding global equities is clearly articulated: "With the continuing growth of China's national interests, its national security is more vulnerable to international and regional turmoil, terrorism, piracy, serious natural disasters and epidemics, and the security of overseas interests concerning energy and resources, strategic sea lines of communication (SLOCs), as well as institutions, personnel and assets abroad, has become an imminent issue."[17] As noted, nationalistic aspirations to reclaim China's historical greatness, coupled with concerns over US efforts to counter its rise through the use of "democratic subversion" and strategic counterbalancing, and the uniquely assertive foreign policy associated with President Xi Jinping, also motivate the PRC's more global, forward-looking, expeditionary military strategy.

It is clear that China's military strategy since 1949, and especially since the opening and economic rise of the PRC dating from the late 1970s, has been dynamic and greatly influenced by the variables of threat assessment, Communist Party and state interests, geography, historical experience, the availability of resources for military modernization, and the changing nature of warfare. Each of the strategies adopted uniquely shaped the direction of PLA modernization.

China's National and Military Strategy Goals

This brief summary of inflection points in the evolution of China's military strategy and force modernization brings the story to the present. How might China's national and military goals evolve over the next several decades? This look into the future is based on the logic undergirding the developments summarized above as well as statements of PRC leaders about the dangers they see and what they hope to achieve. Though speculative, this projection provides a useful basis for anticipating the forces and missions envisioned and for identifying challenges that must be overcome in order to build, deploy, and operate those forces.

The Trump administration's 2017 "National Security Strategy" and 2018 "National Defense Strategy" explicitly characterized the PRC a "revisionist power" that "seeks to displace the United States in the Indo-Pacific region" and as a "strategic competitor."[18] This marked a significant departure from the Obama administration, which emphasized US desire for a constructive and cooperative relationship.[19] Beijing took note with the PRC Ministry of Defense declaring the 2018 "National Defense Strategy" reflected a "Cold War" mentality and was "full of unreal assertions of 'zero-sum' games and confrontations."[20] However, for now the security environment is assessed to be relatively positive for China. That being the case, party leaders are pursuing a national security agenda with the following goals: (1) perpetuating CCP rule; (2) maintaining domestic stability; (3) sustaining economic growth and development; (4) defending national sovereignty and territorial integrity; (5) reacquiring regional preeminence and securing China's status as a great power; and (6) safeguarding China's interests abroad.[21]

President Xi's widely promoted "China Dream" vision of national rejuvenation is, in many respects, a different way of articulating these goals.[22] Realization of this vision is linked to two Chinese centenaries: 2021 (the one-hundredth anniversary of the founding of the CCP) and 2049 (the one hundredth anniversary of the founding of the People's Republic of China). The national objective for 2021 is to achieve a "moderately prosperous society" and establish the requisite conditions for building a fully modern socialist country by 2049. The objectives articulated for this second centenary celebration are ambitious: "New heights are reached in every dimension of material, political, cultural and ethical, social, and ecological advancement. Modernization of China's system and capacity for governance is achieved. China has become a global leader in terms of composite national strength and international influence."[23]

As this quotation indicates, China's leaders aspire to make the PRC at least equal to the most powerful nations in the world, or possibly to surpass all others by the middle of the century. That will require substantial and expensive investments not just in military capabilities but also in economic performance, comprehensive public education, health care and elder care, and nearly every other dimension of modern life. Gains in other areas will be necessary to achieve some of the military goals, but paying for those advances will compete with the escalating costs of maintaining and operating more complex military systems. How well the PLA fares in future budget debates will depend on how leaders assess the international situation and the urgency of domestic challenges (see chapter 9 by Thomas Fingar, this volume). The military almost certainly will not obtain all that it wants, but it is instructive to summarize PLA aspirations because of what they tell us about Beijing's perception of the world and China's place in it, and to illustrate the magnitude of military requirements in the largely zero-sum competition for funding.

The China Dream encompasses "the dream of building a powerful military."[24] President Xi, in his capacity as CMC chairman, and the PLA senior leadership oversee the development and implementation of a multifaceted and ambitious military strategy to support the more comprehensive national security strategy. By the first centenary in 2021, the PLA aims to be entirely mechanized and more fully capable in its application of information technologies and to achieve major improvements in its strategic capabilities. By 2035 the Chinese military is to transform itself into a "modern power" entailing improvements in doctrine, organizational structure, personnel, and weaponry. By the arrival of the second centenary, the goal is for the PLA to be a "top-tiered" force, second to none.[25]

China's armed forces must accomplish many daunting tasks to achieve these objectives. First and foremost is to eliminate endemic corruption. More senior officers have been targeted and removed from the military in the current protracted anticorruption drive than from any other state organization (see chapter 3 by Andrew Wedeman, this volume). Other challenges include greatly improving the norms of professionalism within the officer corps and raising the prestige of career military service. A second cluster of tasks centers on the challenges of developing a doctrine and the enabling capabilities required to prevail in system-versus-system operations featuring information dominance, precision strikes, and joint operations.[26] What this means, in effect, is developing the capability to operate in a manner that approximates the ability of the US armed forces to conduct inherently joint, lethal, flexible, and agile military campaigns.

A third challenging task is to improve PLA operational capabilities to levels that would allow it to compete with the US military in the Western

Pacific and to maintain effective command and control of expeditionary forces deployed outside of Asia. To do so will require, among other things, successful implementation of the organizational reforms launched by President Xi in 2015 and include establishing theater commands, reorganizing the CMC, developing the Strategic Support Force (responsible for space, cyber, and electronic warfare missions), creating the Joint Operations Command, establishing the Overseas Operations Office, forming the Joint Logistics Support Force, and demobilizing personnel.[27] Most of these reforms have been carried out or are in the final stages of implementation, but their impact on PLA performance is not yet known. In addition, given China's dynamic security environment, it is likely that further significant government and military structural reforms will be required if the PLA is to realize the demanding goals it has been directed to achieve by midcentury.

The fourth and last set of significant challenges is for the Chinese military to enhance its offensive and defensive capabilities in the maritime, space, and cyber domains to levels that overmatch, or at least approximate, those of the United States and other potential military rivals. With the rapid advances taking place in a growing number of technologies that may have significant military potential (artificial intelligence, robotics, nanotechnologies, biotechnologies, etc.), China must expand the depth and scope of its defense-related research, development, testing, evaluation, and production enterprises. Doing so will require the establishment of an integrated civilian-military defense industrial system that prizes innovation, attracts financial investment, and places a premium on profit.

Development and Implementation of China's Military Strategy

The pace of China's military modernization has been breathtaking since the mid-1990s, when the party began to allocate far greater resources to the PLA. Rapid improvements were relatively easy to achieve initially because the starting point was so low. Now both aspirations and the challenges of further modernization are greater. Achieving them will be more difficult and more costly. How ambitious goals for military modernization are pursued and/or modified will depend on three factors: (1) the level of strategic ambition and threat perception; (2) resource allocation; and (3) readiness and capabilities of military forces.

LEVEL OF STRATEGIC AMBITION AND THREAT PERCEPTION

The requirement to safeguard vital state interests drives the development of military capabilities. At the same time, however, the fielding of additional and more sophisticated military capabilities can generate new vital interests that were previously not considered because they could not be defended. Simply stated, requirements drive the acquisition of capabilities and the acquisition of capabilities leads to new missions and requirements. In the case of modern China, both factors are in play due to its meteoric economic and military rise. For example, in 1980 the PRC had negligible trade in the Middle East and possessed only an antiquated brown water navy. Less than forty years later, China is a major purchaser of oil and natural gas from the Middle East, invests heavily in infrastructure projects, and is a significant financial lender. It should surprise no one, therefore, that China strives to field the military means needed to protect its rapidly expanding and widespread economic interests.

Greater capability, in the form of recently acquired naval capacity to project modestly sized flotillas and limited strategic airlift to any part of the globe, has influenced the Chinese public and their leaders to view the protection of citizens living overseas as a critical state interest. The PLA's successful noncombatant evacuation operations in Libya in 2011 and Yemen in 2015 likely signal a more interventionist approach to safeguarding Chinese nationals aboard. As an op-ed in China's Communist Party mouthpiece, *Global Times*, noted several days after the Yemen evacuation: "In addition to emergency response, it is very challenging for any government to provide regular safety assurances to its nationals on foreign soil. In this regard, the Chinese government is catching up quickly to meet public demands."[28]

This dynamic interplay between economic interests and military means has informed and will continue to inform how the PLA pursues three of its major military tasks: (1) supporting the completion of China's national reunification (most notably the incorporation of Taiwan into the PRC) and assertion of effective control over its expansive maritime claims in the East and South China Seas; (2) replacing the United States as the dominant military power in the Western Pacific, which requires the further development of capabilities and the weakening of US regional bilateral alliances and partnerships; and (3) securing the nation's ever growing economic interests and protecting the safety of Chinese citizens around world. The United

States looms large in the first two tasks (which entail control of the PRC's near abroad in East Asia and establishment of a sphere of influence in the Western Pacific); the third is often the result of an unanticipated crisis (e.g., noncombatant evacuation of Chinese citizens from a country that suddenly plunges into violent civil war).

The warfighting capacity required to compel Taiwan's reunification and exert maritime control in claimed areas of the East and South China Seas is considerable. Achieving it will require a suite of capabilities that include long-range target acquisition and precision strike systems needed to deny regional access to US and allied forces (often referred to as Anti-Access/Area Denial [A2/AD] capabilities); air, surface, and subsurface forces equipped and arrayed to achieve dominance in critical areas of operations throughout the duration of hostilities; and the means to degrade US command, control, communications, computers, intelligence, surveillance, and reconnaissance (C4ISR). Other potential requirements include sufficient amphibious forces to secure lodgments and achieve campaign objectives; effective command and control of joint land, air, sea, cyber, and space forces; and strategic nuclear forces that could dissuade the United States from contemplating first use in the midst of a rapidly escalating conventional war.

China enjoys a significant and increasingly important advantage in its contest with the United States in the Western Pacific. That advantage is geographic proximity. For example, the disputed Scarborough Shoal (claimed by China and by US treaty ally, the Republic of the Philippines) is 640 miles from the Chinese Navy's South Sea Fleet Headquarters in Zhanjiang, 583 miles from its base in Sanya on Hainan Island and 391 miles from its potential base of operations on Mischief (Panganiban) Reef in the South China Sea. Distances from the United States are much greater. It is 1,924 miles from US Navy Seventh Fleet Headquarters in Yokosuka, Japan, 5,495 miles from US Navy Pacific Fleet Headquarters in Pearl Harbor, and 7,536 miles from US Navy Third Fleet Headquarters in San Diego. Accordingly, as the Chinese Navy closes the technological gap with the US Navy, its ability to achieve quantitative superiority will become more decisive. The PRC's ambitious rate of warship production and establishment of artificial island bases, such as atop the now despoiled Mischief Reef in the South China Sea, seem to indicate a purposeful strategy aimed at achieving military maritime superiority in a conflict related to Taiwan or control of Western Pacific waters.[29]

However, military superiority is much more than a function of quantitative and qualitative material advantage. Doctrine, organization, training, leadership, logistics, and other factors matter greatly. Large complex militaries, such as the PLA, find that aligning and harmonizing the efforts of the numerous bureaucratic actors responsible for these factors is a difficult task. The challenge is achieving bureaucratic unity of purpose. In the absence of agreed-upon mission sets, militaries can flounder. Historically, those faced with a central strategic problem—such as the Wehrmacht during the late 1930s (potentially fighting a two-front war), or the US Army and Air Force during the Cold War (defeating a quantitatively superior Red Army)—have often innovated well (e.g., the Germans developing blitzkrieg doctrine, the US armed forces creating air-land battle doctrine). Therefore, to the extent that PLA leaders are directed to prioritize specific Western Pacific scenarios that involve potential combat with US forces, the pace of Chinese military modernization may quicken.[30]

China's interests and ambitions extend beyond East Asia and its land borders and are now global in scope. Today the PRC is the world's leading trading nation and the second largest foreign direct investor (behind the United States). Predictably, it has begun to design and champion large-scale overseas economic development programs, such as the hugely ambitious Belt and Road Initiative (BRI) (see chapters 10, 11, and 12 by Ho-fung Hung, Christine Wong, and David M. Lampton, respectively). If China's economy continues to grow at moderate-to-rapid rates, its global equities will continue to expand. This will cause the PLA to devote more attention and effort to its ability to control distant sea lines of communication (SLOCs), and deploy quick-response joint expeditionary forces to protect its investments and citizens abroad. It will also seek to gain influence with foreign militaries and secure guaranteed access to foreign facilities by using arms sales and security assistance programs. China's party and military leaders generally regard security competition with the United States in the Western Pacific in zero-sum terms. This causes them to view the perceived deterioration of America's standing in East Asia as positive. The possible end of Pax Americana does not necessarily mean that the PLA will require fewer resources. Indeed, one can be quite certain that at least some in the military and political elite will argue that the PLA must develop capabilities to fill the putative growing security vacuums that could endanger PRC interests now protected in part by US efforts to maintain global stability.

RESOURCE ALLOCATION

Strategy is about the use of means (or resources) available to the state to exercise control over circumstances and geographic locations to protect or advance state interests. Generous funding and confidence that it will continue well into the future almost inevitably lead professional military leaders and planners to advocate more ambitious goals. The PLA has enjoyed double-digit annual budget increases almost every year since the mid-1990s.[31] However, as noted earlier, the Chinese defense budget was meager at the point of departure, and as the economy grew at double-digit rates, the central government had increasing revenues to fund military modernization.[32] Whether this trend will continue is uncertain because of slowing growth and increased attention to the need for greater spending on education, health, social services, and other priority policy areas identified in Premier Li Keqiang's "Report on the Work of the Government" at the March 2018 First Session of the 13th Chinese National People's Congress (NPC).[33]

President Xi Jinping, whose term in office now has no limits, has invested much personal capital to ensure the PLA becomes a world-class military force. The 2018 defense budget, announced just before the NPC session in March (the members of which voted almost unanimously to end the previous two-term limit on the presidency), reflects his prioritization of military modernization. The budget marks the largest increase in three years, 8.1 percent more than the previous year and outpacing overall economic growth by about 1.5 percent.[34]

However, PRC economic growth rates for the foreseeable future will be lower than the double-digit or near-double-digit rates enjoyed between 1982 and 2011 (see chapters 2 and 8 by Barry Naughton and Hongbin Li et al., respectively). Party leaders will face difficult budget and fiscal policy choices as they attempt to address demands that will compete with defense spending. Those competing demands include debt reduction, the creation of social welfare systems (pensions and health care), and environmental protection. An economic recession induced by a deteriorating global economy, or failure to restructure China's economy and place greater emphasis on domestic consumption, or both, could further limit resources available to the PLA.

If party leaders become even more concerned about domestic unrest than they already are, the likely resultant impact on the military would interfere with efforts to improve the PLA's expeditionary capabilities. The Chinese armed forces' strategic tasks include the requirement to "strengthen efforts in operations against infiltration, separatism and terrorism so as to maintain China's political security and social stability."[35] Generally speaking, the military equipment and training required to deal with civil unrest are not the same as those needed to conduct interstate warfare against a capable opponent. Rising popular discontent at some future point due to the party's failure to deliver on its implicit contract with the Chinese people (i.e., uncontested political control in return for material well-being and social stability) would lead President Xi to shift the PLA's attention to what he and his colleagues would view as an existential threat to their regime.

The growing military applications of technologies and products generated in the commercial economy (e.g., robotics, information technology, and artificial intelligence) could ease budget constraints, and China's massive and ongoing expropriation of foreign cutting-edge technology probably will help the PLA to close its technological gap with the US military. So too might success in Beijing's plans to develop indigenous production capacity in key industries with defense applications manifested in the "Made in China 2025" initiative.[36] President Xi has over the past several years called for reforms in the defense industrial sector that could lead to greater economic efficiency, but the impediments to implementation are formidable. They include state-owned industry monopoly power, bureaucratic resistance, outdated pricing mechanisms, and corruption.[37] Moreover, China may be entering an era when the guns-versus-butter debate—that is, having to examine closely the trade-offs between investments in defense and civilian programs—is more complex and politically charged than has been the case in recent decades. Outcomes of this debate will impact military strategy and capabilities. All things considered, unless external threats are perceived to be much more dangerous, decisions on guns-versus-butter issues are likely to favor nonmilitary expenditures.

CAPACITY AND READINESS

China's military strategy will also be shaped by the perceived capacity and readiness of the PLA to perform its expanding and increasingly complex set of missions. The degree to which party and PLA leaders are confident that China's armed forces can accomplish what the military strategy demands will influence their willingness to add new missions. China today is a regional military power with a global nuclear deterrent force. PRC leaders aim to create a PLA second to none by midcentury. This desire appears to be shared by most of the Chinese people. Continued military modernization will encourage adoption of a more expansive strategy. If, however, the Chinese military falters in the effort to transform itself into a force with global reach and able to dominate the Western Pacific, its strategy will be more cautious and aspire to more modest goals.

Improvements in Chinese military readiness and force projection capabilities since the 1990s have been substantial. To secure ascendancy over the US military in East Asia and "go global" will require further improvements in the officer corps, command and control, doctrine, and training. Further improvement of China's military officer corps is constrained, however, by the strict subordination of the PLA to Communist Party control. The famous maxim of Mao Zedong spoken in 1938—"The party commands the gun, and the gun must never be allowed to command the party"—remains a key ruling principle in China.[38] Party leaders require the PLA to allocate valuable time to the ideological education of its cadre, encumber it with a commissar system that leads to the diffusion of command responsibilities, and demand that it remain sensitive to the often changing political priorities of the moment. As a result, Chinese military officers may not enjoy the degree of autonomy needed to become a highly professional corporate body.[39]

President Xi's aggressive campaign to root out corruption within the PLA is of particular note. Over the past five years thirteen thousand officers have been punished, the latest senior target being former Chief of the Joint Staff, General Fang Fenghui.[40] Xi's persistent and determined efforts to instill accountability and integrity within the ranks may be stifling officer initiative and innovation, leadership attributes that are essential on the modern battlefield. An overly hierarchical directive command structure limits the capacity of a military to achieve the integration necessary to conduct horizontally networked warfare. Adding to these challenges, the lack of combat experience across the ranks of the PLA leadership—the Chinese military's last major wartime campaign was against Vietnam in 1979—reduces their level of professional self-confidence, possibly making them more risk averse.

Establishing and maintaining effective command and control over joint forces operating in an expeditionary environment is a challenging task for any military force in the contemporary era. The major PLA organizational reform in 2016 that included the establishment of five joint theater commands in place of the previous seven army-centric military region commands, the creation of a truly joint staff, and the establishment of an army headquarters on par with its sister services, appear to be significant steps toward making the PLA a modern fighting force. PLA communications systems are increasingly top-tier, but the absence of robust joint task forces routinely operating from overseas bases together with allies and partners, as is the norm for the United States armed forces, disadvantages PLA efforts to match the joint command-and-control skills of its principal rival. Indeed, the Chinese military may place an increasing premium on efforts to create such opportunities, as have the Russian armed forces in Syria.

As mentioned earlier, the development of coherent military doctrine is often dependent on intermilitary service consensus on the nature of the threat and the central strategic problem that such a threat poses. The United States military, in the aftermath of the Vietnam conflict, effectively responded to the perceived Soviet threat during the second half of the Cold War by developing innovative air, land, sea, and joint warfighting doctrines, and highly effective training regimens. It struggled in the aftermath of the collapse of the Soviet Union by focusing too much on military theory detached from reality. PLA concentration on specific contingencies in the Western Pacific or concrete global scenarios will likely stimulate more sophisticated thinking about China's military strategy—though at the risk of preparing for the wrong war.

China's military leaders have long recognized that high-quality standards-based training is a critical component of operational readiness. However, for a variety of reasons the PLA has struggled to create a professional culture that embraces such training. Senior officers openly and candidly acknowledge this shortcoming.[41] If not confident that its training doctrine and programs are producing cutting-edge forces, the Chinese high command will be more risk averse and its military strategy more conservative. Military modernization is a complex process with many interrelated aspects. How quickly the PLA is able to transform itself through modernization will have a significant impact on Chinese defense strategy. To use a sports metaphor, a confident coach will welcome the inclusion of tough opponents on his or her team's schedule and will train accordingly. A less confident coach will play it safe and avoid the world-class competition.

The Impact of China's Geopolitical Environment

China's military strategy will ultimately be determined by the choices of party and PLA leaders in Beijing. What they decide will be greatly influenced by the policies and actions of other countries, especially those states whose own security is impacted by PRC actions. States that judge their own security to be affected by China's military modernization can choose to bandwagon with, balance against, or remain neutral in regional and global geopolitical contests involving China. In other words, what China does will have consequences for and elicit responses from other countries. Their responses, in turn, will affect Beijing's geopolitical situation and threat perceptions.

In the Indo-Asia-Pacific region US military presence and purpose, as well as its security relations with key allies and partners, will have a major impact on PLA strategy. While China may seek a Sino-centric Asian security order reminiscent of its imperial past, it cannot achieve this outcome unilaterally. Examples of responses and developments that will influence future Chinese thinking and actions include the possibility—perhaps likelihood—of sustained US efforts to maintain a capable forward military presence in the Western Pacific to deny China the ability to achieve military control of the maritime commons in East and Southeast Asia, choices made by the government of an eventually unified or federated Korean Peninsula regarding its alliance with the United States, and Japan's future defense policies.

China's increasing diplomatic, economic and military activities in South, Southeast, and Central Asia almost certainly will elicit balancing behavior by states in those regions. This is especially true in South Asia, where India worries about the growing Chinese naval presence and base access in the Indian Ocean and Beijing's historically close ties with Pakistan. In Southeast Asia, proximity to China, small size, and the fact that some corrupt autocratic governments are dependent on PRC largesse make meaningful collective action by the Association of Southeast Asian Nations (ASEAN) unlikely.[42] However, ASEAN member states Indonesia, the Philippines, and Vietnam have the world's fourth-, thirteenth-, and fifteenth-largest populations, potentially strong economies, and disputes with China over maritime claims in the South China Sea that make them unlikely candidates for strategic alignment with Beijing. Small but influential Singapore also seems likely to resist becoming enmeshed in the PRC's orbit.

Perhaps of even greater long-term consequence for China's future military strategy is the orientation of Russia. Moscow has historically had to deal with three threats: from the West (Western Europe and the United States), from the South (variously Turkey and Islamic sectarian movements in Central Asia), and the East (Japan and China). Under Putin, Russian security policy has become unbalanced, obsessing on the United States and its NATO partners. Russia's underpopulated and underdeveloped Far East remains highly vulnerable to Chinese influence. In addition, if the BRI is successful in economically connecting Central Asia to China, Russia will likely take countermeasures to reassert control in its traditional sphere of influence.

Characterizing US–Chinese strategic competition as a contemporary example of "the Thucydides Trap" that triggered the epic struggle between the ancient Greek city-states of Sparta and Athens is in vogue but misleading.[43] Nevertheless, the analogy is useful in that it illuminates an important underlying principle of international relations—namely, that states do attempt to balance and/or bandwagon to increase their security in an anarchic world system. China's rapid regional and global rise will induce both behaviors by affected states. But the fact that the PRC does not have an appealing political ideology and is still seen as more threatening than benign make it likely that major regional 35and global powers will choose to balance rather than bandwagon. If so, China will either need to find more cash-strapped allies of convenience that offer basing and access for the PLA or create new inclusive regional security architectures that lower the risks of conflict and the costs of military competition.

What to Expect

The growth of China's military power since the mid-1990s has been remarkable. The PLA is steadily advancing toward its goal of displacing the US armed forces as the preeminent military in East Asia and the Western Pacific, and developing a global reach capable of defending increasingly global interests. While impressive, the gains realized to date were likely more easily achieved than those required in the years ahead if China is to implement its ambitious national and military strategies. Continued robust economic growth would provide the substantial resources the PLA requires for further modernization, but growth is slowing and competition for budgetary resources is increasing. Expanding international trade and investment will create new interests that China's leaders will judge to require PLA protection and additional resources, but the same leaders will also be attentive to satisfying requisites for sustained growth and maintenance of domestic stability and regime legitimacy.

Sustained political and social stability will maintain the domestic conditions required to keep the PLA focused on expeditionary operations; large or widespread protest demonstrations and demands for government action will divert the military from pursuit of that objective. Consolidation of President Xi's and the party's control over the PLA might give way to a more decentralized and networked command-and-control system required to effectively fight high-end wars in the twenty-first century, but fears of factionalism within the military and the party, and determination to maintain tight control of "everything" could perpetuate or tighten constraints on lower-level organizations and officials, including military commands. An American retreat from the Indo-Asia-Pacific region coupled with adept Chinese diplomacy that did not excite balancing behavior by major powers impacted by the PRC's ascent would greatly ease the PLA's task of becoming a world-class force, second to none, by midcentury. But assertions of American decline are greatly overstated, American retreat from the region is highly unlikely, and the geographic and demographic realities that make neighbors wary of China will not change.

Projections of China's future military strength and political influence that assume each of the challenges summarized in this chapter—and many others—will be resolved in ways that result in an early transition to Chinese preeminence are highly problematic. Anticipating slower expansion, modernization, and improvements in readiness seems a safer bet than straight-line projection of past rates of change. This is not an argument for complacency. China's military capabilities today are vastly greater than they were a decade ago and are almost certain to increase further in the years ahead. Countries anticipate that and will hedge and seek to balance, and a few might bandwagon. The strategic situation in the Indo-Asia-Pacific region will remain in flux and China will remain a major player. Whether China plays a stabilizing or destabilizing role remains to be seen.

PART IV

A Comparative Perspective

CHAPTER 14

China's National Trajectory

Andrew G. Walder

To think productively about China's possible futures, it is important to understand how it became what it is today. The most important driver of China's national trajectory has been its remarkably dynamic economy, which over the past thirty years has been the foundation for relatively high levels of popular support, elite unity and consensus, regime stability, and rising national power and international influence. This dynamism has been generated by a hybrid economy combining elements of a system in transition out of Soviet-type socialism, and an export-oriented East–Asian developmental state. China shares similarities with both systems but also exhibits important differences. Understanding this distinctive trajectory—and what could be its looming impasse—provides a foundation for anticipating political developments over the next twenty years.

Discussions of China's possible futures often focus on the most spectacular and least likely of outcomes—regime collapse and democratization. Some appear to conflate the two, as if the first is a precursor to the second. Although these two outcomes have at times occurred in rapid sequence, this has been rare, and the two are perhaps more accurately conceived as polar opposites. Given the wave of regime collapse and democratization in the late 1980s and early 1990s, fascination with such outcomes is understandable, but it narrows our focus and truncates our chain of reasoning, causing us to neglect less dramatic changes that are also important and more predictable. It is on the latter that this chapter concentrates.

Efforts to project China's future inevitably invite comparisons with the economic and political trajectories of other countries—especially the former Soviet Union and similar regimes as well as the rapidly developing economies in East Asia that China's economic rise most closely resembles. Those who write about this subject often have these examples in mind, but such comparisons should not be left implicit nor should they be invoked casually because seemingly close parallels coexist with striking differences. Broad parallels can be instructive, but it is helpful, indeed necessary, to make these comparisons explicit.

The principal conclusion of this chapter is that China's high-growth era is rapidly coming to an end. The past thirty years of spectacular economic expansion have yielded substantial political dividends—a remarkable degree of elite unity, political stability, and high levels of popular support for the Communist Party and the central government. These dividends will inevitably fade as China shifts to more modest growth rates. But they will evaporate if the overdue transition to a new development model is deferred or mishandled, especially if the delay leads to unprecedented economic contraction or a long period of sluggish growth. Considerably slower growth over a sustained period will change many of the assumptions about Chinese politics that we have long taken for granted.

Out of State Socialism

China began its remarkable rise at the very end of the 1970s as a pioneer of market reform and became the most successful example of transition away from a Soviet economic model. All transitional economies have shared three broad characteristics. First, they shift from bureaucratic planning to market allocation of goods and services. Second, they shift from the near-complete dominance of state ownership to a major if not dominant role for some form of private ownership. And third, they abandon economic autarky in favor of integration with global markets.

China, of course, differs from other transitional economies in a number of ways. Privatization of state assets was more gradual and limited. The party has remained in power to guide the reforms, whereas in most other states this economic transition occurred either simultaneous with, or only after, the collapse of Communist power. China's market reforms began at a much lower level of per capita GDP than most other transitional economies (its GDP per capita in 1979 was equal to the Soviet Union's in the late 1920s).[1] Moreover, owing to China's economic structure, the reforms began

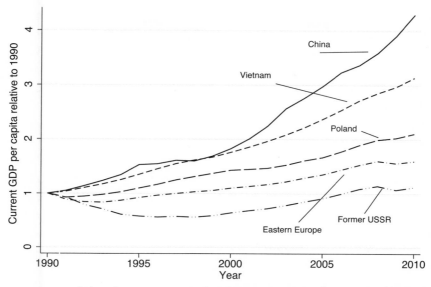

FIGURE 14.1. Index of twenty-year growth trajectories, transitional economies (GDP per capita, US$, PPP, 1990 = 1).

SOURCE: The Maddison Project, http://www.ggdc.net/maddison/maddison-project/home.htm, 2013 version.

with agriculture, not industry. The most obvious way in which China's trajectory has differed from the others, of course, is its spectacular economic growth, which far outpaced all other transitional economies. Figure 14.1 traces the trajectories of these economies from 1990 to 2010. It groups separately the fifteen former Soviet republics, and seven countries in Eastern Europe and their successor states.[2] Only Vietnam comes close to replicating China's trajectory: China's GDP per capita grew more than fourfold, while Vietnam's grew more than threefold. The most successful of the other major economies was Poland, whose economy more than doubled.

What is most noteworthy about the data when they are arrayed in this fashion is that almost all the other economies of this type endured sustained economic downturns. In Eastern Europe the downturns were relatively shallow and lasted an average of five years; in the former Soviet Union they were severe and lasted for more than a decade. We need to explain not only China's sustained high growth rate but also why it (and Vietnam) did not suffer a "transitional recession."

338 ANDREW G. WALDER

The reason China (and Vietnam) avoided these downturns is fundamentally political. You would never guess this by reading the comparative
empirical literature on transitional economies, which has been preoccupied
with debates about policy approaches ("big bang" versus gradualism) and
the different starting points and economic endowments of various countries. The standard approach is to control for country-fixed effects (typically dummy variables for the former USSR and East Asia) in an effort to
explain variations in *average* growth rates over time. This essentially ignores
political trajectories of states, sweeping into the background the collapse
of national state structures, the splitting apart of states into new national
units, and associated consequences like hyperinflation and civil war. These
consequences were most severe in the Soviet Union, where party structures
began to break down four years before it split into fifteen newly independent nations in 1991. They were far less severe in Eastern Europe, which
(except for Yugoslavia) experienced much more rapid and generally peaceful transitions to postcommunism.

Severe political disruptions created steep economic downturns and nega-
tively affected institutional developments for years afterward. Figure 14.2
shows the close temporal connection between the collapse of regimes and
the onset of transitional recessions. It groups three surviving communist regimes (China, Laos, Vietnam), fifteen former Soviet republics, and thirteen
other postcommunist regimes, and traces their annual growth rates from
1989 to 2007.[3] When the data are displayed in this fashion, it is apparent
that the greatest differences across groups are in the initial period from
1989 to 1993, when regimes broke down and states broke apart. Growth
rates returned to positive territory in the former USSR by 1995 and in other
postcommunist states two years earlier. After 1997 differences in average
growth rates across groups were small.[4]

I do not dispute the contribution of sound policy choices in countries
like China and Vietnam. There was nothing automatic about rapid growth
under conditions of political stability; successful reform is not easy even
under the most favorable of initial circumstances. China's effective approach to market reform, and the political dilemmas faced each step of
the way, have been analyzed in convincing detail and its features are well
understood.[5] My point is that one must have a coherent political structure
to develop and implement an economic policy of whatever kind.

China's leaders have by no means taken political stability for granted.
They see it as the foundation for everything that China has accomplished,

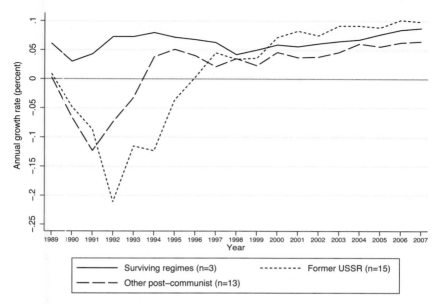

FIGURE 14.2. Annual percentage of change in per capita GDP, transitional economies.

SOURCE: World Bank (2012) and European Bank (1999), in Andrew G. Walder, Andrew Issacson, and Qinglian Lu, "After State Socialism: The Political Origins of Transitional Recessions," *American Sociological Review* 80, no. 2 (April 2015): 444–68.

and as a key to legitimizing the indefinite continuation of a strict and largely unreformed single-party dictatorship. But we need to step back a bit in our examination of China's historical trajectory to ask why China was the first to embark on unorthodox market reforms, and why it was able to carry out such reforms without experiencing severe political disruption. Another way to ask this question is why China's trajectory diverged so sharply from the Soviet Union, where a reform-minded leader tried and failed to accomplish the same thing but unintentionally triggered the political collapse.

Gorbachev faced a very different task than Deng Xiaoping. When he took power in 1985, he was by far the youngest member of the Politburo, having joined it only in 1980. At the time, the Soviet Union was still the world's second largest economy, one of two reigning superpowers. Its civilian and military bureaucracies had been untouched by major purges since the Stalin era, had vested interests in the privileges accorded them, and were a force that stood in the way of reform. Gorbachev decided to go around the structures of the Soviet state, open up the political system, and hold elections for regional assemblies. That fateful decision touched off a wave of nationalist separatism that led to the dismemberment of the Soviet Union a few years later.[6]

China's situation shortly after the death of Mao is a study in contrasts, largely due to the impact of the decade-long Cultural Revolution. Deng Xiaoping was a senior leader of the revolutionary generation who had held high posts in Beijing since 1954. He was the second-highest ranking leader to be purged during the Cultural Revolution and was brought back to Beijing by Mao in 1974 to help restore the economy and stabilize China's governing structures. Deng was purged once again when Mao concluded that he was trying to restore too much of the pre–Cultural Revolution status quo. Deng's combination of revolutionary credentials, deep knowledge of institutions and people, and victimization for opposing Mao's politically induced chaos made him the obvious standard-bearer for a post-Mao rebuilding of the economy and the Chinese state.

Moreover, China was far from the world's second largest economy at the end of the 1970s, and its record of growth was nothing to instill national pride. China had fallen far behind its rivals and presumed enemies, including Japan and South Korea, which like China had been devastated, respectively, by World War II and the Korean War. Figure 14.3 traces the troubled history of China's economic development during the Mao years relative to the other large and impoverished Asian economy, India. China had made greater progress than India during the early 1950s. Starting from a level of development that was lower by some 30 percent of GDP per capita, China had caught up by 1958, only to be thrown backward by the failure of the Great Leap Forward. Having taken several years to recover from the Great Leap, China again pulled even with India in 1966 but was stalled once again by the upheavals of the late 1960s. China had barely caught up with India for the third time in 1978. More than twenty years of progress had been sacrificed to misguided policies. The sorry state of the economy by the mid-1970s, especially in comparison to rapidly developing neighbors in East Asia, undermined any counterarguments to trying a new approach.

One could argue, of course, that market reform would undermine the party's grip on society and the country's political stability. In fact, the reverse process was under way. The Cultural Revolution devastated China's central bureaucracy and party organization, and their restoration and rebuilding were strongly contested until the end of Mao's life. The shift from

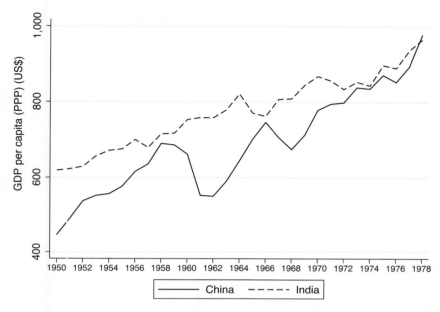

FIGURE 14.3. Growth trajectories of China and India, 1950–78 (GDP per capita, US$, PPP).

SOURCE: The Maddison Project, http://www.ggdc.net/maddison/maddison-project/home.htm, 2013 version.

state planning to market did not imply the weakening of the state, as many observers erroneously understood at the time. One of Deng's primary tasks was to rebuild the administrative capacities of China's central state and the national party organization. He did this in part by returning fallen veteran officials to positions they had lost during the Cultural Revolution. This meant that there was no entrenched bureaucracy with the incentive or capacity to block market reform—Deng was returning to office the very bureaucrats who in the Soviet Union had vested interests in defending the status quo and had the ability to resist. This meant that Deng, unlike Gorbachev, could bundle a political program of state *strengthening* with an agenda of market reform. Deng's program aligned with the interests of bureaucrats who otherwise in a more prosperous and stable socialist state would have stood in the way of his economic program.

Understanding how China's path departed from that of the Soviet Union is of more than historical interest. The key unintended accomplishment of the Cultural Revolution was to ensure that there were no deeply entrenched institutional actors with strong vested interests in the status quo and the political capacity to resist reforms counter to these interests. This made it politically possible for Deng Xiaoping to take China in a very different direction. One cannot make the same statement about China today. Deng's project of rebuilding a strong party-state has been continued by his successors. China's historic growth has created the world's second largest economy; China is now widely considered the only global power with the capacity to rival the United States. Officials high and low have benefitted enormously from these developments, much more so than in the Soviet Union, where private fortunes were never amassed by the families of serving party officials. China as a nation, and a deeply entrenched elite that has benefitted enormously from economic prosperity, potentially has a great deal to lose by a further restructuring and reform of existing institutions.

A Modified East Asian Model

The damage wrought by the Cultural Revolution cleared the ground for the adoption of a radically new model of development. This turned out to be a variant of the East Asian model pioneered by postwar Japan, which at the time was powering the rapid growth of South Korea, Taiwan, and smaller economies in the region.[7] The model had four core features, all of which China shared. The reforms began with an egalitarian rural reform that distributed control of land to farm households, unleashing agricultural development providing a foundation for the commercial and industrial development of rural regions. China disbanded collective farms in the early 1980s, the first and most radical of its reform moves (essentially a replay of the land revolution of the early 1950s, steadily rolled back into collective farms after 1953). The second feature is a strong emphasis on state industrial policy. The third is an emphasis on industrial exports, beginning with low-end products and moving gradually up the technology ladder. And the fourth feature is a prolonged period of "financial repression"—that is, regulated low interest rates on savings and limited financial outlets for households, a managed and undervalued currency to promote exports, and capital controls on financial flows into and out of the country.

China's remarkable growth also closely resembles that of its predecessors in East Asia. One frequently hears claims that no other country in the world has grown as fast as China during its remarkable thirty-year growth

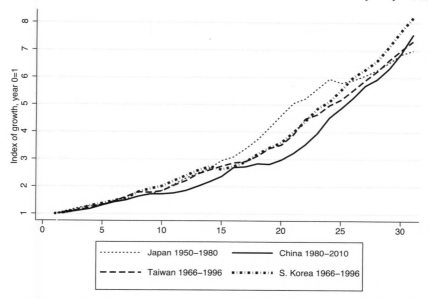

FIGURE 14.4. Index of thirty-year growth trajectories, East Asian economies (GDP per capita, US$ PPP).

SOURCE: The Maddison Project, http://www.ggdc.net/maddison/maddison-project/home.htm, 2013 version.

spurt. In fact, China's growth trajectory largely recapitulates those of Japan, South Korea, and Taiwan during their own fast-growth eras. Figure 14.4 plots an index of growth in GDP per capita (in purchasing power parity) over the fast-growth periods of these economies, with the starting point for each country set at 1. The growth trajectories of all four are closely parallel, and if anything China's lags somewhat behind until the very end. All of them multiplied the size of their economies a remarkable seven- to eight-fold, with South Korea enjoying the largest multiple by a small margin. To be sure, the overall size of the Chinese economy implies an awe-inspiring volume of economic activity, but its *rate* of growth is by no means unprecedented.

Despite these parallels, China evinces striking differences from the East Asian industrialization model. China has relied much more heavily on foreign direct investment and infusions of foreign technologies than did Japan, South Korea, or Taiwan. This reflects the severe damage done to China's higher educational system and technological capacity during the Cultural Revolution and also the paucity of financial capital, foreign exchange, and export capacity of Chinese firms at the outset of reform. Foreign direct investment and joint ventures played very limited roles in the development of South Korea and Taiwan, and virtually no role in Japan, where indigenous firms sought to compete with foreign firms from the beginning and where government policies created barriers to the entry of foreign firms.[8] More important, China has placed much greater emphasis on the continued role of large state-owned corporations, state banks, and state ownership of other key factors of production (especially land and natural resources). Finally, and most obviously, China has a less open and more rigid political system than Japan, and it has strongly resisted the liberalization and democratization that occurred in South Korea and Taiwan near the end of their fast-growth periods. With minor modifications China's political institutions still closely resemble the ones it imported wholesale from the Soviet Union in the 1950s.

There is one additional difference from the other East Asian economies. China began its rapid growth at a significantly lower level of GDP per capita than the others, and it has ended up still well below the level of development achieved by the other economies when they reached the end of their high-growth periods. Figure 14.5 arrays trends in annual GDP per capita for each of the four countries as in Figure 14.3, without indexing the increases relative to the initial year. What is most apparent is that the gap between starting and ending levels of GDP per capita over these thirty-year periods actually increased. Japan, South Korea, and Taiwan had become high-income countries, while China remains in the middle-income category.

These differences with other East Asian economies are at the center of current worries about the future of the Chinese economy. Its long-standing reliance on foreign technology and investment, the continuing heavy role of state ownership in large corporations and the banking system, its bureaucratic-authoritarian party-state (which continues to view high growth rates as a key to political legitimacy), and its still relatively low overall level of GDP per capita, all raise questions about whether the rise of China can be sustained.

Political Dividends of the High-Growth Era

In the early 1840s the young Karl Marx and many of his radical colleagues were disappointed that capitalist development in Prussia had not spurred

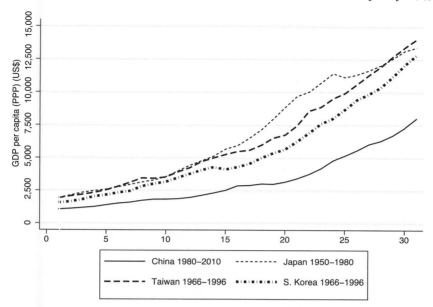

FIGURE 14.5. Thirty-year growth trajectories, East Asian economies (GDP per capita, US$, PPP).

SOURCE: The Maddison Project, http://www.ggdc.net/maddison/maddison-project/home.htm, 2013 version.

progress toward bourgeois democracy. Instead, the authoritarian bent of the German proto-state was becoming ever more pronounced. Most exasperating of all was the fact that the population seemed indifferent to political backsliding on democratic reform and in fact was becoming more nationalistic, proud of the rise of their homeland. In 1843 one of Marx's correspondents complained that "Germans not only tolerated despotism, but tolerated it 'with patriotism.'"[9] One cannot read these words without thinking of contemporary China.

Since the violent repression that crushed nationwide political protests in 1989, and the subsequent acceleration of reform and economic development, the popular movements for democratic reform so prominent in China in the 1980s have become a distant memory. University students powered nationwide campaigns for liberal reform in 1986 and 1989 that were cause for the dismissal of two CCP general secretaries for being soft on liberalization (Hu Yaobang and Zhao Ziyang). Since the mid-1990s, students instead have taken to the streets primarily to express patriotic outrage at the foreign enemies of China—disputes with Japan over islands in the East China Sea, the bombing of their embassy in Belgrade by a NATO warplane, invitations to the Dalai Lama issued by European heads of state, or visits by a Japanese prime minister to the Yasukuni Shrine.[10] The trend reached its height during the worldwide mobilization of Chinese students overseas in 2008, encouraged and even coordinated by Chinese embassies abroad, to protest insults to the nation during the Olympic torch relays and allegedly biased coverage of China by Western news outlets.[11]

The disorienting reversal of student politics is indicative of broader patterns of popular support for the Chinese political system. Since the year 2000, a variety of attitudinal surveys—the World Values Survey, Asian Barometer, and the China Survey—have repeatedly found very high levels of trust in the central government.[12] By a considerable margin these were the highest levels of the countries covered by these surveys, and the absolute levels of support were remarkably high—95 percent in the 2000 wave of the World Values Survey, and 85 percent in the 2008 China Survey. Distrust in China's government is consistently concentrated on lower levels, not on the central state. Although these surveys may overestimate actual support for various dimensions of the political system, there is little reason to suspect that the Chinese political system suffers from a lack of popular legitimacy.[13]

Highly consistent with these findings are separate surveys that gauge perceptions of distributive justice. Contrary to suggestions that rapidly rising levels of income inequality have been a breeding ground for popular anger, three surveys conducted in China from 2004 to 2014 have found little evidence that citizens perceive the economic order as unfair. Compared with the results of identical surveys conducted in Eastern Europe and wealthy democracies, Chinese citizens are considerably more likely to attribute wealth or poverty to hard work and ability, and much less likely to view the wealthy as dishonest or to attribute wealth to unfair advantages.[14]

The list of possible causes of citizen dissatisfaction is long, and there has been no shortage of protests against land seizures, official corruption, abuse of power, inadequate compensation for layoffs, or wage disputes.[15] People who are directly aggrieved by the actions of local officials have shown a clear propensity to protest. But levels of trust and perceptions of fairness remain unusually high. The most obvious reason is the very high rate of increase in incomes and material prosperity during the thirty-year economic boom. Few people are less well-off than they were in the past, and few are not much better off than their parents' generation. There is clear evidence for this speculation in surveys, which reflect a considerable optimism. Chinese are far more likely to report that their incomes have improved over the past five years, and they are far more optimistic about future increases in their income than respondents in either Eastern Europe or wealthy democratic nations. Much more than in these other countries, Chinese citizens agree that "hard work is always rewarded."[16] The connection between rapid economic growth, increasing prosperity, optimism about future prospects, and a sense of popular acceptance of existing political and economic arrangements seems very clear.

The End of the High-Growth Era

For at least a decade many observers in China and abroad, including the country's top leaders, have recognized that its successful development model, which has relied on high levels of investment, moving labor from agriculture to industry, and low industrial wages for export processing, is reaching the end of its run. It must be replaced by a new model, one that is able to reap increasing returns to investment through innovation and greater productivity.

All of the East Asian miracle economies ended their era of fast growth after roughly three decades. As earlier chapters in this volume have detailed, China has enjoyed demographic advantages during its period of high growth that are now largely exhausted. One of them is an unusually pronounced demographic dividend due to the entry into the labor force of large birth cohorts of the 1950s to the mid-1970s. The dependency ratio (nonworking people under age fifteen and over sixty-five per one hundred working-age population) dropped from 80 in 1980 to 36 in 2010. This boosted household savings and rapid increases in investment, helping to spur industrialization. Smaller birth cohorts since the late 1970s have reduced dependents under age fifteen, but as the large earlier cohorts retire, dependency ratios are growing as the population ages rapidly (see chapter 6 by Karen Eggleston, this volume). There were ten workers per retiree in 1990, six in 2010, and the number will drop to four by 2030.[17] As in Japan and South Korea, this will depress the high rates of household savings that powered investment-driven growth.[18]

This implies a shrinking labor force and rising wages in manufacturing, especially export processing. China's labor force has declined steadily since 2010, and industrial wages have risen faster than the rate of economic growth. This cuts into China's long-standing advantage as a low-cost location in global supply chains.[19] Moreover, skill levels are declining due to low rural educational attainment of recent birth cohorts. After the shift from collective to household agriculture, the availability of far higher off-farm incomes lowered rural school enrollments (see chapter 8 by Hongbin Li et al., this volume). Thus labor force skill acquisition necessary for modern manufacturing is declining.[20]

Also important is the large overhang of state-owned enterprises (SOEs). After downsizing and restructuring since the mid-1990s, SOEs now employ less than 20 percent of the labor force but still control 40 percent of industrial assets, worth 145 percent of annual GDP in 2011. By this measure the size of China's state sector is double that of India and Russia, and three times as large as South Korea, which has the largest state sector of any developed country. Unfortunately, China's state sector contributes modestly to GDP relative to the assets it commands. In recent years the state sector is estimated to contribute roughly 35 percent to GDP; the private sector 60 percent.[21] This reflects a poor return on assets: in 2012 the state sector's return on assets was 4.8 percent; the private sector's was 13.2 percent. State firms also contribute remarkably little to China's export capacity. Only 11 percent of exports were from state enterprises in 2013; private firms accounted for just below 40 percent (the remainder was from foreign firms).[22] All of this points to the need to continue the reform and restructuring of the state sector, in particular to force SOEs to confront more serious competition in the core sectors they dominate, either from domestic private or foreign firms. Harder budget constraints would have to be imposed on SOEs that are habitually unable to repay their loans—instead of rolling them over by extending the repayment period. These moves imply further downsizing of the sector through bankruptcy and closures of firms that have poor financial prospects, especially in sectors that suffer from severe overcapacity (see chapter by Barry Naughton, this volume).

Unfortunately, despite reform programs that call for precisely these steps, there has been little progress and a great deal of backtracking.[23] In large part this is due to China's response to the global financial crisis, which led to a 20 percent drop in China's exports in 2008 and mass layoffs in export sectors. The government responded with an enormous stimulus program heavily focused on infrastructure spending, financed by extending loans from state banks primarily to SOEs, and by mandating that local governments help finance these projects, even if it meant they would have to go into debt (see chapter by Jean C. Oi, this volume). These heroic measures propped up China's economy in the short run. During the boom years of 2003–2007 annual growth ranged from 10 percent to 14 percent; the stimulus credit expansion permitted it to hold steady at 9 percent to 10 percent from 2008 to 2010. After this point, despite the massive credit expansion, growth began dropping steadily, to 6.7 percent in 2016.[24]

After the worst of the global financial crisis, China's leaders were faced with a choice. They could curtail credit and reign in debt, which was concentrated especially in the state sector—but this would slow growth even more. Or they could continue to extend credit to indebted firms and hope for a "soft landing" of gradually declining growth rates. Faced with these alternatives, they chose the latter, and they remain in a serious "reform-growth dilemma." Perhaps worse, recent policies regarding state enterprises have emphasized the key role of the state sector and the intensification of Communist Party control over these corporations, executive appointments, and business decisions. Many observers see these as exacerbating the core problems of corporate governance.[25]

In this context the Belt and Road Initiative (BRI), hailed within China as a major strategic foray, does not address these core problems, and in some respects is yet another way to delay reform and may be exposing China to more problems as earlier chapters in this volume have detailed. However impressive as geopolitical strategy, the initiative is mobilizing capital for projects with little prospect for financial returns in the near-term and in fact appears to be motivated in part by desire to absorb excess capacity in loss-making state corporations. Further extending the credit boom into financially risky projects, the BRI delays state-sector reform by propping up overcapacity sectors that are already the most in need of restructuring (see chapters 10 and 12 by Ho-fung Hong and David M. Lampton, respectively, this volume).[26]

As a result, total credit to corporations—private and state-owned—has expanded even as growth rates have dropped; higher levels of investment are generating increasingly smaller returns. The result has been an unprecedented expansion of corporate and total debt, causing many observers to warn that China's debt load is increasing at a rate and to a size that typically precedes major financial crises.[27] By May 2017, China's total debt was equivalent to 327 percent of 2016 GDP; this is more than double the total in 2008, roughly the same level as the United States, though still far lower than Japan's, which is well above 400 percent of annual GDP.[28] The composition of China's debt, unlike those of other leading economies, is predominantly corporate rather than household or government. This leads many observers to believe that the debt load will have a much larger and more direct impact on the "real" economy. Ominously, the rate of increase in overall debt is similar to that in Japan on the eve of its financial crisis and subsequent stagnation in the 1990s.[29]

According to the International Monetary Fund (IMF), SOEs are responsible for 55 percent of corporate debt, despite representing only 22 percent of economic output, with a large percentage of them "essentially on life support." Some 60 percent of the rise in corporate debt since 2008 is due to state-sector borrowing, and the most indebted "zombie" firms are concentrated in state-sector industry in north and northeast China.[30] Nonproductive firms or excess capacity sectors absorb an increasing share of credit, wasting resources and creating ever-larger debt. The debt overhang will depress future economic growth, as increasing shares of new bank loans will be devoted simply to rolling over existing unpaid loans. This is what makes structural reform more urgent—writing off bad debt, shutting down nonviable enterprises, removing implicit guarantees and subsidies to state firms that soften budget constraints, and improving lending standards. Such reforms would slow growth in the short run, but the leadership remains wedded to "strengthening" the state sector and meeting politically mandated growth targets.[31]

Many believe that China can avoid a financial crisis because of state control over the banks, its managed exchange rate, and unusually strong capital controls. Other analysts recognize these systemic brakes on financial panic but warn that China is still vulnerable to the potentially destabilizing consequences of rapidly expanding debt. The implications of mounting debt for China's future are twofold. First, needed state-sector reform and a shift away from investment-driven growth have been delayed. Under normal circumstances such a delay would weaken China's economic advance in the medium term, postponing reforms widely considered essential for the shift to a new development model. These are the issues usually considered in discussions of whether China will have the ability to escape a prospective "middle income trap." The debt problem, however, adds a new dimension to discussions of China's future. Delayed reform has been accompanied by a politically mandated expansion of credit that has burdened China with a rapidly growing and unsustainably large debt level—far more damaging to the country's economic prospects than delaying reform in the absence of a credit boom.

Second, even without a financial crisis, it is clear that future growth is being sacrificed by policies that prioritize the propping up of short-term growth. The only question appears to be whether much lower growth in the future will be accompanied by financial turmoil, short-term downturns, or even Japan-style stagnation. Some argue that "China as a whole is a Ponzi unit," with total interest on outstanding loans double the incremental increase in nominal GDP.[32] Even if a financial crisis can be avoided, continued delay on reforming the state sector, combined with ballooning corporate debt, lead to projections that China's growth rate will decline to 2–3 percent per year within the next decade.[33]

Politics in a Lower-Growth Future

The likely impact of lower growth on the party's popular support can already be foreseen in the same surveys that have reported high levels of trust in the central government. The four rounds of the Asian Barometer Survey, from 2002 to 2015, have shown a steady decline in overall levels of trust. While this decline is observed across all age cohorts, in each survey levels of trust vary systematically by age, with the oldest cohorts having the highest level of trust and the youngest cohort the lowest. More important, the oldest cohorts show the lowest rate of decline in levels of trust, while the youngest cohorts show much more pronounced declines. The downward trend, moreover, is most pronounced among better-educated urban residents, those who have benefitted most from China's economic expansion.[34]

These findings have implications for a future era of lower growth. The oldest cohorts in these surveys experienced life prior to China's economic boom and have seen the greatest improvements in their incomes and standard of living. The youngest cohorts were born and came of age during the boom. The improvements that they have experienced are more modest than those of older generations and they are more likely to take current levels of prosperity for granted. As younger cohorts age in an era of slower growth, slower increases in income, and lower rates of upward mobility, the downward trend in expressed trust toward central authorities is likely to continue and perhaps accelerate.

Analysts have already noted a growing generation gap between pre- and post-1980 birth cohorts, especially among educated urban residents. The younger generation is less nationalistic and less trusting of the central government. Surveys show that they are more skeptical of both central and local governments, and have less interest in politics than personal concerns. However, they are more confident about discussion of public issues, even though their confidence does not often translate into political activism. While this appears to suggest apathy and inactivity, it could also be a portent of a more critical and less obedient citizenry. These survey results are at odds with the perception that younger generations are more nationalistic and patriotic due to "patriotic education" in the school system.[35]

These surveys contain hints that the high levels of popular approval so evident during the high-growth era will be replaced by greater willingness to criticize regime performance. The rapid aging of the population will greatly increase costs for health care and pensions, and if China's public programs are not expanded and improved, they are likely to become major issues of popular concern (see Eggleston chapter, this volume). This is especially the case because of the age structure of the population—virtually all members of the younger generations are from single-child households, and in the absence of strong public programs, health care and support of elderly parents will become a major burden and reduce disposable income. China's government expenditures on health care and pensions as a percentage of GDP are low—roughly half of the average for high-income countries, and rapid population aging creates strong pressures for increasing public expenditures.[36] In this and other areas, lower growth will create increasing pressures for enhanced government performance. These will be especially evident among the two hundred million to three hundred million urbanites with consumer purchasing power that earns them the somewhat misleading label of "middle class." Moreover, faltering performance in social policy will likely further reduce tolerance of official corruption and income inequality. This population is of much greater strategic importance for party power than laid-off industrial workers in rust-belt regions, disgruntled pensioners, and expropriated homeowners and farmers who have generated waves of protest in the past. Large-scale collective action by the citizens of

China's leading cities would be much more challenging than protests by less strategically located populations, and it would present leaders with a much greater dilemma about the use of force versus compromise.[37]

The anticipated redesign of China's fiscal system also contains hidden political risks. The current fiscal system is heavily dependent on taxes on industry, especially large state enterprises—a legacy of the old Soviet system. As growth slows, these revenues will decline. More than two-thirds of government tax revenue comes from taxes on firms. Chinese urban households are dramatically undertaxed from a comparative perspective. Only 6 percent of tax revenue comes from the individual income tax, and as recently as 2018, some report that fewer than 10 percent of Chinese citizens pay any income tax.[38] There is no significant taxation of property, in particular homes or other real estate. The private wealth and much higher household incomes so evident among the top earners in urban areas have barely been tapped. Furthermore, the current system, which precludes local governments from raising revenues through mechanisms like property taxes, has left them indebted to banks at levels that threaten the solvency of the financial system (see chapter 4 by Jean C. Oi, this volume). As growth rates slow and corporate indebtedness strains the fiscal system, additional taxation of households appears inevitable. Prosperous urban households will face significant taxation for the first time, a development likely to alter their expectations and perceptions of government performance because it will occur at precisely the time that demand and costs for health care and elder care will stress family budgets (see Eggleston chapter, this volume).

These trends will also be felt within the Communist Party itself, which has concentrated its recruitment efforts for well over a decade among the highly educated, especially students enrolled in leading universities.[39] The party's real social base is its ninety million members, and generational change is reflected there as well. Older generations of leaders will find themselves under increasing pressure to meet the expectations of the increasingly prosperous and well-educated members that dominate the lower reaches of their organization in urban areas. Many individuals from these backgrounds already occupy positions as party branch secretaries. Their views, experiences, and expectations will not be very different from their nonparty colleagues with similar occupations and living standards.[40] By extension, the party rank and file and many of its lower-level functionaries will also have similar performance expectations for their party's leaders, and they will likely have no more tolerance for high-level corruption than their nonparty counterparts. They also may have progressively less tolerance for strict censorship, demands for ideological conformity, and the suppression of political expression than those outside the party.

More broadly, demographic shifts in a low-growth era will create more severe distributional trade-offs than China's leaders have faced during the high-growth era. Rising expenditures on health care, pensions, and other social programs will come into more direct conflict with spending on the military and internal security. This is especially so because expenditures on internal security are not a response to widespread criminal activity or credible terrorist threats; they are a consequence of Beijing's desire to restrict the circulation of information and suppress independent political expression (see chapter 5 by Xueguang Zhou, this volume). A much more constrained national budget, more modest trade surpluses and foreign exchange reserves in a low-growth era, in all likelihood accompanied by a still painful unwinding of accumulated debt, may well generate serious disagreements over national priorities in the top leadership of a kind that has been largely absent since the late 1980s.

The leadership of a more fiscally and financially constrained China will face tougher choices about its military and security expenditures, the assertiveness of its foreign policy, the design of its taxation system, the survival of large state-owned corporations, and the level and associated costs of monitoring and policing political expression. These issues will all be felt much more acutely in a low-growth era, increasing the likelihood of openly expressed policy differences at the top of the party. To the extent that such differences become evident outside the highest reaches of power, they would, as in the past, activate party members at all levels and stimulate discussion and political expression in the population at large.

The constraints facing a future slow-growth China will not be as severe as those faced by the Soviet Union near the end of its existence. The USSR tried to match US military spending despite having an economy whose GDP in 1987 was only 39 percent as large as the United States, with a GDP per capita only one third as large.[41] China's military and internal security expenditures have risen rapidly, but they are still only a fraction of what the United States spends. More important, the overall size of China's economy is much larger relative to that of the United States than the Soviet Union's ever was—and this is what matters most in considerations of military and economic might. In nominal terms China's GDP is 60 percent the size of the US economy.[42] China therefore has, and will continue to have, a much larger economic foundation for international influence than the Soviet Union at its height.

Nonetheless, China will feel much more constrained in the future by domestic liabilities. With regard to these it is GDP *per capita* that is the most relevant measure. China's current GDP per capita is only 27 percent that of the United States, even less than the Soviet Union's level in 1987, and with a population that is aging much more rapidly. Therefore the trade-off between social spending and military-security expenditures will be much more serious than the overall size of China's economy might suggest.

China's Possible Futures

The force of the argument in this chapter depends on China's future growth trajectory. The high-growth era is already over. The only question is how much lower growth rates will be. The most optimistic scenarios project continuing growth at 4 percent to 5 percent annually, well above anticipated growth rates for China's economic rivals. This would considerably lessen the impact of the trends outlined in this chapter. There are reasons to take these optimistic projections seriously. China's state sector is a problem, but it is considerably smaller than the private sector. Its negative impact will not be as severe as in the Soviet Union, where a stagnating state sector was the entire economy. The Chinese economy is far more open, dynamic, and innovative than the Soviet Union's was at any point. Its large and vibrant private economy has been a driver of improvements in productivity and innovation. And while China shows clear parallels with other high-growth economies in East Asia, it remains at a lower level of urbanization and industrialization than Japan and South Korea at the end of their high-growth eras. China's low level of GDP per capita compared with its predecessors in East Asia, and the massive size and large potential of its domestic consumer economy, suggest that China still has the potential to generate growth at higher levels.

The weight of the argument in this chapter, however, is that these optimistic projections are much less credible now than a decade ago. The demographic changes that will leave China with a rapidly aging population, rising dependency ratios, and smaller and more expensive labor forces are inevitable and already under way. The reform of the state sector seems to have been postponed indefinitely. The recent emphasis on centralizing party control and increasing the state sector's role will exacerbate existing problems. Moves toward a new development model are not yet clearly visible. Most worrying of all is the rapidly accumulating debt load in the corporate sector. The combination of these trends suggests that growth may be well below the optimistic projections, and the burgeoning debt makes a liquidity crisis and even recession a real possibility.

To the extent that these concerns are justified, the chain of reasoning in this chapter permits fairly confident predictions about the changes that will follow. The urban population will have less trust in the central authorities and less tolerance of inequality and official corruption. They will be less optimistic about their life prospects and more demanding when it comes to social policy. A party organization whose membership and lower-level functionaries look increasingly like the more prosperous and well-educated urban citizens will share many of these characteristics, putting new pressures on the party's higher leadership. Party leaders will face greater constraints when it comes to military expenditures and security policy, and rising demands for social expenditures. This will increase the likelihood of open policy differences among top leaders that once again, as in the now distant 1980s, differentiate reformers and liberalizers from conservatives and even hard-line nationalists.

This much we can predict with relative confidence. But there is no firm foundation for predicting the likely outcomes of a more politically dynamic and pluralistic society and party organization. We cannot predict how these strivings will be expressed, or how leaders will react. Interactions among top leaders, both civilian and military, and how their relationships are altered or frayed in the face of political tensions cannot be predicted. If China's political institutions were unexpectedly to break down, it would be even more uncertain what might follow—corrupt personal rule backed by military and security forces (as in Russia); South Korean or Polish-style negotiated transfer of power; or perhaps simply a partial political liberalization. It is quite possible that the party will adapt, liberalize, accommodate, and survive, although certain leaders might instead attempt to double down on repression and doctrinal rigidity.

Macro-level outcomes of this type are the products of micro-level interactions among high-level political actors in changing and often ambiguous circumstances. They are not a linear function of aggregate economic and social trends or levels of popular protest. After all, these outcomes realistically are no more predictable than an American presidential election. But one thing seems clear: the popular support enjoyed by the central government and the party unity that we have learned to take for granted for more than twenty years will no longer be a central feature of the Chinese polity. Change—of some kind—will be in the air.

Notes

Introduction

1. Examples include Martin Jacques, *When China Rules the World: The End of the Western World and the Birth of a New Global Order*, second edition (New York: Penguin, 2012); Jonathan Fenby, *Will China Dominate the 21st Century*, second edition (Cambridge, UK: Polity Press, 2017); Ann Lee, *Will China's Economy Collapse?* (Cambridge, UK: Polity Press, 2017); and Gordon G. Chang, *The Coming Collapse of China* (New York: Random House, 2001).

2. See, for example, Xi Jinping, *The Governance of China* (Beijing: Foreign Languages Press, 2014); and Xi Jinping, *The Governance of China II* (Beijing: Foreign Languages Press, 2017).

3. See, for example, Howard W. French, *Everything under the Heavens: How the Past Helps Shape China's Push for Global* Power (New York: Alfred Knopf, 2017); and James R. Gorrie, *The China Crisis: How China's Economic Collapse Will Lead to a Global Depression* (Hoboken, NJ: John Wiley & Sons, 2013).

4. See, for example, David Shambaugh, *China's Future* (Cambridge, UK: Polity Press, 2016); and Lee, *Will China's Economy Collapse?*

5. For the first articulation of the centenary goals, see "Full Text of Hu Jintao's Report at the 18th Party Congress," November 27, 2012, http://www.china-embassy.org/eng/zt/18th_CPC_National_Congress_Eng/t992917.htm. Reaffirmations can be found in Xi Jinping, "Secure a Decisive Victory in Building a Moderately Prosperous Society in All Respects and Strive for the Great Success of Socialism with Chinese Characteristics for a New Era," delivered at the 19th National Congress of the Communist Party of China, October 18, 2017, http://www.xinhuanet.com/english/download/Xi_Jinping's_report_at_19th_CPC_National_Congress.pdf; and Li Keqiang, "Report on the Work

of the Government," delivered at the First Session of the 13th National People's Congress of the People's Republic of China on March 5, 2018, http://online.wsj .com/public/resources/documents/NPC2018_GovtWorkReport_English.pdf. For illustrative commentary on the significance of the goals, see Shannon Tiezzi, "Why 2020 Is a Make-or-Break Year for China," *The Diplomat*, February 13, 2015, https://thediplomat.com/2015/02/why-2020-is-a-make-or-break-year-for-china/.

6. Beijing ceased referring by name to the drive to achieve preeminence in several areas of advanced technology in late 2018, seemingly in response to complaints and demands from the Trump administration made during the trade dispute that began the previous year. The title of the program may have been dropped but not the quest for technological dominance. For more on 2025 goals, see State Council, "'Made in China 2025' Plan Issued," May 19, 2015, http:// english.gov.cn/policies/latest_releases/2015/05/19/content_281475110703534.htm.

7. Reformers like Zhu Rongji used the excuse of getting ready for China to join the World Trade Organization (WTO) to push through much needed SOE reforms. See Jean C. Oi, ed., *Going Private in China: The Politics of Corporate Restructuring and System Restructuring* (Washington, DC: APARC Brookings, 2011), especially Joo-Youn Jung, "Reinvented Intervention: The Chinese Central State and State-owned Enterprise Reform in the WTO Era," 119–34. See also Barry Naughton, *Growing out of the Plan* (Cambridge, UK: Cambridge University Press, 1995).

8. See Ian Johnson, "China's Lost Decade," *New York Review of Books*, September 27, 2012, http://www.nybooks.com/articles/2012/09/27/chinas-lost -decade/.

9. Cheng Li, *Chinese Politics in the Xi Jinping Era: Reassessing Collective Leadership* (Washington, DC: Brookings Institution, 2016).

10. See, for example, Ezra F. Vogel, *Deng Xiaoping and the Transformation of China* (Cambridge, MA: Belknap Press, 2011), chapter 11; and Harry Harding, *A Fragile Relationship: The United States and China since 1972* (Washington, DC: Brookings Institution, 1992).

11. See, for example, Richard Baum, ed., *China's Four Modernizations: The New Technological Revolution* (Boulder, CO: Westview Press, 1980).

12. Illustrative examples of works examining trade-offs and problems include Vaclav Smil, *The Bad Earth: Environmental Degradation in China* (Armonk, NY: M.E. Sharpe, 1984); Mary E. Gallagher, *Authoritarian Legality in China: Law, Workers, and the State* (Cambridge, UK: Cambridge University Press, 2017); and Jean C. Oi, *Rural China Takes Off: Institutional Foundations of Economic Reform* (Berkeley: University of California Press, 1999).

13. Then premier Wen Jiabao famously characterized China's growth model as "unstable, unbalanced, uncoordinated, and unsustainable" in 2007 and re-

turned to that point in his final report to the National People's Congress. See Wen Jiabao, "Report on the Work of the Government," March 5, 2013, http://on line.wsj.com/public/resources/documents/WenWorkReport_Eng_2013.pdf; and Tom Holland, "Wen and Now: China's Economy is Still 'Unsustainable,'" *South China Morning Post*, April 10, 2017.

14. For a detailed case study of this agility, see Jean C. Oi and Steven M. Goldstein, eds., *Zouping Revisited: Adaptive Governance in a Chinese County* (Stanford, CA: Stanford University Press, 2018).

15. The World Bank classifies countries with per capita incomes of $3,956 to $12,235 as "upper middle income." China's per capita income in 2018 was $9,770. See "China," World Bank Data, https://data.worldbank.org/country/ china?view=chart.

16. See, for example, Linda Glawe and Helmut Wagner, "The Middle-Income Trap: Definition, Theories and Countries Concerned—A Literature Survey," *Comparative Economic Studies* 58 (2016): 507–38, https://link.springer.com/con tent/pdf/10.1057%2Fs41294-016-0014-0.pdf; and Barry Eichengreen, Donghyun Park, and Kwanho Shin, "Growth Slowdowns Redux: New Evidence on the Middle Income-Trap," National Bureau of Economic Research, Working Paper 18673, January 2013, http://www.nber.org/papers/w18673.pdf.

17. For information on graduation to high-income status, see Matt Juden, "Which Countries Have Graduated from Each Income Group and When?" Center for Global Development, March 23, 2016, https://www.cgdev.org/blog/ which-countries-have-graduated-each-income-group-and-when.

18. See, for example, David L. Epstein, Robert Bates, Jack Goldstone, Ida Kristensen, and Sharyn O'Halloran, "Democratic Transitions," *American Journal of Political Science* 50, no. 3 (July 2006): 551–69; and Henry S. Rowen, "When Will the Chinese People Be Free?" *Journal of Democracy* 18, no. 3 (July 2007): 38–52 and works cited therein.

19. See, for example, "Xi Calls for Strengthened Ideological Work in Colleges," *Xinhua*, December 9, 2016, http://www.xinhuanet.com/english/2016 -12/09/c_135891337.htm; and "Document 9: A ChinaFile Translation," China File, November 8, 2013, http://www.chinafile.com/document-9-chinafile-translation.

20. See, for example, Edward S. Steinfeld, *Playing Our Game: Why China's Rise Doesn't Threaten the West* (Oxford: Oxford University Press, 2010).

21. See, for example, Migtali Das and Papa N'Diaye, "Chronicle of a Decline Foretold: Has China Reached the Lewis Turning Point?" International Monetary Fund, IMF Working Paper, January 2013, https://www.imf.org/external/pubs/ft/ wp/2013/wp1326.pdf.

22. See, for example, "China Plus One," *FTI Journal*, February 2013, http:// www.ftijournal.com/article/china-plus-one.

23. See, for example, "Xu Zhangrun's China: 'Licking Carbuncles and Sucking Abscesses,'" *China Change*, August 1, 2018, https://chinachange.org/2018/08/01/xu-zhangruns-china-licking-carbuncles-and-sucking-abscesses/; and Chris Buckley, "As China's Woes Mount, Xi Jinping Faces Rare Rebuke at Home," *New York Times*, July 31, 2018, https://www.nytimes.com/2018/07/31/world/asia/xi-jinping-internal-dissent.html.

24. See, for example, Tianyong Zhou, *The China Dream and the China Path* (Singapore: World Scientific Publishing, 2014).

25. See, for example, Joseph Fewsmith, "The Political and Social Implications of China's Accession to the WTO," *China Quarterly* 167 (September 2001): 573–91, and sources cited therein.

26. See, for example, Xi Jinping, "Address to the First Session of the 12th National People's Congress," March 17, 2013, in Xi, *Governance of China*, vol. 1, 40–46.

27. See Andrew Walder, *China under Mao: A Revolution Derailed* (Cambridge, MA: Harvard University Press, 2015).

28. See, for example, Seth D. Kaplan, "Development with Chinese Characteristics," *The American Interest*, January 3, 2018, https://www.the-american-interest.com/2018/01/03/development-chinese-characteristics/; and Thomas Ambrosio, "The Rise of the 'China Model' and 'Beijing Consensus': Evidence of Authoritarian Diffusion?" *Contemporary Politics* 18, no. 4: 381–99, https://www.tandfonline.com/doi/pdf/10.1080/13569775.2012.728029?needAccess=true.

29. Xi Jinping, "Full Text of Xi Jinping's Report at 19th CPC National Congress," November 3, 2017, http://www.xinhuanet.com/english/special/2017-11/03/c_136725942.htm.

Chapter 1. Xi Jinping and the Evolution of Chinese Leadership Politics

1. Xi Jinping, "Secure a Decisive Victory in Building a Moderately Prosperous Society in All Respects and Strive for the Great Success of Socialism with Chinese Characteristics for a New Era," report on the work of the 18th Central Committee to the CCP's 19th National Congress, *Xinhua* English, October 18, 2017.

2. See, for example, Xu Kangning, "Will China Repeat Japan's 'Lost Decade'?" *People's Daily* (*Renmin Ribao,* 人民日报), August 26, 2011; Wang Xiangwei, "Xi Jinping Might Be the Reformer China Needs—To Surprise the West," *South China Morning Post*, November 19, 2012.

3. On these initiatives under Hu Jintao, see Alice Miller, "Dilemmas of Globalization and Governance," in Roderick MacFarquhar, ed., *The Politics of China: Sixty Years of the People's Republic of China* (New York: Cambridge University Press, 2011), 582–88.

4. For a catalogue of these and other troubles at the end of the Hu era, see Zhou Ruijin 周瑞金, "*Heyi jieyou, weiyou gaige,* 何以解忧，唯有改革" ("Only Reform Can Relieve Our Distress"), *Caijing,* January 16, 2012, 75–83. Zhou, a former deputy editor of *People's Daily,* was the author of a series of articles under the pseudonym "Huangfu Ping" in the early 1990s backing a renewal of reform.

5. The frustrated efforts to advance PLA reform include the repeated attempts to develop command and control structures and processes for effective joint warfare and for addressing China's expanding maritime interests at the expense of the traditional ground forces orientation.

6. On persistent problems of coordination among the PRC's maritime security agencies, see Lyle J. Goldstein, *Five Dragons Stirring up the Sea: Challenge and Opportunity in China's Improving Maritime Enforcement Capabilities,* Center for Naval Warfare Studies, China Maritime Study no. 5 (Newport, RI: Naval War College Press, 2010); and Linda Jakobson, *China's Unpredictable Maritime Security Actors* (Sydney: Lowy Institute, 2014).

7. Bo Xilai was removed as Chongqing party chief on March 15, 2012; suspended from membership in the Politburo on April 10, 2012, as a corruption investigation of him opened; and expelled from the party by a Politburo meeting on September 28, 2012, an outcome ratified by the 17th Central Committee's Seventh Plenum on November 4, 2012, *Xinhua,* March 15, April 10, September 28, and November 4, 2012, respectively. He was convicted of multiple counts of corruption and abuse of office in September 2013.

8. "Firmly March on the Path of Socialism with Chinese Characteristics and Strive to Complete the Building of a Moderately Prosperous Society in All Respects" ("*Jiandingbuyi yanzhe Zhongguo tese shehuizhuyi daolu qianjin wei quanmian jiancheng xiaokang shehui er fendou,*" 坚定不移沿着中国特色社会主义道路前进 为全面建成小康社会而奋斗), report delivered by Hu Jintao to the opening session of the 18th Party Congress, *Xinhua,* November 17, 2012.

9. "CCP Central Committee Decision on Several Major Questions in Comprehensively Deepening Reform" ("*Zhonggong zhongyang guanyu quanmian shenhua gaige ruogan zhongda wenti de jueding,*" 中共中央关于全面深化改革若干重大问题的决定), November 15, 2013, in *Selected Important Documents since the 18th Party Congress* (*Shiba da yilai zhongyao wenxian xuanbian,*十八大以来重要文献选编), vol. 1 (Beijing: Party Literature Office Press, 2014), 511–46.

10. Hu Jintao, "Hold High the Great Banner of Socialism with Chinese Characteristics and Strive for New Victories in Building a Moderately Prosperous Society in All Respects" ("*Gaoju Zhongguo tese shehuizhuyi weida qizhi wei duoqu quanmian jianshe xiaokang shehui xin shengli er fendou,*" 高举中国特色社会主义伟大旗帜为夺取全面建设小康社会新胜利而奋斗), report on the work of the 16th Central Committee to the 17th Party Congress, October 15, 2007, in *Selected*

Important Documents since the 18th Party Congress (*Shiqi da yilai zhongyao wenxian xuanbian,* 十七大以来重要文献选编), vol. 1 (Beijing: Party Literature Office Press, 2009), 1–43; and Hu Jintao, "Firmly March on the Path of Socialism with Chinese Characteristics and Strive to Complete the Building of a Moderately Prosperous Society in All Respects" ("*Jiandingbuyi yanzhe Zhongguo tese shehuizhuyi daolu qianjin wei quanmian jiancheng xiaokang shehui er fendou,*" 坚定不移沿着中国特色社会主义道路前进 为全面建成小康社会而奋斗) report on the work of the 17th Central Committee to the 18th Party Congress, November 8, 2012, in *Selected Important Documents since the 18th Party Congress* (*Shiba da yilai zhongyao wenxian xuanbian,*十八大以来重要文献选编), vol. 1 (Beijing: Party Literature Office Press, 2014), 1–44.

11. The agenda that the Xi leadership has pursued since the 18th Party Congress as reflected in Hu Jintao's report there reflects a broad consensus among the party elite—both active and retired. As such, Xi Jinping had a strong voice in its composition—appropriately, since he was the man designated to lead the effort to implement its agenda—but it did not reflect solely or even entirely his own preferences. See Alice Miller, "The Road to the Eighteenth Congress," *China Leadership Monitor,* no. 36 (January 6, 2012).

12. Xi Jinping, Explanation of the "Several Guidelines for Intra-Party Political Life under the New Situation" and "CCP Regulations for Inner-Party Supervision" ("*Guanyu 'guanyu xin xingshi xia dang nei zhengzhi shenghuo de ruogan zhunze' he 'Zhongguo gongchandang dangnei jiandu tiaoli' de shuoming,*" 关于 '关于新形势下党内政治生活的若干准则' 和 '中国共产党党内监督条例' 的说明), delivered to the 18th Central Committee Sixth Plenum, *Xinhua,* November 2, 2016.

13. For details, see Alice Miller, "The Road to the Third Plenum" and "What They Did on Their Summer Vacation," *China Leadership Monitor,* nos. 42 (October 7, 2013) and 45 (October 21, 2014), respectively.

14. For example, the Jiang Zemin leadership cracked down on agitation by both the party's left wing and by liberal intellectuals and right-leaning dissidents as Beijing undertook concerted pushes simultaneously to transform China's state-owned enterprise sector and join the World Trade Organization (WTO). See Miller, "Dilemmas and Globalization and Governance," 536–48 and 561–66.

15. See Barry Naughton, "Supply-Side Structural Reform at Mid-year: Compliance, Initiative, and Unintended Consequences," *China Leadership Monitor,* no. 51 (August 30, 2016).

16. Joel Wuthnow and Phillip C. Saunders, "Chinese Military Reforms in the Age of Xi Jinping: Drivers, Challenges, and Implications," *China Strategic Perspectives,* no. 10 (Washington, DC: National Defense University Press, 2017), 37–41.

17. By "Deng's orthodox logic of dialectical materialism," I mean Deng's

reversion to the conventional Marxist-Leninist logic of giving priority to the "economic base" over the "superstructure" in contrast to Mao's voluntarist inversion of it. On the Dengist roots of Xi's "new era" concept, see Alice Miller, "Only Socialism Can Save China; Only Xi Jinping Can Save Socialism," *China Leadership Monitor*, no. 56 (May 17, 2018). On the strong continuity of Xi's political approach with Deng Xiaoping's, see Alice Miller, "What Would Deng Do?" *China Leadership Monitor*, no. 52 (February 14, 2017).

18. Across the entire reform era, the party had previously required only one Central Committee plenum to prepare the way for an upcoming inaugural session of the NPC, underscoring the significance and scale of the proposals to be presented to the 13th NPC. The scope of organizational changes adopted there are easily the most extensive of the reform era. The State Council has seen reorganization at every inaugural NPC session since 1982. But this time the modifications extended to the party structure, the State Council and the NPC Standing Committee, state agencies, the Chinese People's Political Consultative Conference, the military and security forces, and mass organizations.

19. "Urgent Tasks of China's Third Generation Collective Leadership," in *Selected Works of Deng Xiaoping*, vol. 3 (Beijing: Foreign Languages Press, 1994), 300–301.

20. "Some Norms for Political Life within the Party" (*"Guanyu dang nei zhengzhi shenghuo de ruogan zhunze,"* 关于党内政治生活的若干准则), adopted at the 11th Central Committee's Fifth Plenum, February 29, 1980, in CCP Central Documents Office, ed., *Selected Important Documents since the Third Plenum* (*San zhong quanhui yilai zhongyao wenxian xuanbian,* 三中全会以来重要文献选编) (Beijing: Central Publishing House, 2011), vol. 1, 363.

21. "Several Guidelines for Intra-Party Political Life under the New Situation" (*"Guanyu xin xingshi xia dang nei zhengzhi shenghuo de ruogan zhunze,"* 关于新形势下党内政治生活的若干准则), adopted at the 18th Central Committee's Sixth Plenum, October 2016, *Xinhua*, November 2, 2016.

22. See, for example, the treatment of Hu's visit to frigid Inner Mongolia, *People's Daily*, (*Renmin Ribao,* 人民日报), January 6, 2003.

23. On the scale of the personality cult around Mao Zedong, see the example of the treatment accorded a Pakistani gift of mangoes to the revered chairman in Edward E. Rice, *Mao's Way* (Berkeley: University of California Press, 1972), 455–57.

24. Cindy Boren, "Kim Jong-il: A Sporting Life," *Washington Post*, December 19, 2011.

25. Xuan Li (*Xuan li* 宣理), "Major Institutional Arrangements for Guaranteeing the Long-Term Stability of the Party and the State" (*"Baozheng dang he guojia changzhijiuan de zhongda zhidu anpai,"* 保证党和国家长治久安的重大制度安排) *People's Daily* (*Renmin Ribao,* 人民日报), March 1, 2018, 3.

Chapter 2. Grand Steerage

1. Liu Qiangdong, "Interview with Qin Shuo," August 19, 2017, http://www .wenxuecity.com/news/2017/08/19/6504690.html. See also Tsinghua University Law Professor Xiang Feng, "AI Will Spell the End of Capitalism," May 3, 2018, *World Post,* https://www.washingtonpost.com/amphtml/news/theworldpost/wp/ 2018/05/03/end-of-capitalism/.

2. Karl Marx, *Economic and Philosophic Manuscripts of 1844* (New York: Prometheus Books, 1988).

3. Xi Jinping, "Secure a Decisive Victory in Building a Moderately Prosperous Society in All Respects and Strive for the Great Success of Socialism with Chinese Characteristics for a New Era," Report to the 19th Party Congress, October 18, 2017, http://www.xinhuanet.com/english/special/2017-11/03/c_13672 5942.htm

4. There are a few examples of programs that might plausibly seem to contradict this assertion. For example, China had a "Western Development Program" and also an industrial policy for semiconductor industry develop-ment. The Western Development Plan was a general regional preferential policy that bundled together a number of existing policy provisions (Barry Naughton, "The Western Development Program," in Barry Naughton and Dali Yang, eds., *Holding China Together: Diversity and National Integration in the Post-Deng Era* (New York: Cambridge University Press, 2004), 253–97. The semiconductor in-dustry policy was an effort to establish a set of tax rebates that would encourage primarily foreign (!) firms to produce in China. Even if the reader prefers to call these "plans," the number is quite small.

5. Chen Ling and Barry Naughton, "An Institutionalized Policy-making Mechanism: China's Return to Techno-Industrial Policy," *Research Policy* 45 (2016): 2,138–52.

6. Junko Yoshida, "Much Ado About China's Big IC Surge; Myth and reality of China's IC fund," *EETimes Online,* June 22, 2017, http://www.eetimes.com/ document.asp?doc_id=1331928 (accessed on September 11, 2019). In addition, after the Chinese corporation ZTE was sanctioned by the United States, it is reported that urgent instructions went out to increase allotments to IC industry funds and accelerate construction.

7. CCP Party Center and State Council, "An Outline of the National Innovation Driven Development Strategy," May 29, 2016, *Xinhua,* http://www .xinhuanet.com/politics/2016-05/19/c_1118898033.htm.

8. Paul Triolo and Jimmy Goodrich, "From Riding a Wave to Full Speed Ahead: As China's Government Mobilizes for AI Leadership, Some Challenges Will Be Tougher Than Others," *New America DigiChina Project Policy Paper,*

February 28, 2018, https://www.newamerica.org/cybersecurity-initiative/digi
china/blog/riding-wave-full-steam-ahead/.

9. The April 2018 draft plan for Xiongan stresses the green city agenda. It
specifies population density limits but has no provisional population targets.
Hebei Provincial Party Committee and Government, "Hebei Xiongan Draft
Plan" ("*Hebei Xiongan xinqu guihua gangya,*" 河北雄安新区规划纲要), April 21,
2018, http://www.xinhuanet.com/2018-04/21/c_1122720132.htm.

10. The calculation and definitions are described in Barry Naughton, "Is
China Socialist?," *Journal of Economic Perspectives* 31, no. 1 (Winter 2017): 1–23.
Official Ministry of Finance data are used to update the calculation through
2018.

11. The OECD unweighted average budget revenue, including social security
contributions, is 34 percent of GDP, coincidentally almost the same as China's
augmented government revenues. Of this, 9 percent of GDP are official social
security revenues, and some countries, like Australia, fund social security out of
general revenues. For the United States the figures are 24 percent of GDP in total
revenues, of which 5.4 percent are social security revenues. These figures include
central, state, and local governments. For more discussion, see Naughton, "Is
China Socialist?," 6.

12. National Bureau of Statistics, *Zhongguo Tongji Zhaiyao 2018* (China
Statistical Abstract 2018) (Beijing: Zhongguo Tongji, 2018), 32.

13. The grand steerage policies contradict statements by Chinese policymakers that seem to advocate a rebalancing toward consumption. At the 19th
Communist Party Congress in November 2017, Xi Jinping declared that the
principal contradiction of the current era is the one "between unbalanced and
inadequate development and the people's ever-growing needs for a better life."

14. Barry Naughton, *The Chinese Economy: Adaptation and Growth*
(Cambridge: MIT Press, 2018), 202–206.

15. Barry Naughton, "The Current Wave of State Enterprise Reform in
China: A Preliminary Appraisal," *Asian Economic Policy Review* 12, no. 2 (July
2017): 282–98.

16. Data are from the private industry group Zero2IPO, https://www.pedata
.cn/ (some data may be behind a paywall).

17. Liu He, ed., *A Comparative Study of the Two Global Crisis* (*Liangci quan-
qiu da weiji de bijiao yanjiu,* 两次全球大危机的比较研究) (Beijing: Zhongguo
Jingji, 2013). This coauthored work won the top economics prize in China in
2012, demonstrating its persuasiveness and impact. A small part of its argument
appears in Liu He, "Overcoming the Great Recession: Lessons from China,"
Harvard Kennedy School, Belfer Center for Science and International Affairs,

July 2014, https://news.harvard.edu/wp-content/uploads/2014/07/comparative_crises_final-web.pdf.

18. National Science Board (US National Science Foundation), *Science and Engineering Indicators 2018,* https://www.nsf.gov/statistics/2018/nsb20181/ (accessed on September 11, 2019).

Chapter 3. Anticorruption Forever?

1. The CPI is available at "Corruption Perception Index 2016," *Transparency International,* January 25, 2017, https://www.transparency.org/news/feature/corruption_perceptions_index_2016. Scores for the CPI are not normally distributed with the result that the median is a better measure of centrality than the mean.

2. The Governance Index is available at "Worldwide Governance Indicators," World Bank, http://info.worldbank.org/governance/wgi/#home (accessed on September 9, 2019).

3. Pew Research Center Global Attitudes Project, "Environmental Concerns on the Rise in China Many Also Worried about Inflation, Inequality, Corruption," Pew Research Center, September 19, 2013, http://www.pewglobal.org/2013/09/19/environmental-concerns-on-the-rise-in-china/; and Richard Wike and Bridget Parker, "Corruption, Pollution, Inequality Are Top Concerns in China Many Worry about Threats to Traditions and Culture," Pew Research Center, September 24, 2015, http://www.pewglobal.org/files/2015/09/Pew-Research-Center-China-Report-FINAL-September-24-2015.pdf. Also see Transparency International, "Global Corruption Barometer, 2017, https://www.transparency.org/news/feature/global_corruption_barometer_citizens_voices_from_around_the_world (accessed on September 9, 2019).

4. In 2014, Bruce J. Dickson found that a majority of those who believed that almost all officials were corrupt and those who said they had paid bribes supported the regime; see Dickson, *The Dictator's Dilemma: The Chinese Communist Party's Strategy for Survival* (New York: Oxford University Press, 2016), 256–57.

5. This was apparently a dispute over money that Neil Heywood felt he was owed for helping Gu Kailai launder bribes from individuals seeking to curry favor with Bo Xilai.

6. In May 2018, Sun Zhengcai was sentenced to life in prison after being convicted of accepting 170 million yuan in bribes.

7. Although the term "tiger" is popularly applied to any senior official charged with corruption, I use the term to refer to civilian officials and party cadres. In addition to this group, Xi Jinping has also pursued corruption within the People's Liberation Army (PLA). As of January 2018, over seventy senior military officers were allegedly investigated or sidelined because of possible corruption. Data on senior PLA officers charged with corruption is less reliable than

that on the civilian tigers. Military officers are generally investigated by the PLA's internal Procuratorate and prosecuted in military courts. The outcomes of those investigations and trials often are not publically reported. In many cases, reports of an investigation appear in the Hong Kong press or overseas media but are not reported by official mainland sources. I will thus refer to this group only in mapping out the temporal development of the crackdown.

8. "CPC Constitution Says 'Fight against Corruption Keeps Going,'" *Xinhua*, October 24, 2017.

9. "In Mass Address, China's Xi Calls for Total Party Loyalty," *Reuters*, January 11, 2018.

10. "Decision of the Standing Committee of the National People's Congress Regarding the Pilot Reform of the National Supervisory System in Beijing, Shanxi, and Zhejiang" ("*Quanguo renmin daibiao changwu weiyuanhui guanyu zai Beijing shi, Shanxi sheng, Zhejiang sheng kaizhan guojia tizhi shidian gongzuo de jueding*," 全国人民代表大会常务委员会关于在北京市、山西省、浙江省开展国家监察体制改革试点工作的决定), http://www.xinhuanet.com//politics/2016-12/25/c_1120184274.htm (accessed on September 9, 2019).

11. "Take Strict Control of the Party in a Comprehensive Manner and Move Forward" ("*Quanmian cong yan zhi dang zai chufa—xie zai shijiu jie zhongyang jiwei er ci quanhui zhaokai zhi ji*," 全面从严治党再出发—写在十九届中央纪委二次全会召开之际), On the occasion of the Second Plenary Session of the 19th Central Committee, January 11, 2018, http://www.chinacourt.org/article/detail/2018/01/id/3153360.shtml.

12. "CPC Has Nearly 89.5m Members," *China Daily*, June 30, 2017.

13. Based on data in the annual work reports of the National Supervisory Commission. The reports are available at http://www.ccdi.gov.cn.

14. Based on annual work reports of the Supreme People's Procuratorate. The reports are available at http://www.spp.gov.cn.

15. Based on annual work reports of the Supreme People's Court. The reports are available at http://www.spc.gov.cn.

16. "Eight-point Regulation," *China Daily*, December 5, 2012, http://cpcchina.chinadaily.com.cn/2012-12/05/content_15991171.htm. Based on the monthly reports by the DIC available at http://fanfu.people.com.cn.

17. "Four Dishes and One Soup: China's Anti-Graft Push Shows a Leadership Increasingly Wary of Public Discontent," *China Economic Review* (January 22, 2013), https://chinaeconomicreview.com/four-dishes-one-soup/.

18. In 1989 nearly a quarter of a century before the Eight-point Regulation, the State Council mandated that official banquets be limited to "one bowl of soup and four other dishes." Ann Scott Tyson, "Chinese Criticize Lavish Feasting," *Christian Science Monitor*, January 4, 1990.

19. Announcements of the expulsion party members frequently include violating the Eight-point Regulation in the list of offenses.

20. "Reported Cases Up 20% in First Half of Year" ("*Shang bannian chachu zhiwu fanzui renshu tongbi zengzhang jin liang cheng,*" 上半年查处职务犯罪人数同比增长近两成), *People.cn,* July 13, 2017, http://legal.people.com.cn/n1/2017/0713/c42510-29401229.html.

21. Report available at "The People's Congress Holds the Second Plenary Meeting to Hear and Consider the 'Two Highs' Report" ("*Rendaihui juxing di er ci quanti huiyi tingqu he shenyi 'liang gao' baogao,*" 人代会举行第二次全体会议听取和审议 "两高" 报告), *China Police Network,* March 9, 2018, http://special.cpd.com.cn/n40115672/n40575470/n40575478/n40634200/c40698457/content.html.

22. The 2019 Procuratorial Work Report did not provide a breakdown of indictments by level.

23. Gu Junshan reportedly gave Xu Caihou's daughter RMB 2 million as a wedding present.

24. Bo Zhiyue, "Were China's Corrupt Officials Plotting a Coup?" *The Diplomat,* April 13, 2015.

25. Alice Miller, "The Trouble with Factions," *China Leadership Monitor* 44 (2015): 1–12.

26. Half of the tigers had been detained by late 2015.

27. The following paragraphs on Gu Junshan are based on Nectar Gan, "China's Disgraced PLA General Gu Junshan Given Suspended Death Sentence for Corruption," *South China Morning Post,* August 10, 2015, http://www.scmp.com/news/china/policies-politics/article/1848264/chinas-disgraced-pla-general-gu-junshan-given-suspended; Jonathan Ansfield, "Leader of China Aims at Military with Graft Case," *New York Times,* March 31, 2014, https://www.nytimes.com/2014/04/01/world/asia/chinese-military-general-charged-in-graft-inquiry.html; and Heyan Wang, "How a PLA General Built a Web of Corruption To Amass a Fortune," *Caixin,* January 16, 2014.

28. "Verdict of the Trial of the First Instance of Bo Xilai," translated in *China Law & Government* 47, no. 5/6 (2015): 25–139.

29. Malcolm Moore, "Chinese Billionaire Linked to Bo Xilai Detained," *The Telegraph,* April 2, 2012, http://www.telegraph.co.uk/news/worldnews/asia/china/9180677/Chinese-billionaire-linked-to-Bo-Xilai-detained.html; and Jun Mai, "Jailed Bo Xilai Ally Was 'In Excellent Condition' before 'Mysterious' Heart Attack," *South China Morning Post,* December 10, 2015, http://www.scmp.com/news/china/policies-politics/article/1889120/jailed-dalian-shide-tycoon-and-bo-xilai-ally-xu-ming.

30. Leslie Hook, "Gu Kailai," *Financial Times,* December 14, 2012, https://www.ft.com/content/8cd36e04-43f1-11e2-a48c-00144feabdc0?mhq5j=e6.

31.   David Barbosa, "China Boss's Fall Puts Focus on a Business Ally," *New York Times*, August 21, 2013, http://www.nytimes.com/2013/08/22/world/asia/china-bosss-fall-puts-focus-on-business-ally.html#story-continues-1.

32.   Lucy Hornsby, "The Parallel Rise of China's Bo Xilai and a Business Ally," *Reuters,* April 25, 2012, http://af.reuters.com/article/worldNews/idAFBRE83OoKK20120425?sp=true.

33.   "Zhou Yongkang Sentenced to Life Imprisonment in the First Instance" ("*Zhou Yongkang yishen bei panchu wuqi tuxing,*" 周永康一审被判处无期徒刑), *Xinhua*, June 11, 2015, http://news.xinhuanet.com/legal/2015-06/11/c_1115590304.htm.

34.   "Ling Jihua Sentenced to Life Imprisonment in the First Instance" ("*Ling Jihua yishen beipan wuqi,*" 令计划一审被判无期), http://news.ifeng.com/a/20160704/49291566_0.shtml.

35.   Data on the amounts of illegal money the tigers were taking in also suggest deep corruption. The data are skewed by some very large amounts. The median amount of bribes and other corrupt monies accepted by individual tigers was RMB 1.84 million a year, a sum that would have been twenty-two times the RMB 84,240 annual salary that Politburo Standing Committee members, including General Secretary Xi Jinping, were reported to have earned in 2014. Luo Wangshu, "Public Employees Get Salary Increase," *China Daily*, January 20, 2015.

36.   "Facts and Figures on CCP Discipline Inspection Work," *China Daily*, October 3, 2017.

37.   The use of central inspection teams actually began in 2003. Yukyung Yeo, "Complementing the Local Discipline Inspection Commissions of the CPP: Empowerment of the Central Inspection Groups," *Journal of Contemporary China* 25, no. 97 (2016): 59–74; and Fenfei Li and Jinting Deng, "The Power and Misuse of Power by China's Local Procuratorates in Anticorruption," *International Journal of Law, Crime, and Justice* 45 (2016): 1–25.

38.   "People's Republic of China Supervision Law (Draft)," *Chinalaw Translate,* June 11, 2017, https://www.chinalawtranslate.com/中华人民共和国监察法 (草案) /?lang=en.

39.   The Anti-Corruption Bureau was established in 1995 in an attempt to improve the Procuratorate's ability to detect and investigate corruption. In 2014 the bureau, which had reportedly struggled for years to cope with the demands of the ongoing anticorruption effort, was upgraded bureaucratically with the appointment of a deputy procurator general to head it. "China Sets Up Anti-Corruption Bureau," *Agence France Press*, November 10, 1995; and Julie Zhu, "China to Form a New Anti-Corruption Bureau," *EJInsight,* November 3, 2014.

40.   Ling Li, "The Rise of the Discipline and Inspection Commission

1927–2012: Anticorruption Investigation and Decision-making in the Chinese Communist Party," *Modern China* 42, no. 5 (2016): 467–82.

41. It is reported, however, that judges often accept confessions obtained by the DIC, reasoning that because the accused signed it, the confession represents proof of guilt.

42. Xuezhi Guo, "Controlling Corruption in the Party: China's Central Discipline Inspection Commission," *China Quarterly* 219 (2014): 597–624.

43. Founded in 2007, the Prevention Bureau's function was never clearly defined. "China Sets Up Anti-Corruption Bureau," *Associated Press,* September 6, 2007; and "China Establishes National Corruption Prevention Bureau," September 13, 2007, http://www.gov.cn/english/2007-09/13/content_748148.htm.

44. Jinting Deng, "The National Supervision Commission: A New Anti-corruption Model in China," *International Journal of Law, Crime and Justice* (2017): 58–73.

45. Josephine Ma, "Revealed: The Far-reaching Powers of China's New Super Anticorruption Agency," *South China Morning Post*, March 13, 2018. Individuals in all of these categories had in fact been prosecuted for corruption prior to 2017.

46. According to Yang Xiaodu, the new commissions will have 10 percent more labor. Nectar Gan, "Corruption Surveillance to Triple as China's New Anti-graft Agency Tightens Screws," *South China Morning Post*, March 6, 2018.

47. Flora Sapio, "*Shuanggui* and Extralegal Detention in China," *China Information* 22, no. 8 (2008): 7–37.

48. Jeremy Daum, "Unsupervised—Initial Thoughts on the Supervision Law," *Chinalaw Translate,* December 20, 2017, https://www.chinalawtranslate.com/unsupervised/?lang=en.

49. Articles 43 and 44, "Supervision Law of the PRC (2018)," *Chinalaw Translate*, November 16, 2017, https://www.chinalawtranslate.com/中华人民共和国监察法（草案）/?lang=en.

50. William Zheng, "China's Corruption Watchdog Probes Officials' Personal Details," *South China Morning Post*, March 2, 2019.

51. The list is the author's paraphrasing of a series of articles that appeared in the *South China Morning Post.*

Chapter 4. Future of Central–Local Relations

1. Adam Liu, "Building Markets within Authoritarian Institutions: The Political Economy of Banking Development in China," PhD dissertation, Department of Political Science, Stanford University, 2018; and Jean Oi and Adam Liu, "Local Government Debt in China," unpublished manuscript.

2. For details of the proliferation of these banks, see Liu, "Building Markets."

The Big 4 banks are the state-owned Bank of Agriculture, the Industrial and Commercial Bank, the Construction Bank, and the Bank of China.

3. See, for example, Jean Oi, "Fiscal Reform and the Economic Foundations of Local State Corporatism in China," *World Politics* 45 (1992): 99–126; and Jean Oi, *Rural China Takes Off: Institutional Foundations of Economic Reform* (Berkeley: University of California Press, 1999).

4. Oi, "Fiscal Reform and the Economic Foundations," 99–126; and Oi, *Rural China Takes Off.*

5. Jean Oi and Zhao Shukai, "Fiscal Crisis in China's Townships: Causes and Consequences," in *Grassroots Political Reform in Contemporary China*, eds. Merle Goldman and Elizabeth Perry (Cambridge, MA: Harvard University Press, 2007), 75–96. Also Lynette Ong, "The Political Economy of Township Government Debt, Township Enterprises and Rural Financial Institutions in China," *The China Quarterly* 186 (June 2006): 377–400.

6. The collapse of the township semiofficial financial institutions is an example of the problems of institutional catchup that the central state continually faced as the economy was in transition and growing rapidly. The banking regulatory system was created to monitor only the state banks and the savings cooperatives under the Agricultural Bank. The new financial institutions that localities created to circumvent the center's credit freeze fell outside of the state's regulatory orbit. It was only when Zhu Rongji took control of these and turned them into urban cooperative banks that they were put under state regulation. While Zhu's actions could have averted future problems, it was already too late for localities.

7. The contingent debt is payment that might be carried by the local governments in the future, such as the local government's guaranteed loans. In earlier periods it also included losses incurred by state-run grain enterprises.

8. See Yang Zhiyong and Yang Zhigang, *30 Years of Chinese Public System Reform* (Shanghai: People's Press of Shanghai, 2008), 41.

9. The localities' expenditure can be divided into two categories: the basic operation costs and the cost for public goods and services. The first category includes the basic personnel wages and basic administrative expenditure, which is called the "food money" by the local governments because this expenditure is critical for the survival of the local government. Oi and Zhao, "Fiscal Crisis in China's Townships," 80.

10. Christine P. W. Wong, *Financing Local Government in the People's Republic of China* (New York: Oxford University Press, 1997).

11. An investigation conducted by the Department of Fiscal and Financial Affairs of the National Development and Reform Commission (NDRC) and the Academy of Macro Economy Research of the NDRC in 2007 showed that

delegating expenditures downward (*shiquan*) was a prevalent phenomenon whether in developed or less-developed areas. Oi and Zhao found that education was one of the most costly expenditures that resulted in local government debt. Oi and Zhao, "Fiscal Crisis in China's Townships."

12. See, for example, Vivienne Shue and Christine Wong, eds., *Paying for Progress in China: Public Finance, Human Welfare and Changing Patterns of Inequality* (New York: Routledge, 2007).

13. ECD/UCLG, *Subnational Governments around the World: Structure and Finance* (2016), 20, https://www.oecd.org/regional/regional-policy/Subnational-Governments-Around-the-World-%20Part-I.pdf (accessed on September 8, 2019).

14. Philippe Wingender, "Intergovernmental Fiscal Reform in China," IMF Working Paper, Asia and Pacific Department, 2018 International Monetary Fund, WP/18/88.

15. In 2012 the center introduced a pilot of a value-added tax (VAT) reform that replaced the business tax. This was implemented nationwide in 2016. Analysts indicate that this further reduced net local tax revenues. See, for example, "Fiscal Policy Reform," China Dashboard Winter 2019—Asia Society Institute and Rhodium Group, https://chinadashboard.asiasociety.org/winter-2019/page/fiscal-affairs (accessed on September 8, 2019).

16. Xun Wu, "China's Growing Local Government Debt Levels," *MIT Center for Finance and Policy* (January 2016): 6.

17. This is detailed in Liu, "Building Markets."

18. See Liu, "Building Markets."

19. Yia-Ling Liu, "From Predator to Debtor: The Soft Budget Constraint and Semi-Planned Administration in Rural China," *Modern China* 3, no. 38 (January 2012): 308–45; Yinqiu Lu and Tao Sun, "Local Government Financing Platforms in China: A Fortune or Misfortune?," IMF Working Paper QP/13/243; and Hui Jin and Isabel Rial, "Regulating Local Government Financing Vehicles and Public-Private Partnerships in China," IMF Working Paper WP/16/187.

20. See, for example, Xin Sun, "Selective Enforcement of Land Regulations: Why Large-Scale Violators Succeed," *The China Journal*, 74, no. 1 (2015): 66–90; Meg Rithmire, "Land Politics and Local State Capacities—The Political Economy of Urban Change in China," *China Quarterly* 216 (December 2013): 872–95; Siu Wai Wong, "Land Requisitions and State-Village Power Restructuring in Southern China," *China Quarterly* 224 (December 2015): 888–908; and Daniel Mattingly, "Elite Capture: How Decentralization and Informal Institutions Weaken Property Rights in Rural China," *World Politics* 68, no.3 (2016): 383–412.

21. Xun Wu, "China's Growing Local Government Debt Levels."

22. Xun Wu, "China's Growing Local Government Debt Levels."

23. Jeremy Wallace, "Juking the Stats? Authoritarian Information Problems in China," *British Journal of Political Science* 46, no. 1 (2016): 11–29.

24. Hu Zejun, "2016 State Council Audit Report on Central Budget and Other Fiscal Revenues and Expenditures," 28th meeting of Standing Committee of 12th National People's Congress (June 23, 2017), "*Guowuyuan guanyu 2016 niandu zhongyang yusuan zhixing he qita caizheng shouzhi de shenji gongzuo baogao," 2017 nian 6 yue 23 ri zai di shier jie quanguo renmin daibiao dahui changwu weiyuanhui di ershiba ci huiyi shang, shenji shu shenji zhang Hu Zejun,* 国务院关于2016年度中央预算执行和其他财政收支的审计工作报告；2017年6月23日在第十二届全国人民代表大会常务委员会第二十八次会议上，审计署审计长 胡泽君.

25. Another report stated local government debt at the end of 2016 was RMB 15.32 trillion (15.32 *wanyi yuan,* 万亿元 [*renminbi,* 人民币]), which seems in line with the quota, if over. That report also stated that local governments had a debt ratio (debt/total fiscal revenue) (*zhaiwu yu'e/zonghe caili,* 债务余额/综合财力) of 80.5 percent. "Chinese Government Debt Ratio Is 36.7%" ("*Zhongguo zhengfu zhaiwu fuzhai lü wei 36.7%,*" 中国政府债务负债率为36.7%), China New Network (*Zhongguo xinwen wang,* 中国新闻网), May 4, 2017.

26. Hu Zejun, "2016 State Council Audit Report on Central Budget."

27. Before, in 2009, under a pilot program the Ministry of Finance issued on behalf of a small number of provinces local bonds. Later, the center allowed a few provinces to issue bonds directly. W. Raphael Lam and Jingsen Wang, "China's Local Government Bond Market," IMF Working Paper, Fiscal Affairs Department, International Monetary Fund September 2018, WP/18/219, https://www.imf.org/~/media/Files/Publications/WP/2018/wp18219.ashx (accessed on September 6, 2019).

28. Wingender, "Intergovernmental Fiscal Reform in China."

29. Lam and Wang, "China's Local Government Bond Market."

30. According to "China Dashboard, Fiscal Affairs, Winter 2019," Asia Society Policy Institute and The Rhodium Group, https://chinadashboard.asiasociety.org/winter-2019/page/fiscal-affairs (accessed on September 8, 2019), local governments "at the end of 2014 had a reported 14.34 trillion RMB ($2.1 trillion) in official debt. Only 256.5 billion RMB ($37 billion) of this remains to be swapped as of October 2018."

31. Lam and Wang, "China's Local Government Bond Market."

32. Timmy Shen and Yu Hairong, "China May Move Up Date for Local Bond Issuances," *Caixin English,* December 18, 2018, https://www.caixinglobal.com/2018-12-18/china-may-allow-local-governments-to-issue-bonds-earlier-than-usual-101360642.html.

33. "Signs of China (2)," *China Change,* September 22, 2018, https://chinachange.org/2018/09/22/signs-of-china-2/.

34. Document 49 from the State Council, "The State Council's guidance on promoting central and local financial power and reform of the division of expenditure responsibility" (Guofa (2016) 49 hao, *"Guowuyuan guanyu tuijin zhongyang yu difang caizheng shiquan he zhichu zeren huafen gaige de zhidao yijian,"* 国发 (2016)49号,"国务院关于推进中央与地方财政事权和支出责任划分改革的指导意见"), http://www.jconline.cn/Contents/Channel_10062/2016/0824/1309865/content_1309865.htm.

35. Xun Wu, "China's Growing Local Government Debt Levels," also states that the mandated shutdown of "non-standardized financing channels, specifically including the LGFV, would be gradually shut down."

36. See Wingender, "Intergovernmental Fiscal Reform in China."

37. "China Punishes 249 'Lazy' Officials for Unspent Funds," *Reuters China,* September 29, 2015.

38. "Less Than 12,000 Civil Servants Resigned in 2015" (*"Ren she bu: 2015 nian gongwuyuan cizhi budao 1.2 wanren,"* 人社部: 2015年公务员辞职不到1.2万人), *Sina News,* June 2016, http://finance.sina.com.cn/roll/2016-06-27/doc-ifxtmwri4609654.shtml.

39. This ratio is a better measurement than the number of applicants because the number of applicants may decrease due to a decrease in the number of vacancies rather than a declining interest in public service jobs. This ratio better captures how attractive the civil service job is among people. Note that these numbers are only for central government civil servant jobs, not jobs in provincial, prefectural, county, or township governments (or applicants to these local jobs). This decrease in ratio is highly statistically significant (p value is almost 0). To determine whether these changes were statistically significant, given that Xi Jinping came to power in November 2012, we calculated the difference in the ratio of number of test takers / number of admitted between 2008–12 and 2013–17.

40. "2018 Civil Servant Examination Test as Seen from this Year's Test Registration Data" (*"Cong linian guokao baoming shuju kan 2018 gongwuyuan kaoshi,"* 从历年国考报名数据看2018国家公务员考试), Official Website for Civil Servant Examination, July 2017, http://www.chinagwy.org/html/xwsz/zyxw/201707/21_204180.html.

41. The common characteristics of those who left included the following: (1) around thirty-five years old, at the division or vice division level (*chuji huo fuchuji,* 处级或副处级); (2) most are in coastal developed regions, such as Beijing, Guangdong, and Zhejiang; and (3) most went into business that is related to their previous job or joined the management of big companies.

42. See Jean C. Oi, "Politics in China's Corporate Restructuring," in Jean C. Oi, ed., *Going Private in China* (Washington, DC: Brookings APARC, 2011).

43. See Lizhi Liu, "From Click to Boom: The Political Economy of E-Commerce in China," PhD dissertation, Department of Political Science, Stanford University, 2018.

44. Document 49 states that "for further fiscal reform, the center will 'minimize' its involvement in managing micro (local) fiscal affairs, take advantage of local governments' advantage in handling local affairs, and, *mobilize and protect local governments' enthusiasm (jijixing,* 积极性*) and pro-activeness (zhudongxing,* 主动性*) in development"* (emphasis mine).

Chapter 5. Social Media and Governance in China

1. Franz Schurmann, *Ideology and Organization in Communist China* (Berkeley: University of California Press, 1968).

2. "Netizen," or network citizen, is the term used to refer to persons who define their identity, at least in part, as a function of their use of the Internet and participation in social media groups.

3. "Cao Guowei: The Number of Self-media Accounts on Weibo and WeChat Has Broken 10 Million" (*"Cao Guowei: Weibo he weixin shang zi meiti zhanghao shu yi po qianwan,"* 曹国伟: 微博和微信上自媒体账号数已破千万), TechWeb.com.cn, December 17, 2015, http://people.techweb.com.cn/2015-12-17/2243255.shtml.

4. Capital Internet Association, *China Weibo Development Report (2016–2017)* (*Shoudu hulianwang xiehui, Zhongguo weibo fazhan baogao,* 首都互联网协会,中国微博发展报告) (Beijing: People's Publishing House, 2017), 6.

5. Capital Internet Association, *China Weibo Development Report (2016–2017)*, 24–25.

6. "Cao Guowei: The Number of Self-media Accounts on Weibo and WeChat Has Broken 10 Million."

7. Xie Bei, *Study of China's Internet in the Era of Micro-communication* (*Xie Bei, wei chuanbo shidai de Zhongguo hulianwang zhengzhi yanjiu,*谢蓓, 微传播时代的中国互联网政治研究) (Beijing: People's Publishing House, 2014), 45.

8. Xie Bei, *Study of China's Internet in the Era of Micro-communication;* Jia Zhemin, *Political Communication in the Internet Age: Government, the Public, and Behavioral Processes* (*Jia Zhemin, hulianwang shidai de zhengzhi chuanbo: Zhengfu, gongzhong yu xingwei guocheng,* 贾哲敏,互联网时代的政治传播: 政府、公众与行为过程) (Beijing: People's Publishing House, 2017); and Capital Internet Association, *China Weibo Development Report (2016–2017)*.

9. Xie Bei, *Study of China's Internet in the Era of Micro-communication.*

10. Xueguang Zhou, *The Institutional Logic of Governance in China: An Organizational Approach* (*Zhou Xueguang, Zhongguo guojia zhili de zhidu luoji: Yige zuzhi xue yanjiu,* 周雪光,中国国家治理的制度逻辑: 一个组织学研究) (Beijing: Sanlian Press, 2017).

11. Andrew G. Walder, *Communist Neo-Traditionalism: Work and Authority in Chinese Industry* (Berkeley: University of California Press, 1986); and Edward Friedman, Paul G. Pickowicz, and Mark Selden, *Chinese Village, Socialist State* (New Haven, CT: Yale University Press, 1991).

12. Kenneth Lieberthal and David M. Lampton, eds., *Bureaucracy, Politics and Decision Making in Post-Mao China* (Berkeley: University of California Press, 1992).

13. Vivienne Shue, *The Reach of the State: Sketches of the Chinese Body Politic* (Stanford, CA: Stanford University Press, 1988).

14. Yongshun Cai, *Collective Resistance in China: Why Popular Protests Succeed or Fail?* (Stanford, CA: Stanford University Press, 2010); Chih-jou Jay Chen, "Growing Social Unrest and Emergent Protest Groups in China," in H.-H. M. Hsiao and C.-Y. Lin, eds., *Rise of China: Beijing's Strategies and Implications for the Asia-Pacific* (New York: Routledge, 2009), 87–106; Elizabeth J. Perry and Mark Selden, eds., *Chinese Society: Change, Conflict and Resistance*, 2nd edition (New York: Routledge, 2003); and Xueguang Zhou and Yun Ai, "Bases of Governance and Forms of Resistance: The Case of Rural China," in D. Courpasson and S. Valls, eds., *The Sage Handbook of Resistance* (Thousand Oaks, CA: Sage Publications, 2016), 443–60.

15. Xueguang Zhou, *The Institutional Logic of China's State Governance.*

16. Capital Internet Association, *China Weibo Development Report (2016–2017).*

17. Sina Weibo Community Management Center (*Xinlang weibo shequ guanli zhongxin,* 新浪微博社区管理中心), "Sina Weibo Community Convention (Trial), Sina Weibo Community Management Regulations (Trial), Sina Weibo Community Committee System (Trial)," ("*Xinlang weibo shequ gongyue (shixing), xinlang weibo shequ guanli guiding (shixing), xinlang weibo shequ weiyuanhui zhidu (shixing)*)," 新浪微博社区公约 (试行)、新浪微博社区管理规定(试行),新浪微博社区委员会制度(试行), https://baike.baidu.com/item/%E6%96%B0%E6%B5%AA%E5%BE%AE%E5%8D%9A%E7%A4%BE%E5%8C%BA%E7%AE%A1%E7%90%86%E8%A7%84%E5%AE%9A%EF%BC%88%E8%AF%95%E8%A1%8C%EF%BC%89 (accessed on September 9, 2019).

18. Jia, *Political Communication in the Internet Age,* chapter 4.

19. Benedict Anderson, *Imagined Communities: Reflections on the Origin and Spread of Nationalism* (New York: Verso, 1983).

20. Xueguang Zhou, "Unorganized Interests and Collective Action in Communist China," *American Sociological Review* 58, no. 1 (1993): 54–73.

21. For further information on this episode, see "The Wukan Incident," Tsinghua University School of Public Management, Societal Management Innovation Research Group ("*Wukan shijian shimo,*" *Qinghua daxue gonggong guanli xueyuan shehui guanli chuangxin ketizu,* "乌坎事件始末," 清华大学公共管

理学院社会管理创新课题组), *China Nonprofit Review* 10 (2012): 1–67; and Jia, *Political Communication in the Internet Age.*

22. See Xie Bei, *Study of China's Internet in the Era of Micro-communication,* 200–25, for detailed documentation and analyses of the role of social media in this episode.

23. "Yang Dacai" (Yang Dacai, 杨达才), Wikipedia, https://zh.wikipedia.org/wiki/%E6%9D%A8%E8%BE%BE%E6%89%8D.

24. "The 50 cent party" (also known as the "50 cent army") is an expression on social media that refers to the large number of helping hands hired by the government to spread selected information or voice official views on social media to sway public opinion.

25. Chen Haibing, "Weibo: Accelerator of a Chinese-style Democratic Process" (*Weibo: Zhongguo shi minzhu jincheng de jiasuqi,* 微博:中国式民主进程的加速器), *Observations and Thoughts (Guancha yu sikao,* 观察与思考).

26. As is the norm nowadays, this policy was not made public but carried out through the chain of command inside the bureaucratic apparatus. During this period WeChat accounts reported many anecdotes where reporters from other media, official or unofficial, were called back while they were traveling to the accident site to report the episode. All media were instructed to use Xinhua News as the source of reporting on the rescue efforts and investigation of this accident.

27. "*Zhongguo hulianwangluo fazhan zhuangkuang tongji baogao*" (July, 2016), by China Internet Information Center ("*Zhongguo hulian wangluo xinxi zhongxin,*" 中国互联网络信息中心), p. 25, http://www.cnnic.cn/hlwfzyj/hlwxzbg/ (accessed on September 9, 2019).

28. Gary King, Jennifer Pan, and Margaret E. Roberts, "How the Chinese Government Fabricates Social Media Posts for Strategic Distraction, Not Engaged Argument," *American Political Science Review* 111, no. 3 (2017): 484–501.

29. Li Peilin, Chen Guangjin, Zhang Yi et al., *Blue Book on China's Society (Li Peilin, Chen Guangjin, Zhang Yideng, shehui lanpishu,* 李培林、陈光金、张翼等, 社会蓝皮书) (Beijing: Social Sciences Literature Press, 2017), 229.

30. See also Didi Kirsten Tatlow, "Chinese Man's Death in Custody Prompts Suspicion of Police Brutality," *New York Times,* May 12, 2016, https://www.nytimes.com/2016/05/13/world/asia/china-lei-yang-police-death.html.

31. Based on a Weibo post dated December 19, 2017.

32. See Lucy Hornby and Archie Zhang, "Beijing's Migrant Expulsion Prompts Civic Outcry," *Financial Times,* November 28, 2017, https://www.ft.com/content/892fb552-d40e-11e7-8c9a-d9c0a5c8d5c9.

33. Gary King, Jennifer Pan, and Margaret Roberts, "How Censorship in China Allows Government Criticism but Silences Collective Expression," *American Political Science Review* 107, no. 2 (2013): 326–43; and King, Pan, and

Roberts, "How the Chinese Government Fabricates Social Media Posts for Strategic Distraction," 484–501.

34. Jennifer Pan and Yiqing Xu, "China's Ideological Spectrum," *Journal of Politics* 80, no. 1 (2017): 254–73, https://www.journals.uchicago.edu/doi/pdfplus/10.1086/694255.

35. Andrew Nathan, "Authoritarian Resilience," *Journal of Democracy* 14, no. 1 (2013): 6–17.

36. Often, information was leaked on the Internet to discredit political opponents or signal major political upheavals. For example, during the sensitive days when Wang Lijun sought political asylum in the US consulate in Chengdu, rumors and speculation were allowed to flow all over the Internet to undermine Bo Xilai's political position.

37. King, Pan, and Roberts, "How the Chinese Government Fabricates Social Media Posts."

38. Xiaotong Fei, *From the Soil: The Foundations of Chinese Society. A Translation of Fei Xiaotong's Xiangtu Zhongguo,* with an introduction and epilogue by Gary G. Hamilton and Wang Zheng (Berkeley: University of California Press, 1992).

39. Charles Tilly, *The Contentious French* (Cambridge, MA: Belknap Press of Harvard University Press, 1986), 9.

40. James C. Scott, *Weapons of the Weak: Everyday Forms of Peasant Resistance* (New Haven, CT: Yale University Press, 1985); James C. Scott, *Domination and the Arts of Resistance: Hidden Transcripts* (New Haven, CT: Yale University Press, 1990); and Timur Kuran, *Private Truths, Public Lies* (Cambridge, MA: Harvard University Press, 1997).

Chapter 6. Demographic and Health Care Challenges

1. Elderly and disabled people frequently require assistance with "activities of daily living" such as dressing, eating, and bathing. These nonmedical services are called "long-term care" or "long-term services and supports."

2. Karen N. Eggleston, Jean C. Oi, Scott Rozelle, Ang Sun, Andrew Walder, and Xueguang Zhou, "Will Demographic Change Slow China's Rise?" *Journal of Asian Studies* 72, no. 3 (2013): 505–18.

3. This section draws from Karen Eggleston, "Health, Education, and China's Demographic Transition since 1950," in Masahiko Aoki and Jinglian Wu, eds., *The Chinese Economy: A New Transition* (New York: International Economics Association, Palgrave-MacMillan, 2012), 150–65.

4. For more details, see, for example, Baochang Gu, Feng Wang, Zhigang Guo, and Erli Zhang, "China's Local and National Fertility Policies at the End of the Twentieth Century," *Population and Development Review* 33, no. 1 (2007):

129–48; and for the historical trajectory, see James Lee and Feng Wang, *One Quarter of Humanity: Malthusian Mythology and Chinese Realities, 1700–2000* (Cambridge: Harvard University Press, 2001).

5. By contrast, in India the proportion of sixty and older will be considerably lower, around 18 percent by 2050. David Bloom and Karen Eggleston, "The Economics of Population Aging in China and India: Introduction to the Special Issue," *Journal of the Economics of Aging* 4 (2014): 1–7.

6. China's fertility rate is so crucial yet controversial that is it worth quoting at length from the estimates of experts. From Quanbao Jiang, Li Xiaomin, Shuzhuo Li, and Marcus W. Feldman, "China's Marriage Squeeze: A Decomposition into Age and Sex Structure," *Social Indicators Research* 127, no. 2 (2016): 793–807 (quote on pp. 797–98): "The total fertility rate (TFR) was 1.22 in the 2000 census, and 1.18 in the 2010 census. The National Bureau of Statistics also adjusted the TFR of 1.22 in 2000 census to 1.4 for internal use (Morgan et al., 2009). Zhao and Chen (2011) accepted a TFR of 1.45 for 2005–2010 in their projection. In the medium scenario of United Nations projection, China's TFR was set at 1.66 from 2010 to 2015, 1.69 for 2015–2020, and 1.72 for 2020–2025 (United Nations, 2013). According to the population at younger ages and projection of births with different TFRs, a TFR of 1.4 is found to ensure a smooth transition between the projected births and younger birth cohorts in the 2010 census. In this paper we adopt two scenarios for TFR, 1.4 and 1.6, and adopt the fertility pattern reported by the 2010 census (PCO, 2012)."

7. Zijuan Shang, Shuzhuo Li, and Marcus W. Feldman, "Fertility, Sex Ratio, and Family Planning Policies in China," in Karen Eggleston, ed., *Policy Challenges from Demographic Change in China and India*, Stanford University Shorenstein Asia-Pacific Research Center series (Washington, DC: Brookings Institution Press, 2016), 33–52.

8. See, for example, the discussion in John Bauer, Feng Wang, Nancy E. Riley, and Xiaohua Zhao, "Gender Inequality in Urban China: Education and Employment," *Modern China* 18, no. 3 (1992): 333–70.

9. For more discussion of this issue, see, for example, Christophe Z. Guilmoto, "Skewed Sex Ratios at Birth and Future Marriage Squeeze in China and India, 2005–2100," *Demography* 49, no. 1 (2012): 77–100, doi: 10.1007/s13524 -011-0083-7; Zhen Guo, Monica Das Gupta, and Shuzhuo Li, "'Missing Girls' in China and India: Trends and Policy Challenges," *Asian Population Studies* 12, no. 2 (2016): 135–55; and Jiang et al., "China's Marriage Squeeze," 793–807.

10. Guilmoto, "Skewed Sex Ratios at Birth and Future Marriage Squeeze" (emphasis added); and Eggleston, *Policy Challenges from Demographic Change in China and India*.

11. Xueyan Yang, Shuzhuo Li, Isabelle Attané, and Marcus W. Feldman,

"On the Relationship between the Marriage Squeeze and the Quality of Life of Rural Men in China," *American Journal of Men's Health* 11, no. 3 (2017): 702–10.

12. For example, one study estimates that "China's marriage market will be confronted with a relatively severe male squeeze. For the decomposition of the cohort aged 30, from 2010 to 2020 age structure will be dominant, while from 2020 through 2034 the contribution of age structure will gradually decrease and that of sex structure will increase. From then on, sex structure will be dominant" (Jiang et al., "China's Marriage Squeeze," 793).

13. Ronald Lee and Andrew Mason, "Population Change and the Economic Security of Older People in Asia," *National Transfer Accounts,* no. 10 (September 2016): 1–3.

14. Projections from the UN Population Division are available numerically and graphically at https://esa.un.org/unpd/wup/Country-Profiles/ and https://esa.un.org/unpd/wpp/Graphs/Probabilistic/EX/FMCOMP/ (accessed on September 6, 2019).

15. See, for example, Feng Wang and Xuejin Zuo, "Inside China's Cities: Institutional Barriers and Opportunities for Urban Migrants," *American Economic Review* 89, no. 2 (1999): 276–80; and Karen Eggleston, Jean Oi, and Yiming Wang, eds., *Challenges in the Process of China's Urbanization*, Stanford University Shorenstein Asia-Pacific Research Center (Washington, DC: Brookings Institution Press, 2017).

16. Indeed, Figure 6.4 shows that despite the scary rhetoric about the fiscal strain from retirement of the baby boomers in the United States, the increase in median age is slower than even Vietnam, with all but India of these large Asian countries becoming older than the United States in the near future, at much lower levels of per capita income. Fiscal strain in the United States arises from the unsustainable financing of entitlement programs, especially Medicare, rather than from "pure demographics."

17. See the discussion in F. Wang and A. Mason, "The Demographic Factor in China's Transition," in L. Brandt and T. G. Rawski, eds., *China's Great Economic Transformation* (Cambridge: Cambridge University Press, 2008), 136–66; and David E. Bloom, David Canning, Linlin Hu, Yuanli Liu, Ajay Mahal, and Winnie Yip, "The Contribution of Population Health and Demographic Change to Economic Growth in China and India," *Journal of Comparative Economics* 38, no. 1 (2010): 17–33.

18. Ronald Lee, Sang-Hyop Lee, and Andrew Mason, "The Demographic Dividend and Population Aging in Asia and the Pacific: Introduction to the Special Issue," *Journal of the Economics of Aging* 8 (December 2016), http://dx.doi.org/10.1016/j.jeoa.2016.03.005.

19. Bloom and Eggleston, "Economics of Population Aging in China and India."

20. David E. Bloom, Somnath Chatterji, Paul Kowal, Peter Lloyd-Sherlock, Martin McKee, Bernd Rechel, Larry Rosenberg, and James P. Smith, "Macroeconomic Implications of Population Aging and Selected Policy Responses" *The Lancet* 385 (2014): 649–57, doi:10.1016/S0140-6736(14)61464-1.

21. This section draws from Karen Eggleston and Victor Fuchs, "The New Demographic Transition: Most Gains in Life Expectancy Now Realized Late in Life," *Journal of Economic Perspectives* 26 (3): 137–56.

22. See discussion in Xuejin Zuo, Guozheng Chen, and Xiaoyan Sun, "Population Aging and Its Impact on Employment," in Xueyuan Tian, ed., *China's Population Aging and the Risk of "Middle-income Trap"* (Singapore: Springer, 2017): 107–23.

23. See the discussion in Xuejin Zuo, "Reforming Pensions to Ensure Equitable and Adequate Retirement Incomes in China," in *Equitable and Sustainable Pensions: Challenges and Experience* (Washington, DC: International Monetary Fund, 2014), 293–312.

24. For more on living arrangements, intergenerational support, and labor supply, see Sen Ma and Fangqi Wen, "Who Coresides with Parents? An Analysis Based on Sibling Comparative Advantage," *Demography* 53, no. 3 (2016): 623–47, doi:10.1007/s13524-016-0468-8; Karen Eggleston, Ang Sun, and Zhaoguo Zhan, "The Impact of Rural Pensions in China on Labor Migration," *World Bank Economic Review* (July 2016), doi:10.1093/WBER/LHW032; Ang Sun, Chuanchuan Zhang, and Xiangting Hu, "Boys, Girls, and Grandparents: The Impact of the Sex of Preschool-Age Children on Family Living Arrangements and Maternal Labour Supply," Asia Health Policy Program working paper no. 44 (October 20, 2017), http://aparc.fsi.stanford.edu/asiahealthpolicy/publication/boys-girls-and-grandparents-impact-sex-preschool-age-children-family-living-arrangements; and Xi Chen, Karen Eggleston, and Ang Sun, "The Impact of Social Pensions on Intergenerational Relationships: Comparative Evidence from China," *Journal of the Economics of Aging* 12 (2018): 225–35.

25. Yin Weimin, "Building a Comprehensive Multi-Level Social Security System" ("*Quanmian jiancheng duocengci shehui baozhang tixi*," 全面建成多层次社会保障体系), *CPC News*, http://theory.people.com.cn/n1/2018/0109/c40531-29752898.html (accessed on April 25, 2018).

26. For example, "Yin Weimin, Minister of human resources and social security, was quoted by Xinhua News Agency as saying on March 1 [2017] that due to heavy employment pressures, the government will take a more cautious approach in formulating the new policy," http://www.chinadaily.com.cn/opinion/2017-03/11/content_28517346.htm (accessed on April 25, 2018).

27. See the discussion in James P. Smith, John Strauss, and Yaohui Zhao, "Healthy Aging in China," *Journal of the Economics of Aging* 4 (2014): 37–43.

28. David E. Bloom, Elizabeth T. Cafiero-Fonseca, Mark E. McGovern, Klaus Prettner, Anderson Stanciole, Jonathan Weiss, Samuel Bakkila, and Larry Rosenberg, "The Macroeconomic Impact of Non-Communicable Diseases in China and India: Estimates, Projections, and Comparisons," *Journal of the Economics of Aging* 4 (2014): 100–11.

29. Smith, Strauss, and Zhao, "Healthy Aging in China."

30. Yi Zeng, Qiushi Feng, Therese Hesketh, Kaare Christensen, and James W. Vaupel, "Survival, Disabilities in Activities of Daily Living, and Physical and Cognitive Functioning among the Oldest-Old in China: A Cohort Study," *The Lancet* 389, no. 10079 (2017): 1619–29.

31. Yanting Li, Yimin Zhang, Shuai Fang, Shanshan Liu, Xinyu Liu, Ming Li, Hong Liang, and Hua Fu, "Analysis of Inequality in Maternal and Child Health Outcomes and Mortality from 2000 to 2013 in China," *International Journal for Equity in Health* 16, no. 1 (2017): Article 66, pp. 1–11, https://equity healthj.biomedcentral.com/track/pdf/10.1186/s12939-017-0558-2 (accessed on September 23, 2019). Also see Hong Liu, Hai Fang, and Zhong Zhao, "Urban-Rural Disparities of Child Health and Nutritional Status in China from 1989 to 2006," *Economics & Human Biology* 11, no. 3 (2013): 294–309.

32. See the discussion of health equity progress and challenges in Jun Yang, José G. Siri, Justin V. Remais, Qu Cheng, Han Zhang, Karen K. Y. Chan, Zhe Sun et al., "The Tsinghua–Lancet Commission on Healthy Cities in China: Unlocking the Power of Cities for a Healthy China, "*The Lancet* 391, no. 10135 (2018): 2140–84, https://www.thelancet.com/journals/lancet/article/PIIS0140-6736(18)30486-0/fulltext.

33. Yang et al., "Tsinghua–Lancet Commission on Healthy Cities in China."

34. Xiaoyan Lei, Xiaoting Sun, John Strauss, Yaohui Zhao, Gonghuan Yang, Perry Hu, Yisong Hu, and Xiangjun Yin, "Reprint of: Health Outcomes and Socio-Economic Status among the Mid-Aged and Elderly in China: Evidence from the CHARLS National Baseline Data," *Journal of the Economics of Aging* 4 (2014): 59–73.

35. See the discussion of health equity progress and challenges in Yang et al., "Tsinghua–Lancet Commission on Healthy Cities in China."

36. Xiaoyan Lei, Nina Yin, and Yaohui Zhao, "Socioeconomic Status and Chronic Diseases: The Case of Hypertension in China," *China Economic Review* 23, no.1 (2012): 105–21.

37. Dana Goldman and James Smith, "Can Patient Self-Management Help Explain the SES Health Gradient?," *Proceedings of the National Academy of Sciences* 99, no. 16 (2012): 10929–34.

38. Shuzhuo Li, Fubin Sun, Quanbao Jiang, Xufeng Zou and Renxian Guan, "Report of the Study on China's Mortality Changes in the 1990s Based on China's 2000 Population Census," Institute for Population and Economy Studies School of Management, Xi'an Jiaotong University, Xi'an, 2004.

39. Yong Cai, "Regional Inequality in China: Mortality and Health," in Deborah Davis and Wang Feng, eds., *Creating Wealth and Poverty in Post-Socialist China* (Stanford, CA: Stanford University Press, 2009), 143–55.

40. This section draws from my congressional testimony in 2014, with policy updates.

41. See report by Yajie Wang on "Experts View on National Health Committee: Approaching Healthy China and Overhaul," eeo.com, March 13, 2018.

42. See Zijuan Shang, Shuzhuo Li, and Marcus W. Feldman, "Fertility, Sex Ratio, and Family Planning Policies in China," in Eggleston, *Policy Challenges from Demographic Change in China and India*, 33–52.

43. See the discussion in Yang et al., "Tsinghua–Lancet Commission on Healthy Cities in China."

44. CEES Research Team, "How Are Chinese Manufacturing Firms Coping with Rising Labor Costs? A Report of China Employer-Employee Survey (CEES), 2015–2016," June 2017, 24.

45. Wenjuan Zhang, "The Development of Long-term Care System in China," Institute of Gerontology, Renmin University of China, presentation at Stanford University, February 2018.

46. Xinhua, "China to Standardize Elderly Care Services Industry," *China Daily,* October 19, 2017, http://www.chinadaily.com.cn/business/2017-10/19/con tent_33452368.htm.

47. See the discussion in Yang et al., "Tsinghua–Lancet Commission on Healthy Cities in China."

48. World Health Organization (WHO), *People's Republic of China Health System Review*, Health Systems in Transition 5, no. 7 (Geneva: Asia Pacific Observatory on Health Systems and Policies, 2015).

49. Yi Zeng et al., "Survival, Disabilities in Activities of Daily Living, and Physical and Cognitive Functioning among the Oldest-old in China."

50. Jack Donahue, Karen Eggleston, and Richard Zeckhauser, "The Dragon, the Eagle, and the Private Sector: Public-Private Collaboration in China and the United States," unpublished manuscript, 2019.

51. Donahue, Eggleston, and Zeckhauser, "Dragon, the Eagle, and the Private Sector."

52. Karen Eggleston, "Innovation and Shortage: The Yin and Yang of the Health Sector," *Acta Oeconomica* 68 (S) (2018): 99–114.

53. Ian Hicks, Lucy Liu, and Linda Zhao, "The Challenges of Cancer Treatment in China," *China Business Review*, January 1, 2011, https://www.china businessreview.com/the-challenges-of-cancer-treatment-in-china/.

54. From Roche: "In collaboration with the Cancer Foundation in China and the Ministry of Health, we launched a patient assistance program (PAP) in August 2011 to address affordability. Under the program, after a patient has taken the first six cycles of Herceptin treatment, Roche donates the next eight cycles through the Cancer Foundation so that patients complete the full course of treatment," http://www.roche.com/sustainability/what_we_do/for_patients/access_to_healthcare/making_innovation_accessible/ath_china_pap.htm.

55. Jui-fen Rachel Lu, Karen Eggleston, and Joseph Tung-Chieh Chang, "Economic Dimensions of Personalized and Precision Medicine in Asia: Evidence from Breast Cancer Treatment in Taiwan," *Economic Dimensions of Personalized and Precision Medicine* (National Bureau of Economic Research, 2018), available as Asia Health Policy Program working paper no. 48, http://aparc.fsi.stanford.edu/asiahealthpolicy/publication/economic-dimensions-personalized-and-precision-medicine-asia-evidence-breast-cancer.

56. See, for example, the interesting analyses in Wei Huang, Xiaoyan Lei, Geert Ridder, John Strauss, and Yaohui Zhao, "Health, Height, Height Shrinkage, and SES at Older Ages: Evidence from China," *American Economic Journal: Applied Economics* 5, no. 2 (2013): 86–121.

57. Xiliu Zhang, "Let General Practitioners Become Community Health Gatekeepers" ("*Rang quanke yisheng chengwei shequ jumin jiankang 'shoumen ren,'* 让全科医生成为社区居民健康"守门人"), *Xinhua Net*, January 22, 2018, http://www.xinhuanet.com/health/2018-01/22/c_1122291599.htm.

58. Policymakers emphasize that the "family doctor contract" is voluntary, and patients must wish to sign up or to stay enrolled after a year's worth of experience with the service, which provides some feedback regarding whether patients find the services worthwhile. Inducements include promises of better access to specialists when deemed medically appropriate, lower copayments or greater access and convenience for medication refills, etc. Officials are taking steps to assure quality and follow-through on the services promised in family doctor "contracts" to achieve the goals of general coverage by 2020.

59. WHO, *People's Republic of China Health System Review*.

60. Karen Eggleston, "Health Care for 1.3 Billion: China's Remarkable Work in Progress," *Milken Institute Review* (second quarter 2012): 16–27.

61. Tiemin Zhai, John Goss, and Jinjing Li, "Main Drivers of Health Expenditure Growth in China: A Decomposition Analysis," *BMC Health Services Research* 17, no. 1 (2017): article 185, pp. 1–9, https://bmchealthservres.biomedcentral.com/track/pdf/10.1186/s12913-017-2119-1.

62. Ronald Lee and Andrew Mason, "Cost of Aging," *Finance & Development* 54, no. 1 (2017): 7–9.

63. The authors estimate that land reform accounted for roughly half of the increase in sex ratios in rural China from 1978 to 1986, or about one million missing girls. Douglas Almond, Hongbin Li, and Shuang Zhang, "Land Reform and Sex Selection in China," *Journal of Political Economy*, 127, no. 2 (April 2019): 560–85.

64. For example, a recent study has documented substantial cognitive impairments among the oldest-old in China, consistent with trends also evident in other studies of mainland China, Hong Kong, and Taiwan. See Yi Zeng et al., "Survival, Disabilities in Activities of Daily Living, and Physical and Cognitive Functioning among the Oldest-old in China."

Chapter 7. Can China Achieve Inclusive Urbanization?

1. Lynette H. Ong, "State-Led Urbanization in China: Skyscrapers, Land Revenue and Concentrated Villages," *China Quarterly* 217 (March 2014): 162–79, https://doi.org/10.1017/S0305741014000010.

2. The middle-income trap is a hotly debated proposition that middle-income countries grow more slowly than richer and poorer countries and often "get stuck" at middle income level, failing to achieve rich country status. https://www.economist.com/special-report/2017/10/05/the-middle-income-trap-has-little-evidence-going-for-it.

3. Adam Tyner and Yuan Ren, "The *Hukou* System, Rural Institutions, and Migrant Integration in China," *Journal of East Asian Studies* 16, no. 3 (November 2016): 331–48, https://doi.org/10.1017/jea.2016.18; and Ren Mu and John Giles, "Village Political Economy, Land Tenure Insecurity, and the Rural to Urban Migration Decision: Evidence from China," World Bank Policy Research Working Paper, no. 7080 (2014), http://papers.ssrn.com/sol3/papers.cfm?abstract_id=2518827.

4. The World Bank defines "inclusive urbanization" mainly as the provision of public and social services to rural migrants equal to what is enjoyed by local urban residents; see World Bank, *Urban China: Toward Efficient, Inclusive, and Sustainable Urbanization* (Washington, DC: World Bank, 2014), 3, http://elibrary.worldbank.org/doi/book/10.1596/978-1-4648-0206-5.

5. Chongming Island was the last rural county of Shanghai to transition to an urban district in January 2017. With that change Chongming residents went from being rural to being urban.

6. Aiqun Hu, "The Global Spread of Neoliberalism and China's Pension Reform since 1978," *Journal of World History* 23, no. 3 (2012): 609–38, https://doi.org/10.1353/jwh.2012.0071.

7. Roger Goodman, Gordon White, and Huck-ju Kwon, eds., *The East Asian Welfare Model: Welfare Orientalism and the State*, ESRC Pacific Asia Programme (New York: Routledge, 1998).

8. Andrew George Walder, *Communist Neo-Traditionalism: Work and Authority in Chinese Industry* (Berkeley: University of California Press, 1988); and Mark W. Frazier, *Socialist Insecurity: Pensions and the Politics of Uneven Development in China* (Ithaca, NY: Cornell University Press, 2010).

9. Shaohua Zhan, "*Hukou* Reform and Land Politics in China: Rise of a Tripartite Alliance," *The China Journal* 78 (2017): 25–49; Joel Andreas and Shaohua Zhan, "*Hukou* and Land: Market Reform and Rural Displacement in China," *Journal of Peasant Studies* 43, no. 4 (July 3, 2016): 798–827, https://doi.org/10.1080/03066150.2015.1078317; and Kristen Looney and Meg Rithmire, "Urbanization with Chinese Characteristics? China's Gamble for Modernization," n.d., 13.

10. Kam Wing Chan et al., *Urbanization with Chinese Characteristics: The Hukou System and Migration* (New York: Routledge, 2018).

11. Development Research Center of the State Council and World Bank, *China 2030: Building a Modern, Harmonious, and Creative High-Income Society* (Washington, DC: World Bank, 2013), http://elibrary.worldbank.org/doi/book/10.1596/978-0-8213-9545-5.

12. World Bank, *Urban China*.

13. In the Chinese context, with its residential registration system (*hukou*), every citizen is tied to a specific place (a city for urban citizens, a county for rural citizens) and to a type of production (agricultural for rural versus nonagricultural for most urban citizens).

14. Dorothy J. Solinger, *Contesting Citizenship in Urban China: Peasant Migrants, the State, and the Logic of the Market* (Berkeley: University of California Press, 1999); Li Zhang, *Strangers in the City: Reconfigurations of Space, Power, and Social Networks within China's Floating Population* (Stanford, CA: Stanford University Press, 2001); Kam Wing Chan, "The Household Registration System and Migrant Labor in China: Notes on a Debate," *Population and Development Review* 36, no. 2 (2010): 357–64; and Fei-Ling Wang, *Organizing through Division and Exclusion: China's Hukou System* (Stanford, CA: Stanford University Press, 2005).

15. World Bank, *Urban China*.

16. Chan et al., *Urbanization with Chinese Characteristics*.

17. Zhan, "*Hukou* Reform and Land Politics in China"; and Andreas and Zhan, "*Hukou* and Land."

18. Ong, "State-Led Urbanization in China"; and Chan et al., *Urbanization with Chinese Characteristics*.

19. Yi Yang, "Highlights of Communique of 4th Plenary Session of CPC Central Committee," *Xinhua News Online*, October 23, 2014, http://news.xinhua net.com/english/china/2014-10/23/c_133737957.htm.

20. There are other types of urban social welfare, including the minimum income guarantee (*dibao,* 低保) and urban resident social insurance. However, these programs provide only the most basic support.

21. Mary Elizabeth Gallagher, *Authoritarian Legality in China: Law, Workers, and the State* (New York: Cambridge University Press, 2017).

22. "Labor Contract Law of P.R. China (promulgated by the Standing Committee of the Nat'l People's Cong., June 29, 2007, Effective Jan. 1, 2008)" ("*Zhonghua renmin gongheguo laodong hetong fa,*" 中华人民共和国劳动合同法), (n.d.), http://www.gov.cn/flfg/2007-06/29/content_669394.htm; and "Social Insurance Law of P.R. China (Promulgated by the Standing Comm. of Nat'l People's Cong., Oct. 28, 2010, Effective July 1, 2011)" ("*Zhonghua remin gongheguo shehui baoxianfa,*" 中华人民共和国社会保险法), (n.d.), http://www.gov.cn/flfg/2010 -10/28/content_1732964.htm; and "Law of the People's Republic of China on mediation and arbitration of labor dispute" ("*Zhonghua remin gongheguo laodong zhengyi tiaojie zhongcai fa zhushi ben,*" 中华人民共和国劳动争议调解仲裁法注释本) (Beijing: Legal Publishing [*Falü chuban she,* 法律出版社], 2008).

23. Gallagher, *Authoritarian Legality in China.*

24. Feng Chen, "Individual Rights and Collective Rights: Labor's Predicament in China," *Communist and Post-Communist Studies* 40, no. 1 (March 2007): 59–79, https://doi.org/10.1016/j.postcomstud.2006.12.006.

25. Dongyu Peng, "The Implementation of the Three Methods Will Have a Far-reaching Influence on the Construction of a Harmonious Society" ("*San fa shishi jiang dui hexie shehui jianshe chansheng shenyuan yingxiang,*" 三法实施将对和谐社会建设产生深远影响), Renmin University of China (*Zhongguo Renda,* 中国人大) April 10, 2008, 18–20.

26. Z. Cheng, R. Smyth, and F. Guo, "The Impact of China's New Labour Contract Law on Socioeconomic Outcomes for Migrant and Urban Workers," *Human Relations* 68, no. 3 (March 1, 2015): 329–52, https://doi.org/10.1177/ 0018726714543480.

27. Chris King-chi Chan, *The Challenge of Labour in China: Strikes and the Changing Labour Regime in Global Factories*, China Policy Series 16 (New York: Routledge, 2010); Eli Friedman, *Insurgency Trap: Labor Politics in Postsocialist China* (Ithaca, NY: ILR Press, an imprint of Cornell University Press, 2014); and Manfred Elfstrom and Sarosh Kuruvilla, "The Changing Nature of Labor Unrest in China," *Industrial & Labor Relations Review* 67, no. 2 (2014): 453–80.

28. Yang Du, Albert Park, and Yaowu Wu, "Informal Employment in Urban China: Measurement and Implications," September 2017.

29. Cheng, Smyth, and Guo, "Impact of China's New Labour Contract Law."

30. Du, Park, and Wu, "Informal Employment in Urban China."

31. Xiaoying Li and Richard B. Freeman, "How Does China's New Labour Contract Law Affect Floating Workers?: China's New Labour Contract Law," *British Journal of Industrial Relations* 53, no. 4 (December 2015): 711–35, https://doi.org/10.1111/bjir.12056.

32. Bingqin Li, Chunlai Chen, and Biliang Hu, "Governing Urbanization and the New Urbanization Plan in China," *Environment and Urbanization* 28, no. 2 (October 2016): 515–34, https://doi.org/10.1177/0956247816647345; and Eli Friedman, "Just-in-Time Urbanization? Managing Migration, Citizenship, and Schooling in the Chinese City," *Critical Sociology* 44, no. 3 (May 2018): 503–18.

33. Jih-Un Kim, "A Bumpy Road to Cities: Analysis of the Obstacles and Limits of China's New Urbanization: China's New Urbanization," *Pacific Focus* 30, no. 3 (December 2015): 372–88, https://doi.org/10.1111/pafo.12057.

34. Cheng, Smyth, and Guo, "Impact of China's New Labour Contract Law."

35. Yiu Por (Vincent) Chen and Yuan Zhang, "A Decomposition Method on Employment and Wage Discrimination and Its Application in Urban China (2002–2013)," *World Development* 110 (October 2018): 1–12, https://doi.org/10.1016/j.worlddev.2018.05.012; and Yih-chyi Chuang and Eric Yan, "Behind the Invisible Wall: What Determine Wage Differentials between Urban and Migrant Workers in China," *International Journal of China Studies* 8, no. 1 (April 2017): 61–91.

36. Meiyan Wang, "Wage Arrears and Discrimination against Migrant Workers in China's Urban Labor Market," in *China Population and Labor Yearbook, Volume 1, The Chinese Academy of Social Sciences Yearbooks: Population and Labor* (Leiden: Brill, 2009), 154–76; and Aaron Halegua, "Getting Paid: Processing the Labor Disputes of China's Migrant Workers," *Berkeley Journal of International Law* 26, no. 1 (2008): 254–322.

37. Mary Gallagher et al., "China's 2008 Labor Contract Law: Implementation and Implications for China's Workers," *Human Relations*, February 17, 2014, https://doi.org/10.1177/0018726713509418; and Aaron Halegua, "Access to Justice for China's Workers," Report Commissioned by the Ford Foundation (New York: U.S.-Asia Law Institute, NYU, July 2016).

38. Yumin Ye, Richard LeGates, and Bo Qin, "Coordinated Urban-Rural Development Planning in China: The Chengdu Model," *Journal of the American Planning Association* 79, no. 2 (April 3, 2013): 125–37.

39. Shih-Jiunn Shi, "Towards Inclusive Social Citizenship? Rethinking China's Social Security in the Trend towards Urban–Rural Harmonisation," *Journal of Social Policy* 41, no. 4 (October 2012): 789–810, https://doi.org/10.1017/S0047279412000517.

40. Shih-Jiunn Shi, "Social Policy Learning and Diffusion in China: The Rise of Welfare Regions?" *Policy and Politics* 40, no. 3 (n.d.): 20; and Zhu Qian, "Resettlement and Adaptation in China's Small Town Urbanization: Evidence from the Villagers' Perspective," *Habitat International* 67 (September 2017): 33–43, https://doi.org/10.1016/j.habitatint.2017.06.013.

41. Andreas and Zhan, "*Hukou* and Land."

42. S. Whiting, "Values in Land: Fiscal Pressures, Land Disputes and Justice Claims in Rural and Peri-Urban China," *Urban Studies* 48, no. 3 (February 1, 2011): 569–87, https://doi.org/10.1177/0042098010390242; Ong, "State-Led Urbanization in China"; and Julia Chuang, "Urbanization through Dispossession: Survival and Stratification in China's New Townships," *Journal of Peasant Studies* 42, no. 2 (March 4, 2015): 275–94, https://doi.org/10.1080/03066150.2014.990446.

43. Li, Chen, and Hu, "Governing Urbanization and the New Urbanization Plan in China."

44. Friedman, "Just-in-Time Urbanization?"

45. Pierre Francois Landry, *Decentralized Authoritarianism in China: The Communist Party's Control of Local Elites in the Post-Mao Era* (Cambridge: Cambridge University Press, 2008).

46. Yuen Yuen Ang, *How China Escaped the Poverty Trap*, Cornell Studies in Political Economy (Ithaca, NY: Cornell University Press, 2016).

47. Ruixue Jia and Huihua Nie, "Decentralization, Collusion, and Coal Mine Deaths," *Review of Economics and Statistics* 99, no. 1 (March 2017): 105–18, https://doi.org/10.1162/REST_a_00563; Peter Lorentzen, Pierre Landry, and John Yasuda, "Undermining Authoritarian Innovation: The Power of China's Industrial Giants," *Journal of Politics* 76, no. 1 (2014): 182–94; and Mary Elizabeth Gallagher, *Contagious Capitalism Globalization and the Politics of Labor in China* (Princeton, NJ: Princeton University Press, 2007), http://site.ebrary.com/id/10477105.

48. Christine Wong, "Paying for the Harmonious Society," *China Economic Quarterly* 14, no. 2 (2010): 20–25; and Siu Wai Wong, "Urbanization as a Process of State Building: Local Governance Reforms in China: Urbanization as a Process of State Building," *International Journal of Urban and Regional Research* 39, no. 5 (September 2015): 912–26, https://doi.org/10.1111/1468-2427.12250.

49. Andreas and Zhan, "*Hukou* and Land"; Chuang, "Urbanization through Dispossession"; and Looney and Rithmire, "Urbanization with Chinese Characteristics? China's Gamble for Modernization."

50. Landry, *Decentralized Authoritarianism in China*; Ching Kwan Lee, *Against the Law: Labor Protests in China's Rustbelt and Sunbelt* (Berkeley: University of California Press, 2007); and Susan H. Whiting, *Power and Wealth*

in Rural China: The Political Economy of Institutional Change, Cambridge Modern China Series (New York: Cambridge University Press, 2001).

51. Yuhua Wang, *Tying the Autocrat's Hands: The Rise of the Rule of Law in China* (New York: Cambridge University Press, 2014).

52. Anita Chan, *China's Workers under Assault: The Exploitation of Labor in a Globalizing Economy* (Armonk, NY: M.E. Sharpe, 2001); Solinger, *Contesting Citizenship in Urban China*; and Ajit Singh and Ann Zammit, "Labour Standards and the 'Race to the Bottom': Rethinking Globalisation and Workers Rights from Developmental and Solidaristic Perspectives," *Oxford Review of Economic Policy* 20 (Spring 2004): 85–104.

53. Hon S. Chan and Jie Gao, "Death versus GDP! Decoding the Fatality Indicators on Work Safety Regulation in Post-Deng China," *China Quarterly* 210 (June 2012): 355–77, https://doi.org/10.1017/S0305741012000379; and Jia and Nie, "Decentralization, Collusion, and Coal Mine Deaths."

54. David Weil, "Individual Rights and Collective Agents: The Role of Old and New Workplace Institutions in the Regulation of Labor Markets," in Richard Freeman, Joni Hersch, Lawrench Mishel, eds., *Emerging Labor Market Institutions for the Twenty-First Century* (Chicago: University of Chicago Press, 2004), 13–44, http://www.nber.org/chapters/c9948.pdf; and Wenjia Zhuang and Kinglun Ngok, "Labour Inspection in Contemporary China: Like the Anglo-Saxon Model, but Different," *International Labour Review* 153, no. 4 (2014): 561–85.

55. Friedman, *Insurgency Trap*; B. Taylor and Q. Li, "Is the ACFTU a Union and Does It Matter?," *Journal of Industrial Relations* 49, no. 5 (November 1, 2007): 701–15, https://doi.org/10.1177/0022185607082217; and Feng Chen, "Between the State and Labour: The Conflict of Chinese Trade Unions' Double Identity in Market Reform," *China Quarterly* 176 (2003): 1006–28.

56. Tom Mitchell and Lucy Hornby, "China Lawyer Trial Begins amid Crackdown on Labour Rights Groups," *Financial Times*, December 14, 2015, http://www.ft.com/intl/cms/s/0/a67e3882-a183-11e5-8d70-42b68cfae6e4.html #axzz48MGabcdu; and Patricia Chen and Mary Gallagher, "Mobilization without Movement: How the Chinese State 'Fixed' Labor Insurgency," *ILR Review*, February 20, 2018, https://doi.org/10.1177/0019793918759066.

57. David Bandurski, *Dragons in Diamond Village: Tales of Resistance from Urbanizing China* (New York: Melville Publishing House, 2016).

58. Zhan, "Hukou Reform and Land Politics in China"; and Andreas and Zhan, "*Hukou* and Land."

59. Chuang, "Urbanization through Dispossession"; and Kristen Looney and Meg Rithmire, "China Gambles on Modernizing Through Urbanization," *Current History* 116, no. 791 (September 2017): 209.

60. Yujeong Yang, "Politics of Inclusion and Exclusion: Dual Pension Regimes in China," PhD dissertation, University of Michigan, 2018. Yang finds that the average residency pension was 280 RMB, while the average employment pension was 1600 RMB.

61. Bandurski, *Dragons in Diamond Village*; and "How the Eviction of Beijing's Migrant Workers Is Tearing at the Fabric of the City's Economy," *South China Morning Post*, January 4, 2018, https://www.scmp.com/news/china/policies -politics/article/2126836/how-eviction-beijings-migrant-workers-tearing-fabric.

62. Xi Jinping, "Full Text of Xi Jinping's Report at 19th CPC National Congress," November 3, 2017, http://www.xinhuanet.com/english/special/2017 -11/03/c_136725942.htm.

63. "Temporary Work," n.d., https://en.wikipedia.org/wiki/Temporary_work (accessed on September 8, 2019).

64. Du, Park, and Wu, "Informal Employment in Urban China."

65. "Report on the Development of the Sharing Economy in China, 2017" ("*Zhongguo fenxiang jingji fazhan baogao*," 中国分享经济发展报告2017), State Information Center and China Internet Association, February 2017.

66. "The Odd Job Economy Has Arrived, How Will Social Insurance Keep Up?" ("*Linggong jingji lai le, shebao ruhe genshang*," 零工经济来了，社保如何跟上), *Economic Daily (Jingji ribao,* 经济日报), January 5, 2018, http://www.xinhua net.com/fortune/2018-01/05/c_1122213098.htm; and Yuan Ming, "Construct New Type of Harmonious Labor Relations in the Internet Age," *China Enterprise News*, April 24, 2018, http://epaper.zqcn.com.cn/attachement/1/2018 -04/24/05/2018042405.pdf.

67. The exception to this is the legislative attention to subcontracting, which is a triangular relationship between an employer, a labor service company, and an employee. However, even in this area there are many loopholes and problems that tend to make the employee vulnerable, with lower pay, small or nonexistent benefits, and lack of employment security.

68. Jiwei Lou, "Full Text of Minister of Finance Lou Ji Wei Speech at Tsinghua University Business School" ("*Caizhengbuzhang Lou Jiwei zai qing-hua jingguan xueyuan yanjiang quanwen*," 财政部长楼继伟在清华经管学院演讲全文), April 24, 2015; "Economist Zhang Weiying Calls for a Decisive Halt in the Implementation of the Labor Contract Law, Says It Hurts the Interests of Workers" ("*Jingji xuejia Zhang Weiying: Laodong hetongfa sunhai gongren de liyi guoduan tingzhi zhixing*," 经济学家张维迎：劳动合同法损害工人的利益果断停止执行), *Caijing*, February 8, 2009; and Wenlong Guo, "The Labor Contract Law Has Made Slackers into Stars," July 23, 2016, http://www.gegugu.com/2016/07/29/ 10719.html.

69. Ian Holliday, "Productivist Welfare Capitalism: Social Policy in East

Asia," *Political Studies* 48, no. 4 (2000): 706–23; Ka Ho Mok and John Hudson, "Managing Social Change and Social Policy in Greater China: Welfare Regimes in Transition?," *Social Policy and Society* 13, no. 2 (April 2014): 235–38, https://doi .org/10.1017/S1474746413000596; and Frazier, *Socialist Insecurity.*

70. Jared Bernstein, "An Interview with Sam Hammond: Free Markets Require Robust Social Insurance," *Washington Post,* May 2, 2018, https:// www.washingtonpost.com/news/posteverything/wp/2018/05/02/an-interview -with-sam-hammond-free-markets-require-robust-social-insurance/?utm_ term=.1381abf3d36b.

71. Yujeong Yang and Mary Gallagher, "Moving In and Moving Up? Labor Conditions and China's Changing Development Model: China's Changing Labor Conditions," *Public Administration and Development* 37, no. 3 (August 2017): 160–75, https://doi.org/10.1002/pad.1800.

72. Bingqin Li, "Social Pension Unification in an Urbanising China: Paths and Constraints," *Public Administration and Development* 34, no. 4 (October 2014): 281–93, https://doi.org/10.1002/pad.1687; and Jin Jiang, Jiwei Qian, and Zhuoyi Wen, "Social Protection for the Informal Sector in Urban China: Institutional Constraints and Self-Selection Behaviour," *Journal of Social Policy* 47, no. 2 (April 2018): 335–57, https://doi.org/10.1017/S0047279417000563.

Chapter 8. Human Capital and China's Future

1. *China Statistical Yearbook 2017* (Beijing: China Statistics Press, 2017).

2. Hongbin Li, Prashant Loyalka, Scott Rozelle, and Binzhen Wu, "Human Capital and China's Future Growth," *Journal of Economic Perspectives* 31, no. 1 (2017): 25–47.

3. On human capital contributions to Chinese growth, see Belton Fleisher, Haizheng Li, and Min Qiang Zhao, "Human Capital, Economic Growth, and Regional Inequality in China," *Journal of Development Economics* 92, no. 2 (2010): 215–31.

4. Li et al., "Human Capital and China's Future Growth."

5. The importance of human capital to economic growth has been recognized for decades. See Gary S. Becker, *Human Capital: A Theoretical and Empirical Analysis with Special Reference to Education,* third edition (Chicago: University of Chicago Press, 1993).

6. See Li et al., "Human Capital and China's Future Growth."

7. See OECD, "Looking to 2060: A Global Vision of Long-Term Growth," *OECD Economics Department Policy Notes,* no. 15 (November 2012); and PricewaterhouseCoopers, "The Long View: How Will the Global Economic Order Change by 2050?" *The World in 2050* (2017).

8. Additional information on the higher demands of emerging industries can

be found in Timothy F. Bresnahan, "Computerisation and Wage Dispersion: An Analytical Reinterpretation," *Economic Journal* 109, no. 456 (1999): 390–415; Timothy F. Bresnahan, Erik Brynjolfsson, and Lorin M. Hitt, "Information Technology, Workplace Organization, and the Demand for Skilled Labor: Firm-level Evidence," *Quarterly Journal of Economics* 117, no. 1 (2002): 339–76; and Lawrence F. Katz and Alan B. Krueger, "Computing Inequality: Have Computers Changed the Labor Market?," *Quarterly Journal of Economics* 113, no. 4 (1998): 1169–1213.

9. OECD, *Education at a Glance 2017: OECD Indicators* (Paris: OECD Publishing, 2017); and Niny Khor, Lihua Pang, Chengfang Liu, Linxiu Zhang, Fang Chang, Di Mo, Prashant Loyalka, and Scott Rozelle, "China's Looming Human Capital Crisis: Upper Secondary Educational Attainment Rates and the Middle Income Trap," *China Quarterly* 228 (2016): 905–26.

10. Khor et al., "China's Looming Human Capital Crisis."

11. Our method is similar to Li et al., "Human Capital and China's Future Growth," but it uses data from 2015 instead of 2014 and considers additional factors related to economic growth. To increase the number of observations, we used the information from neighboring years when the relevant information is not available in a particular year. For example, we use data from 2008–12 for 2010 and data from 2011–14 for 2015. The numbers for China are derived from its population census.

12. We exclude China from our regression analysis to determine how the PRC compares to the rest of the world. We removed outliers from the data (countries with populations in the bottom 3 percentiles or GDP per capita in the top 3 percentiles) that we judged likely to skew our regression estimates. The data were downloaded in September 2017. In our regression analysis we used GDP to weight our data, meaning that we assigned greater weight to the human capital-income relationship of larger countries than to those of smaller nations.

13. This step builds on the work of Eric A. Hanushek and Ludger Woessmann, *The Knowledge Capital of Nations: Education and the Economics of Growth* (Cambridge, MA: MIT Press, 2015); and Li et al., "Human Capital and China's Future Growth." We used the following equation to produce estimates for each year separately:

$$\log(Y_i) = \alpha \cdot Edu_i + \beta \cdot X_i + \varepsilon_i$$

Y_i is the per capita GDP (our measure of income) of each country i. Edu_i is the measure of educational attainment in country i. X_i is the set of other variables that can influence economic growth, such as population size, labor force share, and physical capital.

14. Specifically an additional year of schooling was found to be correlated with 25.1 percent, 25.9 percent, 25.3 percent, and 26.3 percent higher GDP per

capita in 2000, 2005, 2010, and 2015, respectively. The R-squared of these regressions are also high (≥0.667), particularly after 2005 (≥0.720), suggesting that education levels can explain much of the variation in GDP per capita across countries.

15. We also try the specification that uses population as the weight. The results are still very similar.

16. Li et al., "Human Capital and China's Future Growth"; Xiaodong Zhu, "Understanding China's Growth: Past, Present, and Future," *Journal of Economic Perspectives* 26, no. 4 (2012): 103–24; and Loren Brandt and Xiaodong Zhu, "Accounting for China's Growth," IZA Discussion Papers, no. 4764 (2010).

17. See Vikram Nehru and Ashok Dhareshwar, "A New Database on Physical Capital Stock: Sources, Methodology and Results," *Revista de análisis económico–Economic Analysis Review* 8, no. 1 (1993): 37–59.

18. We assume all children younger than age seventeen in the 2010 census attend middle school if they attend primary school.

19. This growth rate is derived using information on admission quotas between 2010 and 2015 and the corresponding cohort size. We allocate the total quota to rural and urban students based on historical allocation information in Population Census 2010. The calculated growth rate for high school enrollment is negative for rural students between 2010 and 2015. To be conservative, we assume no growth.

20. For *normal case I* and the *optimistic case*, we had to make assumptions about how admission quotas are allocated between rural and urban students. Based on the data pattern from the 2010 population census, we assumed the quota share of rural students to be proportional to the population share of rural students, and derived the proportion based on the quota share and population share of the corresponding age group (age fifteen for high school and age eighteen for college in 2007) in the 2010 census.

21. We present the gaps in educational attainment between urban and rural students under the optimistic scenario in Figure 8.A1. The numbers for years after 2007 are estimated.

22. Calculations are based on the national population census 2010.

23. *China Educational Finance Statistical Yearbook* (Beijing: China Statistics Press, 2016).

24. When it comes to attending high school, it is almost impossible for any children with rural *hukou* to attend schools in urban school districts. As a consequence, if a rural student wants to attend high school, he must attend in his home county.

25. We assume the same cost (US$2,420) for one additional enrollment.

Whether kids are migrants does not matter for the cost estimation. What matters is the rate of expansion of the high-school enrollment for migrant kids.

26. Urban kids in the population census 2010 include migrant children living in the urban areas. We add the case that the high school enrollment rate of migrant kids is expanded at the rate of the rural kids. The cost increases a little bit. High school currently is not free in China. Urban kids also need to pay for it. Migrant kids might need to pay more if they can enter high school.

27. These calculations are based on the 2010 population census.

28. Dandan Zhang, Xin Li, and Jinjun Xue, "Education Inequality between Rural and Urban Areas of the People's Republic of China, Migrants' Children Education, and Some Implications," *Asian Development Review* 32, no. 1 (2015): 196–224.

29. On per capita spending on facilities and programs in rural schools, see Wen Wang and Zhirong Jerry Zhao, "Spatial Decomposition of Funding Inequality in China's Basic Education: A Four-Level Theil Index Analysis," *Public Finance and Management* 14, no. 4 (2014): 416. On the difficulty retaining high-quality teachers, see Yi Wei, "Teacher Mobility in Rural China: Evidence from Northwest China," Michigan State University, 2016.

30. *China Educational Finance Statistical Yearbook* (2016).

31. Tanja Sargent and Emily Hannum, "Keeping Teachers Happy: Job Satisfaction among Primary School Teachers in Rural Northwest China," *Comparative Education Review* 49, no. 2 (2005): 173–204; and Yi Wei, "Teacher Mobility in Rural China."

32. Calculation based on *China Educational Finance Statistical Yearbook* (2016) and UNESCO Institute of Statistics (2016). For China the rate increases to 46 percent, 48 percent, and 46 percent for high schools, middle schools, and primary schools, respectively, and the rate in rural areas is about 1 to 2 percentage points higher.

33. Xuehui An, "Teacher Salaries and the Shortage of High-Quality Teachers in China's Rural Primary and Secondary Schools," *Chinese Education & Society* 51, no. 2 (2018): 103–16. It is difficult to say exactly how much because urban teachers often have supplements to their salaries from bonuses given by parents and additional teaching duty in off-school hours.

34. The basic salary of rural teachers is set and paid for by the central government and is equivalent to a civil servant's salary. Additional payments to teachers must come from the local government's budget.

35. Prashant Loyalka, Sean Sylvia, Chengfang Liu, James Chu, and Yaojiang Shi, "Pay by Design: Teacher Performance Pay Design and the Distribution of Student Achievement," *Journal of Labor Economics* 37, no. 3 (2019): 621–62. In this system rural teachers were rewarded for gains made by their students, rela-

tive to other rural students in other schools in the county. When provided with additional incentives, teachers worked harder and spent more time with students during and after class.

36. *China Educational Finance Statistical Yearbook* (2016).

37. Chengfang Liu, Linxiu Zhang, Renfu Luo, Scott Rozelle, Brian Sharbono, and Yaojiang Shi, "Development Challenges, Tuition Barriers, and High School Education in China," *Asia Pacific Journal of Education* 29, no. 4 (2009): 503–20; and Hongbin Li, Lingsheng Meng, Xinzheng Shi, and Binzhen Wu, "Poverty in China's Colleges and the Targeting of Financial Aid," *China Quarterly* 216 (2013): 970–92.

38. Hongmei Yi, Linxiu Zhang, Renfu Luo, Yaojiang Shi, Di Mo, Xinxin Chen, Carl Brinton, and Scott Rozelle, "Dropping Out: Why Are Students Leaving Junior High in China's Poor Rural Areas?," *International Journal of Educational Development*, 32, no. 4 (2012): 555–63; and Hongbin Li, Lei Li, Binzhen Wu, and Yanyan Xiong, "The End of Cheap Chinese Labor," *Journal of Economic Perspectives* 26, no. 4 (2012): 57–74.

39. Susan M. Dynarski, "Does Aid Matter? Measuring the Effect of Student Aid on College Attendance and Completion," *American Economic Review* 93, no. 1 (2003): 279–88; D. M. Linsenmeier, H. S. Rosen, and C. E. Rouse, "Financial Aid Packages and College Enrollment Decisions: An Econometric Case Study," *Review of Economics and Statistics* 88, no. 1 (2006): 126–45; Thomas J. Kane, "Evaluating the Impact of the DC Tuition Assistance Grant Program," *Journal of Human Resources* 42, no. 3 (2007): 555–82; Felipe Barrera-Osorio, Marianne Bertrand, Leigh L. Linden, and Francisco Perez-Calle, "Improving the Design of Conditional Transfer Programs: Evidence from a Randomized Education Experiment in Colombia," *American Economic Journal: Applied Economics* 3, no. 2 (2011): 167–95; Chengfang Liu, Linxiu Zhang, Renfu Luo, Xiaobing Wang, Scott Rozelle, Brian Sharbono, Jennifer Adams et al., "Early Commitment on Financial Aid and College Decision Making of Poor Students: Evidence from a Randomized Evaluation in Rural China," *Economics of Education Review* 30, no. 4 (2011): 627–40; and Prashant Loyalka, Yingquan Song, Jianguo Wei, Weiping Zhong, and Scott Rozelle, "Information, College Decisions and Financial Aid: Evidence from a Cluster-randomized Controlled Trial in China," *Economics of Education Review* 36 (2013): 26–40.

40. Li et al., "Poverty in China's Colleges and the Targeting of Financial Aid."

41. Liu et al., "Development Challenges, Tuition Barriers, and High School Education in China."

42. Di Mo, Linxiu Zhang, Hongmei Yi, Renfu Luo, Scott Rozelle, and Carl

Brinton, "School Dropouts and Conditional Cash Transfers: Evidence from a Randomised Controlled Trial in Rural China's Junior High Schools," *Journal of Development Studies* 49, no. 2 (2013): 190–207; T. Paul Schultz, "School Subsidies for the Poor: Evaluating the Mexican Progresa Poverty Program," *Journal of Development Economics* 74, no. 1 (2004): 199–250; and World Bank, "Conditional Cash Transfers" (Washington, DC: World Bank, 2009). Christopher Cornwell, David B. Mustard, and Deepa J. Sridhar, "The Enrollment Effects of Merit-Based Financial Aid: Evidence from Georgia's HOPE program," *Journal of Labor Economics* 24, no. 4 (2006): 761–86; and Joshua Angrist and Victor Lavy, "The Effects of High Stakes High School Achievement Awards: Evidence from a Randomized Trial," *American Economic Review* 99, no. 4 (2009): 1384–1414.

43. World Bank, "Conditional Cash Transfers."

44. Renfu Luo, Ai Yue, Huan Zhou, Yaojiang Shi, Linxiu Zhang, Reynaldo Martorell, Alexis Medina, Scott Rozelle, and Sean Sylvia, "The Effect of a Micronutrient Powder Home Fortification Program on Anemia and Cognitive Outcomes among Young Children in Rural China: A Cluster Randomized Trial," *BMC Public Health* 17, no. 1 (2017): 738. Long-Shan Xu, Bao-Jun Pan, Jin-Xiang Lin, Li-Ping Chen, Sen-Hai Yu, and Jack Jones, "Creating Health-Promoting Schools in Rural China: A Project Started from Deworming," *Health Promotion International* 15, no. 3 (2000): 197–206; Chengfang Liu, Louise Lu, Linxiu Zhang, Renfu Luo, Sean Sylvia, Alexis Medina, Scott Rozelle, Darvin Scott Smith, Yingdan Chen, and Tingjun Zhu, "Effect of Deworming on Indices of Health, Cognition, and Education among Schoolchildren in Rural China: A Cluster-Randomized Controlled Trial," *American Journal of Tropical Medicine and Hygiene* 96, no. 6 (2017): 1478–89. Mingguang He, Yingfeng Zheng, and Fan Xiang, "Prevalence of Myopia in Urban and Rural Children in Mainland China," *Optometry and Vision Science* 86, no. 1 (2009): 40–44. Gustavo J. Bobonis, Edward Miguel, and Charu Puri-Sharma, "Anemia and School Participation," *Journal of Human Resources* 41, no. 4 (2006): 692–721; and Edward Miguel and Michael Kremer, "Worms: Identifying Impacts on Education and Health in the Presence of Treatment Externalities," *Econometrica* 72, no. 1 (2004): 159–217.

45. On providing children with vitamins and/or nutritious lunches, see Max Kleiman-Weiner, Renfu Luo, Linxiu Zhang, Yaojiang Shi, Alexis Medina, and Scott Rozelle, "Eggs Versus Chewable Vitamins: Which Intervention Can Increase Nutrition and Test Scores in Rural China?," *China Economic Review* 24 (2013): 165–76; Luo et al., "Nutrition and Educational Performance in Rural China's Elementary Schools"; Luo et al., "Effect of a Micronutrient Powder Home Fortification Program on Anemia and Cognitive Outcomes among Young

Children in Rural China." On eyeglasses for the nearsighted, see Xiaochen Ma, Zhongqiang Zhou, Hongmei Yi, Xiaopeng Pang, Yaojiang Shi, Qianyun Chen, Mirjam E. Meltzer, Saskia le Cessie, Mingguang He, Scott Rozelle, Yizhi Liu and Nathan Congdon, "Effect of Providing Free Glasses on Children's Educational Outcomes in China: Cluster Randomized Controlled Trial," *British Medical Journal* 349 (2014): g5740. On deworming medicines, see Chengfang Liu et al., "Effect of Deworming on Indices of Health, Cognition, and Education among Schoolchildren in Rural China." Ai Yue, Lauren Marsh, Huan Zhou, Alexis Medina, Renfu Luo, Yaojiang Shi, Linxiu Zhang, Scott Rozelle, "Nutritional Deficiencies, the Absence of Information and Caregiver Failures: A Qualitative Analysis of Infant Feeding Practices in Rural China." *PloS One* 11, no. 4 (2016): e0153385.

46. Yue et al., "Nutritional Deficiencies, the Absence of Information and Caregiver Failures."

47. Zhao Qiran, Xiaobing Wang, Scott Rozelle, "Better Cognition, Better School Performance? Evidence from Primary Schools in China," *China Economic Review* 55 (2019): 199–217.

48. *Chinese Statistical Yearbook* (2016).

49. Hongbin Li and Li-An Zhou, "Political Turnover and Economic Performance: The Incentive Role of Personnel Control in China," *Journal of Public Economics* 89, no. 9 (2005): 1743–62; and Hehui Jin, Yingyi Qian, and Barry R. Weingast, "Regional Decentralization and Fiscal Incentives: Federalism, Chinese Style," *Journal of Public Economics* 89, no. 9 (2005): 1719–42.

50. Jikun Huang, Scott Rozelle, and Honglin Wang, "Fostering or Striping Rural China: Modernizing Agriculture and Rural to Urban Capital Flows," *The Developing Economies* 44, no. 1 (2006): 1–26.

51. In 2015 about 40 percent of the local government educational expenditure was financed by the earmarked educational expenditure of the central government. However, local governments still have substantial discretion on how to use the earmarked educational funds. Specifically, they can allocate more resources to urban areas. Local governments may also allocate more resources to high schools, which most rural students stop attending. Average government expenditures on students in compulsory education classes are lower than on high-school classes. *China Educational Finance Statistical Yearbook* (2016).

52. To raise the spending on each student in rural areas to the level in urban areas will cost about $6 billion for the current number of rural students at primary and secondary schools. Making high school free costs about $7.4 billion a year for the current number of high school students. Reducing the college tuition by half costs about $16 billion for the current size of college students. All together, these improvements in total would cost about $29 billion.

Chapter 9. Sources and Shapers of China's Foreign Policy

1. See Thomas Fingar, ed., *The New Great Game: China and South and Central Asia in the Era of Reform* (Stanford, CA: Stanford University Press, 2016), chapter 1.

2. See, for example, Zhihua Shen and Yafeng Xia, *Mao and the Sino-Soviet Partnership, 1945–1959: A New History* (Lanham, MD: Lexington Books, 2015), chapter 1; and Wilson Center, *Making of the Sino-Soviet Alliance, 1945–1950*, http://digitalarchive.wilsoncenter.org/collection/181/making-of-the-sino-soviet-alliance-1945-1950 (accessed on August 31, 2019).

3. The collective and selective memory of many Chinese emphasizes the perils of dependency illustrated by the Chinese version of why Moscow terminated its economic assistance and "even took away key blueprints" and the deleterious consequences for China's development. Collective memory also treats the imposition of "containment" policies by the United States as an unprovoked act that proves fundamental American hostility to China's rise and recovery of its rightful place in the region and the world.

4. American officials recognized the implications of the alliance but for a time doubted that the Chinese would accept subordination to Moscow and judged that the alliance would not endure. They were right in the longer term, but the Korean War locked in hostility between the United States and the People's Republic for two decades.

5. For an assessment of Mao's legacy, see Andrew G. Walder, *China under Mao: A Revolution Derailed* (Cambridge, MA: Harvard University Press, 2015).

6. See Ezra F. Vogel, *Deng Xiaoping and the Transformation of China* (Cambridge, MA: Belknap Press, 2011).

7. For broad surveys of Chinese foreign policy see, for example, John W. Garver, *China's Quest: The History of the Foreign Relations of the People's Republic of China* (Oxford: Oxford University Press, 2016); and Robert G. Sutter, *Chinese Foreign Relations: Power and Policy since the Cold War*, fourth edition (Lanham, MD: Rowman & Littlefield, 2016).

8. See, for example, Giovanni Bressi, "China and Western Europe," *Asian Survey* 12, no. 10 (October 1972): 819–45; and Zbigniew Brzezinski, *Power and Principle*, revised edition (New York: Farrar, Straus, Giroux, 1985), chapter 6.

9. See Harry Harding, *A Fragile Relationship: The United States and China since 1972* (Washington, DC: Brookings Institution Press, 1992); and Michael Green, *By More Than Providence: Grand Strategy and American Power in the Asia Pacific since 1783* (New York: Columbia University Press, 2017), chapter 10.

10. This assessment of the free world was codified in the so-called Three Worlds Theory attributed to Mao but articulated by Deng Xiaoping in a speech at the United Nations in 1974. See Deng Xiaoping, "Speech by Chairman of the

Delegation of the People's Republic of China, Deng Xiaoping, at the Special Session of the U.N. General Assembly," April 10, 1974, https://www.marxists.org/reference/archive/deng-xiaoping/1974/04/10.htm.

11. On the traditional strategy, see Yen-p'ing Hao and Erh-min Wang, "Chinese Views of Western Relations, 1840–95," in John K. Fairbank and Kwang-ching Liu, eds., *The Cambridge History of China*, vol. 11, *Late Ch'ing, 1800–1911*, part 2 (Cambridge: Cambridge University Press, 1980), 142–201.

12. See Harding, *Fragile Relationship*; Green, *By More Than Providence*, chapter 10; and Garver, *China's Quest*, chapter 15.

13. See Vogel, *Deng Xiaoping*; and Li Lanqing, *Breaking Through: The Birth of China's Opening-up Policy* (New York: Oxford University Press, 2009).

14. See Fingar, *New Great Game*, chapter 1; and Carol Lee Hamrin, *China and the Challenge of the Future* (Boulder, CO: Westview Press, 1990), chapter 5.

15. See Thomas Fingar, "Sources and Shapers of China's Global Engagement," in Thomas Fingar, ed., *Uneasy Partnerships: China's Engagement with Japan, the Koreas, and Russia in the Age of Reform* (Stanford, CA: Stanford University Press, 2017), chapter 2.

16. The "two decade" window of opportunity opened by this reassessment of the international situation was long enough to allow for significant self-strengthening but only if China seized the probably short-lived opportunity. The implicit message was that there was no time for party leaders to debate the ideological orthodoxy or fine points of the new strategy.

17. See Harding, *Fragile Relationship*, chapter 3; and Green, *By More Than Providence*, chapter 10.

18. See, for example, Vogel, *Deng Xiaoping,* chapter 11; and Henry Kissinger, *On China* (New York: Penguin 2011), chapters 8–12.

19. See Thomas Fingar, "China's Quest for Technology: Implications for Arms Control II," in John H Barton and Ryukichi Imai, eds., *Arms Control II: A New Approach to International Security* (Cambridge, MA: Oelgeschlager, Gunn and Hain, 1981), chapter 10.

20. See, for example, Harding, *Fragile Relationship*, chapters 5–6.

21. The specific modalities of these instruments have changed over time, but they were used in each of the three periods summarized in this chapter and will continue to be used in the future. Their continued relevance reflects the high degree of stability in China's geopolitical situation, prioritization of national objectives, and Beijing's judgments about what can and cannot be achieved.

22. For discussion and sources on the evolution of Chinese views on international regimes see, for example, Elizabeth Economy, "The Impact of International Regimes on Chinese Foreign Policy-Making: Broadening Perspectives and Policies . . . but Only to a Point," in David M. Lampton, ed., *The*

Making of Chinese Security Policy in the Era of Reform (Stanford, CA: Stanford University Press, 2001), 230–53.

23. For discussion of China's changing view of sovereignty see, for example, Bates Gill, *Rising Star: China's New Security Diplomacy*, revised edition (Washington, DC: Brookings Institution Press, 2007), chapter 4.

24. On rules and the US-led order see, for example, G. John Ikenberry, *Liberal Leviathan: The Origins, Crisis, and Transformation of American World Order* (Princeton, NJ: Princeton University Press, 2011), chapters 3–4.

25. What they were doing was the opposite of the "all in" way in which Central European states approached accession to NATO and the European Union.

26. See, for example, John Wilson Lewis and Xue Litai, *Imagined Enemies: China Prepares for Uncertain War* (Stanford, CA: Stanford University Press, 2006).

27. This is still China's highest priority and will remain so for the foreseeable future. The logic applied in this chapter posits that China's ultimate goals are hegemony and prosperity (power and wealth), that management of perceived threats to security and sustained economic growth are the most important instrumental means for achieving ultimate objectives, and that maintenance of internal order and party leadership are requisites for achieving higher-priority instrumental and ultimate goals.

28. See, for example, Evan S. Medeiros, *Reluctant Restraint: The Evolution of China's Nonproliferation Policies and Practices, 1980–2004* (Stanford, CA: Stanford University Press, 2007); and Thomas Fingar, "China's Goals in South Asia," in Fingar, *New Great Game,* chapter 2.

29. Significant increases in China's defense budget did not begin for a few years, but planning for a more modern military force began much earlier. See, for example, Tai Ming Cheung, *Fortifying China: The Struggle to Build a Modern Defense Economy* (Ithaca, NY: Cornell University Press, 2009), chapters 3–4.

30. See Vogel, *Deng Xiaoping*, chapters 20–21; and Zhao Ziyang, *Prisoner of the State* (New York: Simon & Schuster, 2009), part 1.

31. See the essays in Gideon Rose, ed. *Tiananmen and After* (New York: Council on Foreign Relations, 2014).

32. See Green, *By More Than Providence*, chapters 12–13.

33. See, for example, Richard Youngs, *The European Union and the Promotion of Democracy* (Oxford: Oxford University Press, 2002), chapter 6.

34. See Fingar, *New Great Game*, chapter 1.

35. See, for example, Lowell Dittmer and George T. Yu, eds., *China, the Developing World, and the New Global Dynamic* (Boulder, CO: Lynne Rienner, 2010).

36. See Riordan Roett and Guadalupe Paz, ed., *China's Expansion into the Western Hemisphere* (Washington, DC: Brookings Institution Press, 2008); and Robert I. Rotberg, ed., *China into Africa: Trade, Aid, and Influence* (Washington, DC: Brookings Institution Press, 2008).

37. See, for example, Charles E. Ziegler and Rajan Menon, "Neomercantilism and Great Power Energy Competition in Central Asia and the Caspian," *Strategic Studies Quarterly* 8, no. 2 (Summer 2014), 17–41.

38. See John W. Garver, *China and Iran: Ancient Partners in a Post-Imperial World* (Seattle: University of Washington Press, 2006).

39. Saudi Arabia began to develop closer ties with China in the mid-1980s and Israel quickly followed suit. See, for example, Joseph A. Kechichian, "Saudi Arabia and China: The Security Dimension," Middle East Institute, February 9, 2016, http://www.mei.edu/content/map/saudi-arabia-and-china-security-dimension; and Islam Ayyadi and Mohammed Kamal, "China-Israel Arms Trade and Co-operation: History and Policy Implications," *Asian Affairs* 47, no. 2 (2016): 260–73.

40. See Jon B. Alterman and John W. Garver, *The Vital Triangle: China, the United States, and the Middle East* (Washington, DC: Center for Strategic and International Studies, 2008).

41. Another example with direct relevance to Beijing's changing stake in the Middle East is the step-by-step way in which it moved from opposition to support of UN peacekeeping operations. See, for example, Yin He, "China's Changing Policy on UN Peacekeeping Operations," *Institute for Security and Development Policy*, July 2007, http://isdp.eu/content/uploads/publications/2007_he_chinas-changing-policy.pdf; and Stefan Stähle, "China's Shifting Attitude towards United Nations Peacekeeping Operations," *China Quarterly* 195 (September 2008): 631–55.

42. See, for example, Michael D. Swaine, "Perceptions of an Assertive China," *China Leadership Monitor* 32 (Spring 2010), http://carnegieendowment.org/files/CLM32MS1.pdf; and Alastair Iain Johnston, "How New and Assertive Is China's New Assertiveness?" *International Security* 57, no. 4 (Spring 2013): 7–48, and the sources cited therein.

43. See the works cited and arguments summarized in the following articles by Michael D. Swain: "China's Assertive Behavior—Part One: On 'Core Interests," *China Leadership Monitor* 34 (Winter 2011): 1–25; "China's Assertive Behavior—Part Two: The Maritime Periphery" (with M. Taylor Fravel), *China Leadership Monitor* 35 (Summer 2011): 1–29; "China's Assertive Behavior—Part Three: The Role of the Military in Foreign Policy," *China Leadership Monitor* 36 (Winter 2012): 1–17; and "China's Assertive Behavior—Part Four: The Role of the Military in Foreign Crises," *China Leadership Monitor* 37 (Spring 2012): 1–14.

44. See *National Security Strategy of the United States*, December 2017, https://www.whitehouse.gov/wp-content/uploads/2017/12/NSS-Final-12-18-2017-0905.pdf; and Graham Allison, *Destined for War: Can America and China Escape Thucydides Trap?* (New York: Houghton Mifflin Harcourt, 2017).

45. I agree with Johnston's judgment that the magnitude and meaning of the cases cited to prove China's new assertiveness are overstated. See Johnston, "How New and Assertive Is China's New Assertiveness?" For critiques of Allison, see Arthur Waldron, "There Is No Thucydides Trap," *Sunday Times*, June 18, 2017, reprinted in *The Straits Times*, June 18, 2017, http://www.straitstimes.com/opinion/there-is-no-thucydides-trap; and T. J. Pempel, "Thucydides (Clap)Trap," *Global Asia* 10, no. 4 (December 2015): 88–93.

46. For different projections of China's future behavior see, for example, Aaron L. Friedberg, *A Contest for Supremacy: China, America, and the Struggle for Mastery in Asia* (New York: W. W. Norton, 2011); and Thomas Fingar, "China's Vision of World Order," in Ashley J. Tellis and Travis Tanner, eds., *Strategic Asia 2012–13: China's Military Challenge* (Seattle, WA: National Bureau of Asian Research, 2012), 343–73.

47. See Swaine, "Perceptions of an Assertive China" and sources cited therein.

48. See, for example, Yung Chul Park, "The Global Financial Crisis: Decoupling of East Asia—Myth or Reality?" ADB Institute Working Paper 289, June 2011, https://core.ac.uk/download/pdf/6239311.pdf.

49. See, for example, CIGI/Chinese Academy of Social Sciences Task Force, "China and the Financial Crisis," Centre for International Governance Innovation, 2009, https://www.cigionline.org/sites/default/files/task_force_2.pdf (accessed on August 31, 2019).

50. Chinese assertions that the United States seeks to contain China appear regularly. Illustrative examples include Luo Jun, Xinhua Commentary, "US Needs to Discard Containment Fantasy," *Xinhua English*, June 1, 2014; and Xinhua Commentary, "Why China Cannot Back Down in the Doklum Standoff," *Xinhua English*, August 4, 2017. See also Liu Xin and Bai Yunyi, "Most Chinese Feel West's Growing Containment of China, but Optimistic about Future," *Global Times*, December 28, 2018, http://www.globaltimes.cn/content/1133965.shtml.

51. See, for example, Park, "Global Financial Crisis."

52. See the different views of Wu Xinbo, "Understanding the Geopolitical Implications of the Global Financial Crisis," *Washington Quarterly* 33, no. 4 (October 2010): 155–63; and Joseph S. Nye Jr., "American and Chinese Power after the Financial Crisis," *Washington Quarterly* 33, no. 4 (October 2010): 143–53.

53. See commentary of Lyle J. Goldstein, "Does China Think America Is in

Decline?" *National Interest*, January 28, 2016, http://nationalinterest.org/feature/does-china-think-america-decline-15042.

54. See, for example, Mo Shengkai and Chen Yue, "The US-China Thucydides Trap: A View from Beijing," *National Interest*, July 10, 2016, https://nationalinterest.org/feature/the-us-china-thucydides-trap-view-from-beijing-16903; and Shen Jianguang, "China Needs to Prepare for Long-term Rivalry with the US Even If Trade Deal Is Reached," *Global Times Online*, January 9, 2019.

55. See critiques of Allison by Waldron, "There Is No Thucydides Trap"; and Pempel, Thucydides (Clap)Trap."

56. Johnston, "How New and Assertive Is China's New Assertiveness?"

57. See, for example, Zhong Nan, "China Rips into EU for 'Unfair' Dumping Duties," *China Daily*, August 12, 2017, http://www.chinadaily.com.cn/business/2017-08/12/content_30499119.htm.

58. See, for example, Deborah Brautigam and Jyhjong Hwang, "Eastern Promises: New Data on Chinese Loans in Africa, 2000–2014," SAIS China-Africa Research Initiative Working Paper 4, April 2016, https://static1.squarespace.com/static/5652847de4b033f56d2bdc29/t/58ac91ede6f2e1f64a20d11a/1487704559189/eastern+promises+v4.pdf; and Xiaochen Su, "Why Chinese Infrastructure Loans in Africa Represent a Brand-New Type of Neocolonialism," *The Diplomat*, June 9, 2017, http://thediplomat.com/2017/06/why-chinese-infrastructural-loans-in-africa-represent-a-brand-new-type-of-neocolonialism/.

59. See, for example, Harold Trinkunas, "Renminbi Diplomacy? The Limits of China's Influence on Latin America's Domestic Politics," Geoeconomics and Global Issues Paper 3, Brookings Institution, November 2016.

60. See, for example, Christopher K. Johnson, "President Xi Jinping's 'Belt and Road' Initiative," Center for Strategic and International Studies, March 2016, https://csis-prod.s3.amazonaws.com/s3fs-public/publication/160328_Johnson_PresidentXiJinping_Web.pdf.

61. Many cite an article by Wang Jisi as the origin of this idea. See Wang Jisi, "Marching West, China's Geo-strategic Re-balancing, *Global Times* (*Wang Jisi*, 王缉思,"*Xijin, Zhongguo diyuan zhanlüe de zai pingheng*," 西进, 中国地缘战略的再平衡, *Huanqiu Shibao*, 环球时报), October 17, 2012, http://opinion.huanqiu.com/opinion_world/2012-10/3193760.html.

62. See, for example, Gideon Rachman, "China's Strange Fear of a Colour Revolution," *Financial Times*, February 9, 2015, https://www.ft.com/content/9b5a2ed2-af96-11e4-b42e-00144feab7de; and Chris Buckley, "Chinese Propaganda Video Warns of West's 'Devilish Claws,'" *New York Times*, December 22, 2016, https://www.nytimes.com/2016/12/22/world/asia/china-video-communist-party.html?_r=0.

63. See, for example, Robert Kagan, "Not Fade Away: The Myth of American

Decline," *New Republic*, January 10, 2012, https://newrepublic.com/article/99521/america-world-power-declinism.

64. See, for example, Keith B. Richburg, "US Pivot to Asia Makes China Nervous," *Washington Post*, November 16, 2011, https://www.washingtonpost.com/world/asia_pacific/us-pivot-to-asia-makes-china-nervous/2011/11/15/gIQA sQpVRN_story.html?utm_term=.0599a90fff89.

65. See the Center for International Strategic Studies Asia Maritime Transparency Initiative website at https://amti.csis.org.

66. The full quotation attributed to Deng is, "Hide our capacities and bide our time; be good at maintaining a low profile; and never claim leadership." For examples of actions said to depart from this approach, see Elizabeth C. Economy, *The Third Revolution: Xi Jinping and the New Chinese State* (Oxford: Oxford University Press, 2018), chapter 7.

67. David A. Welch and Kobi Logendrarajah, "Is China Still an Outlaw in the South China Sea?" OpenCanada.org, July 29, 2019, https://www.opencanada.org/features/china-still-outlaw-south-china-sea/.

68. See, for example, Robert Keatley, "China's AIIB Challenge: How Should America Respond?" *National Interest*, April 18, 2015, http://nationalinterest.org/feature/americas-big-strategic-blunder-not-joining-chinas-aiib-12666; and Zhiqun Zhu, "China's AIIB and OBOR: Ambitions and Challenges," *The Diplomat*, October 9, 2015, https://thediplomat.com/2015/10/chinas-aiib-and-obor-ambitions-and-challenges/.

69. The efficacy of methods used to limit US pressure was called into question by the policies of the Trump administration.

70. Economy, *Third Revolution*; and Johnston, "How New and Assertive Is China's New Assertiveness?"

71. G. John Ikenberry and Darren Lim, "China's Emerging Institutional Statecraft," April 2017, Brookings Institution; and Medeiros, *Reluctant Restraint*.

72. Economy, *Third Revolution*.

73. See, for example, Office of the United States Trade Representative, "Update Concerning China's Acts, Policies and Practices Related to Technology Transfer, Intellectual Property, and Innovation," November 20, 2018, https://ustr.gov/sites/default/files/enforcement/301Investigations/301%20Report%20Update.pdf.

74. See, for example, "When It Comes to China, Foreign Investors Are Getting 'Promise Fatigue,'" *Reuters*, September 19, 2017, http://fortune.com/2017/09/18/china-politburo-reforms-foreign-investment/.

75. See Fingar, "China's Vision of World Order."

76. See Thomas Fingar, "China's Engagement with South and Central Asia: Patterns, Trends, and Themes," in Fingar, *New Great Game*, chapter 13.

77. This judgment is based in part on my reading of diplomatic history and scholarly studies of international politics, but it is also based on my observations and experience during the fifteen years that I supervised US government analytic work on all countries and issues as assistant secretary of state for intelligence and research, chairman of the National Intelligence Council, and other senior positions in the State Department and Office of the Director of National Intelligence.

78. This prediction is consistent with the course suggested by former Deputy Secretary of State Robert Zoellick when he urged China to act as a "responsible stakeholder" in the international system. See Robert B. Zoellick, "Whither China: From Membership to Responsibility?" Remarks to National Committee on US-China Relations, September 21, 2005, https://2001-2009.state.gov/s/d/former/zoellick/rem/53682.htm.

79. Fingar, "China's Vision of World Order."

Chapter 10. China and the Global South

Versions of this chapter have been presented on several occasions. In addition to comments received at the authors workshop in Beijing, I am thankful to the comments by Akbar Ahmed, Andrew Mertha, James Mittelman, Charles Parton, Sean Starrs, and Mark Thompson. They are not responsible for any mistakes herein.

1. See Joshua C. Ramo, *The Beijing Consensus* (London: Foreign Policy Centre, 2004), for examples of arguments that Beijing's presence in the Global South brings new opportunities and ideas. For China as one of the emerging neocolonial powers, see Patrick Bond, "Sub-imperialism as Lubricant of Neoliberalism: South African 'Deputy Sheriff' Duty within BRICS," *Third World Quarterly* 34, no. 2 (2013): 251–70.

2. Ho-fung Hung, *The China Boom: Why China Will Not Rule the World* (New York: Columbia University Press, 2015), chapter 3.

3. See Hung, *China Boom*, chapter 3.

4. See, for example, Howard W. French, *China's Second Continent: How a Million Migrants Are Building a New Empire in Africa* (New York: Knopf, 2014); and Kevin Gallagher and Roberto Porzecanski, *The Dragon in the Room: China and the Future of Latin American Industrialization* (Stanford, CA: Stanford University Press, 2010).

5. See Giancarlo Corsetti, Paolo Pesenti, and Nouriel Roubini, "What Caused the Asian Currency and Financial Crisis?" *Japan and the World Economy* 11, no. 3 (October 1999): 305–73.

6. Institute of International Finance, "Global Debt Monitor," October 2017,

https://www.iif.com/publication/global-debt-monitor/global-debt-monitor-octo
ber-2017.

7. Hung, *China Boom*, chapter 6.

8. PMI data is compiled by both the Chinese government and private firms
(first HSBC, and then Caixin), enabling crosschecks to determine reliability.
For Chinese government compilation, see National Bureau of Statistics, http://
data.stats.gov.cn/english/easyquery.htm?cn=A01 (accessed on September 5, 2019).
For HSBC/Caixin data, see IHS Market monthly press releases, https://www
.markiteconomics.com/Public/Release/PressReleases (accessed on September 5,
2019).

9. See Ho-fung Hung, "Rise of China and the Global Overaccumulation
Crisis," *Review of International Political Economy* 15, no. 2 (2008): 149–79.

10. See National Development and Reform Commission, *A Report on China's
Outward Investment* (Beijing: People's Daily Press, 2017), Table 1; and Hung,
China Boom, Table 5.4.

11. Alvin Camba and Ho-fung Hung, "China, Africa, and Global Economic
Transformation" in Christopher Alden and Daniel Large, eds., *New Directions in
the Study of Africa and China* (London: Routledge, 2018), chapter 19.

12. Charles Wolf Jr., "The Strategy behind China's Aid Expansion," *Wall
Street Journal,* October 9, 2013, https://www.rand.org/blog/2013/10/the-strategy
-behind-chinas-aid-expansion.html (accessed on September 5, 2019).

13. Deborah Brautigam, "5 Myths about Chinese Investment in Africa,"
Foreign Policy, December 14, 2015, http://foreignpolicy.com/2015/12/04/5-myths
-about-chinese-investment-in-africa/ (accessed on September 5, 2019).

14. Deborah Brautigam, "Ethiopia's Partnership with China." *Guardian,*
December 30, 2011.

15. Christopher Balding, "Venezuela's Road to Disaster Is Littered with
Chinese Cash," *Foreign Policy*, June 6, 2017, http://foreignpolicy.com/2017/06/06/
venezuelas-road-to-disaster-is-littered-with-chinese-cash/ (accessed on September
5, 2019).

16. For example, see the summary of the debate by David Volodzko, "China
and Africa: The Great Debate; The Pros and Cons of China's Presence in Africa,"
The Diplomat, December 7, 2015, https://thediplomat.com/2015/12/china-and
-africa-the-great-debate/ (accessed on September 5, 2019); and Yun Sun, "China's
Aid to Africa: Monster or Messiah?" Brookings Institution, February 7, 2014,
https://www.brookings.edu/opinions/chinas-aid-to-africa-monster-or-messiah/
(accessed on September 5, 2019).

17. See, for example, Gallagher and Porzecanski, *Dragon in the Room*; and
Ching Kwan Lee, *The Specter of Global China: Politics, Labor and Investment in
Africa* (Chicago: University of Chicago Press, 2017).

18. See, for example, D. Michael Shafer, *Winners and Losers: How Sectors Shape the Developmental Prospects of States* (Ithaca, NY: Cornell University Press, 1994); and Gallagher and Porzecanski, *Dragon in the Room.*

19. See Shaun K. Roache, "China's Impact on World Commodity Market," IMF Working Paper (May 2012): 21, http://www.imf.org/external/pubs/ft/wp/2012/wp12115.pdf (accessed on September 5, 2019).

20. Gallagher and Porzencanski, *Dragon in the Room*, 31–32; "Brazil Exports 80 percent of Soy to China in January–August: Agriculture Ministry" *Reuters*, September 14, 2019, https://www.reuters.com/article/us-brazil-agriculture-soy beans/brazil-exports-80-percent-of-soy-to-china-in-january-august-agriculture -ministry-idUSKCN1LU2MT (accessed on September 5, 2019).

21. Maria Jose Haro Sly, "The Argentine Portion of the Soybean Commodity Chain," *Palgrave Communications,* no. 3 (2017): 95, https://www.nature.com/ar ticles/palcomms201795 (accessed on September 5, 2019).

22. Gallagher and Porzencanski, *Dragon in the Room*, 22, passim. Anabel Gonzalez, "Latin America–China Trade and Investment amid Global Tension: A Need to Upgrade and Diversify," Atlantic Council's Adrienne Arsht Latin America Center, December 2018, https://www.atlanticcouncil.org/images/publi cations/Latin-America-China-Trade-and-Investment-Amid-Global-Tensions.pdf (accessed on September 5, 2019).

23. Celine Wang, "China and Zambia's Resource Nationalism," East Asia Forum, March 31, 2017, http://www.eastasiaforum.org/2017/03/31/china-and -zambias-resource-nationalism/ (accessed on September 5, 2019).

24. Lawrence B. Krause, *The Economics and Politics of the Asian Financial Crisis of 1997–98* (New York: Council on Foreign Relations, 1998).

25. Gallagher and Porzencanski, *Dragon in the Room*, 50.

26. Perry Anderson, "Lula's Brazil," *London Review of Books,* March 31, 2011, https://www.lrb.co.uk/v33/n07/perry-anderson/lulas-brazil (accessed on September 5, 2019).

27. Dan Haglund, "In It for the Long Term? Governance and Learning among Chinese Investors in Zambia's Copper Sector," *China Quarterly* 199 (2009): 627–46; and Lee, *Specter of Global China.*

28. Gallagher and Porzencanski, *Dragon in the Room.*

29. Hung, *China Boom*, Figure 3.6

30. See, for example, Howard W. French, *Everything under the Heavens: How the Past Helps Shape China's Push for Global Power* (New York: Knopf, 2017).

31. The term is from G. John Ikenberry, *Liberal Leviathan: The Origins, Crisis, and Transformation of the American World Order* (Princeton, NJ: Princeton University Press, 2011).

32. See, for example, French, *Everything under the Heavens*; and Richard

McGregor, *Asia's Reckoning: China, Japan, and the Fate of US Power in the Pacific Century* (New York: Viking, 2017), chapter 12.

33. Takeshi Hamashita, *China, East Asia, and the World Economy: Regional and Historical Perspectives* (New York: Routledge, 2008); and David C. Kang, *East Asia before the West: Five Centuries of Trade and Tribute* (New York: Columbia University Press, 2010).

34. See William R. Heaton, "China and Southeast Asian Communist Movements: The Decline of Dual Track Diplomacy," *Asian Survey* 22, no. 8 (August 1982): 779–800; and Brautigam, *Dragon's Gift*, 29–40.

35. Ernest Z. Bower, "China's Activities in Southeast Asia and Implications for United States Interests," Statement before the US-China Economic and Security Review Commission, February 4, 2010, https://csis-prod.s3.amazonaws.com/s3fs-public/legacy_files/files/100204_bower_testimony.pdf (accessed on September 5, 2019); James O'Connor, "State Building, Infrastructure Development and Chinese Energy Projects in Myanmar," Irasec's Discussion Papers no. 10, March 2011, http://www.irasec.com/documents/fichiers/46.pdf (accessed on September 5, 2019); and Mark Grimsditch, "China's Investments in Hydropower in the Mekong Region: The Kamchay Hydropower Dam, Kampot, Cambodia," Bank Information Center report, World Bank, 2012, https://www.internationalrivers.org/sites/default/files/attached-files/case_study_china_investments_in_cambodia.pdf.

36. James Reilly, "China's Unilateral Sanctions," *Washington Quarterly* 35, no. 4 (2012): 121–33; and Hung, *China Boom*, chapter 5.

37. See Thomas Fingar, *The New Great Game: China and South and Central Asia in the Era of Reform* (Stanford, CA: Stanford University Press, 2016).

38. See Ilaria Maria Sala, "More Neighbors are Saying 'No Thanks' to Chinese Money—for Now," *Quartz*, December 4, 2017, https://qz.com/1136000/more-neighbors-are-saying-no-thanks-to-chinese-money/ (accessed on September 5, 2019).

39. Maham Hameed, "Infrastructure and Democracy—A Case of China-Pakistan Economic Corridor," *Palgrave Communications,* no. 4 (2018): 64, https://www.nature.com/articles/s41599-018-0115-7 (accessed on September 5, 2019).

40. Saibal Dasgupta, "Pakistan, Nepal, Myanmar Back Away from Chinese Projects," Voice of America, December 4, 2017, https://www.voanews.com/east-asia/pakistan-nepal-myanmar-back-away-chinese-projects (accessed on September 5, 2019).

41. Brautigam, *Dragon's Gift*, 67–70.

42. Brautigam, *Dragon's Gift*.

43. See Hung, *China Boom*, Table 5.7.

44. Howard W. French, "In Africa, an Election Reveals Skepticism of

Chinese Involvement," *The Atlantic*, September 29, 2011, https://www.theatlantic
.com/international/archive/2011/09/in-africa-an-election-reveals-skepticism-of
-chinese-involvement/245832/ (accessed on September 5, 2019).

45. Lamido Sanusi, "Africa Must Get Real about Chinese Ties," *Financial Times,* March 11, 2013, https://www.ft.com/content/562692b0-898c-11e2-ad3f -00144feabdc0 (accessed on September 5, 2019).

46. For example, Brazil has joined the United States to complain about China's currency policy at the World Trade Organization. See Matthew Dalton and Diana Kinch, "Debate on Yuan Manipulation Moves to WTO," *Wall Street Journal*, November 16, 2011.

47. Marianna Parraga and Brian Ellsworth, "Venezuela Falls behind on Oil-for-Loan Deals with China, Russia," *Reuters,* February 9, 2017, https:// www.reuters.com/article/us-venezuela-oil-insight/venezuela-falls-behind-on -oil-for-loan-deals-with-china-russia-idUSKBN15O2BC; https://www.ft.com/ content/562692b0-898c-11e2-ad3f-00144feabdc0.

48. Based on the AIIB website, as of March 6, 2018, https://www.aiib.org/en/ about-aiib/governance/members-of-bank/index.html.

49. Wong Sue-Lin, "China Launches New AIIB Development Bank As Power Balance Shifts," *Reuters,* January 15, 2016, https://www.reuters.com/ article/us-asia-aiib-investment/china-launches-new-aiib-development-bank-as -power-balance-shifts-idUSKCN0UU03Y (accessed on September 5, 2019); and Stewart M. Patrick, "AIIB: Is the Chinese-led Development Bank a Role Model?" Council on Foreign Relations, June 25, 2018, https://www.cfr.org/blog/aiib-chi nese-led-development-bank-role-model (accessed on September 5, 2019).

50. Ana Swanson and Sherey Verma, "Move Over, IMF: BRICS Bank Aims to Rewrite the Rules of Development," *Foreign Policy*, July 11, 2014, http://foreign policy.com/2014/07/11/move-over-imf-brics-bank-aims-to-rewrite-the-rules-of-de velopment/ (accessed on September 5, 2019).

51. Wendy Wu, "AIIB and World Bank Reach Deal on Joint Projects, As China-Led Lender Prepares To Approve US$1.2 Billion of Funds This Year," *South China Morning Post*, April 14, 2016.

52. NYA International 2015, "Kidnapping Risk to Chinese Nationals," *Global Kidnap for Ransom Update*, April 2015, http://www.nyainternational.com/sites/ default/files/no-index/NYA-Global-Kidnap-for-Ransom-Update-April-2015-362 .pdf (accessed on January 3, 2016); and ENR 2014, "Pushback against Chinese Workers Escalates in Africa," *Engineering News Record*, October 14, 2014, http:// www.enr.com/articles/3029-pushback-against-chinese-workers-escalates-in-africa ?v=preview (accessed on September 5, 2019).

53. See Chinese Information Office of the State Council , "The Diversified Employment of China's Armed Forces," Information Office of the State Council,

People's Republic of China, April 2013, http://en.people.cn/90786/8209362.html (accessed on September 5, 2019).

54. Hung, *China Boom*, 141–42.

55. Frontier Services Groups, "Frontier Services Group Strategy Update," press release, December 19, 2017, https://www.prnewswire.com/news-releases/frontier-services-group-strategy-update-607417306.html (accessed on December 30, 2017).

56. "Erik Prince Company To Build Training Center in China's Xinjiang," *Reuters*, January 31, 2019.

Chapter 11. Bold Strategy or Irrational Exuberance?

1. Jonathan Hillman, "China's Belt and Road Initiative: Five Years Later," Statement Before the US-China Economic and Security Review Commission, January 25, 2018, https://csis-prod.s3.amazonaws.com/s3fs-public/publication/ts180125_hillman_testimony.pdf?mSTOaqZbgZdRpx4QWoStıHtIa4fN42uX.

2. "Chronology of China's Belt and Road Initiative," *Xinhua*, June 24, 2018, http://www.xinhuanet.com/english/2016-06/24/c_135464233.htm.

3. Josh Zumbrun and Jon Emont, "China's Financial Reach Leaves Eight Countries Vulnerable, Study Finds," *Wall Street Journal*, March 4, 2018, https://www.wsj.com/articles/chinas-financial-reach-leaves-eight-countries-vulnerable-study-finds-1520190000.

4. Asia-Pacific Economic Cooperation, "Annex D–APEC Connectivity Blueprint for 2015–2025," https://www.apec.org/Meeting-Papers/Leaders-Declarations/2014/2014_aelm/2014_aelm_annexd (accessed on August 27, 2019). The idea of the FTA had been raised earlier by other countries, but it was the push by China that got it back on the agenda.

5. See, for example, Ministry of Foreign Affairs of Japan, "22nd Round of Negotiations for Regional Comprehensive Economic Partnership (RCEP)," April 25, 2018, https://www.mofa.go.jp/press/release/press4e_002009.html.

6. Both the AIIB and the NDB have projected capital commitments of $100 billion. The CEEF began Phase 2 of its operation in 2017, when capital commitment was increased to $10 billion from the initial $1 billion.

7. At this writing, the government is aiming for growth in 2019 to be in the range of 6 percent to 6.5 percent; see "Highlights of Chinese Premier's Government Work Report," March 5, 2019, http://www.ecns.cn/news/politics/2019-03-05/detail-ifzezqac5084324.shtml.

8. "2013 Central Economic Work Conference" ("*Zhongyang jingji gongzuo huiyi, 2013*"中央经济工作回忆, 2013), *Sina News*, http://finance.sina.com.cn/focus/2013zyjjgzhy/ (accessed on August 2, 2018).

9. Tom Miller, *China's Asian Dream: Empire Building along the New Silk Road* (London: Zed Books, 2017).

10. Shannon Tiezzi, "What Did China Accomplish at the Belt and Road Forum?" *The Diplomat*, May 16, 2017, https://thediplomat.com/2017/05/what-did-china-accomplish-at-the-belt-and-road-forum/.

11. Jin Qi's speech in Hong Kong on May 18, 2016, at Belt and Road Summit (*Jin Qi dongshizhang zai "Yidai Yilu" gaofeng luntan de wucan yanjiang,* 金琦董事长在 "一带一路" 高峰论坛的午餐演讲), Silk Road Fund, http://www.silkroadfund.com.cn/cnweb/19930/19938/32726/index.html (accessed on August 27, 2019).

12. Strictly speaking, these funds are not entirely "unencumbered"—this is the amount the central government transfers to local governments to help fund their budgets. Of these transfers, only tax rebates (the returned portion of shared taxes) are set by law or regulation, all the rest are made at the discretion of the central government. With tax rebates having fallen from half of the total at the end of the 1990s to just 12 percent in 2015, broadly speaking, we can call this mostly discretionary.

13. Christine Wong, "China: Public Investment Management under Reform and Decentralization," in *The Power of Public Investment Management: Transforming Resources into Assets for Growth* (Washington, DC: World Bank, 2014), http://hdl.handle.net/10986/21045; and Yougang Chen, Stefan Matzinger, and Jonathan Woetze, "Chinese Infrastructure: The Big Picture," *McKinsey Quarterly*, June 2013, https://www.mckinsey.com/featured-insights/winning-in-emerging-markets/chinese-infrastructure-the-big-picture.

14. The State Council, "China Has 130,000 km of Highways, the Most in the World," August 27, 2017, http://english.gov.cn/news/top_news/2017/08/27/content_281475818432406.htm.

15. "High-speed Rail in China," Wikipedia, https://en.wikipedia.org/wiki/High-speed_rail_in_China (accessed on August 27, 2019).

16. China was ranked twenty-third among 160 countries in infrastructure, and twenty-seventh overall. The only country with a higher LPI score but lower per capita GDP is South Africa.

17. Until 2006 and 2007, China maintained a fixed exchange rate pegged to the US dollar.

18. The China Investment Corporation was established in 2007 as a vehicle to diversify China's foreign exchange holdings.

19. "China Scales Up Financing Support for B&R Initiative," *Xinhua,* May 14, 2017, http://china.org.cn/china/2017-05/14/content_40811348.htm.

20. "Will China's Belt and Road Initiative Outdo the Marshall Plan?" *Economist,* March 8, 2018, https://www.economist.com/finance-and-economics/2018/03/08/will-chinas-belt-and-road-initiative-outdo-the-marshall-plan;

and "Western Firms Are Coining It along China's One Belt, One Road," *Economist,* August 3, 2017, https://www.economist.com/business/2017/08/03/western-firms-are-coining-it-along-chinas-one-belt-one-road.

21. This was the same figure cited by Xi Jinping in his speech at Davos on January 17, 2017. See State Council Information Office, "Full Text: Xi Jinping's Keynote Speech at the World Economic Forum," http://www.china.org.cn/node_7247529/content_40569136.htm.

22. Arthur Kroeber, "Financing China's Global Dreams," *China Economic Quarterly,* (November 2015): 27–36.

23. Gregory Chin and Kevin P. Gallagher, "Coordinated Credit Spaces: The Globalization of Chinese Development Finance," *Development and Change* 50, no. 1 (January 2019): 245–74, doi: 10.1111/dech.12470.

24. This is the practice commonly used for financing infrastructure in China, where banks, including commercial banks, prefer to provide large-scale lending for a bundle of projects. This practice differs markedly from that of multilateral development banks, whose lending is project-based, for one project at a time.

25. Christine Wong, "The Fiscal Stimulus Program and Problems of Macroeconomic Management in China," *OECD Journal on Budgeting* 1, no. 3 (2011): 1–24, doi.org/10.1787/budget-11-5kg3nhljqrjl.

26. Author's calculations.

27. Information from the National People's Congress 2019 Work Report, https://www.china-briefing.com/news/chinas-2019-work-report-growth-target-tax-cuts/ (accessed on April 3, 2019).

28. Estimated at 45 percent of GDP.

29. Yongding Yu, "China's Groundhog Day Growth Pattern," *East Asia Forum Quarterly* (February 2013), https://www.eastasiaforum.org/2013/02/10/chinas-groundhog-day-growth-pattern/.

30. Kan Huo, Wang Changyong, and Jing Wang, "Can Stimulus Light China's Consumer Fire?" *Caijing,* March 6, 2009, http://english.caijing.com.cn/2009-03-06/110114349.html.

31. Belt and Road Portal, "Xinjiang's Construction Plan for Development of a Transport Center on the Silk Road Economic Belt from 2016 to 2030," August 30, 2017, https://eng.yidaiyilu.gov.cn/zchj/dfgg/25503.htm.

32. Henan Provincial Government, "Circular of the People's Government of Henan Province on Issuing the Special Plan for the Development of the 'Silk Road in the Air' from Zhengzhou to Luxemburg (2017–2025)," https://www.yidaiyilu.gov.cn/zchj/dfzc/29573.htm (accessed on March 9, 2018).

33. "Chengdu Five-Year Action Plan for Chengdu to Participate in the 'Belt and Road Initiative' and Promote the 'Go Abroad' Strategy in Enterprises" (*"Chengdu shi rongru 'Yidai Yilu' guojia zhanlüe tuidong qiye 'Zou Chuqu' wu nian*

xingdong jihua" 成都市融入"一带一路"国家战略 推动企业"走出去"五年行动计划),
https://www.yidaiyilu.gov.cn/zchj/jggg/1856.htm (accessed on June 26, 2018).

34. "Action Plan for Quanzhou to Participate in Building the Pioneer Zone for the 21st Century Maritime Silk Road" ("*Quanzhou shi jianshe 21 shiji haishang sichou zhi lu xianxing qu xingdong fangan,*" 泉州市建设21世纪海上丝绸之路先行区行动方案), https://www.yidaiyilu.gov.cn/zchj/jggg/1481.htm (accessed on June 26, 2018).

35. See Christine Wong, "An Update on Fiscal Reform," in R. Garnaut, Cai Fang, and L. Song, eds., *China Update 2018: China's Forty Years of Reform and Development: 1978–2018* (Canberra: Australian National University, 2018), 271–90.

36. Tom Miller, "The Belt and Road to Leadership," *China Economic Quarterly* (June 8, 2017): 9–16. Gavekal Dragonomics.

Chapter 12. All (High-Speed Rail) Roads Lead to China

This chapter reflects preliminary findings of a larger Smith Richardson Foundation–supported project that will result in a book project. David Lampton is collaborating with two colleagues in Southeast Asia, Dr. Selina Ho and Dr. Cheng-Chwee Kuik, in the project. Beyond documentary research encompassing eight countries, this project involves interviewing in all eight countries and beyond. The views expressed in this chapter are preliminary and are Dr. Lampton's. He would like to thank Tiffany Wong for her research assistance; Dr. Thomas Fingar and Professor Jean C. Oi of Stanford University for their editorial and substantive contributions; and Amy Smith Bell for her copyediting.

1. For simplicity we refer to the rail projects under consideration in this chapter as "high-speed," although in China the designation "high-speed" is reserved for systems that operate at 250 kilometers per hour or more, along with other attributes. See Zhenhua Chen and Kingsley E. Haynes, *Chinese Railways in the Era of High-Speed* (Bingley, UK: Emerald Group Publishing, Ltd., 2015), 26.

2. World Bank, "Gross Domestic Savings (% of GDP)," https://data.world bank.org/indicator/NY.GDS.TOTL.ZS (accessed on August 28, 2019).

3. Cui Liru, "Some Thoughts on China's International Strategy," *Contemporary International Relations*, November–December 2011, 6.

4. David M. Lampton, "Notes of Remarks [in Hong Kong] by Joachim von Arnsberg, vice president policy and strategy," Asian Infrastructure Investment Bank, September 8, 2017, 5.

5. Stu Woo, Dan Strumpf, and Betsy Morris, "Huawei, Seen as Possible Spy, Boomed Despite U.S. Warnings," *Wall Street Journal*, January 9, 2018, A8.

6. David M. Lampton notes, Chinese think tanker, "Interview," Washington, DC, September 22, 2017, 3.

7. Luo Wangshu, "Rail System to Grow by 4,000 km in 2018," *China Daily*, January 3, 2018, 1.

8. Brian Wang, "Thailand High Speed Rail Construction Starts," *Next Big Future,* December 2017, https://www.nextbigfuture.com/2017/12/thailand-high-speed-rail-construction-starts.

9. Toru Wakabayashi, "Teikoku Nihon no koutsumou" (Transportation network of Imperial Japan) Seikyuuhsa. It has the subtitle "The Great East Asian Co-Prosperity Zone that was not connected" (correspondence from Seiichiro Takagi, April 18, 2016). David M. Lampton and Cheng-Chwee Kuik, "Conversation with Tun Dr. Mahathir Mohamad," Putrajaya, Kuala Lumpur, June 27, 2016. ASEAN Secretariat, "Master Plan on ASEAN Connectivity," December 2010, https://www.asean.org/storage/images/ASEAN_RTK_2014/4_Master_Plan_on_ASEAN_Connectivity.pdf (accessed on September 4, 2019); Asian Development Bank Institute, *Connecting Asia: Infrastructure for Integrating South and Southeast Asia* (Northampton, MA: Edward Elgar Publishing, Inc., 2016).

10. Xi Jinping, "Secure a Decisive Victory in Building a Moderately Prosperous Society in All Respects and Strive for the Great Success of Socialism with Chinese Characteristics for a New Era," delivered at the 19th National Congress of the Communist Party of China, October 18, 2017, official version by *Xinhua News Agency*, 31.

11. Xi Jinping, "Victory in the New Era," 30.

12. Larry Elliott, "China's Debt Levels Pose Stability Risk, says IMF," *The Guardian,* December 6, 2017, https://www.theguardian.com/world/2017/dec/07/china-debt-levels-stability-risk-imf.

13. David M. Lampton, "Notes of Meeting with very Senior Chinese Economic Leader," Beijing, December 1, 2017, 10–11.

14. David M. Lampton, Chinese think tanker, conference notes, November 11, 2017, 31–32.

15. "Market to Play 'Decisive' Role in Allocating Resources," *Xinhua*, November 2013, http://china.org.cn/china/third_plenary_session/2013-11/12/content_305.

16. Michael G. Plummer, Peter J. Morgan, and Ganeshan Wignaraja, eds., *Connecting Asia: Infrastructure for Integrating South and Southeast Asia*, Asian Development Bank Institute (Cheltenham, UK: Edward Elgar Publishing, Ltd., 2016).

17. Milton and Rose Friedman, *Free to Choose* (San Diego: A Harvest/HBJ Book, 1979), 116.

18. David M. Lampton, "Interview with Engineer," Beijing, July 20, 2016, 7.

19. David M. Lampton, "Interview with Engineer," Beijing, July 20, 2016, 7. Along with my research team, I conducted field visits in the summer of 2017.

20. Wang, "Thailand High Speed Rail Construction Starts."

21. "Chinese Consortium to Bid for High-Speed Rail Project Linking Singapore and Kuala Lumpur," *Straits Times*, December 27, 2017, http://www .straitstimes.com/asia/east-asia/chinese-consortium-to-bid-for-high-speed-rail -project-linking-singapore-and-kuala-lumpur.

22. Stephen E. Ambrose, *Nothing Like It in the World* (New York: Touchstone, 2000), 382. For a somewhat more iconoclastic view of the transcontinental effort in the United States, see Richard White, *Railroaded: The Transcontinentals and the Making of Modern America* (New York: W. W. Norton & Company, 2011), 382.

23. ASEAN Secretariat, "Master Plan on ASEAN Connectivity," chapter 1.

24. David M. Lampton and Cheng-Chwee Kuik, "Conversation with Tun Dr. Mahathir Mohamad," Putrajaya, Kuala Lumpur, June 27, 2016, 9.

25. David M. Lampton and Cheng-Chwee Kuik, "Interview with Malaysian Professor," Malacca City, Malaysia, June 26, 2016, 5–6.

26. Cui, "Some Thoughts on China's International Strategy," 6.

27. David M. Lampton, Selina Ho, and Cheng-Chwee Kuik, "Notes of Meeting with Senior Official," Hanoi, January 5, 2017, 2–3.

28. David M. Lampton, Cheng-Chwee Kuik, and Selina Ho, "Notes of Meeting with Planning Official," Lao PDR, June 6, 2017, 1 and entire interview.

29. In quotations from research team field note interviews, we have used quotation marks within indented quotations adopting the following convention: text without quotation marks indicates that the words are a close paraphrase of what was said, but not necessarily the exact words. Words with quotation marks around them indicate that those words are exactly those used. Cheng-Chwee Kuik, David M. Lampton, and Selina Ho, "Notes of Meeting with Senior Lao Official," June 7, 2017, 5–6.

30. Hu Angang, "China Road and China Dream," Institute for Contemporary China Studies, Tsinghua University, April 2017, 73 and 256.

31. Notes by David M. Lampton, Selina Ho, and Cheng-Chwee Kuik, "Meeting with Policy Researchers," Hanoi, January 5, 2017, 4.

32. Notes by David M. Lampton, Selina Ho, and Cheng-Chwee Kuik, "Meeting with Policy Researchers," Hanoi, January 5, 2017, 3.

33. Notes by David M. Lampton, Selina Ho, and Cheng-Chwee Kuik, "Meeting with Policy Researchers," Hanoi, January 5, 2017, 6–7.

34. MIT mathematician Arnold Barnett was cited by a *New York Times* report as saying, "Chinese high-speed rail has so far established a mortality risk level that equals or exceeds that of the world's safest airlines." See Keith Bradsher,

"Despite a Deadly Crash, Rail System Has Good Safety Record," *New York Times*, September 23, 2013.

35. Emily Guzman, "Huge Safety Flaws Discovered on Shanghai-Yunnan High-Speed Rail," http://www.thatsmags.com/shanghai/post/21388/shanghai-kunming-hsr-tunnel-safety-threat (accessed on January 9, 2018); see also David M. Lampton, "Conversations with Citizens in Kunming and Yunnan," June 19–25, 2016, 1–2.

36. David M. Lampton, "Interview with very Senior Indonesian Official," Jakarta, January 28, 2016, 1. "China's CRRC Corp wins LA Metro Contract Worth up to $647 Million," *Reuters*, March 27, 2017, https://www.reuters.com/article/us-crrc-use/china's-crrc-corp-wins-la; see also David M. Lampton, "Meeting Notes with Rail Corporation Executive," Changchun, Jilin Province, August 10, 2017. Lily Kuo, "Kenya's $3.2 Billion Nairobi-Mombasa Rail Line Opens with Help from China," *Quartz Africa*, June 2, 2017, https://qz.com/996255/kenyas-3-2-billion-nairobi-mombasa-rail-line-opens-with-help-from-china/. "Next Stop Red Sea: Ethiopia Opens Chinese-built Railway to Djibouti," *The Guardian*, October 5, 2016, https://www.theguardian.com/world/2016/oct/06/next-stop-the-red-sea-ethiopia-opens-chinese-built-railway-to-djibouti.

37. David M. Lampton, Selina Ho, Cheng-Chwee Kuik, Interview, Hanoi, January 5, 2017, 5.

38. David M. Lampton, "Notes of Conversation with Think Tanker," February 17, 2016, 5.

39. Nopparat Chaichalearmmongkol, "Railway: Interest Rate Was Sticking Point in Negotiations, Transport Minister Says," *Wall Street Journal*, March 25, 2016, https://www.wsj.com/articles/thailand-calls-off-deal-for-china-to-finance-railway-1458899503.

40. James Kynge, Michael Peel, and Ben Bland, "China's Railway Diplomacy Hits the Buffers," *Financial Times*, July 17, 2017, https://www.ft.com/content/9a4aab54-624d-11e7-8814-0ac7eb84e5f1. This represents 36 percent of an about $16 billion Laotian GDP.

41. David M. Lampton, Selina Ho, and Cheng-Chwee Kuik, "Interview with Professor," Vientiane, June 4, 2017, 3.

42. John McBeth, "Indonesia's High-speed Train, Backed by China, Comes Untracked," *Asia Times*, March 28, 2017.

43. David M. Lampton and Cheng-Chwee Kuik, Interview with "Politician," Kuala Lumpur, June 29, 2016.

44. David M. Lampton, "Interview with Agatha Katz," Washington, DC, November 8, 2017.

45. David M. Lampton and Cheng-Chwee Kuik, Interview with "Politician," Kuala Lumpur, June 29, 2016.

46. David M. Lampton, ed., *Policy Implementation in Post-Mao China* (Berkeley: University of California Press, 1987).

47. David M. Lampton, "Interview with Chinese Security Think Tanker," Washington, DC, September 22, 2017.

48. David M. Lampton and Cheng-Chwee Kuik, "Interview with Politician," Kuala Lumpur, June 29, 2016, 7.

Chapter 13. China's Military Aspirations

1. Drawing from the US Army's definition, "force development" refers to the processes that define military capabilities, design force structures to provide these capabilities, and produce programs that translate organizational concepts based on doctrine, technologies, materiel, manpower requirements, and available resources into integrated armed forces. See US Army, *How the Army Runs: A Senior Leader Reference Handbook 2015–2016* (Carlisle, PA: US Army War College, 2015), 56.

2. H. Richard Yarger and George F. Barber, "The US Army War College Methodology for Determining Interests and Levels of Intensity," US Army War College, Carlisle Barracks, Carlisle, PA, 1997.

3. "China's Military Strategy," Information Office of the State Council of the People's Republic of China, Beijing, 2015.

4. The thesis that rising powers usually emerge on the world stage as strong economic competitors and subsequently develop military capabilities to defend their growing trade and investment interests was popularized by Robert Gilpin, *War and Change in World Politics* (Cambridge: Cambridge Press, 1983); and Paul Kennedy, *The Rise and the Fall of Great Powers* (New York: Vintage Press, 1987).

5. See, for example, David Scott, *China and the International System, 1840–1949: Power, Presence, and Perceptions in a Century of Humiliation* (Albany: State University of New York Press, 2008).

6. "Full Report of Xi Jinping's Report at the 19th CPC National Congress," *China Daily*, November 4, 2017, http://www.chinadaily.com.cn/china/19thcpcnat ionalcongress/2017-11/04/content_34115212.htm.

7. "Xi Attends Parade in Inner Mongolia as PLA Marks Birthday," *China Daily*, July 30, 2017, http://www.chinadaily.com.cn/china/2017-07/30/content _30293445.htm.

8. *Military Terminology of the Chinese People's Liberation Army* (*Zhongguo renmin jiefangjun junyu*, 中国人民解放军军语) (Beijing: PLA Academy of Military Sciences Publishing House), 51.

9. M. Taylor Fravel, "Shifts in Warfare and Party Unity: Explaining China's Changes in Military Strategy," *International Security* 42, no. 3 (Winter 2017–18): 37–83. "China's Military Strategies: An Overview of the 1956, 1980 and 1993

Military Strategic Guidelines," paper prepared for the CAPS-RAND-NDU conference on the PLA, November 2013, Taipei, Taiwan (updated April 2015).

10. See, for example, "The Strategic Thought of Deng Xiaoping," Institute for National Strategic Studies, https://fas.org/nuke/guide/china/doctrine/chin view/chinaptı.html (accessed on September 5, 2019); and Ezra Vogel, *Deng Xiaoping and the Transformation of China* (Cambridge, MA: Belknap Press, 2011), chapter 18.

11. See, for example, Richard Baum, ed., *China's Four Modernizations: The New Technological Revolution* (Boulder, CO: Westview Press, 1980).

12. See James C. Mulvenon, *Soldiers of Fortune: The Rise and Fall of the Chinese Military-Business Complex, 1978–1998* (Armonk, NY: M. E. Sharpe, 2001), 50–69.

13. David Lai and Marc Miller, introduction in Roy Kamphausen, David Lai, and Andrew Scobell, eds., *Beyond the Strait: PLA Missions Other Than Taiwan* (Carlisle, PA: Strategic Studies Institute, US Army War College, 2009), 1–28.

14. M. Taylor Fravel, "China's New Military Strategy: 'Winning Informationized Local Wars,'" *China Brief* 15, no. 13 (July 2, 2015), Jamestown Foundation, https://jamestown.org/program/chinas-new-military-strategy-win ning-informationized-local-wars/.

15. "China's Military Strategy" ("*Zhongguo de junshi zhanlüe,*" 中国的军事战略), *Xinhua Net*, May 26, 2015, http://news.xinhuanet.com/politics/2015-05/26/ c_1115403217.htm.

16. "China's Military Strategy."

17. "China's Military Strategy."

18. "National Security Strategy of the United States of America," December 18, 2017, p. 25, https://www.whitehouse.gov/wp-content/uploads/2017/12/NSS -Final-12-18-2017-0905.pdf; and "Summary of the 2018 National Defense Strategy of the United States of America: Sharpening America's Competitive Edge," 2018, p. 1, https://www.defense.gov/Portals/1/Documents/pubs/2018-National-Defense -Strategy-Summary.pdf.

19. "National Security Strategy," February 2015, https://www.defense.gov/ Portals/1/Documents/pubs/2018-National-Defense-Strategy-Summary.pdf; and "Sustaining U.S. Global Leadership: Priorities for 21st Century Defense," January 2012, http://www.acqnotes.com/Attachments/2012%20National%20 Defense%20Strategy.pdf.

20. "'Cold War' Mentality for U.S. To Play up 'Chinese Military Threat'": Spokesperson, *Xinhua*, January 21, 2018, http://www.xinhuanet.com/english/ 2018-01/21/c_136912454.htm.

21. "Annual Report to Congress: Military and Security Developments Involving the People's Republic of China 2018," US Department of Defense, May

16, 2018, 43, https://media.defense.gov/2018/Aug/16/2001955282/-1/-1/1/2018-china-military-power-report.pdf.

22. Indicating at least the current emphasis placed upon the China Dream vision, the word "dream" was used thirty-one times by Xi in his remarks at the 19th CPC National Congress. Text of Xi Jinping's speech at the 19th CPC National Congress, *Xinhua Net*, October 18, 2017, http://www.xinhuanet.com/english/download/Xi_Jinping's_report_at_19th_CPC_National_Congress.pdf.

23. Xi Jinping's speech at the 19th CPC National Congress.

24. Xi Jinping's speech at the 19th CPC National Congress.

25. Zhao Lei, "PLA To Be World-Class Force by 2050," *China Daily*, October 27, 2017, http://www.chinadaily.com.cn/china/2017-10/27/content_33756453.htm.

26. "China's Military Strategy."

27. Joel Wuthnow and Phillip C. Saunders, *Chinese Military Reforms in the Age of Xi Jinping: Drivers, Challenges, and Implications*, Center for the Study of Chinese Military Affairs Institute for National Strategic Studies China Strategic Perspectives, no. 10 (Washington, DC: National Defense University Press, 2017), 9–23, http://ndupress.ndu.edu/Portals/68/Documents/stratperspective/china/ChinaPerspectives-10.pdf?ver=2017-03-21-152018-430.

28. Liu Yan, "Yemen Evacuation Provokes Debate over Protection Offered by Chinese Passport," *Global Times*, April 10, 2015, http://www.globaltimes.cn/content/916126.shtml.

29. See Ronald O'Rourke, "China Naval Modernization: Implications for US Navy Capabilities—Background and Issues for Congress," *Congressional Research Service*, (December 13, 2017): 3–4, for insights on China's naval shipbuilding program, see https://fas.org/sgp/crs/row/RL33153.pdf.

30. See, for example, James Q. Wilson, *Bureaucracy: What Government Agencies Do and Why They Do It* (New York: Basic Books, 1989), 14–18.

31. See, for example, Anthony H. Cordesman, "Estimates of Chinese Military Spending," Center for Strategic and International Studies, September 21, 2016, https://csis-prod.s3.amazonaws.com/ s3fs-public/publication/160928_AHC_Estimates_Chinese_Military_ Spending.pdf.

32. Cordesman, "Estimates of Chinese Military Spending."

33. Li Keqiang, "Report on the Work of the Government," March 5, 2018, http://cn.wsj.com/photo/WorkReport2018-en.pdf.

34. Scott Neuman, "China Announces Largest Military Spending Increase in 3 Years," National Public Radio, March 5, 2018, https://www.npr.org/sections/thetwo-way/2018/03/05/590845672/china-announces-largest-military-spending-increase-in-three-years.

35. "China's Military Strategy."

36. He Wei and Cheng Yu, "Fresh Impetus for Made in China 2025 Plan,"

China Daily, October 21, 2017, http://usa.chinadaily.com.cn/business/2017-10/21/content_33529649.htm.

37. Tai Ming Cheung, Eric Anderson, and Fan Yang, "Chinese Defense Industry Reforms and Their Implications for US-China Military Technological Competition," Study of Innovation and Technology in China Research Brief, Institute on Global Conflict and Cooperation, January 4, 2017, https://escholarship.org/uc/item/84v3d66k.

38. Mao Zedong, "Problems of War and Strategy," concluding speech at the Sixth Plenary Session of the Sixth Central Committee of the Party, November 6, 1938, in *The Selected Works of Mao Zedong* (Beijing: Foreign Languages Press), https://www.marxists.org/reference/archive/mao/selected-works/volume-2/mswv2_12.htm.

39. Samuel Huntington, *The Soldier and the State: The Theory and Politics of Civil-Military Relations* (Cambridge, MA: Belknap Press of Harvard University Press, 1957), introduced the concept of "objective civilian control"—an institutionalized arrangement granting military leaders professional autonomy in return for policy subordination. The Chinese Communist Party, however, views such autonomy as potentially subversive and threatening to its grip on power.

40. "Chinese Military to Prosecute Former Top General for Graft," *South China Morning Post*, January 9, 2018, http://www.scmp.com/news/china/diplomacy-defence/article/2127513/chinese-military-prosecute-former-top-general-graft.

41. Michael S. Chase, Jeffrey Engstrom, Tai Ming Cheung, Kristen A. Gunness, Scott Warren Harold, Susan Puska, Samuel K. Berkowitz, *China's Incomplete Military Transformation: Assessing the Weaknesses of the People's Liberation Army (PLA)* (Santa Monica, CA: RAND Corporation, 2015), xi, 48, and 50–52, https://www.rand.org/content/dam/rand/pubs/research_reports/RR800/RR893/RAND_RR893.pdf.

42. The ASEAN charter requires consensus for collective action, and achieving consensus on any issue related to China is difficult to achieve.

43. See Graham Allison, *Destined for War: Can America and China Escape Thucydides Trap?* (New York: Houghton Mifflin Harcourt, 2017). For critiques of Allison, see Arthur Waldron, "There Is No Thucydides Trap," *Sunday Times*, June 18, 2017, reprinted in *Straits Times*, June 18, 2017, http://www.straitstimes.com/opinion/there-is-no-thucydides-trap; and T. J. Pempel, "Thucydides (Clap) Trap," *Global Asia* 10, no. 4 (December 2015), 88–93.

Chapter 14. China's National Trajectory

The author is grateful for comments provided by the volume editors; by Qian Yingyi and Zhou Li-An, who served as discussants for this chapter; and by other conference participants.

1. Based on data provided by the Maddison Project, http://www.ggdc.net/maddison/maddison-project/home.htm, 2013 version (accessed on August 27, 2019).

2. Albania, Bulgaria, Czechoslovakia, Hungary, Poland, Romania, and Yugoslavia.

3. The thirteen economies included in this category are Albania, Bulgaria, Cambodia, Croatia, Czech Republic, Hungary, Macedonia, Mongolia, Poland, Romania, Serbia, Slovenia, and Slovakia.

4. The analysis is developed in much greater detail in Andrew G. Walder, Andrew Issacson, and Qinglian Lu, "After State Socialism: The Political Origins of Transitional Recessions," *American Sociological Review* 80, no. 2 (April 2015): 444–68.

5. See, in particular, Barry Naughton, *Growing out of the Plan: Chinese Economic Reform, 1978–1993* (New York: Cambridge University Press, 1995); Barry Naughton, "A Political Economy of China's Economic Transition," in Loren Brandt and Thomas G. Rawski, eds, *China's Great Economic Transformation* (Cambridge: Cambridge University Press, 2008), 91–135; and Nicholas R. Lardy, *Markets over Mao: The Rise of Private Business in China* (Washington, DC: Peterson Institute, 2014).

6. The argument here condenses a much longer presentation in Andrew G. Walder, "Bending the Arc of Chinese History: The Cultural Revolution's Paradoxical Legacy," *China Quarterly* 227 (September 2016): 613–31.

7. This discussion of the East Asian model draws on Arthur Kroeber, *China's Economy: What Everyone Needs To Know* (New York: Oxford University Press, 2016), 9–17.

8. Kroeber, *China's Economy*, 52–56.

9. Quoted in Gareth Stedman Jones, *Karl Marx: Greatness and Illusion* (Cambridge: Harvard University Press, 2016), 145.

10. See, for example, Peter Hays Gries, "Tears of Rage: Chinese Nationalist Reactions to the Belgrade Embassy Bombing," *China Journal* 46 (July 2001): 25–44; Dingxin Zhao, "An Angle on Nationalism in China Today: Attitudes among Beijing Students after Belgrade 1999," *China Quarterly* 172 (December 2002): 885–905; and Jeremy L. Wallace and Jessica Chen Weiss, "The Political Geography of Nationalist Protests in China: Cities and the 2012 Anti-Japanese Protests," *China Quarterly* 222 (June 2015): 403–29.

11. Pál Nyíri, Juan Zhang, and Merriden Varrall, "China's Cosmopolitan Nationalists: 'Heroes' and 'Traitors' of the 2008 Olympics," *China Journal* 63 (January 2010): 25–55.

12. Organized, respectively, by the Institute for Comparative Survey

Research, Vienna; the Center for East Asian Democratic Studies, National Taiwan University; and Texas A&M University.

13. See Lianjiang Li, "Reassessing Trust in the Central Government: Evidence from Five National Surveys," *China Quarterly* 225 (March 2016): 100–21; and Wenfang Tang, "The 'Surprise' of Authoritarian Resilience in China," *American Affairs* 2, no. 1 (Spring 2018): 101–17.

14. Martin King Whyte, "China's Dormant and Active Social Volcanoes," *China Journal* 75 (January 2016): 9–37; and Martin King Whyte, *Myth of the Social Volcano: Perceptions of Inequality and Distributive Justice in Contemporary China* (Stanford, CA: Stanford University Press, 2010).

15. For example, Ching Kwan Lee, "State and Social Protest," *Daedalus* 143, no. 2 (Spring 2014): 124–34; Mary E. Gallagher, "China's Workers Movement and the End of the Rapid-Growth Era," *Daedalus* 143, no. 2 (Spring 2014): 81–95; Feng Chen, "Privatization and Its Discontents in Chinese Factories," *China Quarterly* 185 (March 2006): 42–60; and Lianjiang Li, Mingxing Liu, and Kevin J. O'Brien, "Petitioning Beijing: The High Tide of 2003–2006," *China Quarterly* 210, (June 2012): 313–34.

16. Whyte, "China's Dormant and Active Social Volcanoes," 22.

17. Kroeber, *China's Economy*, 165–67.

18. The model estimates predict a 6 percent decline in the household savings rate by 2030, and a decline in the national savings rate of 4 percent by 2022; see International Monetary Fund (IMF), "People's Republic of China: Selected Issues," IMF Country Report 17/248, August 2017, 15. Demographic trends will have a range of other effects that will inevitably slow growth. See Karen Eggleston et al., "Will Demographic Change Slow China's Rise?" *Journal of Asian Studies* 72, no. 3 (August 2013): 505–18.

19. Kroeber, *China's Economy*, 174–76.

20. Nini Khor et al., "China's Looming Human Capital Crisis: Upper Secondary Education Attainment Rates and the Middle-Income Trap," *China Quarterly* 228 (December 2016): 905–26.

21. Kroeber, *China's Economy*, 99–101.

22. Lardy, *Markets over Mao*, 87, 98.

23. See chapter 2 by Barry Naughton, this volume; and also Nicholas R. Lardy, *The State Strikes Back: The End of Economic Reform in China?* (Washington, DC: Petersen Institute, 2019), 81–97.

24. World Bank, "GDP Growth," https://data.worldbank.org/indicator/NY .GDP.MKTP.KD.ZG?locations=CN (accessed on August 27, 2019).

25. See the analysis of recent government policy in Arthur Kroeber, "Making Sense of the Economic Policy Mess," *China Economic Quarterly* 20, no. 2 (June

2016): 3–6; Barry Naughton, "State Enterprise Reform: Missing in Action," *China Economic Quarterly* 20, no. 2 (June 2016): 15–21; and Barry Naughton, "Supply-Side Structural Reform at Mid-Year: Compliance, Initiative, and Unintended Consequences," *China Leadership Monitor* 51 (Fall 2016), https://www.hoover.org/sites/default/files/research/docs/clm51bn.pdf (accessed on August 27, 2019).

26. Kenneth Sheve and Ruxi Zhang, "One Belt-One Road: Chinese Strategic Investment in the 21st Century," Graduate School of Business, Stanford University, Case P-87, February 2016.

27. See, for example, J. P. Morgan, "China's Financial Sector: Concerns about the Mounting Risks," Emerging Markets Research, July 18, 2013; Goldman Sachs, Investment Strategy Group, "Walled In: China's Great Dilemma," January 2016; IMF, "People's Republic of China: Selected Issues"; Sarah Chan, "China's Corporate Debt: Recent Developments and Implications," Background Brief No. 1223, East Asian Institute, National University of Singapore, February 23, 2017; and Victor Shih, "Financial Instability in China: Possible Pathways and Their Likelihood," *Merics China Monitor*, Mercator Institute for China Studies, October 20, 2017.

28. According to estimates by the Institute of International Finance: see Silvia Amaro, "China's Debt Surpasses 300 Percent of GDP, IIF says, Raising Doubts over Yellen's Crisis Remarks," *CNBC*, June 28, 2017, https://www.cnbc.com/2017/06/28/chinas-debt-surpasses-300-percent-of-gdp-iif-says-raising-doubts-over-yellens-crisis-remarks.html.

29. Goldman Sachs, "Walled In," 23.

30. IMF, "People's Republic," 1, 25–26.

31. See Sarah Y. Tong, "Growth or Structural Reforms? China's Changing Policy Priorities," Background Brief No. 1254, East Asian Institute, National University of Singapore, June 15, 2017; Chan, "China's Corporate Debt"; Naughton, "Supply Side Structural Reform"; and Naughton, "State Enterprise Reform."

32. Shih, "Financial Instability," 4.

33. Goldman Sachs, "Walled In," 4.

34. Wei Shan, "Chinese Citizens' Declining Trust in their Central Government," Background Brief no. 1271, East Asian Institute, National University of Singapore, August 10, 2017.

35. Wei Shan, "How China's Post-1980 Generation Is Politically Different," Background Brief no. 1279, East Asian Institute, National University of Singapore, September 7, 2017.

36. IMF, "People's Republic of China," 14.

37. See Andrew G. Walder, "Popular Protest and Party Rule: China's Evolving Polity," in William C. Kirby, ed., *The People's Republic of China at 60:*

An International Assessment (Cambridge, MA: Harvard University Press, 2011), 133–40.

38. See "What About Representation?," *The Economist* 429 (December 1, 2018): 60–61, for the recent estimate of the percentage of citizens paying income tax. By contrast, close to 73 percent of US citizens pay federal taxes on income, and just under half of federal government revenue comes from individual income taxes. This figure does not include any state or local income taxes, especially local property taxes, which are a major source of local government revenue. The data on the structure of China's fiscal revenue is for 2015, and taken from China's State Administration of Taxation website, http://www.chinatax.gov.cn. See also Thomas Piketty and Nancy Chan, "Income Inequality and Progressive Taxation in China and India," *American Economic Journal: Applied Econometrics* 1, no. 2 (April 2009): 53–63; and Hua Xu and Huiyu Cui, "Personal Income Tax Policy in China and the United States: A Comparative Analysis," *Public Administration Review* 69, supplement (December 2009): S75–S81.

39. See Andrew G. Walder, "The Party Elite and China's Trajectory of Change," *China: An International Journal* 2 (September 2004): 189–209.

40. Bruce Dickson, "Who Wants To Be a Communist? Career Incentives and Mobilized Loyalty in China," *China Quarterly* 217 (March 2014): 42–68. Dickson notes narrow attitudinal differences between party members and others, especially among educated urbanites in prosperous regions.

41. Angus Maddison, "Measuring the Performance of a Communist Command Economy: An Assessment of the CIA Estimates of the USSR," *Review of Income and Wealth* 44, no. 3 (September 1998): 307–23, at 319.

42. The US GDP was 20.5 trillion in current US dollars in 2018, versus 13.5 trillion for China by the same measure. IMF, "World Economic Outlook Data Base, October 2018," https://www.imf.org/external/pubs/ft/weo/2018/02/weo data/weorept.aspx?sy=2016&ey= 2023&scsm=1&ssd=1&sort=country&ds=.&br=1 &pr1.x=57&pr1.y=8&c=924%2C111&s=NGDPD&grp=0&a= (accessed on August 27, 2019).

Index

Page numbers followed by *f* indicate figures; page numbers followed by *n* indicate note numbers; and page numbers followed by *t* indicate tables.

military training, 326–28

mining, 256t, 258–60

Ministry of Industry and Information Technology, 78, 166

miracle economies, East Asian, 347

"miracle growth," 51, 66–69, 274. *See also* economic miracle; Reform and Opening/reform and opening up; reform era

mobile phones, 71–72, 134t

modernization (of China): Africa, other developing countries, and, 248, 265; Chinese Communist Party (CCP) and, 11, 48; corruption and, 105 (*see also* corruption); effects on China, 312; flawed institutions and, 125; foreign policy and, 10, 225–31, 245, 313; and the Global South, 247–48; goals of, 313; inclusive urbanization and, 199; Mao and, 226; pursuit/quest for, 6, 10, 13, 14, 48, 54, 78, 177, 226–31, 233, 248, 265, 319; reform and, 10, 11, 227, 242; Soviet Union and, 226–28, 230, 231; technological, 6; United States and, 227–29, 235, 240. *See also* PLA: modernization

Myanmar, 263–64, 293, 297, 309. *See also* high-speed rail

National Congress of the Communist Party of China, 47; 15th CPC National Congress (1997), 37, 47, 48; 16th CPC National Congress (November 2002), 37, 47. *See also* 18th CPC National Congress; 19th CPC National Congress

National Development and Reform Commission (NDRC), 78, 166, 279, 292, 295

National Health Commission (NHC), 166, 167, 178, 179

National Healthcare Security Administration, 152, 166, 178–79

National People's Congress (NPC), 17, 144. *See also* 13th National People's Congress

national security, threats to, 225, 267

national security strategy, 37, 312, 314, 319, 320

National Supervisory Commission, 103–5; creation of, 84, 102–4

nationalism, 22, 242, 296; decreasing, 352; increasing, 345, 352

nationalist hostility, increasing, 77–78

nationalist separatism, 340

nationalistic aspirations, 315, 318

natural resources: in Africa, 259, 260, 265; export of, 258, 259, 265

Nehru, Vikram, 208

neocolonialism, 247, 288

netizens/network citizens. *See* Internet users/netizens

New Budget Law (2015), 119, 121

New Cooperative Medical Scheme (NCMS), 167

New Development Bank (NDB), 244, 273, 279; finances, 240, 268, 279, 413n6

"new era," 147. *See also* "Xi Jinping Thought for the new era of socialism with Chinese characteristics"

New Generation Artificial Intelligence Development Plan (2017), 56, 69

"new style" urbanization, 180, 181, 189

New Style Urbanization Plan (2014), 181

Ni Fake, 91

Nie Chunyu, 93

19th CPC National Congress (October 2017), 41, 45, 47, 49, 103, 119, 126; Belt and Road Initiative (BRI) and, 292, 295; Xi Jinping's leadership and, 34, 40, 45, 47, 49; Xi Jinping's report to, 33, 54, 196, 315, 367n13, 422n22

Nixon, Richard, 6, 227, 228

nongovernmental organizations (NGOs), labor, 193–94

not-for-profit medical providers, private, 171

nursing homes, 166, 169, 171, 173

Obama, Barack, 238, 241

oil, 249, 267; foreign policy and, 235, 249; from Middle East, 235; Venezuela and, 255, 267

propaganda, 148. *See also* 50 Cent Party/50 Cent Army
Propaganda Department of the Central Committee of CCP, 42; Theory Bureau ("Xuan Li"), 45
protests, 139–41, 345–46, 352–53; Tiananmen Square, 231–34. *See also* civil resistance
province-level units, 301
public services. *See* social services
Publicity Department of CCP. *See* Propaganda Department of the Central Committee of CCP
purchasing manager index (PMI), 250, 251f

Quanzhou (Fujian), 285

race to the bottom, 170, 183, 192–95
railways. *See* high-speed rail
Ran Xinquan, 93, 97
"rebalancing" the economy, 60–61, 367n13
recentralization, 111–12, 126. *See also* centralization; Xi Jinping's leadership: recentralization of power
red culture movement. *See* Maoist revival movement
reform: "critical stage" of essential reforms (*see* "critical stage"); 18th CPC National Congress and, 36, 37–40, 44, 47–48, 122; and modernization, 10, 11, 227, 242; new constraints and choices as China enters deep-water, 8–14; socialism and, 4–5, 10, 11, 33, 341. *See also* comprehensive reform(s); democratic reform; fiscal reforms; PLA: reforms and
Reform and Opening/reform and opening up, 221, 228, 229, 239, 240, 247; and economic growth, 245; and exploitation of PRC-US-USSR strategic triangle, 231; foreign policy requisites and implications (1979–1989), 226–27; goals, 6, 11, 225, 228; launching of, 8, 46, 242; oil and, 249; results of and changes since, 2,

10, 22, 230–32, 312. *See also* "miracle growth"; reform era
reform era, 13, 40, 184, 230, 248, 365n18; the first 40 years of reform, 4–7, 22, 245, 247, 249; trend of openness in, 142; United States and, 229–31, 248. *See also* "miracle growth"; Reform and Opening/reform and opening up
Regional Comprehensive Economic Partnership (RCEP), 273
Ren Zhiqiang, 141–42
renminbi (RMB) diplomacy, 22
research and development (R&D) spending, 71
resistance, civil. *See* civil resistance
reunification, Chinese, 322, 323
Roberts, Margaret, 144
rural–urban disparities. *See* urban–rural disparities
rural–urban harmonization, 189, 190
Russia, 27, 290, 330; military, 315, 316, 328, 330. *See also* former Soviet Union; Soviet Union

safety-net coverage, 152, 177
schools. *See* education; students; teachers
"scientific socialist" model, 11
sea lines of communication (SLOCs), 318, 324
self-initiated media, 132
semiconductor industry, 55, 76, 78, 366n4
service sector, 157, 160, 255
sex ratio at birth (SRB), 156. *See also* gender imbalance
Shi Xinzheng, 218
shuanggui, 103
"silk road," 280
Silk Road Economic Belt, 272, 284–85
Silk Road Fund, 275, 279, 281f
Singapore, 264, 287, 302, 304, 329; railways and, 291, 297, 299, 302–4, 308, 309
Singapore–Kunming Rail Line (SKRL), 299
Sino-Soviet relations, 227, 228, 231, 315, 339, 341; China's fear of Soviet attack, 230, 231; China's perception of Soviet

Failed Democratization in Prewar Japan: Breakdown of a Hybrid Regime
Harukata Takenaka (2014)

New Challenges for Maturing Democracies in Korea and Taiwan
Edited by Larry Diamond and Gi-Wook Shin (2014)

Spending Without Taxation: FILP and the Politics of Public Finance in Japan
Gene Park (2011)

The Institutional Imperative: The Politics of Equitable Development in Southeast Asia
Erik Martinez Kuhonta (2011)

One Alliance, Two Lenses: U.S.-Korea Relations in a New Era
Gi-Wook Shin (2010)

Collective Resistance in China: Why Popular Protests Succeed or Fail
Yongshun Cai (2010)

The Chinese Cultural Revolution as History
Edited by Joseph W. Esherick, Paul G. Pickowicz, and Andrew G. Walder
(2006)